Thus says

𐤉𐤄𐤅𐤄

Let My People Go

Printed July 2007 by
The Graphix Network
4104-C Colben Blvd.
Evans, Georgia
(706) 210-1000

ISBN# 978-0-9795623-0-3
Copyright applied for 7/2007

On the cover of *Let My People Go* is a photo of the ancient almond tree on the very summit of Jebel al Lawz, which is Mount Sinai! This photo was taken by explorers, Jim and Penny Caldwell. Today Madyan is located in northwestern Arabia just like it was at the time of the first Exodus and the real Mount Sinai is located in the land of Madyan (Midyan) where it's always been. The almond tree growing between the two massive granite stones is an excellent candidate for the burning bush of Moses! The burning bush on the summit of this very tall mountain would have shined like a beacon to Moses as he tended Yithro's sheep at the mountain of Elohim.

Shemoth (Exodus) 3

And Mosheh was shepherding the flock of Yithro his father-in-law, the priest of
Midyan. And he led the flock to the back of the wilderness, and came to
Horeb, the mountain of Elohim. 2And the Messenger of 𐤉𐤄𐤅𐤄 appeared to
him in a flame of fire from the midst of a bush. And he looked and saw the
bush burning with fire, but the bush was not consumed. 3And Mosheh said,
"Let me turn aside now, and see this great sight, why the bush does not burn."
4And 𐤉𐤄𐤅𐤄 saw that he turned aside to see, and Elohim called to him from
the midst of the bush and said, "Mosheh! Mosheh!" And he said, "Here I am."
5And He said, "Do not come near here. Take your sandals off your feet, for the
place on which you are standing is set apart ground."

Let My People Go!

Table of Contents

All of Israel Assembled at the 7th Trumpet	1
Title	2
Table of Contents	3
Yahushua's Verse to Remember	4
Foreword	5
What's in a Name?	7
From the Heart	8
Chapter 1 The Good, The Bad, and The Ugly	9
Chapter 2 Israel's Final Exodus	32
Chapter 3 The First Adam	47
Chapter 4 Yahuah's Ten Thousand Year Plan	55
Chapter 5 Rebellion Before the Flood	63
Chapter 6 A New Beginning	90
Chapter 7 The Real Promised Land	121
Chapter 8 The First Exodus from Mitsrayim	131
Chapter 9 The Real OWYAZ	151
Chapter 10 Tribulation of the Righteous	182
Chapter 11 Yahushua Warned Us!	187
Chapter 12 The Prophets Told Us!	196
Chapter 13 The Day of AYAZ	247
Chapter 14 Where Are the Good Shepherds?	327
Chapter 15 Rewards for the Righteous	341
Chapter 16 What Shall We Do?	351
Our Story	357
Around the Arc	364
The Little Red Hen	365
Acknowledgements	370

Yahushua's Verse to Remember!

[24] *"Do not judge according to appearance, but judge with righteous judgment."* Yohanan (John) 7

Foreword

Let's begin by following the Messiah's example. Let's set apart the real name of the creator of the Heavens and the Earth! His name is 𐤉𐤄𐤅𐤄! 𐤉𐤄𐤅𐤄 is the Paleo (ancient) Hebrew name of the heavenly Father! The name 𐤉𐤄𐤅𐤄 is transliterated into the English language as Yahuah. The short version is simply Yah or Yahu! 𐤉𐤄𐤅𐤄 is the <u>only</u> mighty one, who has ever existed, the only mighty one, who exists now, and the only mighty one, who will ever exist anytime in the future! Yahuah's only begotten son's name is written in Paleo Hebrew as OWY𐤄Z! OWY𐤄Z is transliterated into English as Yahushua. Yahushua has provided the Way of salvation for the people 𐤉𐤄𐤅𐤄 calls Israel!

Let My People Go is <u>not</u> a traditional prophecy book! It's certainly <u>not</u> a Left Behind book! I'm sure that Let My People Go will <u>not</u> agree with the prophecy books sold in book stores today. But that doesn't matter at all. Let My People Go is <u>not</u> filled with <u>smooth</u> things that the sheep may <u>want</u> to hear to tickle their ears! And it was <u>not</u> written to make the sheep fall asleep! Instead, it was written to make the **sheep wake up**! Let My People Go is one of a kind to the best of my knowledge. It's a very different book and it's certainly full of surprises! However, Let My People Go repeats the same tough messages that the prophets of 𐤉𐤄𐤅𐤄 taught in antiquity! Let My People Go exhorts the sheep all over the earth to repent of their apostasy against 𐤉𐤄𐤅𐤄! Today thousands of Yahushua's sheep have found their way back to 𐤉𐤄𐤅𐤄. However, most of the sheep in the earth are still in apostasy! They continue to be led astray by a multitude of false shepherds. They have followed mighty ones, who are not mighty ones at all! If your spiritual journey has led you to this humble book, then you must be truly hungry for the truth about the coming Kingdom of 𐤉𐤄𐤅𐤄! OWY𐤄Z and His prophets looked forward to Israel's final Exodus from the nations.

Who are the people called Israel anyway? The people, who 𐤉𐤄𐤅𐤄 calls Israel, love 𐤉𐤄𐤅𐤄 with their whole hearts and they love the face of 𐤉𐤄𐤅𐤄, OWY𐤄Z. Israel will **overcome** all the struggles, all the afflictions, and all the trials, which they will encounter in this present world! The chief love of Israel is to please 𐤉𐤄𐤅𐤄! Israel will guard Yahuah's Commandments, even while they are being tested in Yahuah's furnace of affliction! 𐤉𐤄𐤅𐤄 tests all His children to make sure that their love is genuine! Even Yahuah's only begotten Son, OWY𐤄Z, was tested in Yahuah's furnace of affliction! Shouldn't we also expect to be tested? You know the answer, don't you?

Yahuah's prophets reported that Israel's final Exodus from the nations will be so spectacular and so <u>supernatural</u> that no one will even speak about the 1st Exodus!

Can you imagine a deliverance so spectacular that the 1st Exodus will be completely overshadowed? In the final Exodus of Israel, Yahuah's people will be brought out of all the nations of the Earth! On that Day Israel will return to the real Promised Land, which was promised to Abraham, Isaac, and Jacob. The people called Israel **will struggle** greatly in this present world system, but in the end aYaZ will help them overcome all their afflictions, trials, and tribulations! Israel will be victorious and will be exalted just as OWYaZ was exalted!

Let My People Go was written for **all** the sheep of this world with the hope that they would understand the true Way of aYaZ and **choose** to become members of Yahuah's great assembly called Israel! The messages of Let My People Go may seem extreme and difficult to some people. However, these are extreme times and there's no time for dancing around the truth! I've done my best to be kind and respectful to all the sheep without diluting Yahuah's truth! However, in the end, Let My People Go is what it is! I make no apologies for the messages of aYaZ in the book because these messages will lead the people called Israel to salvation and eternal life. Let My People Go was written for all Israel, but especially for Yahushua's First Fruits, who are being called out of the apostasy to aYaZ right now! Before you dismiss Let My People Go as nonsense, I strongly advise that you to read the whole book, especially Chapter 9 titled, The Real OWYaZ! You won't be sorry! Seek Yahuah's wisdom and understanding, while you read Let My People Go! Then do your own follow-up research! We are living in the days just prior to Yahushua's return! Very, very soon now, OWYaZ will return to reward the righteous and to punish the wicked! But having said all that, I promise you there aren't any space ships, UFOs, nuclear holocausts, or fairy tale raptures in Let My People Go! However, Let My People Go does contain a treasure-trove of wonderful and exciting information about the final Exodus of Israel! The information in Let My People Go is **not** new, but it has been forgotten, hidden, and suppressed for a very long time! The Day of aYaZ will unveil the most spectacular events ever witnessed by mankind! If you **apply** the Scriptures contained in Let My People Go to your own life, then you **will** be prepared for the Day of aYaZ! If OWYaZ finds you spiritually naked, when He returns, then **He** will reject you! If that happens, you will forever regret not seizing this opportunity to prepare yourself! The Day of aYaZ is coming very, very quickly! Prepare yourself by washing your spiritual garments quickly, before it's too late! May aYaZ bless you and keep you safe! And may aYaZ let you see His face, OWYaZ!

What's in a Name?

⁸"I am 𐤉𐤄𐤅𐤄, that is My Name, and My esteem I do not give to another, nor My praise to idols. **Isaiah 42**

And it shall come to pass in the last days, saith 𐤉𐤄𐤅𐤄, I will pour out of my Spirit upon all flesh: and your sons and your daughters shall prophesy, and your young men shall see visions, and your old men shall dream dreams: And on my servants and on my handmaidens I will pour out in those days of my Spirit; and they shall prophesy: And I will shew wonders in heaven above, and signs in the earth beneath; blood, and fire, and vapour of smoke: The sun shall be turned into darkness, and the moon into blood, before that great and terrible day of 𐤉𐤄𐤅𐤄 come: And it shall come to pass, that whosoever shall call on the name of 𐤉𐤄𐤅𐤄 shall be saved. **Acts 2**

From the Heart

My purpose for writing this book is to help the lost sheep to wake up before it's too late! Sometimes the truth hurts, but it has to be told so that the lost sheep will seek the real Good Shepherd, OWYAZ! For thousands of years, false shepherds have deceived the sheep of this earth! These false shepherds are really wolves dressed in sheep's clothing! They have twisted the Scriptures of AYAZ! They use deception to control their own sheep for their own personal gain. Instead of teaching the truth about AYAZ to their sheep, these false shepherds have taught the sheep smooth things. They have <u>not</u> led the sheep down the **narrow** Way of OWYAZ! Multitudes of sheep over many generations have gone to their graves having **missed Yahuah's mark** because of these false shepherds! How very sad that is! Where are the good shepherds? AYAZ hates **all** the idolatrous traditions of men! <u>Mixing</u> bits of Yahuah's truth with pagan traditions, beliefs, and icons **is <u>flatly rejected</u> by AYAZ today just as it was throughout antiquity!** The standards of AYAZ are absolute and unchanging! Our personal opinions are irrelevant! Our family's and friend's personal opinions are irrelevant! Our teacher's personal opinions are irrelevant! The opinions of AYAZ are the only opinions that really matter! AYAZ will do everything possible to draw His sheep out of the contaminated religious traditions of men! AYAZ will pull out all the stops to show us His truth. But at the end of the day, it's still <u>our</u> <u>choice</u>, isn't it? I finally came out of my own spiritual slumber eight years ago! When I understood the deception that has been used to lead the sheep away from AYAZ, I was sick to my stomach! The sheep just don't have good shepherds to lead them along the right Way! There's no doubt that the sheep, who <u>are</u> <u>ensnared</u> in apostasy, do many <u>good</u> <u>works</u> for humanity. They execute seemingly noble programs. They feed the poor and take care of widows, orphans, and the elderly. However, the absolute truth is that all the good works, all the good programs, and all the good intentions are <u>eternally</u> useless, <u>if</u> they are <u>not</u> <u>done</u> in the <u>name of</u> AYAZ with the <u>purpose</u> of <u>drawing</u> <u>men</u> <u>to</u> AYAZ! Help for humanity is sorely needed, but any help that we give is only <u>temporary</u> at best, if we don't introduce every suffering soul to AYAZ! AYAZ has determined what He wants to be called, how He wants to be worshiped, and how we are to live! All these things are of paramount importance to AYAZ! The bottom line is that we must please AYAZ, **not men,** no matter what! Even though multitudes of sheep have wandered away from the real Good Shepherd, there is still time today to repent and to return to the fold of AYAZ! May AYAZ bless you and let you receive the rewards of OWYAZ at the sounding of the 7th Trumpet!

The Good, The Bad, and The Ugly
Chapter 1

³All inhabitants of the world, and you that dwell on the earth: When a banner is lifted up on the mountains, look! And when a ram's horn is blown, hear! **YeshaYahu (Isaiah) 18**

If you are a serious student of the Scriptures, I'm sure that you already realize that we <u>are</u> living in the last days of the times of the nations! We are living in the days just prior to Yahushua's return! Yahushua is the transliterated Hebrew name of our Messiah, <u>not</u> Jesus. Yahushua's name is OWY3Z in Paleo Hebrew! That name is very, very special! The name OWY3Z is set apart to His Father, Yahuah, which is 3Y3Z in Paleo Hebrew! OWY3Z, our Messiah, was born as a Hebrew boy and was raised in a <u>humble</u> Hebrew family. OWY3Z is Yahuah's provision for our salvation, which His name testifies everytime you speak it!

As you look at the world that we live in today, it should be obvious to you that this present world is on a **collision course** with the judgment of 3Y3Z! We are surely living in the last days of this age! The nations rule in rebellion against 3Y3Z! Doesn't this description sound very familiar to you?

1. But know this, that in the last days hard times shall come. ²For men shall be lovers of self, lovers of money, boasters, proud, blasphemers, disobedient to parents, thankless, wrong-doers, ³unloving, unforgiving, slanderers, without self-control, fierce, haters of good, ⁴betrayers, reckless, puffed up, lovers of pleasure rather than lovers of Elohim, ⁵having a form of reverence but denying its power. **2 Timothy**

The Good

Even though there are many ominous signs that signal the end of this present world, Israel should **not** despair! The **GOOD NEWS** is that the return of our Savior, OWY3Z, and the beginning of His Kingdom are imminent! Soon Yahushua's return will become a reality for everyone on the earth. The times we live in today are **frightening**, but the prospect of actually seeing Yahushua's return gives the people, who Yahuah calls Israel, a wonderful reason to **HOPE**!

The Bad

OWY3Z described the times we live in as, "The Times of the Nations". The nations have ruled this world, since the time of Nimrod. Who in the world was Nimrod? Nimrod was Noah's great grandson by way of the line of Ham. Ham was one of Noah's three sons, who survived the Flood with Noah. After the Flood, Nimrod rejected the ways of 3Y3Z, which his great grandfather Noah taught! He became extremely rebellious against the ways of 3Y3Z!

Nimrod became obsessed with conquest and the subjugation of peoples. He was the very first man to train armies for conquest and the world's very first king. Nimrod exerted his control over peoples, even though he was regarded by the common people as their benefactor. Does that sound familiar? After a violent death by the sword, Nimrod became the first man to ever be deified! What does all this Nimrod stuff have to do with us anyway? Semiramis, who was reported to be Nimrod's wife **and mother**, claimed that, after his death Nimrod became one with the sun! That claim set in motion the evolution of the Babylonian Mystery religion, which is still alive and well today all over the world! In fact the Babylonian Mysteries have contaminated all the traditional religions of the earth, which do not serve **ayaz**! This Babylonian Mystery religion is based on the worship of the sun, the moon, and the stars! Believe it or not, it's almost assured that **you** have unknowingly participated in the Babylonian Mystery religion at some point in your life! Semiramis became known as the "Queen of Heaven"! She is the queen mother of the Babylonian Mystery religion, which has enslaved the morally good people of this earth in various degrees of apostasy against **ayaz** for thousands of years! The sad fact is that Nimrod's religious system is still alive and flourishing today in all the counterfeit religions of the earth! However, very soon **OWYAZ** will return to put a **complete** end to the Babylonian Mystery religion and all its daughter religions with all their counterfeit mighty ones! These mighty ones, of course, are actually not mighty ones at all! They are known across the world by a multitude of blasphemous names! However, **OWYAZ** will soon return and set up His government! HalleluYah (Praise Yah!)! **OWYAZ** will soon take up His reign! He will become the undisputed King of the entire Earth! May your Kingdom come on earth as it is in the Heavens! **Isn't that what we pray for, when we pray Yahushua's prayer?** The Patriarchs and the Prophets of **ayaz** yearned throughout antiquity to see the Day of **ayaz**, but it wasn't time. We are a special generation! We live in a special time! Now the Day of **ayaz** is very near. I believe that it will begin **at any time**! If that time arrives before *Let My People Go* is printed, that will be wonderful! Nothing else will matter at all! **OWYAZ** will return with great esteem and great power! **OWYAZ** will gather all His people, Israel, to Himself in a great final worldwide Exodus from the nations! This final worldwide Exodus will occur in phases over a 490 year period, not on one 24 hour day as we reckon time! Yahushua's kingdom will truly be based on **righteousness and justice for all**, not just for the privileged few! When **OWYAZ** returns and puts down all authority, then the wicked will no longer rule this world! HalleluYah! HalleluYah! HalleluYah!

This present world system is terribly broken, isn't it? Nimrod's religious, economic, and political systems still dominate this world. The supporters of Nimrod's religious, economic, and political systems are cursed by ayaz! They have been written down in the Heavens for judgment by **FIRE**!

2 Peter 3
⁵*For they choose to have this hidden from them: that the heavens were of old, and the earth standing out of water and in the water, by the Word of Elohim, ⁶through which the world at that time was destroyed, being flooded with water. ⁷And the present heavens and the earth are treasured up by the same Word, being kept for **FIRE**, to a day of judgment and destruction of wicked men. ⁸But, beloved ones, let not this one matter be hidden from you: that with* ayaz **one day is as a thousand years**, *and* **a thousand years as one day**. ⁹ ayaz *is not slow in regard to the promise, as some count slowness, but is patient toward us, not wishing that any should perish, but that all should come to repentance.* ¹⁰*But the day of* ayaz *shall come as a thief in the night, in which the heavens shall pass away with a great noise, and the elements shall melt with intense heat, and the earth and the works that are in it shall be burned up.* ¹¹*Seeing all these are to be destroyed in this way, what kind of people ought you to be in* set-apart behavior *and* reverence, ¹²*looking for and hastening the coming of the day of Elohim, through which the heavens shall be destroyed, being set on fire, and the elements melt with intense heat!* ¹³*But according to His promise we wait for a renewed heavens and a renewed earth in which righteousness dwells.*

The earth groans for its own release from the bloodshed, the violence, and the curses resulting from the sins committed on its soil by both mankind and the animals! Bloodshed, violence, and perversion are rampant everywhere on the face of the earth! Morally good men, women, and children are dying everyday from diseases and plagues in spite of today's medical technology! Wicked men and women in authority all over the earth oppress the morally good people in every society! Tragically morally good men, women, and children all over the earth defile themselves **unknowingly** by practicing contaminated religious traditions, which were handed down to them by their forefathers! Most of us have inherited errors, lies, and useless traditions from our own ancestors! I'm sorry, but it's true! Close only counts in the game called Horse-Shoes! ayaz is not playing Horse-Shoes!

YirmeYahu 16

[19] O ayaz, my strength and my stronghold and my refuge, in the day of distress the gentiles shall come to You from the ends of the earth and say, "*Our fathers have inherited only falsehood, futility, and there is no value in them.*" [20] *Would a man make mighty ones for himself, which <u>are not mighty ones</u>?*

It's very sad, but most of the morally good people of the earth today are spiritually naked and they **don't even realize it**! The vast majority of the morally good people of this world, **including myself**, have at some point in their lives been participants in counterfeit religious systems that are in complete rebellion against ayaz and His Ways!

Hosea 4:6

My people are destroyed for lack of knowledge: because thou hast rejected knowledge, I will also reject thee, that thou shalt be no priest to me: seeing thou hast forgotten the law of thy Elohim, I will also forget thy children.

Counterfeit religious systems have fallen away from the truth of ayaz. They have created their own **hybrid** doctrines that are mixtures of **partial** truths, errors, and outright lies. I certainly **never intended** to participate in any religion that was contaminated with the worship of the sun, the moon, and the stars. Most of us have inherited religious practices from our ancestors. Unless the Ruach HaQodesh **(the set apart Spirit of Truth)** guides us, we don't have enough knowledge to detect the cleverly disguised practices of pagan sun worship, which are blended into today's religious traditions. I was ensnared with a vast multitude of very good people in a religious system that was in actuality in rebellion against the ways of ayaz for 43 years. That particular <u>system</u> was Christianity, but it could have been <u>any</u> of the other contaminated religions of the earth, which trace their real origin to the worship of the sun, the moon, and the stars! Unfortunately, **we have all been rebels against** ayaz and His ways! Most of us have been just plain ignorant and naïve! We have all been **confused** and **made the fool of** by the various false religious systems operating in the earth! These systems teach apostasy against ayaz to unsuspecting morally **good** people! We have all fallen victims to satan's bait and switch tactics just like Adam and Hawwah did in the Garden of Paradise on the heavenly Mount Zion! There's only been one son of Adam, who was completely innocent! Of course that was OWYaz! OWYaz, our Passover Lamb, suffered incredible pain and humiliation for Israel! OWYaz showed us the **right Way** to go! This same OWYaz will soon return to **JUDGE** both the people and the animals of the earth for all the bloodshed, the violence, and the rebellion committed against ayaz! Both the Righteous and the wicked will be judged!

Everyone will receive their just reward for their own actions! The wicked will receive terrible shame, terrible agony, terrible torture, a terrible physical death, and finally a complete destruction in Yahuah's Lake of Fire, which burns **hotter than fire**! That fire burns hot enough to destroy both the body and the spirit of a person. Ultimately the wicked will be totally destroyed in the Lake of Fire, which the Scriptures call the **Second Death**! The Second Death is Yahuah's complete and final punishment. It is exponentially worse than the physical death of our body of flesh. In this present world, the Righteous will experience many troubles, many afflictions, many rejections, and many hardships, but in the world to come, the Righteous will receive eternal life with OWY3Z! Our eternal life with OWY3Z will be filled with the most wonderful blessings that 3Y3Z could create! HalleluYah! HalleluYah! HalleluYah! The Scriptures teach that 3Y3Z will accept His Righteous children and treat them **better** than sons and daughters! The Righteous will live in Yahushua's presence forever in His set apart city, the New Yahrushalayim, which was named in honor of 3Y3Z! The New Yahrushalayim is a city **not made with human hands**, but it was prepared for the Righteous by OWY3Z! The New Yahrushalayim is stored in the heavens for Israel! It's ready to be revealed to Israel by OWY3Z on the Day of 3Y3Z at the sounding of the 7th Trumpet! Life with OWY3Z will be so **fabulous** that mere words cannot describe the joy and the blessings that will belong to the Righteous!

Yahuah's Ruach HaQodesh, which is Yahuah's Spirit of Truth, is calling for Yahuah's people, Israel, to come out of the Babylonian Mystery religion and her daughter religions now. **Come out NOW, don't wait!** Why is it **so** important to come out of apostasy against 3Y3Z now? 3Y3Z is setting apart His people now for their future roles in Israel's worldwide Exodus! Your ticket is available now! It's free of charge to you because OWY3Z has **already prepaid the cost of your ticket!** That price was paid by OWY3Z, when **He** suffered incredible physical pain, incredible rejection, incredible humiliation, and finally a cruel death hanging on a tree! Right now front row tickets are still available as well as upper deck tickets. Would you rather be on the front row or would you rather be in the upper deck to witness a great event? To get a front row seat, you must come out of the world's apostasy now, before OWY3Z returns! If you wait too long, then you might **not** be able to get in the action at all! If that happens, then you will miss the greatest celebration of all time, when the King of Kings takes His crown and begins to reign on the earth! OWY3Z is Yahuah's Champion and He will prevail! Claim your ticket now, **while you still can** or be forever sorry that you were blinded to the truth and failed to act!

The situation that a person will find himself in, when OWYAZ returns, is determined by the actions that he takes **now** before OWYAZ arrives! If a person comes out of the world's apostasy now and follows the Way of OWYAZ, then he will be spared from the coming hour of trial, which will soon come upon the whole world!

Revelation 3
[7] *"And to the messenger of the assembly in Philadelphia write, 'He (Yahushua, OWYAZ) who is set-apart, He who is true, He who has the key of Dawid, He who opens and no one shuts, and shuts and no one opens, says this:* [8]*"I know your works – see, I have set before you an open door, and no one is able to shut it – that you have little power, yet* **have guarded My Word, and have not denied My Name**. [9]*"See, I am giving up those of the congregation of Satan, who say they are Yehudim and are not, but lie. See, I am making them come and worship before your feet, and to know that I have loved you.* [10]*"Because you have guarded My Word of endurance,* **I also shall guard you from the hour of trial which shall come upon all the world, to try those who dwell on the earth.**

The people, who listen to Yahuah's call and respond <u>now</u> by putting Yahushua's **words into action** in their lives, are destined **to be conformed to the image of** OWYAZ in this life and later in the world to come! Everyday morally good people **choose** to stay mired in Nimrod's religious apostasy! Sadly most of the morally good people of this earth are completely blinded to the Truth! They are spiritually deaf, because **they have repeatedly refused Yahuah's calls many times in their lives!** They have not answered the call of AYAZ. It's AYAZ, who determines, when time has run out! If a person repeatedly chooses to hold on to the lies of apostasy over Yahuah's truth, then they have made their decision, haven't they? They love the lies of apostasy more than Yahuah's truth! That will be the reason that they will **not** be chosen by OWYAZ!

Matthew 22
For many are called, but few are chosen.

It has been my experience that most people will **not** change, even when they are faced with the Truth! Most morally good people love the lies of apostasy more than Yahuah's truth! How sad that is! After repeated rejections of the Ruach HaQodesh's promptings, AYAZ will give a person over to complete spiritual blindness and deafness! AYAZ has a wonderful plan to restore all Israel to the original Promised Land! The Promised Land that I'm referring to here is the very same Promised Land, which was promised to Abraham, Isaac, and Jacob! This return to the real Promised Land will be **completely supernatural!**

It has **nothing** whatsoever to do with the present day State of Israel! The State of Israel was formed **completely by the efforts of powerful men in 1947**! You're probably thinking, "How can that be?". Keep reading and you'll find out the Truth about the real Promised Land of 𝐚𝐘𝐚𝐙 as well as the counterfeit Promised Land in today's State of Israel!

Where does one start in his quest for the Truth? The best place to start is to first determine, who it is that you actually serve! If you are not following the Commandments of 𝐚𝐘𝐚𝐙 and, if you don't love the names of 𝐚𝐘𝐚𝐙 and 𝐎𝐖𝐘𝐚𝐙 with all your heart, then you are not **completely** following the Ways of the Elohim of the Scriptures! We should all desire to please 𝐚𝐘𝐚𝐙 and 𝐎𝐖𝐘𝐚𝐙 by obeying the 3rd Commandment!

Exodus 20
[7] *"You do not bring the Name of 𝐚𝐘𝐚𝐙 your Elohim to naught, for 𝐚𝐘𝐚𝐙 does not leave the one unpunished, who brings His Name to naught.*

We should worship 𝐚𝐘𝐚𝐙 and 𝐎𝐖𝐘𝐚𝐙 by using their real <u>set</u> <u>apart</u> names, not the names that men have substituted over the years! When you meet someone for the very first time, you introduce yourself by your proper name to that person. Then the other person acknowledges your name and introduces himself by his proper name. After you each know the others personal name, then you can cultivate a lasting relationship with each other. Tragically in this world, the real <u>personal</u> names of 𝐚𝐘𝐚𝐙 and 𝐎𝐖𝐘𝐚𝐙 have been suppressed and nearly forgotten for at least 2,200 years! One of the most important tasks that 𝐎𝐖𝐘𝐚𝐙 performed during His earthly ministry was to <u>restore</u> the personal name of 𝐚𝐘𝐚𝐙 to Israel! At that time Yahuah's name had been intentionally suppressed by the **religious leaders** of that day and nearly forgotten **just as it has been in our time**! Read how 𝐎𝐖𝐘𝐚𝐙 discussed His assignment to reintroduce the name of 𝐚𝐘𝐚𝐙 in John 17. In this prayer 𝐎𝐖𝐘𝐚𝐙 was praying for His disciples then as well as for all the future believers of Israel! Thankfully that includes us today, doesn't it?

John 17
[6] *"I have revealed <u>Your</u> <u>Name</u> to the men whom You gave Me out of the world. They were Yours, and You gave them to Me, and they have guarded Your Word.* [26] *"And I have made <u>Your</u> <u>Name</u> known to them, and shall make it known, so that the love with which You loved Me might be in them, and I in them."*

Psalms 22
[22] *I make known <u>Your Name to My brothers</u>; In the midst of the assembly.*

I am a fellow servant of 𝔄𝓨𝔄𝒵 and O𝓦𝓨𝔄𝒵! I am very proud and thankful to know them by their personal names! I love the name of 𝔄𝓨𝔄𝒵! I wish that I could have been named with a name that would bring honor to 𝔄𝓨𝔄𝒵, but my parents didn't understand. Well guess what! 𝔄𝓨𝔄𝒵 has promised to give every member of Israel a new name, when O𝓦𝓨𝔄𝒵 returns! HalleluYah! HalleluYah! HalleluYah!

The Ugly

If you are a Christian, then you know the Father's and Son's names as "God" and "Jesus". Sadly, these are counterfeit names with pagan origins! Their real names were <u>swapped out by men</u> many years ago! There is a disclaimer in most English Bibles about the swap of the father's name. As many sincere believers are discovering today, the words "God" and "Jesus" are **NOT** their real set apart names at all! There is absolutely <u>no</u> power whatsoever in those names to save any man or a woman! In fact, the words "God" and "Jesus" are not only counterfeit, but even the two names themselves have ties to pagan sun worship! That's disgusting to me! I'm offended that men would have ever imagined to swap the real names for pagan names! Have they no respect or fear of 𝔄𝓨𝔄𝒵 at all? We have all been fooled by counterfeit religious systems, which <u>on the surface seem good</u>, but in reality they lead to complete destruction! The counterfeit religious systems appear to be solid ground, but they are really very, very **thin ice**! If you keep walking on very thin ice long enough, then you will **surely** fall through! The counterfeit religious systems are also like bear traps! A bear trap looks like the surrounding good ground to the bear! It looks good and solid. The bear trap is camouflaged by the trapper, who in the case of our apostasy is satan. Satan designs <u>all</u> his counterfeits to look like <u>good solid</u> ground! However, once the bear steps on the bear trap, down, down, down he goes into a pit, which is full of spikes! The bear is impaled on the spikes and doomed to die a horrible death! The religious systems of mankind are **all bear traps**! Some are disguised better than others! Today's Christianity and Judaism are the best bear traps on earth because they contain <u>so many</u> elements of truth! <u>But</u> those elements of truth <u>have been mixed</u> with outright <u>lies</u> and <u>useless traditions of men</u>! <u>Some</u> congregations of Messianic Judaism still refuse to use the set apart names because they choose to observe useless traditions of men instead! How crazy is that? Messianic Judaism <u>can</u> also be a bear trap, if the system suppresses the set apart names, but holds on to the useless **rabbinical** teachings of men! Many sincere and wonderful sheep participate in all those religions, but they are **flawed** because they omit certain elements of the Way of 𝔄𝓨𝔄𝒵, while they cling to <u>fables</u> and <u>useless traditions of men</u> instead! **Clean** <u>is</u> **clean** and **unclean** <u>is</u> **unclean** to 𝔄𝓨𝔄𝒵!

These religious systems contain a lot of camouflage that make them look very, very solid, but underneath, **beware, beware, beware!** Christianity and Judaism are contaminated because of their adoption of pagan traditions, icons, names, and useless manmade traditions! **Mixing is mixing! Contamination is contamination! Clean is clean and unclean is unclean!** I'm very familiar with radioactive contamination. Radioactive contamination is the presence of radioactive materials in <u>unwanted places</u>. Radioactive materials emit cell damaging ionizing radiation, which destroy human cells in body tissues and organs! Ionizing radiation will kill you, when received in high doses! Radioactive contamination is not visible. When it's on a surface, you can't see it at all. You can't smell it. Everything looks good. However, if you come in contact with radioactive contamination, then <u>it gets on you</u> and you become contaminated! You are <u>no</u> <u>longer clean</u>, <u>but you don't even know that you are contaminated</u>! You are now contaminated because the radioactive contamination is on your body and it's <u>killing your cells</u>, even though you can't see it! You surely <u>did not intend</u> on getting contaminated, but you touched something that was contaminated! And the worse part about radioactive contamination is that the whole time that the contamination is on your body, the ionizing radiation is killing the cells of your skin, tissues, and organs! If you breath in airborne particles of contamination, then the radioactive contamination gets inside of you! That is even more dangerous because the radioactive particles will kill the cells of your lungs and vital organs from the inside out! The behavior of radioactive contamination serves as a great analogy for the apostasy that contaminates today's religious systems! Believe it or not these systems are in direct opposition against the Ways of 𝕌𝕐𝔸𝕑! Just like radioactive contamination, the apostasy in today's religious systems is very, very difficult to detect without the right equipment! Just like radioactive contamination, the apostasy against 𝕌𝕐𝔸𝕑 will destroy you from the inside out, **if you swallow it**! If you participate in any religious system in opposition to the ways of 𝕌𝕐𝔸𝕑, then in Yahuah's eyes, you are contaminated or defiled! Clean is clean and unclean is unclean! 𝕌𝕐𝔸𝕑 has determined that He will **not** accept **any religious contamination in our hearts and minds, if we want to be found perfect!**

Haggai 2
"Thus said 𝕌𝕐𝔸𝕑 of hosts, 'Now, ask the priests concerning the Torah, saying, [12] "If one bears set-apart meat in the fold of his garment, and with the edge he <u>touches</u> bread or stew, or wine or oil, or any food, is it set-apart?" And the priests answered and said, "No."

Haggai 2, cont.
¹³And Haggai said, "If someone defiled by a dead body <u>touches</u> any of these, is it defiled?" And the priests answered and said, "It is defiled."
¹⁴And Haggai answered and said, " 'So is this people, and so is this nation before Me,' declares ayaz, <u>'and so is every work of their hands. And whatever they bring near there is defiled</u>.

But the **Good News** is that we can <u>all</u> be washed clean by Yahuah's Ruach HaQodesh! We can be cleansed and forgiven thanks to OWYAZ! We don't have to stay defiled and unclean! Turn around and repent now, if you are still mired in apostasy! Follow the Way of OWYAZ! Strive to be found perfect before ayaz! Contrary to popular opinion, **it is attainable.** Many patriarchs of ayaz like Seth, Enoch, Noah, Abraham, David, and many, many others have been found perfect by ayaz.

Matthew 5
Be ye therefore perfect, even as your Father which is in heaven is perfect.

Colossians 1
Whom we preach, warning every man, and teaching every man in all wisdom; that we may present every man perfect in the Messiah OWYAZ

Psalm 37
Mark the perfect man, and behold the upright: for the end of that man is peace.

ayaz has set His standards high! It's Yahuah's standards that we must be concerned about, <u>not</u> the preacher's standards, <u>not</u> the Pope's standards, <u>not</u> a friend's standards, and <u>not</u> our relative's standards! We were created to be Qodesh! That means that we are to be set apart as uncontaminated vessels to honor ayaz! A little leaven spoils the whole loaf! That's the problem. The shepherds of the contaminated religious systems, have suppressed the true nature of their religious systems from the good sheep under their control! These false shepherds strive to maintain control over their sheep and to <u>preserve</u> <u>their</u> <u>own</u> <u>careers</u> by preaching their system's faith and message, which they agreed to in most cases, when they graduated from their seminary or religious school! At the end of the day, it's all about money and security for them! It apparently doesn't matter to them that their system's message is in direct conflict with the Ways of ayaz and OWYAZ! These false shepherds are in denial of the real truth, just like Bill Clinton was in denial of his relationship with an intern. Don't just take my word, study to show yourself approved!

Study the history and doctrines of mankind's religious systems for yourself! See if their doctrines really match the Way of Yahuah described in the Scriptures! Study the life and actions of Constantine, the Roman Emperor! He was very instrumental in amalgamating bits of truth with pagan traditions. Constantine had the audacity to change the day of Yahuah's Sabbath to the Day of the Sun! Read Alexander Hislop's, *The Two Babylons,* and see for yourself where the traditions of the Roman Catholic **(universal)** Church originated. That Church preserved the Babylonian Mysteries and forced the nations under her power to drink out of her cup containing the wine of her iniquities against ayaz. Go to any good library and search the internet for the truth yourself. You can read about apostasy against ayaz as long as your heart desires! The Catholic Church has been the main force that has preserved the Babylonian Mysteries, but the Protestant denominations are not innocent either. They continued to embrace many aspects of the Babylonian Mysteries in their denominations, after the Protestant Reformation. Clean is clean and unclean is unclean! All the peoples of the earth have been guilty of apostasy, all of us! None of us has been completely innocent! Apostasy is apostasy and it's all rebellion to ayaz! Many reading *Let My People Go* including myself, followed the Christian religious system with enthusiasm instead of the right Way of ayaz for many years! I **certainly thought that I was doing the right thing**! Unfortunately, I trusted the false Shepherds. I was too lazy to do my own research! What a mistake that was! I am very sorry that I was so ignorant, so naïve, and so rebellious against ayaz and Owyaz!

Zephaniah 1

²*"I shall snatch away all from the face of the earth," declares* ayaz ³*"I snatch away man and beast, I snatch away the birds of the heavens, and the fish of the sea, and the stumbling-blocks, with the wrong, when I shall cut off man from the face of the earth," declares* ayaz. ⁴*"And I shall stretch out My hand against Yehudah, and against all the inhabitants of Yahrushalayim, and* cut off every trace of Ba'al **(Baal is translated as Lord in English)** *from this place, the names of the* idolatrous priests, *with the priests,* ⁵*and those bowing down to the host of the heavens on the house-tops, and those bowing themselves, swearing by* ayaz *and swearing by Malkam;* ⁶*and those who turn away from following* ayaz, *and who have not sought* ayaz *or inquired of Him."* ⁷Hush! in the presence of the Master ayaz. *For the day of* ayaz *is near, for* ayaz *has prepared a slaughter, He has set apart His invited ones.* ⁸*"And it shall be, in the day of the slaughter of* ayaz, *that I shall punish the rulers and the sons of the sovereign, and all such as are clad in foreign garments.* ⁹*"And I shall punish on that day all who leap over the threshold, who fill their masters' houses with violence and deceit.*

Zephaniah 1, cont.
[10]"And on that day there shall be," declares 𐤀𐤄𐤅𐤄, "the sound of a cry from the Fish Gate, and of a howling from the Second Quarter, and of a great crashing from the hills. [11]"Howl, you inhabitants of Maktesh, for all the merchant people shall be silenced, all those weighing out silver shall be cut off. [12]"And at that time it shall be, that I search Yahrushalayim with lamps and punish the men who are settled on their dregs, who say in their heart, '𐤀𐤄𐤅𐤄 does no good, nor does He evil.' [13]"And their wealth shall become plunder, and their houses laid waste. And they shall build houses, but not inhabit them, and they shall plant vineyards, but not drink their wine." [14]Near is the great day of 𐤀𐤄𐤅𐤄, near and hurrying greatly, the noise of the day of 𐤀𐤄𐤅𐤄. Let the mighty man then bitterly cry out! [15]That day is a day of wrath, a day of distress and trouble, a day of waste and ruin, a day of darkness and gloominess, a day of clouds and thick darkness, [16]a day of ram's horn and alarm – against the walled cities and against the corner towers.
[17]"And I shall bring distress on men, and they shall walk like blind men – because they have sinned against 𐤀𐤄𐤅𐤄, and their blood shall be poured out like dust and their flesh like dung." [18]Neither their silver nor their gold shall be able to deliver them in the day of the wrath of 𐤀𐤄𐤅𐤄. And by the fire of His jealousy all the earth shall be consumed, for He makes a sudden end of all those who dwell in the earth.

Every last one of us has sinned and rebelled against Yahuah's Way countless times! I was completely mired in apostasy just a few years ago and I didn't know anything was wrong! I accepted as the truth everything that the false shepherds taught! Sadly the desire for wealth, power, security, and control have contaminated Christianity! I love Christians with my whole heart and I am willing to give my life, if necessary, so that as many Christians as possible can know the Truth about 𐤀𐤄𐤅𐤄! I know that the vast majority of the morally good people in churches today never intended to engage in any kind of apostasy or sun worship against 𐤀𐤄𐤅𐤄! How could this switch have occurred then? After Yahushua's disciples were no longer on the scene, Constantine, pulled the old **switch-r-rue** on the good people of the earth! Since that time, the deception has just gotten worse and worse until today the good people of the earth can no longer even discern the counterfeit nature of their own religious traditions! It seems impossible to them that Christianity, which seems so good and wholesome, is actually a deadly **PAGAN counterfeit**! I guess it's human nature, but people like to be spoon fed. Religious organizations have created vast amounts of wealth and business infrastructures to control their sheep. These institutions have generated huge amounts of tax free revenue for themselves by spoon feeding counterfeit traditions of men to their sheep instead of the real Truth of 𐤀𐤄𐤅𐤄!

This diabolical form of big business has been going on for many, many centuries! Today large numbers of pastors are multi-millionaires! Many travel around the world in private jets! Have these shepherds laid up treasures for themselves on earth by marketing their own fables instead of the Good News of ayaz and owyaz? Are these false shepherds following the Way of owyaz? Are these shepherds messengers of ayaz or **are they wolves masquerading in sheep's clothing**? Who calls these shepherds into apostasy against ayaz? ayaz and owyaz certainly did not call them! Ask yourself these questions? **Da-a, don't let them make merchandise of you anymore!** They are **not** Yahuah's messengers because they don't bear Yahuah's good fruit! They are the messengers of Baal! Their lies are deadly bear traps to anyone, who would walk that way! Their uncontrolled desires have made them fat with the spoils that they have fleeced from their own sheep! Obviously they serve their "god" for money and the security of their own careers!

Matthew 6
[19]"*Do not lay up for yourselves treasures on earth, where moth and rust destroy and where thieves break in and steal,* [20]*but lay up for yourselves treasures in heaven, where neither moth nor rust destroys and where thieves do not break in and steal.* [21]"*For where your treasure is, there your heart shall be also.* [24]"*No one is able to serve two masters, for either he shall hate the one and love the other, or else he shall cleave to the one and despise the other. You are not able to serve Elohim and mammon.*[z]

We are all accountable for what we do, especially when we learn the real Truth about the world's apostasy! If you blow off Yahuah's knowledge of the Truth, then you blow it off **AT YOUR OWN PERIL**! Once you are convicted of the truth, then you are accountable for what you do with that knowledge! If you choose to ignore Yahuah's call to change repeatedly, then you will be held accountable on the Day of Judgment! If you reject Yahuah's call repeatedly, then ayaz will finally **give up on you** entirely! ayaz will give you over to complete spiritual blindness! If you are a father like me, then you have the responsibility to guide your family to ayaz, **not away from Him**! Every father of Israel is **the high priest in his home** and should guide his family along Yahuah's Way, not the way of Baal! It's the father's responsibility to lovingly lead his family along Yahushua's narrow Way even though it's a very hard and afflicted Way! You are the good shepherd for your family! Lead your family with joy and gladness along the Way of owyaz! We must all search diligently and determine what the real truth of ayaz is for ourselves!

In my family's case, we had to experience many troubles and afflictions before we were finally humbled by 𐤉𐤄𐤅𐤄! 𐤉𐤄𐤅𐤄 has put our family in His furnace of affliction! He used many troubles and afflictions in this present world to humble and finally break us! Thankfully as a result, I became very, very hungry for the truth. Consider Romans 8:28! 𐤉𐤄𐤅𐤄 will use the same kinds of **hard** things in your life to get your attention, if He has to! 𐤉𐤄𐤅𐤄 loves you so very much! He works diligently to bring you back to His Way. 𐤉𐤄𐤅𐤄 proved His ultimate love for us by sending 𐤉𐤄𐤅𐤔𐤏 to suffer terribly, terribly for you and me! HalleluYah! HalleluYah! HalleluYah! Check out every word in *Let My People Go* for yourself! I dare You! 𐤉𐤄𐤅𐤔𐤏 will reveal His Ways to anyone, black, white, or anywhere in between! Yahuah's Way is **OPEN** to anyone, who has a humble and contrite heart before 𐤉𐤄𐤅𐤄! After 𐤉𐤄𐤅𐤔𐤏 reveals His Ways to you, then it's your decision what to do with Yahuah's Truth. Then it's crunch time! Your decisions on what to do then will be the most important decisions that you will ever make! It's where the rubber meets the road! Once you know the Truth, then you must act on it for 𐤉𐤄𐤅𐤔𐤏! If you decide to make the changes needed to line yourself up with the Scriptures, then **trust** 𐤉𐤄𐤅𐤄 to show you what needs to be done day by day. If you know the Way of 𐤉𐤄𐤅𐤄 and still make a conscious decision to ignore and suppress the Truth, then You have just rejected 𐤉𐤄𐤅𐤄! That's **rebellion** against 𐤉𐤄𐤅𐤄 and His desires! If you never truly repent during your lifetime, then you will be judged as a willful apostate, just like Nimrod!

What's in a Name?

When you learn the names of the 𐤉𐤄𐤅𐤄 and 𐤉𐤄𐤅𐤔𐤏, then you have just learned **the two most important words** that will ever exist in any language! The collection of writings referred to as *The Dead Sea Scrolls* contain the set apart names in Hebrew, both in modern Hebrew and in the older Paleo Hebrew. Paleo Hebrew is the uncontaminated original language of Adam. The old scrolls stored in the Qumran caves near the Dead Sea were set apart because they had the names 𐤉𐤄𐤅𐤄 and 𐤉𐤄𐤅𐤔𐤏 written on them. Righteous men in antiquity would not destroy those scrolls because they contained the name of 𐤉𐤄𐤅𐤄, even though the scrolls were worn out. **Now that's respect for the 3rd Commandment!** That's the real reason that the Dead Sea Scrolls came into existence in the first place!

Exodus 20 (Commandment #3)
^{7}"*You do not bring the Name of* 𐤉𐤄𐤅𐤄 *your Elohim to naught, for* 𐤉𐤄𐤅𐤄 *does not leave the one unpunished, who brings His Name to naught.*

This commandment warns against those, who would hide or replace the true name of ayaz! It also warns against those, who would use the name lightly, who would swear false oaths by it, or who would not show the name of ayaz the respect, which it deserves! If you don't learn anything else from this book other than the knowledge of the set apart names of ayaz and owyaz, then that knowledge alone is **priceless** to your soul! **The Scriptures state that there are no other names by which men can be saved!**

Acts 4
Be it known unto you all, and to all the people of Israel, that by the name of **owyaz** *the Messiah of Nazareth, whom ye crucified, whom* **ayaz** *raised from the dead, even by him doth this man stand here before you whole. This is the <u>stone which was set at naught of you builders</u>, which is become the head of the corner. <u>Neither is there salvation in any other: for there is none other name</u> under heaven given among men, whereby we must be saved.*

Romans 10
For whosoever shall call upon the name of **ayaz** *shall be saved.*

John 3
[16]*"For Elohim so loved the world that He gave His only brought-forth Son, so that everyone who believes in Him should not perish but possess everlasting life.* [17]*"For Elohim did not send His Son into the world to judge the world, but that the world through Him might be saved.* [18]*"He who believes in Him is not judged, but he who does not believe is judged already, because he has not believed in the <u>Name of the only brought-forth Son of Elohim</u>.*

John 1
[12]*But as many as received Him, to them He gave the authority to become children of Elohim, to those believing in <u>His Name</u>,* [13]*who were born, not of blood nor of the desire of flesh nor of the desire of man, but of Elohim.*

If you do love **ayaz** and **owyaz**, this book will really excite you! Some information in this book will **surprise and even shock you**! When you see something new in *Let My People Go* that contradicts what you have traditionally believed, then **force yourself to remain completely neutral and totally objective**! Please humor me and continue reading, then later put on your own private detective hat and check out everything in *Let My People Go* for yourself! Do your own follow-up research. Whatever you do, **Do Not** automatically dismiss something just because it's different from your religious preprogramming!

I have found in my own studies that Yahuah's truth usually lies **somewhere other** than the popularly held religious opinions of apostate Christianity, Judaism, or even the very close Messianic Judaism. Whatever the teachers, preachers, and authors, are teaching, who are in apostasy against ᎪᏕᎯᏃ, look in a different direction **(most often 180° opposite)** for the real truth of ᎪᏕᎯᏃ! ᎪᏕᎯᏃ does have a great sense of humor! ᎪᏕᎯᏃ purposely chooses the rather <u>ordinary</u>, <u>simple</u>, and <u>weak</u> things in this world to confound the wise! That's why ᎪᏕᎯᏃ chose me of all people to write *Let My People Go* and not some PHD from Harvard!

1 Corinthians 1
²⁶For look at your calling, brothers, that there were not many wise according to the flesh, not many mighty, not many noble. ²⁷But Elohim has chosen the <u>foolish matters of the world</u> to put to <u>shame the wise</u>, and Elohim has chosen the weak of the world to put to shame the strong.

ᎪᏕᎯᏃ simply will **not** reveal His real secrets to the false prophets and the false teachers, who have sold out the way of ᎪᏕᎯᏃ for the way of Balaam! Instead of walking in Yahushua's narrow Way, they have sold out for their own personal gain. Remember, you are looking for Yahuah's Truth. You are embarking on a life and death **(your life and your family's lives)** quest for the truth of ᎪᏕᎯᏃ! Most of the prophecy writers today don't understand prophecy because their underlying motives are completely materialistic! ᎪᏕᎯᏃ rightly judges our hearts and minds! ᎪᏕᎯᏃ knows the difference between clean motives and unclean motives. False prophets have their own motives and personal agendas, which include the accumulation of wealth at the expense of the sheep. These false prophets fleece their own sheep! Most market popularly held beliefs about prophecy, which are far, far from the truth of ᎪᏕᎯᏃ. These false prophets copy each others thoughts and ideas! The false prophets have been blinded by ᎪᏕᎯᏃ because of their repeated failures to respond, when ᎪᏕᎯᏃ has called them to come out of their own apostasy! Why are these false prophets blinded? It's because their real motives for writing their books are **not** pure! They're motives are **not** consistent with Yahuah's desires! Unfortunately most write for their own personal gain! They wouldn't write at all, if there was no money in it for them! Most have chosen the way of Balaam! I have to write *Let My People Go* for ᎪᏕᎯᏃ, even if no one ever buys or reads a single copy! It's a fabulous privilege for me to write *Let My People Go* for ᎪᏕᎯᏃ and OWYᎯᏃ!

2 Peter 2

¹²But these, like natural unreasoning beasts, having been born to be caught and destroyed, blaspheme that which they do not know, shall be destroyed in their destruction, ¹³being about to receive the wages of unrighteousness, deeming indulgence in the day a pleasure, spots and blemishes, reveling in their own deceptions while they feast with you, ¹⁴having eyes filled with an adulteress, and unable to cease from sin, enticing unstable beings, having a heart trained in greed, children of a curse, ¹⁵having left the right way they went astray, having followed the way of Bil'am the son of Be'or, who loved the wages of unrighteousness, ¹⁶but he was rebuked for his transgression: a dumb donkey speaking with the voice of a man restrained the madness of the prophet. ¹⁷These are fountains without water, clouds driven by a storm, to whom the blackest darkness is kept forever. ¹⁸For speaking arrogant nonsense, they entice through the lusts of the flesh, through indecencies–the ones who have indeed escaped from those living in delusion, ¹⁹promising them freedom, though themselves being slaves of corruption, for one is a slave to whatever overcomes him. ²⁰For, after they have escaped the defilements of the world through the knowledge of the Master and Savior OWYᴚZ Messiah, they are again entangled in them and overcome, the latter end is worse for them than the first. ²¹For it would have been better for them not to have known the way of righteousness, than having known it, to turn from the set-apart command delivered unto them. ²²For them the proverb has proved true, "A dog returns to his own vomit," and, "A washed sow returns to her rolling in the mud."

Jude 1:11

¹¹Woe to them! Because they have gone in the way of Qayin **(Cain)**, and gave themselves to the delusion of Bil'am for a **reward**, and perished in the rebellion of Qorah.

Most writers care more about selling books than restoring the Truth of ᎪYᴚZ. The plans that ᎪYᴚZ has for the return of OWYᴚZ <u>far</u> exceed the current popular spins in today's prophecy books! In fact, if you read those books, they will actually be **stumbling blocks** to your understanding! You don't want to be like the five virgins in the parable of OWYᴚZ, who were not ready for the Bridegroom at His return! These virgins were <u>not prepared</u> and were ultimately <u>rejected</u>! If you have already <u>completely</u> sold out to OWYᴚZ, then you already have Yahuah's seed deposited inside of you! Yahuah's set apart Spirit, the Ruach HaQodesh, teaches us Yahuah's Ways! His Ruach HaQodesh will guide you to ᎪYᴚZ step by step and will comfort you, <u>when you are put in Yahuah's furnace of affliction</u>!

1 John
²⁷ But the anointing which you have received from Him stays in you, and you have no need that anyone should teach you. But as the same anointing does teach you concerning all, and is true, and is no falsehood, and even as it has taught you, you stay in Him.

Our salvation is a **continual work in progress**! We will <u>not</u> be perfected until OWY∆Z returns at the 7th Trumpet to assume His reign of the earth! At that time the Righteous will experience a complete rebirth **(We will be literally born again!)** into incorruptible bodies! I hope, when you read *Let My People Go*, that Yahuah's Ruach HaQodesh will stir you up like never before! I pray that every reader will become hungry and thirsty for the Truth contained in Yahuah's Scriptures and that every reader will choose to become members of the commonwealth of Israel!

Restoration
The people, who are sincerely hungry for the Truth about ∆Y∆Z and OWY∆Z, as well as those, who have **already** joined Israel are my target readers! It's <u>not</u> good enough to hear the Truth, we must **love** ∆Y∆Z enough **to act** on the Truth! Since Yahushua's twelve disciples left the scene, the world has lapsed into greater and greater confusion and apostasy! Confusion, hatred, darkness, greed, and useless traditions of men have dominated every religious system in the entire world! This not only includes all the outright pagan religions of this world, which don't acknowledge the Scriptures at all, but also traditional Christianity, traditional Judaism, and even some congregations in Messianic Judaism! Pagan practices, icons, and useless traditions of men have become syncretized with Yahuah's true instructions and ordinances! This mixing has resulted in the real Truth being <u>diluted</u> and blended with seemingly harmless traditions and errors! We must examine ourselves <u>objectively</u> against **Yahuah's standards, not our own standards**! Hybrid replacements seem good and acceptable to men, but in reality they are unclean to ∆Y∆Z! ∆Y∆Z has deemed hybrid replacements **totally unacceptable**! Remember what happened, when Aaron's sons Nadab and Abihu offered strange fire and incense before ∆Y∆Z instead of what ∆Y∆Z instructed!

²*And fire came out from* ∆Y∆Z *and consumed them, and they died before* ∆Y∆Z! **Leviticus 10**

In the 1800's Alexander Hislop tried his best to expose the pagan traditions in the world's religious systems in his classic book, *The Two Babylons*. In recent years other men and women of Israel have written very good books that follow up where Alexander Hislop left off.

These books further expose apostasy and restore the knowledge of the set apart names to Israel. These men have opened themselves up to much criticism from the religious establishment, where Yahuah's real messages are <u>not</u> popular at all! The messages of ᚐYᚐZ and OWYᚐZ have <u>never</u> been popular with any of man's religious institutions at any time! Lew White has written a wonderful book called *Fossilized Customs*. *Fossilized Customs* is a very straight forward book, which goes a long way to expose apostasy! It leads many morally good people to repent and to follow the Way of OWYᚐZ! Other great books include, *Come Out of Her My People* by C.J. Koster, the *Come to the Light* series by Todd Bennett, and the Paleo Name Versions (PNV) by Todd Effren! I am so grateful to ᚐYᚐZ for providing each of these men of Israel! I'm sure that ᚐYᚐZ is raising up others as I write *Let My People Go*! These books all show how the world's religious systems have become contaminated with pagan practices, icons, and useless traditions of men! Thankfully good books like these are being written in our times! People are beginning to search and question the status quo for themselves! There is a very small remnant of people today, **who <u>do</u> <u>respond</u> to Yahuah's call**! They do make the necessary changes in their lives! HalleluYah! These people are the good ground that OWYᚐZ talked about to His disciples!

Luke 18

[15]"And that on the <u>good soil</u> are those who, <u>having heard the word</u> <u>with a noble and good heart, retain it</u>, and **<u>bear fruit with endurance</u>**.

This remnant of Israel love the Truth of ᚐYᚐZ! They are very hungry and thirsty! The sad part is that millions and millions of morally good and sincere people over many thousands of years have been deceived by trickery! They have fallen into religious snares, which were dug by the adversaries of ᚐYᚐZ! It saddens me to think about all the good people, who went to their graves being mislead by the false shepherds! The false shepherds led them in the wrong direction for their own personal gain in this world! The religious traditions of men have led multitudes of men to **accept lawlessness**, which ᚐYᚐZ **has always rejected**! ᚐYᚐZ is the same mighty one in the past, present, and future! ᚐYᚐZ is unchanging and transcends time itself! It's impossible for ᚐYᚐZ to change outside of His own character! Lawlessness is transgression against Yahuah's instructions and ordinances, Yahuah's Torah! The Torah of ᚐYᚐZ contains Yahuah's Instructions, His Ordinances, and His Commandments! Christians have been led to believe <u>by</u> <u>their</u> <u>false</u> <u>shepherds</u> that Yahuah's standards have <u>somehow</u> changed at different times for different peoples! Pastors instruct their sheep **every Sunday** that the Torah, which they **smugly** call the Law, is for Jews only!

Instead of truth, these shepherds teach their sheep that they are now covered under a new special covenant outside of Yahuah's **covenant with Israel**! **Hel-lo-o, nothing could be further from the Truth**! The Scriptures actually state that the evidence of our faith and our love for OWYAZ is that we obey Yahuah's Commandments, period! Like Forrest Gump said, "There's nothing more to say about that!" The case should be closed, but it's not, because the false shepherds continue to confuse the morally good sheep! Morally good people have been led to believe that a formal seminary degree equates into a person, who can rightly interpret the Scriptures! **That's a Big, Big, Big mistake!** False shepherds with fancy degrees from famous schools of secular learning have been leading good sheep further and further into the apostasy for thousands of years instead of guarding the Truth contained in the Yahuah's Scriptures! We all will be held accountable for what **we have done in this world**! Sellers of illegal drugs are judged much harsher than the drug users today! In the same way the false shepherds will be judged much harsher by OWYAZ! They will be held to a much higher standard because of their knowledge and their willful rebellion against AYAZ! **Woe, Woe, Woe, be it to the false Shepherds!**

Do You Have A Love For The Truth?

I will warn you now that many subjects that I will discuss in *Let My People Go* will be totally new to you, even if you study the Scriptures diligently! Some of the information will probably shock you! The book will certainly will not line up with popularly held prophetic teachings. In writing this book my concern was not pleasing people or being in the mainstream of this world's popular religious thought! Today the false shepherds teach smooth things that are easy to accept by people, who really don't like to study for themselves! The smooth things that they teach involve little or no personal sacrifice or effort to implement! Messages about struggles, trials, tribulations, sufferings, rejections, and afflictions are not preached very often, even though OWYAZ warned us that our lives would be very hard and greatly afflicted, if we choose to follow His Way!

Matthew 7
[13]"*Enter in through the narrow gate! Because the gate is wide – and the way is broad – that leads to destruction, and there are many, who enter in through it.* [14]"*Because the gate is narrow and the way is <u>hard pressed</u>[b] which leads to life, and there are few, who find it.* [15]"*But beware of the false prophets, who come to you in sheep's clothing, but inwardly they are savage wolves.*
[b] **Or the way is afflicted.**

Instead of the hard Truth, the false shepherd's of today **preach prosperity, prosperity, and more prosperity in this world**, which is in direct opposition with Yahushua's messages!

Matthew 19:24 *And again I say unto you, It is easier for a camel **(Mistranslated, camel should be rope.)** to go through the eye of a needle, than for a rich man to enter into the kingdom of* ᎥᎩᏃ.

Matthew 6 *Lay **not** up for yourselves treasures upon earth, where moth and rust doth corrupt, and where thieves break through and steal: But lay up for yourselves treasures in heaven, where neither moth nor rust doth corrupt, and where thieves do not break through nor steal:*

When you follow Yahushua, you should **expect** rejection and persecution from this present world's religious system! When you truly decide to become a doer of the Word and follow the instructions of ᎥᎩᏃ, then you will find yourself going against the grain of this world's religious, social, and economic systems! If you truly love OWᎩᏃ, then you will truly learn what it means to be set apart to ᎥᎩᏃ!

Scoffers
2 Peter
This is now, beloved ones, the second letter I write to you, in which I stir up your sincere mind, to remember ²the words previously spoken by the set-apart prophets, and of the command of the Master and Savior, spoken by your emissaries, ³knowing this first: that mockers shall come in the last days with mocking, walking according to their own lusts, ⁴and saying, "Where is the promise of His coming? For since the fathers fell asleep, all continues as from the beginning of creation." ⁵For they choose to have this hidden from them: that the heavens were of old, and the earth standing out of water and in the water, by the Word of Elohim, ⁶through which the world at that time was destroyed, being flooded with water. ⁷And the present heavens and the earth are treasured up by the same Word, being kept for fire, to a day of judgment and destruction of wicked men.

We **should expect** in light of the above Scripture that the majority of people in our time **will scoff at the notion that OWᎩᏃ is about to return**! They've heard it all before! People have felt that way for centuries, right? Beware least you be found naked by OWᎩᏃ! Let's be honest, most people don't really believe that things will ever change, do they? Most people believe that things will just keep on going somehow! The material presented in *Let My People Go* will no doubt be spurned by the rich, the famous, the powerful, and most of the religious scholars of this world! They will view this information as nonsense! It's a threat to their empires!

The religious authorities were the biggest adversaries of OWY3Z during His ministry! So shouldn't the people of OWY3Z today also expect that the traditional religious authorities will be their adversaries too! **Anyone** searching for the real Way of OWY3Z should expect stumbling blocks and opposition from the traditional religious authorities of our time!

Study to Show Yourself Approved!

Please get the best literal translation of the Scriptures that you can to study. Find a good literal translation, which has the Set Apart Names restored. My personal favorites are *The Scriptures* by the Institute of Scripture Research, which I predominately used in *Let My People Go*, and *The Restoration Scriptures* by Your Arms to Israel Publishing. I also love to read Todd Effren's *Paleo Name Versions*. They have blessed my heart! Todah Todd! Thank you so much! Taking the Scriptures out of their intended context is one of the main tactics that the wolf shepherds have used for thousands of years in order to twist the context of a Scripture passage to suit their selfish purposes! Read and study the Scriptures in their original context! The writers of the Scriptures were all Hebrews, so get a translation true to the original Hebraic context of the Scriptures! Don't skip around too much. Read the Scriptures as a complete scroll of text just like they were written by the author. Read the books of Scriptures through, over and over and over. Make notes in the margins for later comparison. Other books that will help you understand the Scriptures are also available! These books include *The Book of Enoch* and *The Book of Yashar*! Both *The Book of Enoch* and *The Book of Yashar* are directly quoted from in the Scriptures! *The Book of Adam and Eve* and *The Cave of Treasures* are also very old writings, which should be evaluated with discernment, but do contain very useful information, when checked against the Scriptures! These two books will give the reader useful insight and clues into what actually occurred before the Flood. All these writings were handed down from generation to generation. Of course some things were altered to some extent, but they have survived the ravages of time. I love reading them! Without a doubt, liberties were taken with all these writings, but the same can be said of every English translation of the Scriptures including the King James Bible! I suspect alterations of all these books were done **intentionally** to suit man's religious agendas, but some may have been done unintentionally! Who am I to say? But, Israel has the very best teacher! He's able to unravel every twist and tangle! OWY3Z will show us the right way to go!

2 Thessalonians 2

⁹*The coming of the lawless one is according to the working of Satan, with all power and signs and wonders of falsehood,* ¹⁰*and with <u>all deceit of unrighteousness</u> in those perishing, because **they did not receive the love of the truth** in order for them to be saved.*

To follow 𝐀𝐘𝐀𝐙 in this day and time, a person must have a passionate love for the truth! 𝐀𝐘𝐀𝐙 hates lies and Yahuah's people must be extremely zealous, when it comes to searching for the Truth! In order to objectively read *Let My People Go* you must determine <u>right</u> <u>now</u> to become as <u>neutral, unbiased, and open-minded</u> as you possibly can! If you have already determined to dismiss anything that's not consistent with your present beliefs, then you are wasting your time reading *Let My People Go!* But, if you STOP reading, then you may have missed an opportunity to climb out of the religious snares of apostasy that you may be trapped in! The information in *Let My People Go* is only new in the context of the time that we live in today. The Prophets of 𝐀𝐘𝐀𝐙 were instructed by the Word of 𝐀𝐘𝐀𝐙, OWY𝐀𝐙. OWY𝐀𝐙 commanded them to write what they heard and saw so that the Righteous of future generations would understand Yahuah's plans for mankind. The truth of 𝐀𝐘𝐀𝐙 has been hidden and replaced with the fables conceived by wicked men over thousands of years! To recover real wisdom and understanding about 𝐀𝐘𝐀𝐙, a person must diligently search out the Truth for himself! **There is no short cut**! A lot of **work is required**! You should <u>not</u> trust anyone to do this righteous **work** for you! If you will put forth the effort, then OWY𝐀𝐙 has promised that He will reward you! You can find Yahuah's treasure of great value, if you search for OWY𝐀𝐙 with your whole heart! Then you will love the truth of 𝐀𝐘𝐀𝐙 and guard it with your very life! One day every human being that has ever lived will be judged by OWY𝐀𝐙! He will judge everyone using the Torah of 𝐀𝐘𝐀𝐙 as His **standard**! Everyone of us will be judged on **how we have lived our lives in this present world**! We must be prepared! We must not be completely overcome by the cares of this present world to the extent that we ignore the weightier matters of **life**! How can we be ready? We must live our lives in a manner that pleases 𝐀𝐘𝐀𝐙 **now, before** OWY𝐀𝐙 **comes**! How do we please 𝐀𝐘𝐀𝐙? We must humble ourselves and make a life changing decision to follow Yahushua's Way no matter what happens! Choose to travel Yahushua's narrow way! Go that Way! Yahushua's Way is very afflicted! Very few people will travel that Way! **But in the end, if you choose to tough it out and follow** OWY𝐀𝐙**, then you will <u>not</u> be ashamed!** If you finish this race of patient endurance well, then at the sound of the 7th trumpet, you will **shine** like a bright morning star just like OWY𝐀𝐙!

Israel's Final Exodus
Chapter 2

> ⁶"I shall say to the north, 'Give them up!' And to the south, 'Do not keep them back!' Bring My sons from afar, and My daughters from the ends of the earth–⁷all those who are called by My Name, whom I have created, formed, even made for My esteem."
> YeshaYahu (Isaiah) 43

Have you ever seen the Charlton Heston movie called *The Ten Commandments*? *The Ten Commandments* has always been one of my favorite movies! I can still visualize Charlton Heston, who played Moses, standing on the shore of the Sea with the army of the Pharaoh in hot pursuit! Moses has the rod of ᴀYᴀZ outstretched over the Sea! There **appears** to be no escape for the Israelites! But, just in time, ᴀYᴀZ parts the Sea! The Sea forms a wall of water on the right side and on the left side leaving a dry road for Israel to cross! Wouldn't those events have been wonderful spectacles to have witnessed first hand? After the Israelites arrived at Mount Sinai, ᴀYᴀZ gave Moses His Ten Commandments! Can you imagine what it must have been like, when ᴀYᴀZ came down on the top of Mount Sinai! The Mountain was on fire and trembling from the presence of ᴀYᴀZ! Mount Sinai was covered with fire, darkness, and thick clouds! ᴀYᴀZ spoke directly to the Israelites from the midst of the fire that covered the Mountain, similar to the way OWYᴀZ spoke to Moses from the burning bush!

Exodus 19
And it came to pass on the third day in the morning, that there were thunders and lightnings, and a thick cloud upon the mount, and the voice of the trumpet exceeding loud; so that all the people that were in the camp trembled. And Moses brought forth the people out of the camp to meet with Elohim; and they stood at the nether part of the mount. And mount Sinai was altogether on a smoke, because ᴀYᴀZ descended upon it in fire: and the smoke thereof ascended as the smoke of a furnace, and the whole mount quaked greatly. And when the voice of the trumpet sounded long, and waxed louder and louder, Moses spake, and Elohim answered him by a voice. And ᴀYᴀZ came down upon mount Sinai, on the top of the mount: and ᴀYᴀZ called Moses up to the top of the mount; and Moses went up.

ᴀYᴀZ spoke the Ten Commandments to the multitude of Israel gathered below Mount Sinai! Yahuah's voice <u>thundered</u> from the Heavens above the top of Mount Sinai as ᴀYᴀZ spoke directly to the people gathered at the base of the Mountain!

Yahuah's voice was so awesome that from that time forward, the Israelites insisted that Moses mediate between them and 𝐀𝐘𝐀𝐙! They didn't want 𝐀𝐘𝐀𝐙 to speak directly to them anymore! Those events were awesome and the people were terrified!

Exodus 20

And Elohim spake all these words, saying, I am 𝐀𝐘𝐀𝐙 thy Elohim, which have brought thee out of the land of Mitsrayim, out of the house of bondage. Thou shalt have no other elohim before me. Thou shalt not make unto thee any graven image, or any likeness of any thing that is in heaven above, or that is in the earth beneath, or that is in the water under the earth: Thou shalt not bow down thyself to them, nor serve them: for I 𝐀𝐘𝐀𝐙 thy Elohim am a jealous Elohim, visiting the iniquity of the fathers upon the children unto the third and fourth generation of them that hate me; And shewing mercy unto thousands of them that love me, and keep my commandments. Thou shalt not take the name of 𝐀𝐘𝐀𝐙 thy Elohim in vain; for 𝐀𝐘𝐀𝐙 will not hold him guiltless that taketh his name in vain. Remember the sabbath day, to keep it holy. Six days shalt thou labor, and do all thy work: But the seventh day is the sabbath of 𝐀𝐘𝐀𝐙 thy Elohim: in it thou shalt not do any work, thou, nor thy son, nor thy daughter, thy manservant, nor thy maidservant, nor thy cattle, nor thy stranger that is within thy gates: For in six days 𝐀𝐘𝐀𝐙 made heaven and earth, the sea, and all that in them is, and rested the seventh day: wherefore 𝐀𝐘𝐀𝐙 blessed the sabbath day, and hallowed it. Honor thy father and thy mother: that thy days may be long upon the land which 𝐀𝐘𝐀𝐙 thy Elohim giveth thee. Thou shalt not kill. Thou shalt not commit adultery. Thou shalt not steal. Thou shalt not bear false witness against thy neighbor. Thou shalt not covet thy neighbor's house, thou shalt not covet thy neighbor's wife, nor his manservant, nor his maidservant, nor his ox, nor his ass, nor any thing that is thy neighbor's. And all the people saw the thunderings, and the lightnings, and the noise of the trumpet, and the mountain smoking: and when the people saw it, they removed, and stood afar off. And they said unto Moses, Speak thou with us, and we will hear: but let not Elohim speak with us, lest we die. And Moses said unto the people, Fear not: for Elohim is come to prove you, and that his fear may be before your faces, that ye sin not.

Is Yahuah's arm to short to save us today? Yahuah's arm, OWYAZ, is not to short to deliver Yahuah's people, Israel, from the nations today! 𝐀𝐘𝐀𝐙 is about to return the captivity of Israel, but this time 𝐀𝐘𝐀𝐙 will rescue Israel from all four corners of the earth! Have you ever wished that you could have been there to see those fabulous signs and wonders described in the Scriptures? If the answer is "yes", then you are going to be thrilled as you read *Let My People Go!*

𐤀𐤉𐤄𐤅, El Shaddai, **(from Shadah, Mighty One of the Mountain)**, has saved His greatest signs and wonders for Yahushua's return, which is coming very soon! Just think about that! You can witness wonderful things that you never even imagined possible, if you make the right choices now! If you love 𐤀𐤉𐤄𐤅 with all your heart and guard His Commandments, then you too can stand before 𐤀𐤉𐤄𐤅 and OWY𐤀𐤉 at the foot of Mount Sinai just like Moses did! How can that be possible? How do I know that there is a worldwide Exodus for Israel? The final Exodus for Israel is a central theme in the prophetic writings of the Scriptures! 𐤀𐤉𐤄𐤅 says that this final Exodus will **completely overshadow the 1st Exodus** to the point that no one will even speak of the 1st Exodus!

YirmeYahu 16
[14] "Therefore see, the days are coming," declares 𐤀𐤉𐤄𐤅, "when it is no longer said, 𐤀𐤉𐤄𐤅 lives who brought up the children of Yisra'el from the land of Mitsrayim,' [15] but, 𐤀𐤉𐤄𐤅 lives who brought up the children of Yisra'el from the land of the north and from all the lands where He had driven them.' For I shall bring them back into their land I gave to their fathers.

The earth and all of Yahuah's creation longs for its release from the curses of sin! The people called Israel from all the generations will be assembled together in one place at one time at the sounding of the 7th Trumpet of Revelation!

YirmeYahu 23
[7] "Therefore, see, the days are coming," declares 𐤀𐤉𐤄𐤅, "when they shall say no more, 'As 𐤀𐤉𐤄𐤅 lives who brought up the children of Yisra'el out of the land of Mitsrayim,' [8] but, 'As 𐤀𐤉𐤄𐤅 lives who brought up and led the seed of the house of Yisra'el out of the land of the north and from all the lands where I had driven them. And they shall dwell on their own soil."

In this final spectacular ingathering of Israel back to the real Promised Land, Yahuah's overcomers, Israel, are not only going to Mount Sinai like they did in the 1st Exodus, but Israel will ultimately enter into Yahushua's New Yahrushalayim! The New Yahrushalayim is Yahuah's set apart city founded on Mount Zion in the heavens! Of course today the New Yahrushalayim and Mount Zion are hidden from our vision, but Yahuah will bring them down out of the heavens into **everyone's** vision over the Mountains of Israel, when OWY𐤀𐤉 returns at the 7th Trumpet! The New Yahrushalayim is the set apart city not made with human hands, which Israel will ultimately inhabit as it descends to the earth! 𐤀𐤉𐤄𐤅 will finally remove the veil from our eyes at the sounding of the 7th Trumpet!

Everyone on the planet will be able to see the heavenly Mount Zion as it descends back to the wilderness and its pre-Flood position over the Set Apart Mountain of ᎪᏆᎪᏃ! Remember Yahuah will restore everything! ΟᎳᎩᎪᏃ has created the New Yahrushalayim for His Bride! It comes down out of the Heavens into our vision above the Mountains of Israel at the sounding of the 7th Trumpet, when ΟᎳᎩᎪᏃ returns to rescue His people! Rescue Israel from what you say! Keep reading *Let My People Go* and you'll understand Yahuah's plan for His great Day! The New Yahrushalayim will be visible in the Heavens as it descends to the Earth to its designated place in the wilderness, after the sounding of the 7th Trumpet! At the sounding of the 7th Trumpet, **Mount Zion** will be seen in the heavens as she descends! Mount Zion will give birth to a Son, ΟᎳᎩᎪᏃ! ΟᎳᎩᎪᏃ will return to rescue and gather all Israel to His wedding banquet!

Abraham Looked For a City *Not* *Made* With Human Hands!
Hebrews 11

By faith Abraham, when he was called to go out into a place which he should after receive for an inheritance, obeyed; and he went out, not knowing whither he went. By faith he sojourned in the land of promise, as in a strange country, dwelling in tabernacles with Isaac and Jacob, the heirs with him of the same promise: For <u>he looked for a city which hath foundations, whose builder and maker is</u> ᎪᏆᎪᏃ. *Through faith also Sara herself received strength to conceive seed, and was delivered of a child when she was past age, because she judged him faithful who had promised. Therefore sprang there even of one, and him as good as dead, so many as the stars of the sky in multitude, and as the sand which is by the sea shore innumerable. These all died in faith, not having received the promises, but having seen them afar off, and were persuaded of them, and embraced them, and confessed that they were strangers and pilgrims on the earth. For they that say such things declare plainly that they seek a country. And truly, if they had been mindful of that country from whence they came out, they would have had the chance to return. But now they desire a better country, that is, an heavenly: wherefore* ᎪᏆᎪᏃ *is not ashamed to be called their Elohim: for he hath prepared for them a city.*

Hebrews 12
For ye are not come unto the Mount that might be touched, and that burned with fire, nor unto blackness, and darkness, and tempest, And the sound of a trumpet and the voice of words; which voice they that heard entreated that the word should not be spoken to them any more:

Hebrews 12, cont.
*(For they could not endure that which was commanded, And if so much as a beast touch the mountain, it shall be stoned, or thrust through with a dart: And so terrible was the sight, that Moses said, I exceedingly fear and quake:) But ye are come unto mount Zion, and unto the city of the living Elohim, the Heavenly Yahrushalayim, and to an innumerable company of angels **(messengers)**, __To the general assembly and assembly of the firstborn__, which are written in heaven, and to* ᎪYᎯZ *the Judge of all, and to the spirits of just men made perfect, And to* OWYᎯZ *the mediator of the new covenant, and to the blood of sprinkling, that speaketh better things than that of Abel. See that ye refuse not him that speaketh. For if they escaped not who refused him that spake on earth, much more shall not we escape, if we turn away from him that speaketh from heaven: Whose voice then shook the earth: but now he hath promised, saying,* **Yet once more I shake not the earth only, but also heaven.** *And this word, Yet once more, signifieth the removing of those things that are shaken, as of things that are made, that those things which cannot be shaken may remain.*

OWYᎯZ appears at the sounding of the 7th Trumpet riding on the clouds to deliver His First Fruits, His Barley, who are trapped! They are under siege in the __authentic__ Yahrushalayim, which has been sacked by the beast! At the sound of the 7th Trumpet OWYᎯZ will lead all of Israel, His overcomers, to His camp at Mount Sinai for the final 3½ years of Daniel's 490 year prophecy! When the 7th Trumpet sounds, OWYᎯZ will split the Mount of Olives and provide a Way of escape for Israel through the Mountains just like He parted the Sea in the 1st Exodus! OWYᎯZ will rescue the First Fruits of Israel and lead them to Mount Sinai along with a great assembly from all the generations of Israel! After the 7th Trumpet sounds, the Scriptures teach that OWYᎯZ will hand pick fishermen and hunters from those, who have escaped from the rebuilt Yahrushalayim, to send to the nations! These emissaries will fish out and hunt every last one of Yahushua's people **(His Wheat)**, who are trapped in the nations! Yahushua's Wheat will be harvested out of all the nations, where they are being oppressed by the beast of Revelation! Israel's final Exodus will be completely __supernatural__ and **has __nothing whatsoever to do with today's modern State of Israel__!** Israel's worldwide Exodus is not to be confused with the __man__-made attempt to gather Jews into a Zionist state __called__ Israel! Keep reading! Stay neutral! Don't judge by appearances! Today's State of Israel is man's attempt to preempt Yahuah's __supernatural__ Exodus! In fact today's State of Israel **is actually __not__ even located in the __authentic__ location of the land promised to Abraham, Isaac, and Jacob!**

Today's Zionist State of Israel was planned and executed by powerful men, not ᴭYᴭZ! It is doomed to failure despite the fact that many sincere people have put their faith in it! ᴭYᴭZ doesn't need man's money, technology, armies, jet aircraft, or helicopters to gather His people back to the Promised Land! Israel's first Exodus was all supernatural and Israel's final Exodus will be **even more** supernatural! The final Exodus will exceed all of our expectations! How do I know? Because the Scriptures say so! The final Exodus will be so spectacular that the first Exodus won't even be spoken of in the future! Can you imagine a deliverance that will be so awesome that it will completely overshadow the 1st Exodus? That means that the signs and wonders of the coming Exodus will completely overshadow the ten plagues of Mitsrayim, the parting of the Sea, and the destruction of Pharaoh's army! How can that be possible? Because the Scriptures clearly say that it will happen! The Scriptures teach that the final Exodus is soon to come! I can't wait! How about You?

The Final Exodus in the Scriptures!
Jeremiah 16
Therefore, behold, the days come, saith ᴭYᴭZ, *that it shall no more be said,* ᴭYᴭZ *liveth, that brought up the children of Israel out of the land of Mitsrayim; But,* ᴭYᴭZ *liveth, that brought up the children of Israel from the land of the north, and from all the lands whither he had driven them: and I will bring them again into their land that I gave unto their fathers. Behold, I will send for many fishers, saith* ᴭYᴭZ, *and they shall fish them; and after will I send for many hunters, and they shall hunt them from every mountain, and from every hill, and out of the holes of the rocks. For mine eyes are upon all their ways: they are not hid from my face, neither is their iniquity hid from mine eyes. And first I will recompense their iniquity and their sin double; because they have defiled my land, they have filled mine inheritance with the carcasses of their detestable and abominable things. O* ᴭYᴭZ, *my strength, and my fortress, and my refuge in the day of affliction, the Gentiles shall come unto thee from the ends of the earth, and shall say, Surely our fathers have inherited lies, vanity, and things wherein there is no profit. Shall a man make elohim unto himself, and they are no elohim? Therefore, behold, I will this once cause them to know, I will cause them to know mine hand and my might; and* **they shall know that my name is ᴭYᴭZ.**

Jeremiah 23
Woe be unto the pastors that destroy and scatter the sheep of my pasture saith ᴭYᴭZ! *Therefore thus saith* ᴭYᴭZ *Elohim of Israel against the pastors that feed my people; Ye have scattered my flock, and driven them away, and have not visited them: behold, I will visit upon you the evil of your doings, saith* ᴭYᴭZ.

Jeremiah 23, cont.

And I will gather the remnant of my flock out of all countries whither I have driven them, and will bring them again to their folds; and they shall be fruitful and increase. And I will set up shepherds over them which shall feed them: and they shall fear no more, nor be dismayed, neither shall they be lacking, saith **ayaz**. Behold, the days come, saith **ayaz**, that I will raise unto David a righteous Branch, and a King shall reign and prosper, and shall execute judgment and justice in the earth.

In his days Judah shall be saved, and Israel shall dwell safely: and this is his name whereby he shall be called, **ayaz** OUR RIGHTEOUSNESS. Therefore, behold, the days come, saith **ayaz**, that they shall no more say, **ayaz** liveth, which brought up the children of Israel out of the land of Mitsrayim; But, **ayaz** liveth, which brought up and which led the seed of the house of Israel out of the north country, and from all countries whither I had driven them; and they shall dwell in their own land.

Jeremiah 31

Behold, I will bring <u>them from the north country, and gather them from the coasts of the earth</u>, and with them the blind and the lame, the woman with child and her that travaileth with child together:<u> a great company shall return thither</u>. They shall come with weeping, and with supplications will I lead them: I will cause them to walk by the rivers of waters in a straight way, wherein they shall not stumble: for I am a father to Israel, and Ephraim is my firstborn. Hear the word of **ayaz**, O ye nations, and declare it in the isles afar off, and say, <u>He that scattered Israel will gather him, and keep him, as a shepherd doth his flock</u>. For **ayaz** hath redeemed Jacob, and ransomed him from the hand of him that was stronger than he. Therefore <u>they shall come and sing in the height of Zion</u>, and shall flow together to the goodness of **ayaz**, for wheat, and for wine, and for oil, and for the young of the flock and of the herd: and their soul shall be as a watered garden; and they <u>shall not sorrow any more at all</u>. Then shall the virgin rejoice in the dance, both young men and old together: for I will turn their **mourning into joy**, and **will comfort them, and make them rejoice from their sorrow**. And I will satiate the soul of the priests with fatness, and my people shall be satisfied with my goodness, saith **ayaz**. Behold, the days come, saith **ayaz**, that I will <u>make a new covenant</u> with the house of Israel, and with the house of Judah: Not according to the covenant that I made with their fathers in the day that I took them by the hand to bring them out of the land of Mitsrayim; which my covenant they brake, although I was an husband unto them, saith **ayaz**:

Jeremiah 31, cont.
But this shall be the covenant that I will make with the house of Israel; After those days, saith 𐤀𐤉𐤄𐤅, *I <u>will put my law in their inward parts</u> and <u>write it in their hearts</u>; and will be their Elohim, and they shall be my people. And they shall teach no more every man his neighbor, and every man his brother, saying, Know* 𐤀𐤉𐤄𐤅: *for they shall all know me, from the least of them unto the greatest of them, saith* 𐤀𐤉𐤄𐤅; *for I will forgive their iniquity, and I will remember their sin no more.*

Jeremiah 32
*Behold, <u>I will gather them</u> out of all countries, whither I have driven them in mine anger, and in my fury, and in great wrath; and **I will bring them again unto this place**, and I will cause them to dwell safely: And they shall be my people, and I will be their Elohim: And I will give them one heart, and one way, that they may fear me for ever, for the good of them, and of their children after them: And I will make an everlasting covenant with them, that I will not turn away from them, to do them good; but I will put my fear in their hearts, that they shall not depart from me. **Yea, I will rejoice over them to do them good, and I will plant them in this land <u>assuredly with my whole heart and with my whole soul</u>**! For thus saith* 𐤀𐤉𐤄𐤅; *Like as I have brought all this great evil upon this people, <u>so will I bring upon them all the good that I have promised them.</u>*

Verse 41 of Jeremiah 32 reveals <u>just how important to</u> Yahuah's heart the regathering of His remnant people, Israel, really is! 𐤀𐤉𐤄𐤅 <u>promises</u> that He will gather and restore His people with **His whole Heart and soul**! That's one of the most powerful statements of Yahuah's will in the entire Scriptures! What an astounding verse! Who can measure the depth of Yahuah's heart and soul! Yahuah's heart and soul are unsearchable, infinite, boundless, and without measure! 𐤀𐤉𐤄𐤅 says that He desires with His whole heart to return His people, Israel, from their captivity in the nations back to the original Promised Land! This is an expression of Yahuah's boundless love for Israel! This is the same love that 𐤀𐤉𐤄𐤅 demonstrated, when **He chose** to humble His only Son, 𐤏𐤅𐤄𐤅𐤔, and offer Him as our Passover Lamb! That same love for Israel motivated 𐤏𐤅𐤄𐤅𐤔 **to humble Himself and endure immeasurable pain, suffering, and rejection, when He came as our Passover Lamb!** Israel's final Exodus will happen soon, but it will <u>not</u> happen as a result of man's efforts and scheming!

Jeremiah 33
Behold, I will bring it health and cure, and I will cure them, and will reveal unto them the abundance of peace and Truth.

Jeremiah 33

And I will cause the captivity of Judah and the captivity of Israel to return, and will build them, <u>as at the first</u>. And I <u>will cleanse them from all their iniquity</u>, whereby they have sinned against me; and I will pardon all their iniquities, whereby they have sinned, and whereby they have transgressed against me. And it shall be to me a name of joy, a praise and an honor before all the nations of the earth, which shall hear all the good that I do unto them: and they shall fear and tremble for all the goodness and for all the prosperity that I procure unto it. Thus saith ayaz; again there shall be heard <u>in this place</u>, which ye say shall be <u>desolate</u> without man and without beast, even in the cities of Judah, <u>and in the streets of Yahrushalayim, that are desolate, without man, and without inhabitant, and without beast,</u> The voice of joy, and the voice of gladness, the voice of the bridegroom, and the voice of the bride, the voice of them that shall say, Praise ayaz of hosts: for ayaz is good; for his mercy endureth for ever: and of them that shall bring the sacrifice of praise into the house of ayaz. For I will cause to return the captivity of the land, as at the first, saith ayaz. Thus saith ayaz of hosts; <u>Again in this place, which is desolate without man and without beast</u>, and in all the cities thereof, shall be an habitation of shepherds causing their flocks to lie down. In the cities of the mountains, in the cities of the vale, and in the cities of the south, and in the land of Benjamin, and in the places about Yahrushalayim, and in the cities of Judah, shall the flocks pass again under the hands of him that telleth them, saith ayaz. Behold, the days come, saith ayaz, that I will perform that good thing which I have promised unto the house of Israel and to the house of Judah. In those days, and at that time, will I cause the Branch of righteousness **(Yahushua)** to grow up unto David; and he shall execute judgment and righteousness in the land. In those days shall Judah be saved, and Yahrushalayim shall dwell safely: and this is the name wherewith she shall be called, ayaz our righteousness.

Jeremiah 50

In those days, and in that time, saith ayaz, <u>the children of Israel shall come</u>, they and the children of <u>Judah together, going and weeping</u>: they shall go, and seek ayaz their Elohim. They shall ask the way to Zion with their faces thitherward, saying, Come, and let us join ourselves to ayaz in a perpetual covenant that shall not be forgotten. My people hath been <u>lost sheep</u>: their <u>shepherds</u> <u>have caused</u> <u>them to go astray</u>; they have turned them away on the mountains: they have gone from mountain to hill, <u>they have forgotten their resting place</u>. All that found them have devoured them: and their adversaries said, We offend not, because they have sinned against ayaz, the habitation of justice, even ayaz, the hope of their fathers.

Jeremiah 50, cont.
And I will bring Israel again to his habitation, and he shall feed on Carmel and Bashan, and his soul shall be satisfied upon mount Ephraim and Gilead. In those days, and in that time, saith **ayaz***, the iniquity of Israel shall be sought for, and there shall be none; and the sins of Judah, and they shall not be found: for* <u>I will pardon them whom I reserve</u>.

Not only has **ayaz** offered His redemption to the twelve tribes of Israel, but He has offered His **OWYaz** to all the nations of the earth!

Isaiah 49
⁵*And now said* **ayaz** *– who formed Me from the womb to be His Servant, to bring Ya'aqob back to Him, though Yisra'el is not gathered to Him, yet I am esteemed in the eyes of* **ayaz***, and My Elohim has been My strength –* ⁶*and He says, "Shall it be a* **small matter** *for You to be My Servant to raise up the tribes of Ya'aqob, and to bring back the preserved ones of Yisra'el? And I shall give You as a light to the gentiles, to be My deliverance to the ends of the earth!"*[i]

As you can see, the theme of Israel's end time Exodus is the central theme of all the prophecy in the Scriptures. Hundreds more references about Israel's end time Exodus are to be found in the Scriptures! Israel must understand, **who they are**! Who is Israel anyway? Everyone, who is hungry for the Truth, needs to search out the answer to that question for themselves! Batya Wooten has written a very good book called *Who is Israel* on the subject, which I recommend! *Who is Israel* will be a good starting point for your research! The Scriptures teach that, if you really love **ayaz** and **OWYaz**, then you will desire to please them by obeying the Commandments and Ordinances of **ayaz**! When you make your mind up to really seek Yahuah's ways, then **ayaz** will surely reveal them to you! When **ayaz** begins to reveal His ways to you, then you will realize how twisted man's religious traditions have become! You will be upset that you ever followed them! At that time you will be faced with many decisions! Now here's the difficult part! If you truly follow the ways of **ayaz**, you will **not** feel comfortable participating in the errors of man's religious systems anymore! If you make a decision to continue to be a willing participant in the religious apostasy of men, then you have rejected the Truth of the Scriptures! You have <u>**loved the lies**</u> of apostasy more than **ayaz**! That really says it all, doesn't it? I hope that this book will make those decisions easier! Again if you really love **ayaz** and His son, **OWYaz**, you will want to please them by obeying their instructions, not man's religious traditions! **ayaz** calls His people, Israel!

Israel will have the Torah of **ayaz** written on their hearts! Israel will love Yahuah's Torah and they will love Yahuah's name! Israel will <u>not</u> give Yahuah's Commandments up for anything, even if they cost them their own lives! When the Romans sacked Yahrushalayim for the last time in 135 CE, the Romans completely leveled the city to the ground! That is **<u>still</u>** the present condition of the **<u>real</u>** Yahrushalayim to this day! **ayaz** has determined that the real Yahrushalayim will remain in ruins in the dust of northwestern Saudi Arabia and will remain uninhabited, until **owyaz** returns to harvest His Barley! Am I saying that the city called Jerusalem in the State of Israel is not the real Yahrushalayim of the Scriptures? **Yes, that's exactly what I am saying** and you can prove it to yourself as you read *Let My People Go*! That's absurd you say! Stay neutral and keep reading! Remember **Yahushua's Verse to Remember**! In fact, you might want to read that Scripture passage again before reading every chapter of this book because there are many more surprises, but I did promise you that there won't be any UFOs or atomic holocausts! No, it's not absurd to say that the real Yahrushalayim lies in ruins without any inhabitants because that's what **ayaz** taught! **ayaz** communicated that message through His prophets time and time again! It's what the Scriptures teach! The Romans took heavy losses trying to suppress the revolts of the Jewish zealots! The Romans hated the Jews! They knew very well how much the Jews loved their precious Promised Land and especially their beloved city, Yahrushalayim! The Romans devised and executed a dastardly plan, which they knew would hurt the Jews in the worst possible way! At that time the Romans exiled as many Jews as possible from the real Promised Land! They killed all the remaining zealots and their families (more than 500,000)! Then the Romans moved the borders of the real Promised Land **<u>north</u>**! They established a **<u>counterfeit</u>** Promised Land in today's Palestine and built a new Roman city called Aelia Capitolina! That counterfeit city is today's Jerusalem in the State of Israel! That is the truth! The Romans knew that after many Jewish generations had died off, there would be no more eye witnesses, who could identify the authentic location of the real Promised Land! The Jews living in Europe and the Middle East would **<u>no longer know</u>** that a **switch-r-rue <u>had even occurred</u>**! The vast Roman resources and propaganda system were used over many centuries to wipe out any knowledge that could be used to reestablish the real boundaries of the authentic Promised Land! In 1947, after many generations of Jewish exile in the nations, powerful Zionist entities made agreements with world super-powers!

They **revived** the dastardly lie, when they called for all the Jews in every nation to relocate to the recreated Promised Land in Palestine! Some sincere spiritual Jews, who cling to the promises of Yahuah's end time Exodus, refuse to relocate to Palestine because they know that the plan is **not** from ayaz! Many righteous Jews believe that it would be a sin of rebellion to prematurely end their own exile, before ayaz ends it! After the final Roman destruction of Yahrushalayim, many Jews migrated into Palestine where all the bloodshed is happening today! Other Jews were still living in western Arabia as late a 622 CE where they had fled, after their exile by the Romans! Jews went south back to the land of Mitsrayim in western Arabia, which was the real place of origin of the 1st Exodus! Over time many Jews moved even further south in Arabia as far as today's Yemen! Mitsrayim was located in today's western Saudi Arabia and encompassed the area of today's Mecca and Medina! Many Jewish families fled from the area around Mecca and Medina! They migrated all the way down to today's Yemen first to escape the persecution of the Romans and later to escape the persecution of the Muslims! During the time of Mohammed and afterwards, Jewish tribes around Mecca and Medina were severely taxed, oppressed, tortured, raped, and killed! Today, the remaining Jewish families have assimilated completely into the people of Arabia or they have fled into other countries far away from Saudi Arabia completely! The last Jews were evacuated from Yemen in 1947 and flown to the modern State of Israel! Today, the seed of Abraham are still scattered throughout the entire world! Jews have been thoroughly assimilated into all the nations across the entire earth! Yahuah's people, Israel, including those living in Palestine, **are still in exile** from the real Promised Land! They will not return until OWYaZ leads them home! The assimilation of Jews into the nations was so complete that most of the Northern Tribes have completely forgotten their own ethnic identity! Many people with Jewish bloodlines live in the nations, but they don't know about their own Jewish heritage! However, ayaz does know where every drop of Jewish blood is today! All the seed of Abraham, who have circumcised hearts and love ayaz and OWYaZ, will return one day to Yahuah's Promised Land in northwestern Saudi Arabia as well as any other person in the nations, who will embrace Yahuah's Covenant with Israel! Read what Isaiah and Paul had to say about the people called Israel!

Isaiah 56
Thus saith ayaz, Keep ye judgment, and do justice: for my salvation is near to come, and my righteousness to be revealed. Blessed is the man that doeth this, and the son of man that layeth hold on it; that keepeth the sabbath from polluting it, and keepeth his hand from doing any evil.

Isaiah 56, cont.
Neither let the son of the stranger, that hath joined himself to 𐤀𐤉𐤄𐤅, *speak, saying,* 𐤀𐤉𐤄𐤅 *hath utterly separated me from his people: neither let the eunuch say, Behold, I am a dry tree. For thus saith* 𐤀𐤉𐤄𐤅 *unto the eunuchs that* **keep my sabbaths**, *and* **choose the things that please me**, *and take hold of my covenant; Even unto them will I give in mine house and within my walls a place and a name better than of sons and of daughters: I will give them an everlasting name, that shall not be cut off.* **Also the sons of the stranger, that join themselves to** 𐤀𐤉𐤄𐤅, **to serve him, and to** *love the name* **of** 𐤀𐤉𐤄𐤅, **to be his servants, every one that keepeth the sabbath from polluting it, and taketh hold of my covenant; Even them will I bring to my holy mountain**, *and make them joyful in my house of prayer: their burnt offerings and their sacrifices shall be accepted upon mine altar; for mine house shall be called an house of prayer for all people.*

Ephesians 2
Wherein in time past ye walked according to the course of this world, according to the prince of the power of the air, the spirit that now worketh in the children of disobedience: Among whom also we all had our conversation in times past in the lusts of our flesh, fulfilling the desires of the flesh and of the mind; and were by nature the children of wrath, even as others. But 𐤀𐤉𐤄𐤅, *who is rich in mercy, for his great love wherewith he loved us, Even when we were dead in sins, hath quickened us together with the Messiah, (by favor ye are saved;) And hath raised us up together, and made us sit together in heavenly places in the Messiah* OWY𐤄𐤅: *That in the ages to come he might shew the exceeding riches of his favor in his kindness toward us through the Messiah* OWY𐤄𐤅. *For by favor are ye saved through faith; and that not of yourselves: it is the gift of* 𐤀𐤉𐤄𐤅: *Not of works, lest any man should boast. For we are his workmanship, created in the Messiah* OWY𐤄𐤅 *unto good works, which* 𐤀𐤉𐤄𐤅 *hath before ordained that we should walk in them. Wherefore remember, that ye being in time past Gentiles in the flesh, who are called Uncircumcision by that which is called the Circumcision in the flesh made by hands; That at that time ye were without the Messiah, being aliens from the* **Commonwealth of Israel**, *and strangers from the covenants of promise, having no hope, and without Elohim in the world: But now in the Messiah* OWY𐤄𐤅 *ye who sometimes were far off are made nigh by the blood of the Messiah. For he is our peace, who hath made both one, and hath broken down the middle wall of partition between us;*

Ephesians 2, cont.
Having abolished in his flesh the enmity, even the law of commandments contained in ordinances; for to make in himself of twain one new man, so making peace; And that he might reconcile both unto ayaz *in one body by the stake, having slain the enmity thereby: And came and preached peace to you which were afar off, and to them that were nigh. For through him we both have access by one Spirit unto the Father. Now therefore ye are no more strangers and foreigners, but fellow citizens with the saints, and of the household of* ayaz*; And are built upon the foundation of the apostles and prophets,* owyaz *the Messiah himself being the chief corner stone; In whom all the building fitly framed together groweth unto a holy temple in* ayaz*: In whom ye also are builded together for a habitation of Elohim through the Spirit.*

ayaz is calling out to His people, Israel, all over the world **right now, Jewish blood or not**, to embrace His Covenant and to become part of the people that He calls Israel! The people, Israel, are Yahuah's overcomers! ayaz is calling all His people, who are scattered in the nations to embrace His Covenant and His owyaz, **His salvation**! Most people all over the world are in religious systems that were taught to them by their forefathers! ayaz knows what has to be done in our lives regardless of our backgrounds to bring us to a knowledge of the real Truth! All we have to do is to be willing to make the changes as His Ruach HaQodesh convicts our hearts that **changes are needed**! You will find that once you make your mind up to follow Yahuah that ayaz will create a powerful love for His Torah in your Heart! ayaz will **circumcise** your heart by spiritually cutting away the desires of lust, vanity, and the love of idolatrous traditions such as Christmas, Easter, Halloween, and Valentine's Day! When owyaz writes His desires on your heart, you will positively know the right Way to go day by day! After all the searching, you will find Yahushua's narrow Way! However, Yahushua's Way is very tough! It's a very afflicted Way! Few will ever travel it, but those, who do travel it to the end, will walk on the heights of Israel with owyaz!

SUMMARY

The most important two names **ever named** are those of ayaz and owyaz! These are the **only** two names in which salvation can be attained! The names of "God and Jesus" are **NOT** the real names of our heavenly Father and His Son at all! They were switched many years ago by selfish men! Wicked men have always found ways to control others by using false religious practices enforced by physical violence! **The names of "God and Jesus" are not only incorrect, but worse still, they are terrible abominations to** ayaz!

Those two names are linked to the worship of the sun, the moon, and the stars! They are contaminated with pagan practices! A central theme of all the prophecy in the Scriptures is that there will be a final worldwide Exodus for Israel to the real Promised Land! Israel's worldwide Exodus will usher in Yahushua's kingdom and it will bring an end to the nation's rule of themselves! Israel's final Exodus will be completely **SUPERNATURAL** and has no relationship at all with the present day State of Israel, which is satan's counterfeit! The Scriptures teach that Israel's final Exodus will make people forget the signs and wonders done by ayaz during the 1st Exodus from Mitsrayim! The people called Israel by ayaz, (not to be confused with today's State of Israel), are scattered all over the earth to this very day! None of Yahuah's people are in the real Promised Land even today! Israel is still in exile far away from the real Promised Land! **ayaz is enforcing Israel's exile, no one else**! Israel's exile was the result of their continued harlotry with foreign nations and their sun deities! When OWYaz came they were blinded to the Truth of His identity! The masses of Israel were spiritually blinded and did not even recognize their own deliverer, when OWYaz came as Israel's Passover Lamb! Only a remnant of people recognized OWYaz, when He came! A remnant recognized OWYaz because they **did not** judge OWYaz by what they **saw** in His physical appearance, but instead they trusted what OWYaz said and what He did as the evidence of His true identity!

At the appointed time, OWYaz will return to deliver the First Fruits of Israel and bring them back to the Promised Land! ayaz will send OWYaz to bring back the First Fruits of Israel from the nations! Yes, OWYaz returns **first** to gather His Barley into His barn! Then many, many years later at the sounding of the 7th Trumpet, OWYaz will return to rescue His **Barley**, who will be trapped and under siege in the rebuilt Yahrushalayim! Then OWYaz will gather His **Wheat**! His Wheat will will be scattered in the nations and will be severely oppressed in Nimrod's system! I am very certain that many of the sheep, who will read *Let My People Go,* will be a part of Yahushua's Barley Harvest! HalleluYah! HalleluYah! HalleluYah! Congratulations, if that's you! Finish this race of patient endurance well!

The First Adam
Chapter 3

Book of Adam and Eve

¹ ayaz said to Adam, "I have ordained on this earth days and years, and you and your descendants shall live and walk in them, until the days and years are fulfilled; when I shall send the Word that created you, and against which you have transgressed, the Word that made you come out of the garden, and that raised you when you were fallen. 2 Yes, the Word that will again save you when the five and a half days are fulfilled." 3 But when Adam heard these words from ayaz, and of the great five and a half days, he did not understand the meaning of them. 4 For Adam was thinking there would be only five and a half days for him until the end of the world. 5 And Adam cried, and prayed to ayaz to explain it to him. 6 Then ayaz in his mercy for Adam who was made after His own image and likeness, explained to him, that these were 5,000 and 500 years; and how One would then come and save him and his descendants.

Adam lived 930 years and was an extremely righteous man! He knew the significance of his disobedience of Yahuah's commandment for himself and for all the future generations of mankind! Adam and Hawwah, who is known as Eve today, grieved terribly for their sin and they mourned greatly over their loss of Paradise! In the book of Genesis limited information is given about Adam's life, before and after his expulsion from the Garden! The early chapters of Genesis are written in less detail than the later chapters! As a result everyone should examine and carefully consider all creditable sources of information about the lives of the Patriarchs, before the Flood in order to better understand the overview presented in the book of Genesis! Remember men determined, which writings to canonize into the Scriptures! That does not mean that other writings don't have spiritual merit! Of course, other writings should be examined and carefully evaluated! Wicked men have altered virtually all the old writings about ayaz including most of the English translations of the Scriptures to suit their own purposes, even though ayaz put a curse on those, who would add to or take away from His Words! Have men no shame and no fear of ayaz? Over thousands of years, men have destroyed, suppressed, and hidden much information that is pertinent to the Scriptures! In this chapter I have included many passages from *The Scriptures* as well as passages from other books like *The Book of Adam and Eve*, *The Cave of Treasures*, and *The Book of Yashar*! It's my hope that you will evaluate all these writings with discernment!

Look for spiritual merit! Use these writings to increase your understanding of the time before the Flood! It's very clear that 𝐚𝐘𝐚𝐙 loved Adam and Hawwah very, very much! Yahushua's first promises of redemption were made to Adam as you will see in Genesis and in *The Book of Adam and Eve*! I personally believe that Adam and Hawwah were the two most repentant people, who have ever lived! They were the first to experience Paradise in the Garden of Eden on the Heavenly Mount Zion! When they lost their privilege to remain in the Garden, Adam's and Hawwah's remorse was extremely severe and almost to death! They understood very well the consequences of their original sin on themselves and their posterity! The Scripture says that 𝐚𝐘𝐚𝐙 created Adam from the dust of the Earth in His own image! Adam is a fabulous man!

Genesis 1
And Elohim said, Let us make man in our image, after our likeness: and let them have dominion over the fish of the sea, and over the fowl of the air, and over the cattle, and over all the earth, and over every creeping thing that creepeth upon the earth. So Elohim created man in his own image, in the image of Elohim created he him; male and female created he them.

Genesis 2
And 𝐚𝐘𝐚𝐙 Elohim <u>formed man of the dust of the ground</u>, and breathed into his nostrils the breath of life; and man became a living soul. And 𝐚𝐘𝐚𝐙 Elohim planted a garden eastward in Eden; and <u>there he put the man whom he had formed</u>.

Adam was created from the dust of the earth! <u>Then</u> Adam was taken and <u>placed in</u> the Garden! Where was this Garden? The answer to this question will be fundamental to your understanding of the Scriptures! The Garden was <u>not</u> a place on this earth, but a place on the heavenly Mount Zion!

Genesis 2
And 𝐚𝐘𝐚𝐙 Elohim took the man, and <u>put him into the Garden of Eden</u> to dress it and to keep it. And 𝐚𝐘𝐚𝐙 Elohim commanded the man, saying, Of every tree of the garden thou mayest freely eat: But of the tree of the knowledge of good and evil, thou shalt not eat of it: for in the day that thou eatest thereof thou shalt surely die. And 𝐚𝐘𝐚𝐙 Elohim said, It is not good that the man should be alone; I will make him an help meet for him. And out of the ground 𝐚𝐘𝐚𝐙 Elohim formed every beast of the field, and every fowl of the air; and brought them unto Adam to see what he would call them: and whatsoever Adam called every living creature, that was the name thereof.

Genesis 2, cont.

And Adam gave names to all cattle, and to the fowl of the air, and to every beast of the field; but for Adam there was not found a help meet for him. And אYAZ Elohim caused a deep sleep to fall upon Adam and he slept: and he took one of his ribs, and closed up the flesh instead thereof; And the rib, which אYAZ Elohim had taken from man, made he a woman, and brought her unto the man. And Adam said, This is now bone of my bones, and flesh of my flesh: she shall be called Woman, because she was taken out of Man.

Adam was created out of the dust of a Set Apart earthly Mountain! We know that Mountain in the Scriptures as Mount Sinai! Remember, when Moses was instructed to take his shoes off at the burning bush because that place was set apart ground! Adam was taken to the Garden of Eden, after he was created from the earth on the summit of Mount Sinai! That's why Mount Sinai is set apart to אYAZ! But where was this Garden? Bible scholars today teach that the Garden was on the terrestrial earth in the fertile crescent of the Middle East! That seems logical, doesn't it? Remember Yahushua's "**Verse To Remember**"! However, even though that may sound reasonable, that was not Yahuah's plan! The earth that Adam was formed from was from Mount Sinai, which was located in the Land that אYAZ was later to promise to Abraham! However, the Garden of Eden was not on the earth at all! *No*, this is not science fiction! Keep reading and stay neutral! It is a fact! Nowhere do the Scriptures teach that the Garden was on the Earth! אYAZ created Adam to fellowship with Him in a beautiful Garden that He planted on the heavenly Mount Zion, where **Yahuah's** **throne** **is** now and where it has **always been**! Think about it! If the Garden was on the Earth in Iraq or anywhere else, then Cherubim **would still** be guarding its entrance with a flaming sword so that mankind could not reenter the Garden prematurely! If the Garden of Eden was on the earth, then **man would need to quarantine that section of the earth because the Cherubim would be destroying everyone, who approached the entrance to the Garden!** We haven't heard of anyone in Iraq or any other earthly place being killed by Cherubim with a flaming sword, have we? No, no, no, please wake up to the truth! Look beyond appearances! Study to show yourself approved! Haven't you always heard the words "Mount Zion" and never really understood where or what Mount Zion is? Yahuah's throne is located on Mount Zion right now! אYAZ lives on top of the Heavenly Mount Zion, not Mount Olympus! The Earth is Yahuah's footstool and the heavens are His throne! That throne is located at the summit of the heavenly Mount Zion!

Isaiah 66
Thus saith **𐤄𐤅𐤄𐤉**, <u>The heaven is my throne, and the earth is my footstool</u>: where is the house that ye build unto me? And where is the place of my rest?

When Adam and Hawwah sinned they were sent out of the Garden of Eden to till the ground from which Adam was taken! That location was on top of an earthly Mountain, Mount Sinai! This particular earthly mountain was the most set apart place **on the earth** at that time! Adam and Hawwah had to leave the Set Apart Garden in the Heavens on Mount Zion! They were forced to leave that paradise! Adam and Hawwah fell to a lower place both literally and spiritually! Their abode now was to be the summit of an earthly mountain, Mount Sinai! Mount Sinai is one of Yahuah's Set Apart Mountains on the earth, which He calls the Mountains of Israel! Four mountains of **𐤄𐤅𐤄𐤉** are set apart in the Scriptures! They all exist in the Promised Land in northwestern Saudi Arabia! I will personally stand on all four as you will, if you follow Yahushua's Way! These mountains are known as Mount Sinai, Mount Carmel, the Mount of Olives, and Mount Moriah!

Genesis 3
Therefore **𐤄𐤅𐤄𐤉** Elohim sent him forth from the Garden of Eden, to till the ground from whence he was taken. So he drove out the man; and he placed at the east of the Garden of Eden Cherubim, and a flaming sword which turned every way, to keep the way of the tree of life.

Adam and Hawwah became terrified, when they left the Garden on the Heavenly Mount Zion and saw the rough landscape of the earth below! The earth could not compare to the beautiful landscape of Yahuah's Garden! Adam and Hawwah could no longer live on the heavenly Mount Zion, until the time of their redemption was accomplished! After Adam transgressed Yahuah's commandment by eating from the Tree of Knowledge of Good and Evil, Adam and Hawwah were placed on the top of Mount Sinai! The summit of Sinai was to be their abode! Mount Sinai was the best place that Adam could have been on the earth! Adam was as close to Mount Zion as you could get! He was before Yahuah's face! The earthly Mount Sinai was set apart and special to **𐤄𐤅𐤄𐤉**. Remember how **𐤄𐤅𐤄𐤉** instructed Moses to remove his shoes because he was on set apart ground!

Exodus 3
^{3}And Mosheh said, "Let me turn aside now, and see this great sight, why the bush does not burn." ^{4}And **𐤄𐤅𐤄𐤉** saw that he turned aside to see, and Elohim called to him from the midst of the bush and said, Mosheh! Mosheh!" And he said, "Here I am."

Exodus 3, cont.
⁵And He said, *"Do not come near here. Take your sandals off your feet, for the place on which you are standing is set-apart ground."* ⁶And He said, *"I am the Elohim of your father, the Elohim of Abraham, the Elohim of Yitshaq, and the Elohim of Ya'aqob."*

Mount Sinai was the place where ayaz assembled the Israelites and gave His Commandments in the 1ˢᵗ Exodus! Mount Sinai was a very tall Mountain and reached into the clouds at the time of Adam! Its summit <u>was</u> just below the skirts of the heavenly Mount Zion! At the time of Adam's fall, Mount Zion was still visible from the summit of Mount Sinai because sin had <u>not yet multiplied on the earth</u>! However violence, wickedness, and sexual perversion spread rapidly across the earth from the time of Adam, until the Flood! At the time of the Flood every thought and action of mankind was entirely wicked! Only Noah was found perfect in his ways! As these sins increased to epic proportions, the separation grew between the heavenly Mount Zion and the summit of Mount Sinai! After the Flood, Mount Zion <u>was no longer visible at all</u>! This explains Isaiah's and John's descriptions of the heavenly Mount Zion and the New Yahrushalayim descending out of the heavens on the Day of ayaz at the sounding of the 7ᵗʰ Trumpet! The summit of Mount Zion is Yahuah's most Qodesh place **(most set apart place)**! Today the visible confirmation of the existence of Mount Zion's is veiled to us! At this time the Most Set Apart place, Mount Zion, is hidden from our human vision! However, that veil will be lifted at the sound of the 7ᵗʰ Trumpet, when OWYaz returns to rescue His Barley and guides all His people, Israel, back to the heavenly Mount Zion and the New Yahrushalayim!

Every believer should read *the Book of Adam and Eve* and decide for themselves about the merit of this book! While this ancient book has not been labeled as Scripture, I believe that this book does provide valuable insight into what early people believed happened before the Flood! One of the very important themes given in *the Book of Adam and Eve* is the promise that was made by OWYaz to Adam and Hawwah of their future redemption! OWYaz promised to redeem Adam, after 5,500 years! When I first read *the Book of Adam and Eve* I didn't know what to think about the 5,500 year milestone because it did not line up with today's popular religious opinions. However, as I have researched everything that I could find on the subject, I am convinced that OWYaz did in fact come at the 5,500 year mark from Adam regardless of what the experts say! Stay neutral and keep reading! I believe that the recording of days by mankind has been hopelessly mired in error! I believe that the calendars have been manipulated many times to suit the purposes of men throughout history!

Wicked men have gone to great lengths and used everything at their disposal to confuse everything that might lead other men to a true knowledge of 𝐚𝐘𝐚𝐙!

Book of Adam and Eve

Chapter 3 - Concerning the promise of the great five and a half days.
𝐚𝐘𝐚𝐙 said to Adam, "I have ordained on this earth days and years, and you and your descendants shall live and walk in them, until the days and years are fulfilled; when I shall send the Word that created you, and against which you have transgressed, the Word that made you come out of the garden, and that raised you when you were fallen. Yes, the Word that will again save you when the five and a half days are fulfilled." But when Adam heard these words from 𝐚𝐘𝐚𝐙, and of the great five and a half days, he did not understand the meaning of them. 4 For Adam was thinking there would be only five and a half days for him until the end of the world. And Adam cried, and prayed to 𝐚𝐘𝐚𝐙 to explain it to him. Then 𝐚𝐘𝐚𝐙 in his mercy for Adam who was made after His own image and likeness, explained to him, that these were **5,000 and 500 years**; and how One would then come and save him and his descendants.

Yahushua's Covenant with Adam

Chapter 14
Then Adam said to 𝐚𝐘𝐚𝐙: "O Elohim, take You my soul, and let me not see this gloom any more; or remove me to some place where there is no darkness." But 𝐚𝐘𝐚𝐙 the Elohim said to Adam, "Indeed I say to you, this darkness will pass from you, every day I have determined for you, until the fulfillment of My covenant; when I will save you and bring you back again into the garden, into the house of light you long for, in which there is no darkness. I will bring you to it -- in the kingdom of heaven." Again The Word of 𝐚𝐘𝐚𝐙 said to Adam, "All this misery that you have been made to take on yourself because of your transgression, will not free you from the hand of Satan, and will not save you. But I will. **When I shall come down from heaven, and shall become flesh of your descendants, and take on Myself the infirmity from which you suffer, then the darkness that covered you in this cave shall cover Me in the grave, when I am in the flesh of your descendants.**

Chapter 21   The First Sacrifice on the Set Apart Mountain
Then Adam and Eve went in search of the garden. And the heat beat like a flame on their faces; and they sweated from the heat, and cried before the Elohim. But the place where they cried was close to a high mountain, facing the western gate of the garden. Then Adam threw himself down from the top of that mountain; his face was torn and his flesh was ripped; he lost a lot of blood and was close to death.

Book of Adam and Eve
The First Sacrifice on the Set Apart Mountain, cont.

Meanwhile Eve remained standing on the mountain crying over him, thus lying. And she said, "I don't wish to live after him; for all that he did to himself was through me." Then she threw herself after him; and was torn and ripped by stones; and remained lying as dead. But the merciful ayaz, *who looks over His creatures, looked at Adam and Eve as they lay dead, and He sent His Word to them, and raised them. And said to Adam, "O Adam, all this misery which you have brought on yourself, will have no affect against My rule, neither will it alter the covenant of the 5,500 years."*

Chapter 23

Then Adam cried more and said, "O ayaz, *have mercy on me,* **so far as to take on yourself, that which I will do.**" *But* ayaz *withdrew His Word from Adam and Eve. Then Adam and Eve stood on their feet; and Adam said to Eve, "Strengthen yourself, and I also will strengthen myself." And she strengthened herself, as Adam told her. Then Adam and Eve took stones and placed them in the shape of an altar; and they took leaves from the trees outside the garden, with which they wiped, from the face of the rock, the blood they had spilled. But that which had dropped on the sand, they took together with the dust with which it was mingled and offered it on the altar as an offering to* ayaz. *Then Adam and Eve stood under the Altar and cried, thus praying to* ayaz, *"Forgive us our trespass and our sin, and look at us with Thine eye of mercy. For when we were in the garden our praises and our hymns went up before you without ceasing. But when we came into this strange land, pure praise was not longer ours, nor righteous prayer, nor understanding hearts, nor sweet thoughts, nor just counsels, nor long discernment, nor upright feelings, neither is our bright nature left us. But our body is changed from the likeness in which it was at first, when we were created. Yet now look at our blood which is offered on these stones, and accept it at our hands, like the praise we used to sing to you at first, when in the garden." And Adam began to make more requests of* ayaz.

The First Sacrifice Is Accepted

Chapter 24 *Then the merciful* ayaz, *good and lover of men, looked at Adam and Eve, and at their blood, which they had held up as an offering to Him; without an order from Him for so doing. But He wondered at them; and accepted their offerings. And* ayaz *sent from His presence a bright fire, that consumed their offering. He smelled the sweet savor of their offering, and showed them mercy.*

The First Sacrifice Is Accepted

Chapter 24, cont.

Then came the Word of ayaz to Adam, and said to him, "O Adam, as you have shed your blood, so will I shed My own blood when I become flesh of your descendants; and as you died, O Adam, so also will I die. And as you built an altar, so also will I make for you an altar of the earth; and as you offered your blood on it, so also will I offer My blood on an altar on the earth. And as you sued for forgiveness through that blood, so also will I make My blood forgiveness of sins, and erase transgressions in it. And now, behold, I have accepted your offering, O Adam, but the 'days' of the covenant in which I have bound you are not fulfilled. When they are fulfilled, then will I bring you back into the Garden. Now, therefore, strengthen your heart; and when sorrow comes over you, make Me an offering, and I will be favorable to you."

Summary

Adam was the beginning of the Righteous line of ayaz! He was one of the most Righteous men, who has ever lived and certainly the most repentant! The original promises made by OWYaz were made to Adam! So Yahushua's love for Adam must be immense! OWYaz loves Adam and Hawwah very, very much and did <u>not</u> forget His promises to them, when He came 5,500 years later as our Passover Lamb! Adam lived on the same soil from which he was formed, after he fell spiritually and physically from the heavenly Garden of Eden on Mount Zion to the earthly Mount Sinai! Adam lived on the summit of the set apart mountain of ayaz, Mount Sinai, which is in today's northwestern Saudi Arabia! In the book of Exodus Mount Sinai was the place where the <u>Ten Commandments were given</u> to Moses and it was the place where ayaz chose to <u>betroth Israel</u>! What a coincidence!

Yahuah's Ten Thousand Year Plan
Chapter 4

Today prophecy teachers copy each other's words just like the Scriptures said they would! Most teach about a 7,000 year plan of "god"! By their calculations OWY3Z would have returned at the 6,000 year mark! But, what happened? Where is OWY3Z? Do you remember the Y-2K scare? Well, we know that OWY3Z did not come in spite of all the fuss, don't we? Many religious people were expecting OWY3Z to return at the 6,000 year mark to begin His 1,000 year reign on earth! By their calculations, 4,000 years have passed from the time of Adam to the Messiah's first coming and 2000 years have passed since! That sounded reasonable, didn't it? It's still a very popular prophecy teaching even today! I suggest that you look for the real truth in another direction! ƎY3Z doesn't reveal mysteries to people, whose only desire is to exploit the Truth for fame and fortune! Exchanging the Truth of ƎY3Z for fame and fortune is the path that Balaam followed! Eternal damnation lies at the end of that road! Much can be learned about Yahuah's overall plan from *The Book of Enoch*! It's an extremely important writing and should be read by anyone, who really loves ƎY3Z! I personally believe that *The Book of Enoch* was inspired by ƎY3Z, but you need to evaluate it for yourself! Compare its messages to the messages contained in the Scriptures! Many fragmented copies of *The Book of Enoch* were found in the 11 Qumran Caves with the other Dead Sea Scrolls. This book was quoted from in the book of Jude! *The Book of Enoch* was very well known by OWY3Z, the prophets, and all the Righteous of Israel! But it was not canonized! Wicked men have tried to suppress wisdom and understanding about ƎY3Z for a very long time! *The Book of Enoch*, when read in conjunction with the Scriptures, is a treasure trove of wisdom and understanding about Yahuah's plan! In *The Book of Enoch* each one thousand year period is equated to one week! The book summarizes each week in Yahuah's 10,000 year plan! OWY3Z came in the sixth week, 5,500 years from the fall of Adam! We are currently living in the **middle of the 8th week**, which is approximately 7,500 years from Adam's fall! According to Enoch, OWY3Z **will return in the 8th 1,000 year week to judge the wicked and reward the Righteous**!

Book of Enoch Chapter 91

$_3$And Enoch began to recount from the books and said: 'I was born the seventh in the **first week**, While judgment and righteousness still endured. $_4$And after me there shall arise in the **second week** great wickedness, And deceit shall have sprung up; And in it there shall be the first end. **(Genesis 6)**

Book of Enoch Chapter 91, cont.
*And in it a man shall be saved; And after it is ended unrighteousness shall grow up, And a law **(Noah's Law)** for the sinners.* ₅*And after that in the **third week** at its close, a man shall be elected **(Abraham)** a plant of righteous judgment, And his posterity shall become the plant of righteousness for evermore.* ₆*And after that in the **fourth week**, at its close, Visions of the holy and righteous shall be seen, and a law for all generations **(10 Commandments given at Sinai)**.* ₇*And after that in the **fifth week**, at its close, The house of glory and dominion shall be built for ever.* ₈*And after that in the **sixth week (5,500 years)** all who live in it shall be blinded, and the hearts of all of them shall godlessly forsake wisdom **(Yahushua)** And in it a man shall ascend **(Yahushua ascends to His Father)**; And at its close the house of dominion shall be burnt with fire **(Destruction of Yahrushalayim 135 CE)**, And the whole race of the chosen root shall be dispersed.* ₉*And after that in the **seventh week** shall an apostate generation arise **(the church)**. And many shall be its deeds and all its deeds shall be apostate.* ₁₀*And at its close shall be elected the elect righteous of the eternal plant of righteousness, To receive sevenfold instruction concerning all His creation.* ₁₁*For who is there of all the children of men that is able to hear the voice of the Holy One* ᐊYᐊZ *without being troubled? And who can think His thoughts? And who is there that can behold all the works* ₁₂*of heaven? And how should there be one who could behold the heaven, and who is there that could understand the things of heaven and see a soul or a spirit and could tell thereof, or ascend and see* ₁₃*all their ends and think them or do like them? And who is there of all men that could know what is the breadth and the length of the earth, and to whom has been shown the measure of all of them?* ₁₄ *Or is there any one who could discern the length of the heaven and how great is its height, and upon what it is founded, and how great is the number of the stars, and where all the luminaries rest? And after that there shall be another, the **eighth week**, that of righteousness, And a **sword shall be given to it that a righteous judgment** may be executed on the oppressors, And sinners shall be delivered into the hands of the righteous. **(Return of Yahushua, OWYᐊZ, to Judge the Nations)*** ₁₃*And at its close they shall acquire houses through their righteousness, And a house shall be built for the Great King in glory for evermore,* ₁₄*And all mankind shall look to the path of uprightness. And after that, in the **ninth week**, the righteous judgment shall be revealed to the whole world, And all the works of the godless shall vanish from all the earth, And the world shall be written down for destruction. **(Renewed Earth)***

Book of Enoch
10,000 Year Plan of 𝐚𝐘𝐚𝐙
Chapter 91, cont.

₁₅And after this, in the **tenth week** in the seventh part, There shall be the great eternal judgment,**(Great White Throne Judgment)** In which He will execute vengeance amongst the angels. ₁₆And the first heaven shall depart and pass away, And a new heaven shall appear, **(New Heaven created)** And all the powers of the heavens shall give sevenfold light. ₁₇And after that there will be many weeks without number for ever, And all shall be in goodness and righteousness, And sin shall no more be mentioned for ever.

Each week represents 1,000 years! Enoch was born the seventh Patriarch from Adam in the **1ˢᵗ** week! In the **2ⁿᵈ** week, the watchers, who were men born into the spiritual line of Adam and Seth, rebelled against 𝐚𝐘𝐚𝐙 on top of the set apart Mountain! These rebellious sons of Elohim came down from the top of Mount Sinai where they had lived, since 𝐚𝐘𝐚𝐙 commanded Adam to dwell there! These watchers were driven by animal lust and chose wives for themselves from the children of Cain, who lived in the plains below Mount Sinai! These events are described in Genesis 6! After this terrible rebellion against 𝐚𝐘𝐚𝐙 occurred, violence and wickedness increased exponentially on the earth! 𝐚𝐘𝐚𝐙 allotted 120 years for mankind to repent! However, immorality and lawlessness became more and more prolific, until Yahuah's patience was finally exhausted! Wickedness and violence got so bad that 𝐚𝐘𝐚𝐙 determined to end that world and its people with a Flood! When the 120 year grace period was over, Noah and his family were the only people spared from the waters of the Deluge! In the **3ʳᵈ** period of 1,000 years, Abraham was chosen to be the father of many nations! He was chosen to be the Righteous seed of Israel! In the **4ᵗʰ** 1,000 year period, the First Exodus occurred! Israel was led out of Mitsrayim in northwestern Arabia **back** to Yahuah's Set Apart Mountain, Mount Sinai! At Mount Sinai 𝐚𝐘𝐚𝐙 gave Israel His eternal commandments! Yahuah's Torah instructs us how to live in this world in a way that pleases 𝐚𝐘𝐚𝐙! When we **choose** to live by Yahuah's Torah, we **prove** that we love 𝐚𝐘𝐚𝐙! Our obedience to His instructions gives 𝐚𝐘𝐚𝐙 great pleasure! That's not legalism, that's true love! In the **5ᵗʰ** 1,000 year period, the House of Glory was built! In the **6ᵗʰ** 1,000 year period, OWY𝐚𝐙 came at exactly the 5,500 year mark just as He promised Adam that He would! Of course at that time, OWY𝐚𝐙 became our kinsman redeemer, when He offered Himself as our Passover Lamb! But for some reason the masses of Israel were blinded to His true identity! After Yahushua's resurrection, He appeared to many of His disciples, then OWY𝐚𝐙 ascended back to Yahuah's throne on the heavenly Mount Zion!

In the 7th 1,000 year period apostasy greatly escalated against ayaz! About 321 CE this apostasy became institutionalized first by Constantine, the Roman Emperor, and later by the Roman Church! Since that time, multitudes of false shepherds have had a fine time twisting the truth of the Scriptures for their own selfish purposes! Constantine with the help of the church fathers amalgamated elements of Scripture with pagan customs, rituals, feasts, and icons! This mixing has completely engulfed the church with apostasy! Today large parts of the world are still in bondage to the false system of worship that was propagated by the Roman Church! That is how Christianity came to be <u>contaminated</u>! Sun worship has crept into <u>every</u> Christian denomination! However, the worship of the Sun, the Moon, and the stars has also contaminated all the other manmade religions of the world as well! At the appointed time in the 8th 1,000 year period, OWYAZ will return to render a righteous judgment against the wicked of the earth! At that time the Righteous of the earth will <u>become</u> the <u>head</u> and <u>not</u> the tail <u>as they are today</u>! Make no mistake about it, until that time, the Righteous will be oppressed by the wicked! Israel will be at the bottom of this present world's power infrastructure! By definition the Righteous do **not** have Type A personalities! Type A people will do anything to gain power and material possessions <u>for themselves</u> in this screwed up world, won't they? In contrast, OWYAZ taught servant-hood and self sacrifice! The wicked want to be served and don't mind oppressing others to sustain their fat lifestyles! Don't believe the false shepherds, who preach doctrines of material prosperity in this life! Material prosperity in this present world **was not** what OWYAZ taught! In fact OWYAZ exhorted Israel to layup for themselves treasures in the heavens! These treasures will be revealed at Yahushua's coming at the 7th Trumpet blast! All of Yahushua's people have suffered afflictions and struggles, since Yahushua suffered and sacrificed Himself at His first coming! ayaz determined that the **suffering servant** pattern of Yahushua's life would be followed by all Yahushua's future sheep, after His sacrifice! Don't fool yourself, Israel will experience a **lot** of troubles and afflictions, until OWYAZ returns! That is the destiny of Israel in this world! But in the world to come, when OWYAZ returns, the Righteous will be **exalted** with OWYAZ! OWYAZ will keep His covenant with all Israel! At the sound of the 7th Trumpet, OWYAZ will raise the Righteous dead from their graves and fulfill His promise to them concerning their resurrection! At that time all the Righteous of Israel from all the ages will be gathered to one place at one time to celebrate Yahushua's wedding banquet! What a day that will be! OWYAZ will bring back all of Israel to the authentic Promised Land! OWYAZ will vanquish all the wicked and will reign on the earth as King of Kings! Finally, absolute justice will prevail!

Satan and all of Yahuah's adversaries will be confined to the Abyss for 1,000 years, while they await their final judgment in the Lake of Fire! The knowledge of ᴀYᴀZ will abound across the whole earth! No one will be able to claim ignorance about ᴀYᴀZ and the Torah anymore! Men will live to be hundreds of years old <u>again</u> similar to the days, before the Flood! In the **9th** 1,000 year period satan will be let out of the Abyss <u>one more time</u> to test the people of the earth before the final Judgment is executed! The adversary will stir up rebellion in the earth for the last time, but ᴀYᴀZ sends fire from the Heavens and quickly snuffs out that rebellion! Satan is thrown into Topheth, the Lake of Fire! The Earth is renewed! The Set Apart city, the New Yahrushalayim, will come down and join with the Earth! The two will become one, Echad, united! There will be no separation anymore between Yahuah's throne and Yahuah's footstool!

Book of Enoch
And after these things there will be weeks **(1,000 year periods)** *without number! And the first heaven shall depart and pass away, And a new heaven shall appear, And all the powers of the heavens shall give sevenfold light. ₁₇And after that there will be many weeks without number for ever, And all shall be in goodness and righteousness, And sin shall no more be mentioned for ever.*

Revelation 21
And I saw a new heaven and a new earth: for the first heaven and the first earth were passed away; and there was no more sea. And I John saw the holy city, New Yahrushalayim, coming down from ᴀYᴀZ *out of heaven, prepared as a bride adorned for her husband. And I heard a great voice out of heaven saying,* **<u>Behold, the tabernacle of</u>** ᴀYᴀZ **<u>is with men</u>, and he will dwell with them, and they shall be his people, and** ᴀYᴀZ **himself shall be with them, and be their Elohim.** *And* ᴀYᴀZ *shall wipe away all tears from their eyes; and there shall be no more death, neither sorrow, nor crying, neither shall there be any more pain: for the former things are passed away. And he that sat upon the throne said, Behold, I make all things new. And he said unto me, Write: for these words are true and faithful. And he said unto me, It is done. I am Alpha and Omega, the beginning and the end. I will give unto him that is athirst of the <u>fountain of the water of life freely</u>. He that overcometh shall inherit all things; and I will be his Elohim, and he shall be my son. But the fearful, and unbelieving, and the abominable, and murderers, and whoremongers, and sorcerers, and idolaters, and all liars, shall have their part in the lake which burneth with fire and brimstone: which is the second death. And there came unto me one of the seven angels which had the seven vials full of the seven last plagues, and talked with me, saying, Come hither, I will shew thee the bride, the Lamb's wife.*

Revelation 21, cont.
And he carried me away in the spirit to a great and high mountain, and shewed me that great city, the holy Yahrushalayim, descending out of heaven from ayaz, having the glory of ayaz: and her light was like unto a stone most precious, even like a jasper stone, clear as crystal; And had a wall great and high, and had twelve gates, and at the gates twelve angels, and names written thereon, which are the names of the twelve tribes of the children of Israel: On the east three gates; on the north three gates; on the south three gates; and on the west three gates. And the wall of the city had twelve foundations, and in them the names of the twelve apostles of the Lamb. And he that talked with me had a golden reed to measure the city, and the gates thereof, and the wall thereof. And the city lieth foursquare, and the length is as large as the breadth: and he measured the city with the reed, twelve thousand furlongs. The length and the breadth and the height of it are equal. And he measured the wall thereof, an hundred and forty and four cubits, according to the measure of a man, that is, of the angel. And the building of the wall of it was of jasper: and the city was pure gold, like unto clear glass. And the foundations of the wall of the city were garnished with all manner of precious stones. The first foundation was jasper; the second, sapphire; the third, a chalcedony; the fourth, an emerald; The fifth, sardonyx; the sixth, sardius; the seventh, chrysolite; the eighth, beryl; the ninth, a topaz; the tenth, a chrysoprasus; the eleventh, a jacinth; the twelfth, an amethyst. And the twelve gates were twelve pearls; every several gate was of one pearl: and the street of the city was pure gold, as it were transparent glass. And I saw no temple therein: for ayaz El-Shaddai and the Lamb are the temple of it. And the city had no need of the sun, neither of the moon, to shine in it: for the glory of ayaz did lighten it, and the Lamb is the light thereof. And the nations of them which are saved shall walk in the light of it: and the kings of the earth do bring their glory and honour into it.

In the **10th** 1,000 year period in the seventh part the great eternal Judgment of all time occurs! But the Righteous Elect have no need to worry! In this judgment they <u>do</u> <u>not</u> need to fear the second death, the Lake of Fire! However, for all the others the books of the heavens will be opened! The deeds of mankind and all of Yahuah's heavenly adversaries will be weighed **against Yahuah's Torah** and a righteous judgment will be rendered!

Revelation 20
And the devil that deceived them was cast into the lake of fire and brimstone, where the beast and the false prophet are, and shall be tormented day and night for ever and ever.

Revelation 20, cont.
And I saw a great white throne, and him that sat on it, from whose face the earth and the heaven fled away; and there was found no place for them. And I saw the dead, small and great, stand before 𐤀𐤅𐤄𐤉*; and the books were opened: and another book was opened, which is the book of life:* **and the dead were judged out of those things which were <u>written in the books</u>, according to their works.** *And the sea gave up the dead which were in it; and death and hell delivered up the dead which were in them: and they were judged every man according to their works. And death and sheol were cast into the lake of fire.* **<u>This is the second death</u>**. *And whosoever was not found written in the book of life was cast into the lake of fire.*

Book of Enoch
Chapter 18
*And I saw a deep abyss, with columns of heavenly fire, and among them I saw columns of fire fall, which were beyond measure alike towards the height and towards the depth. And beyond that abyss I saw a place which had no firmament of the heaven above, and no firmly founded earth beneath it: there was no water upon it, and no birds, but it was a waste and horrible place. I saw there seven stars like great burning mountains, and to me, when I inquired regarding them, The angel said: 'This place is the end of heaven and earth: this has become a **<u>prison</u>** for the stars and the host of heaven. And the stars which roll over the fire are they which have transgressed the commandment of the Lord in the beginning of their rising, because they did not come forth at their appointed times. And He was wroth with them, and bound them till the time when their guilt should be consummated (even) for **<u>ten thousand years</u>**.'*

Chapter 19
And Uriel said to me: 'Here shall stand the watchers who have connected themselves with women **(Genesis 6)**, *and their spirits assuming many different forms* **(evil or unclean spirits)** *are defiling mankind and shall lead them astray into sacrificing to demons as gods, (here shall they stand,) till the day of the great judgement in which they shall be judged till they are made an end of. And the women also of the angels who went astray shall become sirens.' And I, Enoch, alone saw the vision, the ends of all things: and no man shall see as I have seen.*

Summary
𐤀𐤅𐤄𐤉 has a ten thousand year plan for man, not a seven thousand year plan! Yahuah's plan is still in operation today and will culminate with the final judgment of <u>all</u> of Yahuah's adversaries, after 10,000 years!

Yahuah's plan was described by Enoch, who was the 7th Righteous patriarch from Adam! *The Book of Enoch* has been studied by the Righteous of Israel for many, many generations, but has been flatly rejected by the religious scholars of the world's apostate religious systems! Many fragments of *The Book of Enoch* were among the Dead Sea Scrolls found in the Qumran caves in 1947! In the *Book of Adam and Eve*, OWYAZ promised Adam that He would redeem him, after 5,500 years had transpired! OWYAZ kept His promise to Adam and to all the Righteous of Israel, who lived and died before OWYAZ gave up His last breath on the Passover tree! As I write *Let My People Go,* we are living somewhere in the middle of the 8th 1,000 year period! Enoch said that OWYAZ would return again to render His righteous judgment on the wicked and to reward His Righteous in the 8th 1,000 year period! We are very, very close! Teshuba, repent, wash your garments! Yahushua's righteous judgment is very soon to come! I'm very, very excited! Are you excited?

Rebellion Before The Flood
Chapter 5

And it came to be, when men began to increase on the face of the earth, and daughters were born to them, ²that the sons of Elohim saw the daughters of men, that they were good. And they took wives for themselves of all whom they chose. ³And ayaz said, "My Spirit shall not strive with man forever in his going astray. He is flesh, and his days shall be one hundred and twenty years." ⁴The Nephilim were on the earth in those days, and also afterward, when the sons of Elohim came in to the daughters of men and they bore children to them. Those were the mighty men who were of old, the men of name. ⁵And ayaz saw that the wickedness of man was great in the earth, and that every inclination of the thoughts of his heart was only evil continually. ⁶And ayaz was sorry that He had made man on the earth, and He was grieved in His heart. Bereshith 6 (Genesis)

Genesis is one of my favorite books in all the Scriptures! In the book of Genesis the foundations for Israel are laid! Genesis records the generations of the first ten Patriarchs, before the Flood! These first ten Patriarchs were incredibly righteous men, who were **(and still are)** zealous for ayaz! I love and admire these great men because they spent incredible amounts of time praising ayaz and interceding for the people under their care on top of Yahuah's set apart Mountain, Mount Sinai! These great men have been <u>overlooked</u> by most people today because only a very small amount of information is given about each Patriarch in Genesis 5! Only Noah is discussed in any detail and that description is in connection with the Flood! These ten men were absolutely increditable! As we have already discussed, Yahushua's love for Adam was so great that OWYaz promised Adam that He would offer His own blood for him and all his seed! Seth was the son of Adam! Seth's people on top of Mount Sinai worshiped ayaz like never before or since! They were very happy and content! Enoch was so righteous that ayaz translated him straight into Paradise on Mount Zion, before he experienced death! Enosh, Kainan, Mahalalel, Yared, Methusalah, and all the others set the bar very, very high by their obedience to ayaz! We truly do have a great cloud of witnesses! I know that these great men sit in positions of authority on Mount Zion today because of their righteous leadership, before the Flood! The first ten Patriarchs in the order of their birth are Adam, Seth, Enosh, Kainan, Mahalalel, Yered, Hanok **(Enoch)**, Methushelah, Lamek, and Noah! Not a lot of detail is given in Genesis about these ten Patriarchs! However, good information is available for your consideration in several other books!

The Book of Adam and Eve, The Cave of Treasures, and *The Book of Enoch* all give information for us to ponder about the events that occurred before the Flood! These books are important to read, even though they were **not** canonized as Scripture by men! Even though not considered Scripture, these writings do give us valuable insight into what our ancestors believed occurred, before the Flood! Like all books including the Scriptures, the potential always exists for men to add to, take away from, or twist anything written! *The Book of Adam and Eve, The Cave of Treasures,* and *The Book of Enoch* all discuss events that occurred before the Flood! All the accounts are very similar! Translation errors, language differences, omissions, and tampering by men over the years have caused some confusion, but Yahuah's Ruach HaQodesh will give you discernment, when you read these books! Taken together these books can give you a good understanding of what people in the past believed happened, before the Flood! I have included several chapters from *The Book of Adam and Eve* and *The Book of Enoch* so that you can evaluate them for yourself and get a better understanding of what people at the time of Yahushua's ministry believed happened, before the Flood! The events recorded in the Scriptures concerning Cain and Able are important for us to understand today! After Cain murdered Able, Cain descends Mount Sinai and lives in the plains below, away from the Righteous! Seth enforced the first separation of the Righteous from the wicked! The Righteous were called the sons of Elohim! From the time of Seth until the Flood, the sons of Elohim were instructed by each Patriarch to stay on top of Mount Sinai and to separate themselves from the descendents of Cain!

Genesis 4
And Adam knew Eve his wife; and she conceived, and bare Cain, and said, I have gotten a man from ayaz*. And she again bare his brother Abel. And Abel was a keeper of sheep, but Cain was a tiller of the ground. And in process of time it came to pass, that Cain brought of the fruit of the ground an offering unto* ayaz*. And Abel, he also brought of the firstlings of his flock and of the fat thereof. And* ayaz *had respect unto Abel and to his offering: But unto Cain and to his offering he had not respect. And Cain was very wroth, and his countenance fell. And* ayaz *said unto Cain, Why art thou wroth? and why is thy countenance fallen? If thou doest well, shalt thou not be accepted? If thou doest not well, sin lieth at the door. And unto thee shall be his desire, and thou shalt rule over him. And Cain talked with Abel his brother: and it came to pass, when they were in the field, that Cain rose up against Abel his brother, and slew him. And* ayaz *said unto Cain, Where is Abel thy brother?*

Genesis 4, cont.
And he said, I know not: Am I my brother's keeper? And he said, What hast thou done? The voice of thy brother's blood crieth unto me from the ground. And now art thou cursed from the earth, which hath opened her mouth to receive thy brother's blood from thy hand; when thou tillest the ground, it shall not henceforth yield unto thee her strength; a fugitive and a vagabond shalt thou be in the earth. And Cain said unto ᎯYᎯZ, My punishment is greater than I can bear. Behold, thou hast driven me out this day from the face of the earth; and from thy face shall I be hid; and I shall be a fugitive and a vagabond in the earth; and it shall come to pass, that every one that findeth me shall slay me.

Genesis 5 discusses the first ten generations of the Righteous line of Adam! This was the beginning of the family tree of OWYᎯZ! Cain's descendents through Lamech are given separately in Chapter 4 and are **not** part of the Righteous line of Adam!

Yahuah's Righteous Line of Adam
Genesis 5
This is the book of the generations of Adam. In the day that Elohim created man, in the likeness of Elohim made he him; Male and female created he them; and blessed them, and called their name Adam, in the day when they were created. And Adam lived an hundred and thirty years, and begat a son in his own likeness, after his image; and called his name Seth: And the days of Adam after he had begotten Seth were eight hundred years: and he begat sons and daughters: And all the days that Adam lived were nine hundred and thirty years: and he died. And Seth lived an hundred and five years, and begat Enos: And Seth lived after he begat Enos eight hundred and seven years, and begat sons and daughters: And all the days of Seth were nine hundred and twelve years: and he died. And Enos lived ninety years, and begat Cainan: And Enos lived after he begat Cainan eight hundred and fifteen years, and begat sons and daughters: And all the days of Enos were nine hundred and five years: and he died. And Cainan lived seventy years, and begat Mahalaleel: And Cainan lived after he begat Mahalaleel eight hundred and forty years, and begat sons and daughters: And all the days of Cainan were nine hundred and ten years: and he died. And Mahalaleel lived sixty and five years, and begat Jared: And Mahalaleel lived after he begat Yered eight hundred and thirty years, and begat sons and daughters:
And all the days of Mahalaleel were eight hundred ninety and five years: and he died. And Yered lived an hundred sixty and two years, and he begat Enoch: And Yered lived after he begat Enoch eight hundred years, and begat sons and daughters:

Genesis 5, cont.
And all the days of Yered were nine hundred sixty and two years: and he died. And Enoch lived sixty and five years, and begat Methuselah: And Enoch walked with Elohim after he begat Methuselah three hundred years, and begat sons and daughters: And all the days of Enoch were three hundred sixty and five years: <u>And Enoch walked with Elohim: and he was not; for Elohim took him</u>. And Methuselah lived an hundred eighty and seven years, and begat Lamech: And Methuselah lived after he begat Lamech seven hundred eighty and two years, and begat sons and daughters: And all the days of Methuselah were nine hundred sixty and nine years: and he died. And Lamech lived an hundred eighty and two years, and begat a son: And he called his name Noah, saying, This same shall comfort us concerning our work and toil of our hands, because of the ground which ayaz hath cursed. And Lamech lived after he begat Noah five hundred ninety and five years, and begat sons and daughters: And all the days of Lamech were seven hundred seventy and seven years: and he died. And Noah was five hundred years old: and Noah begat Shem, Ham, and Japheth.

The details in *The Book of Adam and Eve* about the events before the Flood are almost identical to the description given in *The Cave of Treasures*! *The Book of Enoch* is also very consistent in its description of the events surrounding the sons of Elohim and even adds more detail concerning these watchers! These **men** were born to be sons of Elohim, but they <u>spurned</u> Yahuah's heritage for sexual gratification with the daughters of Cain! These sons of Elohim were called watchers because they watched the daughters of Cain below the mountain for a whole year before they acted out their rebellion! As a result of their watching, they were seduced! This rebellion led to a huge escalation in violence and wickedness of all kinds against ayaz! These books describe the plotting and scheming of the watchers against Yahuah's Commandments as well as the watcher's descent from the top of Yahuah's set apart Mountain! These watchers descended Mount Sinai and sexually defiled themselves with the daughters of Cain below! This is the scenario that Genesis 6 is describing! The *Book of Enoch* describes Yahuah's judgment of these watchers and their reprobate off-spring! In *the Book of Enoch* the words "sons of Elohim" were translated as angels! This has contributed to a lot of confusion surrounding the events of Genesis 6! **These watchers were men and not heavenly <u>angels</u> at all!** They were born into the righteous family line of Adam and Seth, which was traceable back through the first ten Patriarchs! These watchers should have valued their righteous heritage and the <u>privilege</u> to live at the top of the set apart Mountain, before the face of ayaz!

The seed of the Patriarchs on top of the Mountain were created to be sons and daughters of 𐤀𐤉𐤄𐤆! They were created to be Righteous messengers, not wicked and perverse like Cain's descendents below! They were created to be sons of 𐤀𐤉𐤄𐤆 and members of His set apart family! However, these watchers rejected all of those wonderful blessings! They were overcome with animal desire for the women of Cain below! The watchers' rebellion was not only sexual, but it was a rejection of their righteous birthright as Yahuah's children! Therefore it was a blatant rejection of 𐤀𐤉𐤄𐤆, Himself! Essentially the watchers rejected the privilege to belong to Yahuah's family! Remember, after the Flood, when Esau gave up his birthright to Jacob for a bowl of soup! Esau did not value his own birthright either, but traded it for a lowly bowl of soup! What a costly bowl of soup that was! Because Esau disrespected his righteous estate as the first born son of Isaac in Yahuah's righteous line, the Scriptures say that 𐤀𐤉𐤄𐤆 hated Esau, but loved Jacob! The rebellion of the watchers culminated, when twenty sons of Elohim, assembled and plotted their rebellion against 𐤀𐤉𐤄𐤆! The names of these twenty are given in *The Book of Enoch*! These twenty reprobates plotted against 𐤀𐤉𐤄𐤆! They each made a voluntary decision to give up their own righteous birthright, just like Esau did later! They came down from the set apart Mountain to be with the daughters of Cain! They choose wives for themselves and defiled themselves with the daughters of Cain **just like wild beasts in heat**! Even though Yared and Enoch pleaded with these sons of Elohim zealously to repent from their wicked plans, the watchers would **not** listen and they descended Yahuah's set apart Mountain, never to reascend! Below they committed grievous sins against 𐤀𐤉𐤄𐤆 and against their own bodies! Over time one group after another of Yahuah's people descended the set apart Mountain to mix with Cain's descendents in the plains below! This heartbreak had to really hurt 𐤀𐤉𐤄𐤆 and OWY𐤄𐤆! Finally, only Noah and his family were left at the time of the Flood! As a father of four children this bothers me greatly because I can only imagine the pain and disappointment that 𐤀𐤉𐤄𐤆 and OWY𐤄𐤆 felt as each group of their children descended Mount Sinai! Tremendous wickedness, violence, and sexual perversion resulted from those sad events! Those events angered 𐤀𐤉𐤄𐤆 so much that He determined to destroy mankind and all the creatures that breathed the breath of life with a Flood! Because of the nature of their rebellion, 𐤀𐤉𐤄𐤆 determined that there would be no forgiveness for the watchers, **ever**! At this very moment Azazel and the rest of the watchers, who gave up their Righteous heritage for wild animal lust in this world, are chained in the Abyss of the Earth awaiting their final Judgment!

Genesis 6
And it came to be, when men began to increase on the face of the earth, and daughters were born to them, ²that the <u>sons</u> <u>of</u> <u>Elohim</u> saw the daughters of men, that they were good. And they took wives for themselves of all whom they chose. ³And **aYaZ** said, My Spirit shall not strive with man forever in his going astray. He is flesh, and his days shall be one hundred and twenty years." ⁴The Nephilim were on the earth in those days, and also afterward, when the sons of Elohim came in to the daughters of men and they bore children to them. Those were the mighty men who were of old, the men of name. ⁵And **aYaZ** saw that the wickedness of man was great in the earth, and that every inclination of the thoughts of his heart was only evil continually. ⁶And **aYaZ** was sorry that He had made man on the earth, and He was grieved in His heart. ⁷And **aYaZ** said, "I am going to wipe off man whom I have created from the face of the earth, both man and beast, creeping creature and birds of the heavens, for I am sorry that I have made them.

Book of Adam and Eve
Adam predicts the Flood!

Chapter 8
1. When our father Adam saw that his end was near, he called his son Seth, who came to him in the Cave of Treasures, and he said unto him: 2. "O Seth, my son bring me your children and your children's children, that I may shed my blessing on them ere I die." 3. When Seth heard these words from his father Adam, he went from him, shed a flood of tears over his face, and gathered together his children and his children's children, and brought them to his father Adam. 4. But when our father Adam saw them around him, he wept at having to be separated from them. 5. And when they saw him weeping, they all wept together, and fell upon his face saying, "How shalt thou be severed from us, O our father? And how shall the earth receive thee and hide thee from our eyes?" Thus did they lament much, and in like words. 6. Then our father Adam blessed them all, and said to Seth, after he had blessed them: 7. "O Seth, my son, thou knowest this world - that it is full of sorrow, and of weariness; and thou knowest all that has come upon us, from our trials in it I therefore flow command thee in these words: to keep innocency, to be pure and just, and trusting in **aYaZ**; and lean not to the discourses of haSatan, nor to the apparitions in which he will show himself to thee. 8. But keep the commandments that I give thee this day; then give the same to your son Enos; and let Enos give it to his son Cainan; and Cainan to his son Mahalaleel; so that this commandment abide firm among all your children.

Book of Adam and Eve, cont.
Adam predicts the Flood!

9 "0 Seth, my son, the moment I am dead take ye my body and wind it up with myrrh, aloes, and cassia, and leave me here in this Cave of Treasures in which are all these tokens which 𐤉𐤄𐤅𐤄 gave us from the garden. 10 "0 my son, hereafter shall a flood come and overwhelm all creatures, and leave out only eight souls. 11 "But, 0 my son, let those whom it will leave out from among your children at that time, take my body with them out of this cave; and when they have taken it with them, let the oldest among them command his children to lay my body in a ship until the flood has been assuaged, and they come out of the ship. 12 Then they shall take my body and lay it in the middle of the earth, shortly after they have been saved from the waters of the flood. 13 "For the place where my body shall be laid, is the middle of the earth ; 𐤉𐤄𐤅𐤄 shall come from thence and shall save all our kindred. 14 "But now, 0 Seth, my son, place yourself at the head of your people; tend them and watch over them in the fear of 𐤉𐤄𐤅𐤄; and lead them in the good way. Command them to fast unto 𐤉𐤄𐤅𐤄; and make them understand they ought not to hearken to haSatan, lest he destroy them. 15 "Then, again, sever your children and your children's children from Cain's children; do not let them ever mix with those, nor come near them either in their words or in their deeds." 16 Then Adam let his blessing descend upon Seth, and upon his children, and upon all his children's children. 17 He then turned to his son Seth, and to Eve his wife, and, said to them, "Preserve this gold, this incense, and this myrrh, that 𐤉𐤄𐤅𐤄 has given us for a sign; for in days that are coming, a flood will overwhelm the whole creation. But those who shall go into the ark shall take with them the gold, the incense, and the myrrh, together with my body; and will lay the gold, the incense, and the myrrh, with my body in the midst of the earth. 18 "Then, after a long time, the city in which the gold, the incense, and the myrrh are found with my body, shall be plundered. But when it is spoiled, the gold the incense, and the myrrh shall be taken care of with the spoil that is kept; and naught of them shall perish, until the Word of 𐤉𐤄𐤅𐤄, made man shall come; when kings shall take them, and shall offer to Him, gold in token of His being King; incense, in token of His being 𐤉𐤄𐤅𐤄 of heaven and earth; and myrrh, in token of His passion. 19 "Gold also, as a token of His overcoming haSatan, and all our foes; incense as a token that He will rise from the dead, and be exalted above things in heaven and things in the earth; and myrrh, in token that He will drink bitter gall; and feel the pains of hell from haSatan. 20 "And now, 0 Seth, my son, behold I have revealed unto thee hidden mysteries, which 𐤉𐤄𐤅𐤄 had revealed unto me. Keep my commandment, for yourself, and for your people."

Book of Adam and Eve
Chapter 11 Seth

1. After the death of Adam and of Eve, <u>Seth severed his children, and his children's children, from Cain's children</u>. Cain and his seed went down and dwelt westward, below the place where he had killed his brother Abel. 2 But Seth and his children, dwelt northwards upon the mountain of the Cave of Treasures, in order to be near to their father Adam. 3 And Seth the elder, tall and good, with a fine soul, and of a strong mind, stood at the head of his people; and tended them in innocence, penitence, and meekness, and did not allow one of them to go down to Cain's children. 4 But because of their own purity, they were named **"Children of ᴀYᴀZ,"** and they were with ᴀYᴀZ, instead of the hosts of angels who fell; for they continued in praises to ᴀYᴀZ, and in singing psalms unto Him, in their cave - the Cave of Treasures. 5 Then Seth stood before the body of his father Adam, and of his mother Eve, and prayed night and day, and asked for mercy towards himself and his children; and that when he had some difficult dealing with a child, He would give him counsel. 6 But Seth and his children did not like earthly work, but gave themselves to heavenly things; for they had no other thought than praises, doxologies, and psalms unto ᴀYᴀZ. 7 Therefore did they at all times hear the voices of angels, praising and glorifying ᴀYᴀZ; from within the garden, or when they were sent by ᴀYᴀZ on an errand, or when they were going up to heaven. 8 For Seth and his children, by reason of their own purity, heard and saw those angels. Then, again, the garden was not far above them, but only some fifteen spiritual cubits. 9 Now one spiritual cubit answers to three cubits of man, altogether forty-five cubits. 10 Seth and his children dwelt on the mountain below the garden; they sowed not, neither did they reap; they wrought no food for the body. not even wheat; but only offerings. They ate of the fruit and of trees well flavored that grew on the mountain where they dwelt. 11 Then Seth often fasted every forty days, as did also his eldest children. For the family of Seth smelled the smell of the trees in the garden, when the wind blew that way. 12 They were happy, innocent, without sudden fear, there was no jealousy, no evil action, no hatred among them. **<u>There was no animal passion</u>**, from no mouth among them went forth either foul words or curse ; neither evil counsel nor fraud . For the men of that time never swore, but under hard circumstances, when men must swear, they swore by the blood of Abel the just. 13 But they constrained their children and their women every day in the cave to fast and pray, and to worship the most High ᴀYᴀZ. They blessed themselves in the body of their father Adam, and anointed themselves with it. 14 And they did so until the end of Seth drew near.

Adam and Eve
Seth

Chapter 12

1. Then Seth, the just, called his son Enos, and Cainan, son of Enos, and Mahalaleel, son of Cainan, and said unto them: 2 "As my end is near, I wish to build a roof over the altar on which gifts are offered." 3 They hearkened to his commandment and went out, all of them, both old and young, and worked hard at it, and built a beautiful roof over the altar. 4 And Seth's thought, in so doing, was that a blessing should come upon his children on the mountain; and that he should present an offering for them before his death. 5 Then when the building of the roof was completed, he commanded them to make offerings. They worked diligently at these, and brought them to Seth their father who took them and offered them upon the altar; and prayed 𐤀𐤉𐤄𐤅 to accept their offerings, to have mercy on the souls of his children, and to keep them from the hand of haSatan. 6 And 𐤀𐤉𐤄𐤅 accepted his offering, and sent His blessing upon him and upon his children. And then 𐤀𐤉𐤄𐤅 made a promise to Seth, saying, "At the end of the great five days and a half, concerning which I have made a promise to thee and to your father, I will send My Word and save thee and your seed." 7 Then Seth and his children, and his children's children, met together, and came down from the altar, and went to the Cave of Treasures - where they prayed, and blessed themselves in the body of our father Adam, and anointed themselves with it. 8 But Seth abode in the Cave of Treasures, a few days, and then suffered - sufferings unto death. 9 Then Enos, his first - born son, came to him, with Cainan, his son, and Mahalaleel, Caiman's son, and Jared, the son of Mahalaleel, and Enoch, Jared's son, with their wives and children to receive a blessing from Seth. 10 Then Seth prayed over them, and blessed them, and adjured them by the blood of Abel the just, saying, "I beg of you my children, not to let one of you go down from this Holy and pure Mountain. 11 Make no fellowship with the children of Cain the murderer and the sinner, who killed his brother; for ye know, O my children, that we flee from him, and from all his sin with all our might because he killed his brother Abel." 12 After having said this, Seth blessed Enos, his first - born son, and commanded him habitually to minister in purity before the body of our father Adam, all the days of his life; then, also, to go at times to the altar which he Seth had built. And he commanded him to feed his people in righteousness, in judgment and purity all the days of his life. 13 Then the limbs of Seth were loosened; his hands and feet lost all power; his mouth became dumb and unable to speak; and he gave up the ghost and died the day after his nine hundred and twelfth year; on the twenty - seventh day of the month Abib; Enoch being then twenty years old.

Adam and Eve
Seth

Chapter 12, cont.
14 Then they wound up careful the body of Seth, and embalmed him with sweet spices, and laid him in the Cave Treasures, on the right side of our father Adam's body, and they mourned for him forty days. They offered gifts for him, as they had done for our father Adam. 15 After the death of Seth, Enos rose at the head of his people, whom he fed in righteousness, and judgment, as his father had commanded him. 16 But by the time Enos was eight hundred and twenty years old, Cain had a large progeny; for they married frequently, being given to animal lusts; until the land below the mountain, was filled with them.

Adam and Eve
The children of Cain

1. In those days lived Lamech the blind, *who was of the sons of Cain. He had a son whose name was Atun, and they two had much cattle. 2 But Lamech was in the habit of sending them to feed with a young shepherd, who tended them; and who, when coming home in the evening wept before his grandfather, and before his father Atun and his mother Hazina, and said to them, "As for me, I cannot feed those cattle alone, lest one rob me of some of them, or kill me for the sake of them." For* **among the children of Cain, there was much robbery, murder and sin.** *3 Then Lamech pitied him, and he said, "Truly, he when alone, might be overpowered by the men of this place." 4 So Lamech arose, took a bow he had kept ever since he was a youth, ere he became blind, and he took large arrows, and smooth stones, and a sling which he had, and went to the field with the young shepherd, and placed himself behind the cattle; while the young shepherd watched the cattle. Thus did Lamech many days. 5 Meanwhile Cain, ever since* ᚐᛦᚐᛰ *had cast him off, and had cursed him with trembling and terror, could neither settle nor find rest in any one place; but wandered from place to place. 6 In his wanderings he came to Lamech's wives, and asked them about him. They said to him, "He is in the field with the cattle." 7 Then Cain went to look for him; and as he came into the field, the young shepherd heard the noise he made, and the cattle herding together from before him, 8 Then said he to Lamech, "0 my Elohim, is that a wild beast or a robber?" 9 And Lamech said to him, "Make me understand which way he looks, when he comes up. 10 Then Lamech bent his bow, placed an arrow on it, and fitted a stone in the sling, and when Cain came out from the open country, the shepherd said to Lamech, "Shoot, behold, he is coming." 11 Then Lamech shot at Cain with his arrow and hit him in his side. And Lamech struck him with a stone from his sling, that fell upon his face, and knocked out both his eyes; then Cain fell at once and died.*

Adam and Eve
The children of Cain

12 Then Lamech and the young shepherd came up to him, and found him lying on the ground. And the young shepherd said to him, "It is Cain our grandfather, whom thou hast killed, 0 my Elohim!"18 Then was Lamech sorry for it, and from the bitterness of his regret, he clapped his hands together, and struck with his flat palm the head of the youth, who fell as if dead; but Lamech thought it was a feint; so he took up a stone and smote him, and smashed his head until he died.

Book of Adam and Eve
Death of Enos

Chapter 14

When Enos was nine hundred years old, all the children of Seth, and of Cainan, and his first-born, with their wives and children, gathered around him, asking for a blessing from him. He then prayed over them and blessed them, and prayed [adjured] them by the blood of Abel the just saying to them, "Let not one of your children go down from this Holy Mountain, and let them make NO fellowship with the children of Cain the murderer." Then Enos called his son Cainan and said to him, "See, 0 my son, and set your heart on your people, and establish them in righteousness, and in innocence; and stand ministering before the body of our father Adam, all the days of your life." After this Enos entered into rest, aged nine hundred and - five years and Cainan wound him up, and laid him in the Cave of Treasures on the left of his father Adam; and made offerings for him, after the custom of his fathers. The offspring of Adam continue to keep the Cave of Treasures as a family shrine. After the death of Enos, Cainan stood at the head of his people in righteousness and innocence, as his father had commanded him; he also continued to minister before the body of Adam, inside the Cave of Treasures. Then when he had lived nine hundred and ten years, suffering and affliction came upon him. And when he was about to enter into rest, all the fathers with their wives and children came to him, and he blessed them, and adjured them by the blood of Abel, the just, saying to them, "Let not one among you go down from this Holy Mountain; and make NO fellowship with the children of Cain the murderer." Mahalaleel, his first - born son, received this commandment from his father, who blessed him and died. Then Mahalaleel embalmed him with sweet spices, and laid him in the Cave of Treasures, with his fathers; and they made offerings for him, after the custom of their fathers.

Book of Adam and Eve
Mahalal'el

Chapter 16

Then stood over his people, and fed them in righteousness and innocence, and watched them to see they held no intercourse with the children of Cain. He also continued in the Cave of Treasures praying and ministering before the body of our father Adam, asking 𐤀𐤉𐤀𐤆 for mercy on himself and on his people; until he was eight hundred and seventy years old, when he fell sick. Then all his children gathered unto him, to see him, and to ask for his blessing on them all, ere he left this world. Then Mahalaleel arose and sat on his bed, his tears streaming down his face, and he called his eldest son Jared, who came to him. He then kissed his face, and said to him, "O Jared, my son, I adjure thee by Him who made heaven and earth, to watch over your people, and to feed them in righteousness and in innocence; and not to let one of them go down from this Holy Mountain to the children of Cain, lest he perish with them. "Hear, O my son, hereafter there shall come a great destruction upon this earth on account of them; 𐤀𐤉𐤀𐤆 will be angry with the world, and will destroy them with waters. "But I also know that your children will not hearken to thee, and that they will go down from this mountain and hold intercourse with the children of Cain, and that they shall perish with them. "O my son! teach them, and watch over them, that no guilt attach to thee on their account. " Mahalaleel said, moreover, to his son Jared, "When I die, embalm my body and lay it in the Cave of Treasures, by the bodies of my fathers; then stand you by my body and pray to 𐤀𐤉𐤀𐤆; and take care of them, and fulfill your ministry before them, until you enterest into rest yourself." Mahalaleel then blessed all his children; and then lay down on his bed, and entered into rest like his fathers.

Now up unto this time, the sons of the Righteous on top of the Mountain had remained separated from the children of Cain! This was to change during the reign of Yered! Yered was a very righteous man, but the watchers rebelled during his watch! Two hundred sons of the Elohim rebelled and gave up an eternal life of blessing and fellowship with 𐤀𐤉𐤀𐤆 for the animal flesh of the daughters of Cain! These young men should have been so thankful to be before the face of 𐤀𐤉𐤀𐤆 and so close to Paradise on top of Yahuah's Set apart Mountain! They were so close to the Garden that sometimes they could smell the wonderful fragrances wafting from Paradise on the heavenly Mount Zion! Why would they do something so foolish? These young watchers gave up so much back then because of their uncontrolled animal lust! As a result, they have suffered in darkness and in chains ever since! But their worst punishment is yet to come!

They still have Yahuah's Lake of Fire to look forward to, which 𐤀𐤉𐤀𐤆 calls the second death! That's a very frightening prospect to me! And don't forget, the watchers have no hope of forgiveness! They gave it all up for their <u>unbridled animal lust</u> for the daughters of Cain, who lived in the plains below the Set Apart Mountain! When the watchers comsumated their rebellion against 𐤀𐤉𐤀𐤆, they became like horses in heat! They did exactly what all the previous Patriarchs and Yered warned them **not to do**! Two hundred of these sons of Elohim were called 'Watchers" by Enoch because they watched the daughters of Cain below the Mountain for over a year! These watchers made a pact with each other in which they agreed to carry out their wicked plans <u>together</u>! Their rebellion was a perfect example of planned iniquity against 𐤀𐤉𐤀𐤆! These rebels descended Mount Sinai and took wives from the seductive children of Cain below! This was direct rebellion against Yahuah's Word! **Their rebellion amounted to them rejecting 𐤀𐤉𐤀𐤆 as their Father and choosing instead the adversary, satan!** They behaved like ravenous beasts! After they finished with their perverse sexual acts with the daughters of Cain, these watchers tried to go back up to Yahuah's Mountain! However, they were not able to ascend the Mountain anymore because 𐤀𐤉𐤀𐤆 caused the stones of His Mountain to flame up and block their way! All of these events were well known by all the patriarchs of Israel, but are largely overlooked and misunderstood in our time!

Book of Adam and Eve
The children of Yered are led astray.

*1 Then Yahuah revealed to him again the promise He had made to Adam; He explained to him [the mystery of the] 5500 years, and revealed unto him the mystery of His Word [made flesh] coming upon the earth. 2 And 𐤀𐤉𐤀𐤆 said to Jared, "As to that fire which you hast taken from the altar to light the lamp withal, let it abide with you to give light to the bodies; and let it not come out of the cave, until the body of Adam comes out of it. 3 But, 0 Jared, take care of the fire, that it burn bright in the lamp; neither go you again out of the cave until you receivest an order through **a vision**, and **NOT in an apparition**, when seen by thee. 4 "Then command again thy people not to hold intercourse with the children of Cain, and not to learn their ways; for I am 𐤀𐤉𐤀𐤆 who loves <u>not</u> hatred and works of iniquity." 5 𐤀𐤉𐤀𐤆 gave also many other **commandments** to Jared, and blessed him. And then withdrew His Word from him. 6 Then Yered drew near with his children, took some fire, and came down to the cave, and lighted the lamp before the body of Adam; and he gave his people commandments as 𐤀𐤉𐤀𐤆 had told him to do. 7 This sign happened to Yered at the end of his four hundred and fiftieth year; as did also many other wonders, we do not record.*

Book of Adam and Eve
The children of Yered are led astray.

But we record only this one for shortness sake, and in order not to lengthen our narrative. 8 And Yered continued to teach his children eighty years; but after that they began to transgress the commandments he had given them, and to do many things without his counsel. They began to go down from the Holy Mountain one after another, and to mix with the children of Cain, in foul fellowships. 9 Now the reason for which the children of Yered went down the Holy Mountain, is this, that we will now reveal unto you.

Seduction of the Watchers

1. After Cain had gone down to the land of dark soil, and his children had multiplied therein, there was one of them, whose name was Genun, son of Lamech the blind who slew Cain. 2 But as to this Genun, haSatan came into him in his childhood; and he made sundry trumpets and horns, and string instruments, cymbals and psalteries, and lyres and harps, and flutes; and he played on them at all times and at every hour. 3 And when he played on them, haSatan came into them, so that from among them were heard beautiful and pleasing sounds, that ravished the heart. 4 Then he gathered companies upon companies to play (on their instruments) on them [to form a band]; and when they played, it pleased well the children of Cain, who inflamed themselves with sin among themselves, and burnt as with fire; while haSatan inflamed their hearts, one with another, and increased lust among them. 5 haSatan also taught Genun to bring strong drink out of corn; and this Genun used to bring together companies upon companies in drink-houses; and brought into their hands all manner of fruits and flowers; and they drank together. 6 Thus did this Genun multiply sin exceedingly; he also acted with pride, and taught the children of Cain to commit all manner of the grossest wickedness, which they knew not; and put them up to manifold doings which they knew not before. 7 Then haSatan, when he saw that the youth yielded to Genun and hearkened to him in every thing he told them, he rejoiced greatly, and increased Genun's understanding until he took iron and with it made weapons of war. 8 Then when they were drunk, hatred and murder increased among them; one man used violence against another to teach him evil, taking his children and defiling them before him. 9 And when men saw they were overcome, and saw others that were not overpowered, those who were beaten came to Genun, took refuge with him, and he made them his confederates.

Book of Adam and Eve, cont.

10 Then sin increased among them greatly; until a man committed incest with his own sister, or daughter, or mother, and others; or the daughter of his father's sister, so that there was no more distinction of relationship, and they no longer knew what is iniquity; but did wickedly, and the earth was defiled with sin; and they angered 𐤀𐤉𐤄𐤆 the Great Judge, who had created them. 11 But Genun gathered together companies upon companies, that played on horns and on all the other instruments we have already mentioned, at the foot of the Holy Mountain; and they did so in order that the children of Seth the righteous, who were on the Holy Mountain should hear it. (and being seduced with music). 12 But when the children of Seth heard the noise, they wondered, and came by companies, and stood on the top of the mountain to look at those below; and they did thus a whole year. 13 When, at the end of that year, Genun saw that they were being won over to him little by little, haSatan entered into him [Genun], and taught him to make dyeing stuffs for garments of divers patterns, and made him understand how to dye crimson and purple and what not. 14 And the sons of Cain who wrought all this, and shone in beauty and gorgeous apparel, gathered together at the foot of the mountain in splendor, with horns and gorgeous dresses, and horse races, committing all manner of abominations. 15 Meanwhile the children of Seth, who were on the Holy Mountain, prayed and praised 𐤀𐤉𐤄𐤆, in the place of the hosts of angels who had fallen; wherefore 𐤀𐤉𐤄𐤆 had called them 'angels [or elohim, see psalms],'" because He rejoiced over them greatly. 16 But after this, they no longer kept His commandment, nor held by the promise He had made to their fathers; but they relaxed from their fasting and praying, and from the counsel of Yered their father. And they kept on gathering together on the top of the mountain, to look upon the children of Cain, from morning until evening, and upon what they did, upon their beautiful dresses and ornaments. 17 Then the children of Cain looked up from below, and saw the children of Seth, standing in troops on the top of the mountain; and they called to them to come down to them. 18 But the children of Seth said to them from above, "We don't know the way." Then Genun, the son of Lamech, heard them say they did not know the way, and he bethought himself how he might bring them down. 19 Then haSatan appeared to him by night, saying, "There is no way for them to come down from the mountain on which they dwell; but when they come tomorrow, say to them, 'Come ye to the western side of the mountain; there you will find the way of a stream of water, that comes down to the foot of the mountain, between two hills; come down that way to us.'"

Book of Adam and Eve, cont.
Seduction of the Watchers

20 Then when it was day, Genun blew the horns and beat the drums below the mountain, as he was wont. The children of Seth heard it, and came as they used to do. 21 Then Genun said to them from down below, "Go to the western side of the mountain, there you will find the way to come down." 22 But when the children of Seth heard these words from him, they went back into the cave to Jared, to tell him all they had heard. 23 Then when Yered heard it, he was grieved; for he knew that they would transgress his counsel. 24 After this a hundred men of the children of Seth gathered together, and said among themselves, "Come, let us go down to the children of Cain, and see what they do, and enjoy ourselves with them." 25 But when Yered heard this of the hundred men, his very soul was moved, and his heart was grieved. He then arose with great fervor, and stood in the midst of them, and adjured them by the blood of Abel the just, "Let not one of you go down from this holy and pure mountain, in which our fathers have ordered us to dwell." 26 But when Yered saw that they did not receive his words, he said unto them, "0 my good and innocent and holy children, know that when once you go down from this holy mountain, 𐤀𐤉𐤄𐤆 will not allow you to return again to it." 27 He again adjured them, saying, "I adjure by the death of our father Adam, and by the blood of Abel, of Seth, of Enos, of Cainan, and of Mahalaleel, to hearken to me, and NOT to go down from this holy mountain; for the moment you leave it, you will be reft of life and of mercy; and you shall no longer be called 'children of 𐤀𐤉𐤄𐤆,' but 'children of the devil.' 28 But they would not hearken to his words. 29 Enoch at that time was already grown up, and in his zeal for 𐤀𐤉𐤄𐤆, he arose and said, "Hear me, 0 ye sons of Seth, small and great-when ye transgress the commandment of our fathers, and go down from this holy mountain-ye shall not come up hither again for ever." 30 But they rose up against Enoch, and would not hearken to his words, but went down from the Holy Mountain. 31 And when they looked at the daughters of Cain, at their beautiful figures, and at their hands and feet dyed with color, and tattooed in ornaments on their faces, the fire of sin was kindled in them. 32 Then haSatan made them look most beautiful before the sons of Seth, as he also made the sons of Seth appear of the fairest in the eyes of the daughters of Cain, so that the daughters of Cain lusted after the sons of Seth like ravenous beasts, and the sons of Seth after the daughters of Cain, until they committed abomination with them. 33 But after they had thus fallen into this defilement, they returned by the way they had come, and tried to ascend the Holy Mountain. But they could not, because the stones of that holy mountain were of fire flashing before them, by reason of which they could not go up again.

Book of Adam and Eve, cont.
Seduction of the Watchers

34 And ayaz was angry with them, and repented of them because they had come down from glory, and had thereby lost or forsaken their own purity or innocence, and were fallen into the defilement of sin. 35 Then ayaz sent His Word to Yered, saying, "These your children, whom you didst call 'My children,' - behold they have transgressed My commandment, and have gone down to the abode of perdition, and of sin. Send a messenger to those that are left, that they may not go down, and be lost." 36 Then Yered wept before the Elohim, and asked of Him mercy and forgiveness. But he wished that his soul might depart from his body, rather than hear these words from ayaz about the going down of his children from the Holy Mountain. 37 But he followed Yahuah's order, and preached unto them not to go down from that holy mountain, and not to hold intercourse with the children of Cain. 38 But they heeded not his message, and would not obey his counsel.

Book of Adam and Eve
Sons Go Astray!

1. After this another company gathered together, and they went to look after their brethren; but they perished [in sin] as well as the ones before them had. And so it was, company after company, until only a few of them were left. 2 Then Yered sickened from grief , and his sickness was such that the day of his death drew near. 3 Then he called Enoch his eldest son, and Methuselah Enoch's son, and Lamech the son of Methuselah, and Noah the son of Lamech.

THE FALL OF THE CHILDREN OF SETH

The picture above is from *The Forgotten Books of Eden!* This picture depicts the decent of the sons of Elohim from the set apart Mountain of ayaz! These sons of Elohim were descendants of the line of Seth! They were called "Watchers" because they watched the daughters of Cain in the valley below the Mountain for one year before they acted out their rebellion against ayaz! Some modern translators have called these sons of Elohim, "angels"! This mistranslation has caused the events of Genesis 6 to be widely misunderstood! These sons of Elohim rejected the privilege of being in the Righteous family line of Seth! This amounted to a complete rejection of the family of ayaz in exchange for temporary sensual pleasures with the daughters of Cain! These reprobate watchers descended the Mountain, after being seduced by the daughters of Cain! After their decent, wickedness and violence increased on the earth at an exponential rate, until ayaz could no longer stand it! As a result of the extremely wicked acts of men and beasts that followed this rebellion, ayaz determined to destroy all the men and beasts from off the face of the earth with a Flood! Of course only Noah and his family were spared! These events are described in Genesis 6, 2 Peter 2: 4-5, and Jude 1:6 of the Scriptures as well as *The Book of Enoch, The Book of Adam and Eve,* and *The Cave of Treasures!*

Book of Adam and Eve
Sons Go Astray, cont.!

4 And when they were come to him he prayed over them and blessed them, and said to them, "Ye are righteous, innocent sons; go ye not down from this holy mountain; for behold, your children and your children's children have gone down from this holy mountain, and have estranged themselves from this holy mountain, through their abominable lust and transgression of Yahuah's commandment. 5 "But I know, through the power of ᴀYᴀZ that He will not leave you on this holy mountain, because your children have transgressed His commandment and that of our fathers, which we had received from them. 6 "But, 0 my sons, ᴀYᴀZ will take you to a strange land, and ye never shall again return to behold with your eyes this garden and this holy mountain. 7 "Therefore, 0 my sons, set your hearts on your own selves, and keep the commandment of ᴀYᴀZ which is with you. And when you go from this holy mountain, into a strange land which ye know not, take with you the body of our father Adam, and with it these three precious gifts and offerings, namely, the gold, the incense, and the myrrh; and let them be in the place where the body of our father Adam shall lay. 8 "And unto him of you who shall be left, 0 my sons, shall the Word of ᴀYᴀZ come, and when he goes out of this land he shall take with him the body of our father Adam, and shall lay it in the middle of the earth, the place in which salvation shall be wrought." 9 Then Noah said unto him, "Who is he of us that shall be left?" 10 And Yered answered, "you art he that shall be left. And you shalt take the body of our father Adam from the cave, and place it with thee in the ark when the flood comes. 11 "And your son Shem, who shall come out of your loins, he it is who shall lay the body of our father Adam in the middle of the earth, in the place whence salvation shall come." 12 Then Yered turned to his son Enoch, and said unto him "you, my son, abide in this cave, and minister diligently before the body of our father Adam all the days of your life; and feed your people in righteousness and innocence." 13 And Yered said no more. His hands were loosened, his eyes closed, and he entered into rest like his fathers. His death took place in the three hundred and sixtieth year of Noah, and in the nine hundred and eighty-ninth year of his own life; on the twelfth of Takhsas on a Friday. 14 But as Yered died, tears streamed down his face by reason of his great sorrow, for the children of Seth, who had fallen in his days. 15 Then Enoch, Methuselah, Lamech and Noah, these four, wept over him; embalmed him carefully, and then laid him in the Cave of Treasures. Then they rose and mourned for him forty days.16 And when these days of mourning were ended, Enoch, Methuselah, Lamech and Noah remained in sorrow of heart, because their father had departed from them, and they saw him no more.

Book of Adam and Eve
Enoch

1. But Enoch kept the commandment of Yered his father, and continued to minister in the cave. 2 It is this Enoch to whom many wonders happened, and who also wrote a celebrated book; but those wonders may not be told in this place. 3 Then after this, the children of Seth went astray and fell, they, their children and their wives. And when Enoch, Methuselah, Lamech and Noah saw them, their hearts suffered by reason of their fall into doubt full of unbelief; and they wept and sought of ayaz mercy, to preserve them, and to bring them out of that wicked generation. 4 Enoch continued in his ministry before the Elohim three hundred and eighty-five years, and at the end of that time he became aware through the grace of ayaz, that ayaz intended to remove him from the earth. 5 He then said to his son, "0 my son, I know that ayaz intends to bring the waters of the Flood upon the earth, and to destroy our creation. 6 "And ye are the last rulers over this people on this mountain; for I know that not one will be left you to beget children on this holy mountain; neither shall any one of you rule over the children of his people; neither shall any great company be left of you, on this mountain." 7 Enoch said also to them, "Watch over your souls, and hold fast by your fear of ayaz and by your service of Him, and worship Him in upright faith, and serve Him in righteousness, innocence and judgment, in repentance and also in purity." 8 When Enoch had ended his commandments to them, ayaz transported him from that mountain to the land of life, to the mansions of the righteous and of the chosen, the abode of Paradise of joy, in light that reaches up to heaven; light that is outside the light of this world; for it is the light of ayaz, that fills the whole world, but which no place can contain. 9 Thus, because Enoch was in the light of ayaz, he found himself out of the reach of death; until ayaz would have him taken. 10 Altogether, not one of our fathers or of their children, remained on that holy mountain, except those three, Methuselah, Lamech, and Noah. For all the rest went down from the mountain and fell into sin with the children of Cain. Therefore were they forbidden that mountain, and none remained on it but those three men.

Chapter 6 The Book of Enoch

$_1$And it came to pass when the children of men had multiplied that in those days were born unto $_2$them beautiful and comely daughters. And the watchers, **(sons of Elohim)** the children of the heaven, saw and lusted after them, and said to one another: 'Come, let us choose us wives from among the children of men $_3$and beget us children.' And Semjâzâ, who was their leader, said unto them: 'I fear ye will not $_4$indeed agree to do this deed, and I alone shall have to pay the penalty of a great sin.

The Book of Enoch

Chapter 6, cont.
And they all answered him and said: 'Let us all swear an oath, and all bind ourselves by mutual imprecations $_5$not to abandon this plan but to do this thing.' Then sware they all together and bound themselves $_6$by mutual imprecations upon it. And they were in all two hundred; who descended in the days of Yered on the summit of Mount Hermon, and they called it Mount Hermon, because they had sworn $_7$and bound themselves by mutual imprecations upon it. And these are the names of their leaders: Samîazâz, their leader, Arâkîba, Râmêêl, Kôkabîêl, Tâmîêl, Râmîêl, Dânêl, Êzêqêêl, Barâqîjâl, $_8$Asâêl, Armârôs, Batârêl, Anânêl, Zaqîêl, Samsâpêêl, Satarêl, Tûrêl, Jômjâêl, Sariêl. These are their chiefs of tens.

Chapter 7
$_1$And all the others together with them took unto themselves wives, and each chose for himself one, and they began to go in unto them and to defile themselves with them, and they taught them charms $_2$and enchantments, and the cutting of roots, and made them acquainted with plants. And they $_3$became pregnant, and they bare great giants, whose height was three thousand ells: Who consumed $_4$all the acquisitions of men. And when men could no longer sustain them, the giants turned against $_5$them and devoured mankind. And they began to sin against birds, and beasts, and reptiles, and $_6$fish, and to devour one another's flesh, and drink the blood. Then the earth laid accusation against the lawless ones.

Chapter 8
$_1$And Azâzêl taught men to make swords, and knives, and shields, and breastplates, and made known to them the metals of the earth and the art of working them, and bracelets, and ornaments, and the use of antimony, and the beautifying of the eyelids, and all kinds of costly stones, and all $_2$colouring tinctures. And there arose much godlessness, and they committed fornication, and they $_3$were led astray, and became corrupt in all their ways. Semjâzâ taught enchantments, and root-cuttings, 'Armârôs the resolving of enchantments, Barâqîjâl (taught) astrology, Kôkabêl the constellations, Êzêqêêl the knowledge of the clouds, Araqiêl the signs of the earth, Shamsiêl the signs of the sun, and Sariêl the course of the moon. And as men perished, they cried, and their cry went up to heaven.

Chapter 9
$_1$And then Michael, Uriel, Raphael, and Gabriel looked down from heaven and saw much blood being $_2$shed upon the earth, and all lawlessness being wrought upon the earth.

The Book of Enoch

Chapter 9, cont.
And they said one to another: 'The earth made without inhabitant cries the voice of their crying and making suit up to the gates of heaven. $_3$And now to you, the holy ones of heaven, the souls of men make their suit, saying, "Bring our cause $_4$before the Most High."' And they said to the Lord of the ages: 'Lord of lords, God of gods, King of kings, and God of the ages, the throne of Thy glory (standeth) unto all the generations of the $_5$ages, and Thy name holy and glorious and blessed unto all the ages! Thou hast made all things, and power over all things hast Thou: and all things are naked and open in Thy sight, and Thou seest all $_6$things, and nothing can hide itself from Thee. Thou seest what Azâzêl hath done, who hath taught all unrighteousness on earth and revealed the eternal secrets which were (preserved) in heaven, which $_7$men were striving to learn: And Semjâzâ, to whom Thou hast given authority to bear rule over his associates. And they have gone to the daughters of men upon the earth, and have slept with the $_9$women, and have defiled themselves, and revealed to them all kinds of sins. And the women have $_{10}$borne giants, and the whole earth has thereby been filled with blood and unrighteousness. And now, behold, the souls of those who have died are crying and making their suit to the gates of heaven, and their lamentations have ascended: and cannot cease because of the lawless deeds which are 11 wrought on the earth. And Thou knowest all things before they come to pass, and Thou seest these things and Thou dost suffer them, and Thou dost not say to us what we are to do to them in regard to these.'

Chapter 10
$_1$Then said the Most High, the Holy and Great One spake, and sent Uriel to the son of Lamech, $_2$and said to him: 'Go to Noah and tell him in my name "Hide thyself!" and reveal to him the end that is approaching: that the whole earth will be destroyed, and a deluge is about to come $_3$upon the whole earth, and will destroy all that is on it. And now instruct him that he may escape $_4$and his seed may be preserved for all the generations of the world.' And again the ᎦᎩᎫᏃ said to Raphael: 'Bind Azâzêl hand and foot, and cast him into the darkness: and make an opening $_5$in the desert, which is in Dûdâêl, and cast him therein. And place upon him rough and jagged rocks, and cover him with darkness, and let him abide there for ever, and cover his face that he may 6,7 not see light. And on the day of the great judgment he shall be cast into the fire.

Chapter 10, cont.

The Book of Enoch

And heal the earth which the angels have corrupted, and proclaim the healing of the earth, that they may heal the plague, and that all the children of men may not perish through all the secret things that the $_8$Watchers have disclosed and have taught their sons. And the whole earth has been corrupted $_9$through the works that were taught by Azâzêl: to him ascribe all sin.' And to Gabriel said the ᐊYᗺZ: 'Proceed against the bastards and the reprobates, and against the children of fornication: and destroy [the children of fornication and] the children of the Watchers from amongst men [and cause them to go forth]: send them one against the other that they may destroy each other in $_{10}$battle: for length of days shall they not have. And no request that they (i.e. their fathers) make of thee shall be granted unto their fathers on their behalf; for they hope to live an eternal life, and $_{11}$that each one of them will live five hundred years.' And the ᐊYᗺZ said unto Michael: 'Go, bind Semjâzâ and his associates who have united themselves with women so as to have defiled themselves $_{12}$with them in all their uncleanness. And when their sons have slain one another, and they have seen the destruction of their beloved ones, bind them fast for seventy generations in the valleys of the earth, till the day of their judgment and of their consummation, till the judgment that is $_{13}$for ever and ever is consummated. In those days they shall be led off to the Abyss of fire: and $_{14}$to the torment and the prison in which they shall be confined for ever. And whosoever shall be condemned and destroyed will from thenceforth be bound together with them to the end of all $_{15}$generations. And destroy all the spirits of the reprobate and the children of the Watchers, because $_{16}$they have wronged mankind. Destroy all wrong from the face of the earth and let every evil work come to an end: and let the plant of righteousness and Truth appear: and it shall prove a blessing; the works of righteousness and Truth' shall be planted in Truth and joy for evermore. $_{17}$And then shall all the righteous escape, And shall live till they beget thousands of children, And all the days of their youth and their old age shall they complete in peace. $_{18}$And then shall the whole earth be tilled in righteousness, and shall all be planted with trees and $_{19}$be full of blessing. And all desirable trees shall be planted on it, and they shall plant vines on it: and the vine which they plant thereon shall yield wine in abundance, and as for all the seed which is sown thereon each measure (of it) shall bear a thousand, and each measure of olives shall yield $_{20}$ten presses of oil. And cleanse thou the earth from all oppression, and from all unrighteousness, and from all sin, and from all godlessness: and all the uncleanness that is wrought upon the earth $_{21}$destroy from off the earth.

The Book of Enoch

Chapter 10, cont.
And all the children of men shall become righteous, and all nations ₂₂shall offer adoration and shall praise Me, and all shall worship Me. And the earth shall be cleansed from all defilement, and from all sin, and from all punishment, and from all torment, and I will never again send (them) upon it from generation to generation and for ever.

Chapter 11
₁And in those days I will open the store chambers of blessing which are in the heaven, so as to send ₂them down upon the earth over the work and labor of the children of men. And Truth and peace shall be associated together throughout all the days of the world and throughout all the generations of men.'

Now you should have a better understanding about the events that prompted the Flood! And you know that the watchers were sons of Elohim, who gave up their glorious futures for their uncontrolled animal lust for the seductive daughters of Cain!

2 Peter 3
⁴For if Elohim did not spare the messengers who sinned, but sent them to Tartaros, and delivered them into chains of darkness, to be kept for judgment..

Jude 1
⁶And the messengers who did not keep their own principality, but left their own dwelling, He has kept in everlasting shackles under darkness for the judgment of the great day.

Now you know that these Watchers were not angels at all, but descendents of the Righteous line of Seth! These Watchers taught the daughters of men secrets, which accelerated all kinds of sin and wickedness! ayaz was sorry that He had created mankind! As a result, ayaz decided to destroy the earth with the Flood! Azazel was a ring-leader of the Watchers! **That's why his name comes up on the Day of Atonement every year.** ayaz determined that all sin should be attributed to Azazel because his actions accelerated the growth of sin and violence in the earth exponentially!

The Cave of Treasures
Saying Goodbye to the Mountain

And Noah, his grandson, embalmed the body of Methuselah with myrrh, and cassia, and stakte, and Noah and his sons buried him in the Cave of Treasures; and they and their wives made mourning for him forty days.

The Cave of Treasures
Saying Goodbye to the Mountain

And when the days of his mourning had passed, Noah went into the Cave of Treasures, and embraced and kissed the holy bodies of Seth, and Ânôsh, and Kainân, and Mahlâlâîl, and Yârêd, and Methuselah, and Lamech his father, and he was greatly moved and tears gushed from his eyes. And Noah carried the body of our father Adam, and (the body of) Eve, and his firstborn Shem carried the gold, and Ham carried the myrrh, and Japhet the frankincense, and they went forth from the Cave of Treasures. And as they were coming down from that holy mountain they were smitten sorely with grief: and they wept in agony because they were to be deprived of that holy place, and the habitation of their fathers. And weeping painfully, and wailing sorrowfully, and enveloped in gloom, they said, "Remain in peace! O holy Paradise, thou habitation of our father Adam. He went forth from thee alive, but stripped (of glory) and naked. And behold, at his death he was deprived of thy nearness. He and his progeny were cast out into exile in that land of curses, to pass their days there in pain, and sicknesses, and in labor, and in weariness, and in trouble. Remain in peace, O Cave of Treasures! Remain in peace, O habitation and inheritance of our Fathers! Remain ye in peace, O our Fathers and Patriarchs! Pray ye for us, O ye who live in the dust, ye friends and beloved ones of the Living 𐤀𐤉𐤀𐤆. Pray ye for the remnant of your posterity which is left. O ye who have propitiated God, make supplication unto Him on our behalf in your prayers. Remain in peace, O Ânôsh! Remain ye in peace, O ye ministers of 𐤀𐤉𐤀𐤆, Kainân, and Mahlâlâîl, and Yârêd, and Methuselah, and Lamech, and Enoch! Cry out in sorrow on our behalf. Remain in peace, O Haven and Asylum of the Angels! O ye our Fathers, cry out in sorrow on our behalf, because ye will be deprived of our society! And we will cry out in sorrow, because we are cast out into a bare land, for our habitation will be with the wild beasts." And as they were coming down from that holy mountain, **they kissed the stones thereof, and embraced the delectable trees thereof.** And in this wise they came down, and they wept with great sorrow, and shed scalding (or bitter) tears, and suffering sorely they descended to the plain. And Noah went into the Ark, and deposited the body of Adam in the middle thereof, and he placed these offerings upon it

Psalms 102
Israel's Return to Zion!

But thou, O 𐤀𐤉𐤀𐤆, *shalt endure for ever; and thy remembrance unto all generations. Thou shalt arise, and have mercy upon Zion: for the time to favor her, yea, the set time, is come.* **For thy servants take pleasure in her stones, and favor the dust thereof.**

Psalms 102, cont.

So the heathen shall fear the name of ayaz, and all the kings of the earth thy glory. When ayaz shall build up Zion, he shall appear in his glory. He will regard the prayer of the destitute, and not despise their prayer. This shall be written for the generation to come: and the people which shall be created shall praise YAH. For he hath looked down from the height of his sanctuary; from heaven did ayaz behold the earth; To hear the groaning of the prisoner; to loose those that are appointed to death; To declare the name of ayaz in Zion, and his praise in Yahrushalem; When the people are gathered together, and the kingdoms, to serve ayaz.

Summary

In order to understand the final Exodus of Israel, it is very important to know as much as possible about Adam as well as the other nine Patriarchs, before the Flood! These ten Patriarchs were extremely righteous men! They were called sons of ayaz! These Righteous men should be greatly admired, **but are largely ignored by most people today**! People today don't even know the first ten Patriarch's names! These Righteous men have **not** received the respect and the honor, which they really deserve! It saddens me to think how these Righteous men have been so overlooked and so forgotten by mankind! The world only remembers Adam for the first sin! People completely overlook all the Righteous deeds that Adam did the rest of his life and the righteous way that he shepherded his people! Until the Flood the first ten Patriarchs lived on top of Yahuah's set apart Mountain, Mount Sinai! When Adam sinned in the Garden of Eden, he was living in Paradise on the heavenly Mount Zion, not on the earth! When Adam and Hawwah rebelled against Yahuah's instruction, they could no longer live in the Garden in the direct presence of OWYaz! So ayaz instructed them to leave the Garden! He placed Adam and Hawwah on top of His set apart earthly Mountain, Mount Sinai! Adam was created from the soil on top of Mount Sinai! During the time of Yered, the sons of Elohim, who were descendents of the Righteous line of Adam, rebelled against ayaz! They descended Mount Sinai and took wives of Cain's descendants, who lived below the Mountain! As a result of this rebellion against ayaz, violence, fornication, cannibalism, and perversion of every kind escalated and eventually overwhelmed the whole earth! After a 120 year grace period, ayaz judged those great sins by sending the Flood! As you know, ayaz saved only Noah and his family! Many years later, after the time of Joseph, the Israelites were in bondage in a place called Mitsrayim! Mitsrayim was located in today's northwestern Saudi Arabia, not in Egypt as people believe!

𐤉𐤄𐤅𐤄 used His servant Moses to lead the Israelites back to this very same set apart Mountain, Mount Sinai, to receive His Torah! Why is all this important for us today? Today, the Righteous seed of 𐤉𐤄𐤅𐤄 are scattered throughout <u>every</u> nation of the entire Earth! Yahuah's people, Israel, are awaiting Yahushua's return and their final Exodus back to the real Promised Land! Yahuah's people are living in bondage in the Babylonian systems of the world! They are scattered and far away from their real <u>home</u> in the Promised Land! This Babylonian world system is ruled by the adversaries of 𐤉𐤄𐤅𐤄! But there is **Good News** for Israel! OWYAZ and His messengers have proclaimed this good news for thousands of years and they still proclaim it today! **The Good News is that OWYAZ is coming soon to judge the wicked and to reward the righteous of the earth**! Yes, OWYAZ will <u>reward</u> the Righteous and <u>destroy</u> the wicked! OWYAZ will turn this world right side up instead of up side down! When 𐤉𐤄𐤅𐤄 returns, He will lead His people back to their Promised Land in the Mountains of Israel! Israel will see many signs and wonders that we can't even imagine of today! However, the rest of the world, not under Yahuah's wings of protection, will experience terrible, terrible plagues during the "Tribulation of the Sinners" just like the people of Mitsrayim experienced during the 1st Exodus! OWYAZ knows how to protect His Righteous remnant just like He did in the 1st Exodus! 𐤉𐤄𐤅𐤄 will use the Trumpet plagues to torture the wicked and to evoke repentance in those still trapped in apostasy! However, most of the blinded sheep will still cling to the false religious traditions of this world to the very end! Those, who survive, will see Yahushua's Kingdom established! But those, who refuse to repent and acknowledge the names of 𐤉𐤄𐤅𐤄 and OWYAZ, will face the <u>unbridled</u> <u>wrath</u> of 𐤉𐤄𐤅𐤄, which will be poured out on the wicked and the unrepentant in seven bowl judgments!

A New Beginning
Chapter 6

⁸By belief, Abraham obeyed when he was called to go out to the place which he was about to receive as an inheritance. And he went out, not knowing where he was going. ⁹By belief, he sojourned in the land of promise as a stranger, dwelling in tents with Yitshaq and Ya'aqob, the heirs with him of the same promise, ¹⁰for he was looking for the city having foundations, whose builder and maker is Elohim. Ibrim (Hebrews) 11

After the Flood, 𐤀𐤅𐤄𐤆 started over with Noah's family! It was a new beginning for humanity! The Righteous seed of 𐤀𐤅𐤄𐤆 were preserved through Noah and his son Shem! Shem's line was set apart by 𐤀𐤅𐤄𐤆!

Genesis 8

And it came to pass in the six hundredth and first year, in the first month, the first day of the month, the waters were dried up from off the earth: and Noah removed the covering of the ark, and looked, and, behold, the face of the ground was dry. And in the second month, on the seven and twentieth day of the month, was the earth dried. And Elohim spake unto Noah, saying, Go forth of the ark, thou, and thy wife, and thy sons, and thy sons' wives with thee. Bring forth with thee every living thing that is with thee, of all flesh, both of fowl, and of cattle, and of every creeping thing that creepeth upon the earth; that they may breed abundantly in the earth, and be fruitful, and multiply upon the earth. And Noah went forth, and his sons, and his wife, and his sons' wives with him: Every beast, every creeping thing, and every fowl, and whatsoever creepeth upon the earth, after their kinds, went forth out of the ark. And Noah built an altar unto 𐤀𐤅𐤄𐤆; and took of every clean beast, and of every clean fowl, and offered burnt offerings on the altar. And 𐤀𐤅𐤄𐤆 smelled a sweet savor; and 𐤀𐤅𐤄𐤆 said in his heart, I will not again curse the ground any more for man's sake; for the imagination of man's heart is evil from his youth; neither will I again smite any more every thing living, as I have done. While the earth remaineth, seedtime and harvest, and cold and heat, and summer and winter, and day and night shall not cease.

After the flood, Noah and his son Shem continued to teach righteousness, however Ham and His children chose **not** to walk in the ways of 𐤀𐤅𐤄𐤆. The heart of Ham became very wicked and extremely perverted!

Genesis 9

And Elohim blessed Noah and his sons, and said unto them, Be fruitful, and multiply, and replenish the earth.

Genesis 9, cont.

And the fear of you and the dread of you shall be upon every beast of the earth, and upon every fowl of the air, upon all that moveth upon the earth, and upon all the fishes of the sea; into your hand are they delivered. Every moving thing that liveth shall be meat for you; even as the green herb have I given you all things. But <u>flesh with the life thereof, which is the blood thereof, shall ye not eat</u>. And surely your blood of your lives will I require; at the hand of every beast will I require it, and at the hand of man; at the hand of every man's brother will I require the life of man. <u>Whoso sheddeth man's blood, by man shall his blood be shed</u>: for in the image of Elohim made he man. And you, be ye fruitful, and multiply; bring forth abundantly in the earth, and multiply therein And Elohim spake unto Noah, and to his sons with him, saying, And I, behold, I establish my covenant with you, and with your seed after you; And I will establish my covenant with you; neither shall all flesh be cut off any more by the waters of a flood; <u>neither shall there any more be a flood to destroy the earth</u>. And Elohim said, This is the token of the covenant which I make between me and you and every living creature that is with you, for perpetual generations: I do set my bow in the cloud, and it shall be for a token of a covenant between me and the earth. And it shall come to pass, when I bring a cloud over the earth, that the bow shall be seen in the cloud: And I will remember my covenant, which is between me and you and every living creature of all flesh; and the waters shall no more become a flood to destroy all flesh. And the bow shall be in the cloud; and I will look upon it, that I may remember the everlasting covenant between Elohim and every living creature of all flesh that is upon the earth. And Elohim said unto Noah, This is the token of the covenant, which I have established between me and all flesh that is upon the earth. And the sons of Noah, that went forth of the ark, were Shem, and Ham, and Japheth: and Ham is the father of Canaan. These are the three sons of Noah: and of them was the whole earth overspread. And Noah began to be an husbandman, and he planted a vineyard: And he drank of the wine, and was drunken; and he was uncovered within his tent. And Ham, the father of Canaan, saw the nakedness of his father, and told his two brethren without. And Shem and Japheth took a garment, and laid it upon both their shoulders, and went backward, and <u>covered the nakedness of their father</u>; and their faces were backward, and they saw not their father's nakedness. And Noah awoke from his wine, and knew what his younger son had done unto him. And he said, Cursed be Canaan; a servant of servants shall he be unto his brethren. And he said, Blessed be 𐤀𐤇𐤉𐤄 Elohim of Shem; and Canaan shall be his servant. Elohim shall enlarge Japheth, and he shall dwell in the tents of Shem; and Canaan shall be his servant.

What exactly did Ham do to his father Noah that resulted in Noah cursing Canaan? Ham did **not** just look at his father, while Noah was naked! Ham's sin against his father was sexual in nature! To fully understand what Ham actually did, we must examine the phrase "uncover his father's nakedness" in its Hebraic context! Of course, we should look in the Torah for the answer! Leviticus 18 defines all types of sexual sin!

Chapter 18

And ayaz spoke to Mosheh, saying, ^{2}"Speak to the children of Yisra'el, and say to them, 'I am ayaz your Elohim. ^{3}'Do not do as they do in the land of Mitsrayim, where you dwelt. And do not do as they do in the land of Kena'an, where I am bringing you, and do not walk in their laws. ^{4}'Do My right-rulings and guard My laws, to walk in them. I am ayaz your Elohim. ^{5}'And you shall guard My laws and My right-rulings, which a man does and lives by them. I am ayaz. ^{6}'No one is to approach anyone of his own flesh to uncover his nakedness. I am ayaz. ^{7}'The nakedness of your father or the nakedness of your mother you do not uncover. She is your mother, you do not uncover her nakedness. ^{8}'**The nakedness of your father's wife you do not uncover, it is your father's nakedness.** ^{9}'The nakedness of your sister, the daughter of your father, or the daughter of your mother, whether born at home or else- where, their nakedness you do not uncover. ^{10}'The nakedness of your son's daughter or your daughter's daughter, their nakedness you do not uncover, for theirs is your own nakedness. ^{11}'The nakedness of your father's wife's daughter, brought forth by your father, she is your sister, you do not uncover her nakedness. ^{12}'The nakedness of your father's sister you do not uncover, she is your father's flesh. ^{13}'The nakedness of your mother's sister you do not uncover, for she is your mother's flesh. ^{14}'The nakedness of your father's brother you do not uncover, you do not approach his wife, she is your aunt. ^{15}'The nakedness of your daughter-in- law you do not uncover, she is your son's wife, you do not uncover her nakedness. ^{16}'The nakedness of your brother's wife you do not uncover, it is your brother's nakedness. ^{17}'The nakedness of a woman and her daughter you do not uncover, nor do you take her son's daughter or her daughter's daughter, to uncover her nakedness. They are her relatives – it is wickedness. ^{18}'And do not take a woman as a rival to her sister, to uncover her nakedness while the other is alive. ^{19}'And do not approach a woman to uncover her nakedness in her monthly separation of uncleanness. ^{20}'And do not have intercourse with the wife of your neighbor, to defile yourself with her. ^{21}'And do not give any of your offspring to pass through to Molek. And do not profane the Name of your Elohim. I am ayaz. ^{22}'And do not lie with a male as with a woman, it is an abomination.

Chapter 18, cont.
²³'And do not have intercourse with any beast, to defile yourself with it. And a woman does not stand before a beast to mate with it, it is a perversion. ²⁴'Do not defile yourselves with all these, for by all these the nations are defiled, which I am driving out before you. ²⁵'Thus the land became defiled, therefore I punished it for its crookedness, and the land vomited out its inhabitants. ²⁶'But you, you shall guard My laws and My right-rulings, and not do any of these abominations, the native nor stranger who sojourns among you, ²⁷because the men of the land who were before you have done all these abominations, and thus the land became defiled, ²⁸'So let not the land vomit you out for defiling it, as it vomited out the nations that were before you. ²⁹'For whoever does any of these abominations, those beings who do them shall be cut off from among their people. ³⁰'And you shall guard My Charge, so as not to do any of these abominable practices which were done before you, so as not to defile yourselves by them. I am 𐤉𐤄𐤅𐤄 your Elohim.' "

Ham raped his very own mother, while Noah was sleeping. Cainan was the child that resulted from that incestuous union. That's why Noah spoke the curse over Cainan! Obviously that was a very wicked sin committed by Ham! Over time Ham became more and more wicked! He even followed the ways of Cain! Ham had several sons, but the most notable was named Cush! Cush was also very, very wicked. Cush had a son in his old age named Nimrod! Nimrod has been a huge stumbling block to mankind to this very day! Nimrod was a mighty rebel in the face of 𐤉𐤄𐤅𐤄 He taught ways that were in direct opposition to Yahuah's Ways! The practice of having sexual relations with your mother became a standard of behavior in pagan circles down through the ages! It is believed that Nimrod married his own mother, whose name was Semiramis! Nimrod was the first to set himself up as a lord over masses of people! He trained military forces to subjugate peoples! Nimrod used technology, the human intellect, and the human will to build weapons and fortifications for the conquest of nations! He oppressed people for his own selfish purposes! Nimrod used conquest and technology to increase his power and wealth! Even though Nimrod oppressed people, his subjects saw him as their benefactor! They felt secure under his control and protection!

Genesis 9
⁶And the sons of Ham: Kush, and Mitsrayim, and Put, and Kena'an. ⁷And the sons of Kush: Seba, and Hawilah, and Sabtah, and Ra'mah, and Sabteka. And the sons of Ra'mah: Sheba and Dedan. ⁸And Kush brought forth Nimrod, he began to be a mighty one on the earth.

Genesis 9, cont.
⁹*He was a mighty hunter before* 𝐘𝐀𝐇, *therefore it is said, "Like Nimrod the mighty hunter before* 𝐘𝐀𝐇*."* ¹⁰*And the beginning of his reign was Babel, and Erek, and Akkad, and Kalneh, in the land of Shin'ar.*

The most detailed information on Nimrod is contained in *The Book of Yashar!* *The Book of Yashar* is referred to in the Scriptures at least two times (Joshua 10:12-14 and 2 Samuel 1:17-18)! Read *The Book of Yashar* for yourself! You'll enjoy it and it will increase your spiritual hunger! Nimrod knew that 𝐘𝐀𝐇 was the El Shaddai (Mighty One of the Mountain), who Noah worshiped! Even though Nimrod was Noah's great grandson, he completely rejected the ways of 𝐘𝐀𝐇 just like the sons of Elohim had rejected 𝐘𝐀𝐇, before the Flood! Nimrod certainly **was not** created in the image of his great grandfather, Noah! Instead, he was created in the image of his father, Cush, and his grandfather, Ham, who were both very wicked and perverted! Nimrod should have followed the ways of Noah, but he chose instead to give up the righteous heritage of Noah for fame, wealth, and power in this world! Nimrod had heard about the Flood many times from his great grandfather Noah and from his grandfather Ham! However, Nimrod decided to rebel against the instructions of 𝐘𝐀𝐇 and do things His way! Doesn't that sound familiar? We've all been there and done that haven't we? Nimrod no doubt had heard Noah tell the story of creation and the fall of Adam from the Garden of Delights more than once! Nimrod became the very first conqueror of this world! He was the first man to train armies for conquest! He actually believed that he could be a mighty one like 𝐘𝐀𝐇! Ironically all the strange elohim, who are the mighty ones worshiped by men today, are traceable to Nimrod and his wife Semiramis! Nimrod planned to defeat 𝐘𝐀𝐇 by storming Yahuah's heavenly abode on the heavenly Mount Zion! His subjects constructed a mighty siege tower that went up into the heavens! Nimrod and the other sons of Ham decided to build a manmade mountain called "the Tower of Babel" on the plains of Shinar! Nimrod and the sons of Ham conceived a wicked plan! First Nimrod planned to construct this massive siege tower, "the Tower of Babel"! Then they planned to ascend the tower up into the heavenly Mount Zion and to take Zion by force! The tower of Babel was a technological counterfeit of the real set apart Mountain of 𝐘𝐀𝐇! Nimrod had heard about Yahuah's set apart Mountain all his life! Nimrod and the other sons of Ham wanted to make a name for themselves by using their technology to conquer the Heavenly Mount Zion! Nimrod used bricks, bituminous tar, and the toil of men to build his mountain! Nimrod's mountain was a counterfeit of Yahuah's set apart Mount Sinai, where the sons of Elohim had lived, before the Flood!

Nimrod knew that **𝐚𝐘𝐚𝐙** did not allow the watchers to reascend Mount Sinai, when they rebelled, before the Flood, and he knew that any rebel, after the Flood, could never ascend into the heavenly Mount Zion either! Nimrod believed that the only way that he and his followers could live on the Heavenly Mount Zion was to conquer it! Therefore they used their technology to construct their own mountain or tower into the heavens for the purpose of conquering Mount Zion! Nimrod believed that from his Tower of Babel he could mount an assault against **𝐚𝐘𝐚𝐙** and the heavenly Mount Zion! Of course we know that **𝐚𝐘𝐚𝐙** thwarted Nimrod's wicked plans in a most unusual way! **OWY𝐚𝐙** confused the speech of Nimrod's laborers! Confusion abounded so much so that Nimrod's workers fought and killed each other! Of course, the work stalled much to the embarrassment of Nimrod!

Book of Yashar
Nimrod the Conqueror

*23 And Cush the son of Ham, the son of Noah, took a wife in those days in his old age, and she brought forth a son, and they called his name Nimrod, saying, At that time the sons of men again began to rebel and transgress against Elohim and the child grew up, and his father loved him extremely, for he was the son of his old age. 24 And the garments of skin which The Almighty made for Adam and his wife, when they went out of the garden, were given to Cush. 25 For after the death of Adam and his wife, the garments were given to Enoch, the son of Yered, and when Enoch was taken up to Elohim he gave them to Methuselah, his son. 26 And at the death of Methuselah, Noah took them and brought them to the ark, and they were with him until he went out of the ark. 27 And in their going out, Ham stole those garments from Noah his father, and he took them and hid them from his brothers. 28 And when Ham had his firstborn Cush, he gave him the garments in secret, and they were with Cush many days. 29 And Cush also concealed them from his sons and brothers, and when Cush had begotten Nimrod, he gave him those garments through his love for him, and Nimrod grew up, and when he was 20 years old he put on those garments. 30 And Nimrod became strong when he put on the garments, and The Almighty gave him might and strength, and he was a mighty hunter in the earth, yes, he was a mighty hunter in the field, and he hunted the animals and he built altars, and he offered upon them the animals before **𝐚𝐘𝐚𝐙**. 31 And Nimrod strengthened himself, and he rose up from among his brothers, and he fought the battles of his brothers against all their enemies round about. 32 And **𝐚𝐘𝐚𝐙** delivered all the enemies of his brothers in his hands, and The Almighty prospered him from time to time in his battles, and he ruled upon earth.*

Book of Yashar
Nimrod the Conqueror

33 Therefore it became current in those days, when a man ushered forth those that he had trained up for battle, he would say to them, Like The Almighty did to Nimrod, who was a mighty hunter in the earth, and who succeeded in the battles that prevailed against his brothers, that he delivered them from the hands of their enemies, so may The Almighty strengthen us and deliver us this day. 34 And when Nimrod was 40 years old, at that time there was a war between his brothers and the children of Japheth, so that they were in the power of their enemies. 35 And Nimrod went forth at that time, and he assembled all the sons of Cush and their families, about 460 men, and he hired also from some of his friends and acquaintances about 80 men, and be gave them their hire, and he went with them to battle, and when he was on the road, Nimrod strengthened the hearts of the people that went with him. 36 And he said to them, Do not fear, neither be alarmed, for all our enemies will be delivered into our hands, and you may do with them as you please. 37 And all the men that went were about 500, and they fought against their enemies, and they destroyed them, and subdued them, and Nimrod placed standing officers over them in their respective places. 38 And he took some of their children as security, and they were all servants to Nimrod and to his brothers, and Nimrod and all the people that were with him turned homeward. 39 And when Nimrod had joyfully returned from battle, after having conquered his enemies, all his brothers, together with those who knew him before, assembled to make him king over them, and they placed the regal crown upon his head. 40 And he set over his subjects and people, princes, judges, and rulers, as is the custom among kings. 41 And he placed Terah the son of Nahor the prince of his host, and he dignified him and elevated him above all his princes. 42 And while he was reigning according to his heart's desire, after having conquered all his enemies around, he advised with his counselors to build a city for his palace, and they did so. 45 And all nations and tongues heard of his fame, and they gathered themselves to him, and they bowed down to the earth, and they brought him offerings, and he became their lord and king, and they all lived with him in the city at Shinar, and Nimrod ruled in the earth over all the sons of Noah, and they were all under his power and counsel. 46 And all the earth was of 1 tongue and words of union, but Nimrod did not go in the ways of ayaz, and he was more wicked than all the men that were before him, from the days of the flood until those days. 47 And he made images of elohim's of wood and stone, and he bowed down to them, and he rebelled against ayaz, and taught all his subjects and the people of the earth his wicked ways; and Mardon his son was more wicked than his father.

Genesis 11
The Tower of Babel

And the whole earth was of one language, and of one speech. And it came to pass, as they journeyed from the east, that they found a plain in the land of Shinar; and they dwelt there. And they said one to another, Go to, let us make brick, and burn them thoroughly. And they had brick for stone, and slime had they for mortar. And they said, Go to, let us build us a city and a tower, whose top may reach unto heaven; and let us make us a name, lest we be scattered abroad upon the face of the whole earth. And ayaz came down to see the city and the tower, which the children of men builded. And ayaz said, Behold, the people is one, and they have all one language; and this they begin to do: and now nothing will be restrained from them, which they have imagined to do. Go to, let us go down, and there confound their language, that they may not understand one another's speech. So ayaz scattered them abroad from thence upon the face of all the earth: and they left off to build the city. Therefore is the name of it called Babel; because ayaz did there confound the language of all the earth: and from thence did ayaz scatter them abroad upon the face of all the earth.

Yashar
The Tower of Babel

21 And all the princes of Nimrod and his great men took counsel together; Phut, Egypt, Cush and Canaan with their families, and they said to each other, Come let us build ourselves a city and in it a strong tower, and its top reaching heaven, and we will make ourselves famed, so that we may reign upon the whole world, in order that the evil of our enemies may cease from us, that we may reign mightily over them, and that we may not become scattered over the earth on account of their wars. 22 And they all went before the king, and they told the king those words, and the king agreed with them in this affair, and he did so. 23 And all the families assembled consisting of about 600,000 men, and they went to seek an extensive piece of ground to build the city and the tower, and they sought in the whole earth and they found none like 1 valley at the east of the land of Shinar, about 2 days' walk, and they journeyed there and they lived there. 24 And they began to make bricks and burn fires to build the city and the tower that they had imagined to complete. 25 And the building of the tower was to them a transgression and a sin, and they began to build it, and while they were building against ayaz, The Almighty of heaven, they imagined in their hearts to war against him and to ascend into heaven.

Yashar
The Tower of Babel, cont.

26 And all of those people and all the families divided themselves in 3 parts; the 1st said We will ascend into heaven and fight against him; the 2nd said, We will ascend to heaven and place our own elohims there and serve them; and the 3rd part said, We will ascend to heaven and strike him down with bows and spears; and The Almighty knew all their works and all their evil thoughts, and he saw the city and the tower which they were building. 27 And when they were building they built themselves a great city and a very high and strong tower; and on account of its height the mortar and bricks did not reach the builders in their ascent to it, until those who went up had completed a full year, and after that, they reached to the builders and gave them the mortar and the bricks; so was it done daily. 28 And behold, those ascended, and others descended the whole day; and if a brick should fall from their hands and get broken, they would all weep over it, and if a man fell and died, none of them would look at him. 29 And אYaZ knew their thoughts, and it came to pass when they were building they cast the arrows toward the heavens, and all the arrows fell upon them filled with blood, and when they saw them they said to each other, Surely we have killed all those that are in heaven. 30 For this was from אYaZ in order to cause them to err, and in order; to destroy them from off the face of the ground. 31 And they built the tower and the city, and they did this thing daily until many days and years were elapsed. 32 And The Almighty said to the 70 angels who stood foremost before him, to those who were near to him, saying, Come let us descend and confuse their tongues, that one man will not understand the language of his neighbor, and they did so to them. 33 And from that day following, they forgot each man his neighbor's tongue, and they could not understand to speak in 1 tongue, and when the builder took from the hands of his neighbor lime or stone which he did not order, the builder would cast it away and throw it upon his neighbor, that he would die. 34 And they did so many days, and they killed many of them in this manner. 35 And אYaZ struck the 3 divisions that were there, and he punished them according to their works and designs; those who said, We will ascend to heaven and serve our elohim, became like apes and elephants; and those who said, We will assault the heaven with arrows, אYaZ killed them, one man through the hand of his neighbor; and the 3rd division of those who said, We will ascend to heaven and fight against him, אYaZ scattered them throughout the earth. 36 And those who were left among them, when they knew and understood the evil which was coming upon them, they forsook the building, and they also became scattered upon the face of the whole earth.

Yashar
The Tower of Babel, cont.

37 And they ceased building the city and the tower; therefore he called that place Babel, for there 𐤀𐤍𐤀𐤆 confounded the Language of the whole earth; behold it was at the east of the land of Shinar. 38 And as to the tower which the sons of men built, the earth opened its mouth and swallowed up 1/3rd part thereof, and a fire also descended from heaven and burned another 3rd, and the other 3rd is left to this day, and it is of that part which was aloft, and its circumference is 3 days' walk. 39 And many of the sons of men died in that tower, a people without number.

Well for now, that's enough talk about Nimrod and the rest of the rebellious descendents of Ham! Let's talk about Yahuah's Righteous planting, Abraham, instead! Abraham is the polar opposite of Nimrod! Abraham is a giant among men! I can't wait to meet Abraham in person! Genesis 11 gives Israel the genealogy of the Righteous line from Shem to Abraham!

Genesis 11
These are the generations of <u>Shem</u>: Shem was an hundred years old, and begat Arphaxad two years after the flood: And Shem lived after he begat Arphaxad five hundred years, and begat sons and daughters. And <u>Arphaxad</u> lived five and thirty years, and begat Salah: And Arphaxad lived after he begat <u>Salah</u> four hundred and three years, and begat sons and daughters. And Salah lived thirty years, and begat <u>Eber</u>: And Salah lived after he begat Eber four hundred and three years, and begat sons and daughters. And Eber lived four and thirty years, and begat <u>Peleg</u>: And Eber lived after he begat Peleg four hundred and thirty years, and begat sons and daughters. And Peleg lived thirty years, and begat <u>Reu</u>: And Peleg lived after he begat Reu two hundred and nine years, and begat sons and daughters. And Reu lived two and thirty years, and begat <u>Serug</u>: And Reu lived after he begat Serug two hundred and seven years, and begat sons and daughters. And Serug lived thirty years, and begat <u>Nahor</u>: And Serug lived after he begat Nahor two hundred years, and begat sons and daughters. And Nahor lived nine and twenty years, and begat <u>Terah</u>: And Nahor lived after he begat Terah an hundred and nineteen years, and begat sons and daughters. And Terah lived seventy years, and begat <u>Abram</u>, Nahor, and Haran. Now these are the generations of Terah: Terah begat <u>Abram</u>, Nahor, and Haran; and Haran begat Lot. And Haran died before his father Terah in the land of his nativity, in Ur of the Chaldees. And Abram and Nahor took them wives: the name of <u>Abram's wife was Sarai</u>; and the name of Nahor's wife, Milcah, the daughter of Haran, the father of Milcah, and the father of Iscah. But Sarai was barren; she had no child.

Genesis 11, cont.
And Terah took Abram his son, and Lot the son of Haran his son's son, and Sarai his daughter in law, his son Abram's wife; and they went forth with them from Ur of the Chaldees, to go into the land of Canaan; and they came unto Haran, and dwelt there.

Abraham Called!

Genesis 12
And ᚨYᚨZ said to Abram, Go yourself out of your land, from your relatives and from your father's house, to a land which I show you. ²"And I shall make you a great nation, and bless you and make your name great, and you shall be a blessing! ³"And I shall bless those who bless you, and curse him who curses you. And in you all the clans of the earth shall be blessed." ⁴So Abram left, as ᚨYᚨZ had commanded him, and Lot went with him. And Abram was seventy-five years old when he set out from Haran. ⁵And Abram took Sarai his wife and Lot his brother's son, and all their possessions that they had gathered, and the beings whom they had acquired in Haran, and they set out for the land of Kena'an. And they came to the land of Kena'an. ⁶And Abram passed through the land to the place of Shekem, as far as the terebinth tree of Moreh. At that time the Kena'anites were in the land. And Abram passed through the land to the place of Shekem, as far as the terebinth tree of Moreh. At that time the Kena'anites were in the land. ⁷And ᚨYᚨZ appeared to Abram and said, "To your seed I give this land." And he built there an altar to ᚨYᚨZ, who had appeared to him. ⁸And from there he moved to the mountain east of Beyth El, and he pitched his tent, with Beyth El on the west and Ai on the east. And he built there an altar to ᚨYᚨZ, and called on the Name of ᚨYᚨZ.

I have often wondered **what Abraham did** that caused ᚨYᚨZ to select him of all the people of the earth to be the father of many nations. Keep reading and you will understand, why ᚨYᚨZ chose Abraham! The *Book of Yashar* gives information that would explain why Abraham was chosen! I admire Abraham greatly! He's definitely got my vote!

Book of Yashar
Abraham Takes a Stand Against Idolatry!

Chapter 11.
1 And Nimrod, son of Cush, was still in the land of Shinar, and he ruled over it and lived there, and he built cities in the land of Shinar. 2 And these are the names of the 4 cities which he built, and he called their names after the occurrences that happened to them in the building of the tower.

Book of Yashar
Abraham Takes a Stand Against Idolatry!

3 And he called the first Babel, saying, Because ayaz there confounded the language of the whole earth; and the name of the 2nd he called Erech, because from there The Almighty dispersed them. 4 And the 3rd he called Eched, saying there was a great battle at that place; and the 4th he called Calnah, because his princes and mighty men were consumed there, and they vexed ayaz, they rebelled and transgressed against him. 5 And when Nimrod had built those cities in the land of Shinar, he placed in them the remainder of his people, his princes and his mighty men that were left in his kingdom. 6 And Nimrod lived in Babel, and he there renewed his reign over the rest of his subjects, and he ruled securely, and the subjects and princes of Nimrod called his name Amraphel, saying that at the tower his princes and men fell through his means. 7 And notwithstanding this, Nimrod did not return to ayaz, and he continued in wickedness and teaching wickedness to the sons of men; and Mardon, his son, was worse than his father, and continued to add to the abominations of his father. 8 And he caused the sons of men to sin, therefore it is said, From the wicked goes forth wickedness. 9 At that time there was war between the families of the children of Ham, as they were living in the cities which they had built. 10 And Chedorlaomer, king of Elam, went away from the families of the children of Ham, and he fought with them and he subdued them, and he went to the 5 cities of the plain and he fought against them and he subdued them, and they were under his control. 11 And they served him 12 years, and they gave him a yearly tax. 12 At that time died Nahor, son of Serug, in the 49th year of the life of Abram son of Terah. 13 And in the fiftieth year of the life of Abram son of Terah, Abram came forth from the house of Noah, and went to his father's house. 14 And Abram knew ayaz, and he went in his ways and instructions, and ayaz The Almighty was with him. 15 And Terah his father was in those days, still captain of the host of king Nimrod, and he still followed strange elohims. 16 And Abram came to his father's house and saw 12 elohims standing there in their temples, and the anger of Abram was stirred up when he saw those images in his father's house. 17 And Abram said, As ayaz lives, these images will not remain in my father's house; so will ayaz who created me do to me if in 3 days' time I do not break them all. 18 And Abram went from them, and his anger burned within him. And Abram hurried and went from the chamber to his father's outer court, and he found his father sitting in the court, and all his servants with him, and Abram came and sat before him.

Book of Yashar
Abraham Takes a Stand Against Idolatry!
Chapter 11, cont.

19 And Abram asked his father, saying, Father, tell me where is The Almighty who created heaven and earth, and all the sons of men upon earth, and who created you and me. And Terah answered his son Abram and said, Behold those who created us are all with us in the house. 20 And Abram said to his father, My lord, shew them to me I pray you; and Terah brought Abram into the chamber of the inner court, and Abram saw, and behold the whole room was full of elohims of wood and stone, 12 great images and others less than they without number. 21 And Terah said to his son, Behold, these are them who created all that you see upon earth, and who created me, and you, and all mankind. 22 And Terah bowed down to his elohims, and he then went away from them, and Abram, his son, went away with him. 23 And when Abram had gone from them he went to his mother and sat before her, and he said to his mother, Behold, my father has shown me those who made heaven and earth, and all the sons of men. 24 Now, therefore, hurry and fetch a kid from the flock, and make of it savory meat, that I may bring it to my father's elohims as an offering for them to eat; perhaps I may thereby become acceptable to them. 25 And his mother did so, and she fetched a kid, and made savory meat thereof, and brought it to Abram, and Abram took the savory meat from his mother and brought it before his father's elohims, and he drew nigh to them that they might eat; and Terah his father, did not know of it. 26 And Abram saw on the day when he was sitting among them, that they had no voice, no hearing, no motion, and not one of them could stretch forth his hand to eat. 27 And Abram mocked them, and said, Surely the savory meat that I prepared has not pleased them, or perhaps it was too little for them, and for that reason they would not eat; therefore tomorrow I will prepare fresh savory meat, better and more plentiful than this, in order that I may see the result. 28 And it was on the next day that Abram directed his mother concerning the savory meat, and his mother rose and fetched 3 fine kids from the flock, and she made of them some excellent savory meat, such as her son was fond of, and she gave it to her son Abram; and Terah his father did not know of it. 29 And Abram took the savory meat from his mother, and brought it before his father's elohims into the chamber; and he came nigh to them that they might eat, and he placed it before them, and Abram sat before them all day, thinking perhaps they might eat. 30 And Abram viewed them, and behold they had neither voice nor hearing, nor did one of them stretch forth his hand to the meat to eat. 31 And in the evening of that day in that house Abram was clothed with the spirit of The Almighty.

Book of Yashar
Abraham Takes a Stand Against Idolatry!
Chapter 11, cont.

32 And he called out and said, Woe to my father and this wicked generation, whose hearts are all inclined to vanity, who serve these idols of wood and stone which can neither eat, smell, hear nor speak, who have mouths without speech, eyes without sight, ears without hearing, hands without feeling, and legs which cannot move; like them are those that made them and that trust in them. 33 And when Abram saw all of those things his anger was stirred up against his father, and he hurried and took a hatchet in his hand, and came to the chamber of The Almightys, and he broke all his father's elohims. 34 And when he had done breaking the images, he placed the hatchet in the hand of the great elohim which was there before them, and he went out; and Terah his father came home, for he had heard at the door the sound of the striking of the hatchet; so Terah came into the house to know what this was about. 35 And Terah, having heard the noise of the hatchet in the room of images, ran to the room to the images, and he met Abram going out. 36 And Terah entered the room and found all the idols fallen down and broken, and the hatchet in the hand of the largest, which was not broken, and the savory meat which Abram his son had made was still before them. 37 And when Terah saw this his anger was greatly stirred up, and he hurried and went from the room to Abram. 38 And he found Abram his son still sitting in the house; and he said to him, What is this work you have done to my elohims? 39 And Abram answered Terah his father and he said, Not so my lord, for I brought savory meat before them, and when I came nigh to them with the meat that they might eat, they all at once stretched forth their hands to eat before the great one had put forth his hand to eat. 40 And the large one saw their works that they did before him, and his anger was violently stirred up against them, and he went and took the hatchet that was in the house and came to them and broke them all, and behold the hatchet is yet in his hand as you see. 41 And Terah's anger was stirred up against his son Abram, when he spoke this; and Terah said to Abram his son in his anger, What is this tale that you have told? You speak lies to me. 42 Is there, in these elohims, spirit, soul, or power to do all you have told me? Are they not wood and stone, and have I not myself made them, and can you speak such lies, saying that the large elohim that was with them struck them? It is you that did place the hatchet in his hands, and then say he struck them all. 43 And Abram answered his father and said to him, And how can you then serve these idols in whom there is no power to do any thing? Can those idols in which you trust deliver you? Can they hear your prayers when you call upon them?

Book of Yashar
Abraham Takes a Stand Against Idolatry!
Chapter 11, cont.

Can they deliver you from the hands of your enemies, or will they fight your battles for you against your enemies, that you should serve wood and stone which can neither speak nor hear? 44 And now surely it is not good for you nor for the sons of men that are connected with you, to do those things; are you so silly, so foolish or so short of understanding that you will serve wood and stone, and do after this manner? 45 And forget ayaz, The Almighty who made heaven and earth, and who created you in the earth, and thereby bring a great evil upon your souls in this matter by serving stone and wood? 46 Did not our fathers in days of old sin in this matter, and ayaz, The Almighty of the universe brought the waters of the flood upon them and destroyed the whole earth? 47 And how can you continue to do this and serve elohims of wood and stone, who cannot hear, or speak, or deliver you from oppression, thereby bringing down the anger of The Almighty of the universe upon you? 48 Now therefore my father refrain from this, and bring not evil upon your soul and the souls of your household. 49 And Abram hurried and sprang from before his father, and took the hatchet from his father's largest idol, with which Abram broke it and ran away. 50 And Terah, seeing all that Abram had done, hurried to go from his house, and he went to the king and he came before Nimrod and stood before him, and he bowed down to the king; and the king said, What do you want? 51 And he said, I beseech you my lord, to hear me: Now 50 years back a child was born to me, and so has he done to my elohims and so has he spoken; and now therefore, my lord and king, send for him that he may come before you, and judge him according to the law, that we may be delivered from his evil. 52 And the king sent 3 men of his servants, and they went and brought Abram before the king. And Nimrod and all his princes and servants were that day sitting before him, and Terah sat also before them. 53 And the king said to Abram, What is this that you have done to your father and to his elohims? And Abram answered the king in the words that he spoke to his father, and he said, The large elohim that was with them in the house did to them what you have heard. 54 And the king said to Abram, Had they power to speak and eat and do as you have said? And Abram answered the king, saying, And if there be no power in them why do you serve them and cause the sons of men to err through your follies? 55 Do you imagine that they can deliver you or do anything small or great, that you should serve them? And why will you not sense The Almighty of the whole universe, who created you and in whose power it is to kill and keep alive? 56 O, foolish, simple, and ignorant king, woe to you forever.

Book of Yashar
Abraham Takes a Stand Against Idolatry!
Chapter 11, cont.

57 I thought you would teach your servants the upright way, but you have not done this, but have filled the whole earth with your sins and the sins of your people who have followed your ways. 58 Do you not know, or have you not heard, that this evil which you do, our ancestors sinned in it in days of old, and the eternal The Almighty brought the waters of the flood upon them and destroyed them all, and also destroyed the whole earth on their account? And will you and your people rise up now and do like to this work, in order to bring down the anger of אYaZ, The Almighty of the universe, and to bring evil upon you and the whole earth? 59 Now therefore put away this evil deed which you do, and serve The Almighty of the universe, as your soul is in his hands, and then it will be well with you. 60 And if your wicked heart will not listen to my words to cause you to forsake your evil ways, and to serve the eternal elohim then will you die in shame in the latter days, you, your people and all who are connected with you, hearing your words or walking in your evil ways. 61 And when Abram had ceased speaking before the king and princes, Abram lifted up his eyes to the heavens, and he said, The Lord sees all the wicked, and he will judge them. 62 And the king's servants took Abram and his brother, and they stripped them of all their clothes excepting their lower garments which were upon them.

Book of Yashar
Chapter 12

23 And they bound their hands and feet with linen cords, and the servants of the king lifted them up and cast them both into the furnace. 24 And אYaZ loved Abram and he had compassion over him, and אYaZ came down and delivered Abram from the fire and he was not burned. 25 But all the cords with which they bound him were burned, while Abram remained and walked about in the fire. 26 And Haran died when they had cast him into the fire, and he was burned to ashes, for his heart was not perfect with אYaZ; and those men who cast him into the fire, the flame of the fire spread over them, and they were burned, and 12 men of them died. 27 And Abram walked in the midst of the fire 3 days and 3 nights, and all the servants of the king saw him walking in the fire, and they came and told the king, saying, Behold we have seen Abram walking about in the midst of the fire, and even the lower garments which are upon him are not burned, but the cord with which he was bound is burned.

Book of Yashar

Chapter 12, cont.

28 And when the king heard their words his heart fainted and he would not believe them; so he sent other faithful princes to see this matter, and they went and saw it and told it to the king; and the king rose to go and see it, and he saw Abram walking to and fro in the midst of the fire, and he saw Haran's body burned, and the king wondered greatly. 29 And the king ordered Abram to be taken out from the fire; and his servants approached to take him out and they could not, for the fire was round about and the flame ascending toward them from the furnace. 30 And the king's servants fled from it, and the king rebuked them, saying, Do it quickly and bring Abram out of the fire that you will not die. 31 And the servants of the king again approached to bring Abram out, and the flames came upon them and burned their faces so that 8 of them died. 32 And when the king saw that his servants could not approach the fire lest they should be burned, the king called to Abram, O servant of The Almighty who is in heaven, go forth from amidst the fire and come hither before me; and Abram listened to the voice of the king, and he went forth from the fire and came and stood before the king. 33 And when Abram came out the king and all his servants saw Abram coming before the king, with his lower garments upon him, for they were not burned, but the cord with which he was bound was burned. 34 And the king said to Abram, How is it that you were not burned in the fire? 35 And Abram said to the king, The Almighty of heaven and earth in whom I trust and who has all in his power, he delivered me from the fire into which you did cast me. 36 And Haran the brother of Abram was burned to ashes, and they sought for his body, and they found it consumed. 37 And Haran was 82 years old when he died in the fire of Casdim. And the king, princes, and inhabitants of the land, seeing that Abram was delivered from the fire, they came and bowed down to Abram.

Abraham leaves Haran and is led by ayaz to Beth El, which means the house or the abode of the Mighty One! Later Beth El in the Scriptures became a small settlement located adjacent to the Mountain of ayaz, Mount Sinai. Shiloh was on the North side of that Mountain, Beth El was on the East side. ayaz repeatedly takes Abraham, Isaac, and Jacob to Beth El to His Set Apart Mountain, where each Patriarch would have their own personal encounters with OWYaz!

Genesis 12

And ayaz said to Abram, Go yourself out of your land, from your relatives and from your father's house, to a land which I show you.

Genesis 12, cont.
[2]"And I shall make you a great nation, and bless you and make your name great, and you shall be a blessing! [3]"And I shall bless those who bless you, and curse him who curses you. And in you all the clans of the earth shall be blessed." [4]So Abram left, as ayaz had commanded him, and Lot went with him. And Abram was seventy-five years old when he set out from Haran. [5]And Abram took Sarai his wife and Lot his brother's son, and all their possessions that they had gathered, and the beings whom they had acquired in Haran, and they set out for the land of Kena'an. And they came to the land of Kena'an. [6]And Abram passed through the land to the place of Shekem, as far as the terebinth tree of Moreh. At that time the Kena'anites were in the land. And Abram passed through the land to the place of Shekem, as far as the terebinth tree of Moreh. At that time the Kena'anites were in the land. [7]And ayaz appeared to Abram and said, "To your seed I give this land." And he built there an altar to ayaz, who had appeared to him. [8]And from there he moved to the mountain east of Beyth El, and he pitched his tent, with Beyth El on the west and Ai on the east. And he built there an altar to ayaz, and called on the Name of ayaz.

The Cave of Treasures has some very interesting information about Melchisedek, who was the High Priest of ayaz at the time of Abraham! Melchisedek was stationed at Salem at Yahuah's direction, which was given to Shem! Salem was later called Yahrushalayim in the Scriptures! After Abraham's defeat of the Kings and the rescue of Lot, Yahuah's high priest, Melchisedek, came out to bless Abraham!

Cave of Treasures
And Noah lived three hundred and fifty years after he came forth from the Ark. And when he was sick unto death, Shem, and Ham, and Japhet, and Arpakhshar (Arphaxad), and Shâlah (Salah) gathered together unto him. And Noah called Shem, his firstborn, and said unto him privily, "Take heed, my son Shem, unto what I say unto thee this day. When I am dead, go into the Ark, wherein thou hast been saved, and bring out the body of our father Adam, and let no man have knowledge of what thou doest. And take with thee from this place provision for the way, bread and wine, and take with thee Melchisedek, the son of Mâlâkh, because him hath ayaz chosen from among all your descendants that he may minister before Him in respect of the body of our father Adam. And take the body and place it in the center of the earth, and make Melchisedek to sit down there. And the Angel of ayaz shall go before you, and shall show you the way wherein ye shall go, and also the place wherein the body of Adam shall be deposited, which is, indeed, the center <u>of the earth</u>. There the four quarters of the earth embrace each other.

Cave of Treasures

For when ᴀYᴀZ *made the earth His power went before it, and the earth, from [its] four quarters, ran after it, like the winds and the swift breezes, and there His power stood still and was motionless.* <u>There shall redemption be made for Adam, and for all his posterity.</u> *Now this story, or mystery, was handed down to us from Adam in all generations Adam commanded Seth, and Seth commanded Ânôsh (Enos), and Ânôsh commanded Kaînân (Cainan), and Ḵaînân commanded Mahlâlâîl, and Mahlâlâîl commanded Yârêd, and Yârêd commanded Enoch, and Enoch commanded Methuselah, and Methuselah commanded Lamech; and behold, I command thee this day. And take heed that this story is never mentioned again in all your generations. Get thee up, and take the body of Adam, and deposit it secretly in the place which* ᴀYᴀZ *shall show thee until the day of redemption."* And when Noah had given all these commands unto his son Shem, he died, [being] nine hundred and fifty years old, in the month of Îyâr (May), on the second day thereof, at the second hour of the first day of the week. And Shem his son embalmed him, and buried him in the city which he had built (i.e. Themânôn), and they made a mourning for him forty days.

Cave of Treasures
The Departure of Shem with the body of Adam.

And after the death of Noah Shem did as his father had commanded him. And he went into the Ark by night, and brought out the body of Adam therefrom, and he sealed the Ark with his father's seal, and no man perceived. And he called Ham and Japhet, and said unto them, "My brethren, my father commanded me to go up and travel over the earth, even to the sea and I am to see what the rivers are like, and then return unto you. And behold, my wife and the children of my house are with you; let your eyes be upon them." And his brethren said unto him, "Take with thee a company of men from the camp, for the land is a desert waste, and is shorn of inhabitants, and there are wild beasts therein." And Shem said unto them, "The Angel of the Lord shall go up with me, and he shall save me from every evil thing"; and his brethren said unto him, "Go in peace, and may ᴀYᴀZ of our Fathers be with thee." And Shem said unto Mâlâkh (the brother of Shâlâh (Salah), the son of [Cainan] and [grand]son of Arphaxad), the father of Melchisedek, and Yôzadhâḵ, his mother, "Give ye me Melchisedek, that he may go up with me, and be a consolation for me on the road." And Mâlâkh and Yôzadhâḵ, his mother, said unto Shem, "Take [him] and go in peace."

Cave of Treasures
The Departure of Shem with the body of Adam.

And Shem gave commands unto his brethren, and said unto them, "My brethren, my father made me swear that neither I, nor any of your descendants, should go into the Ark," and he sealed the Ark with his seal, and said unto them, "Let no man go near it." And Shem took the body of Adam and Melchisedek, and went forth by night from among his people, and behold, the Angel of the 𐤀𐤉𐤄𐤆, who was going before them, appeared unto them. And their journey was very speedy, because the Angel of 𐤀𐤉𐤄𐤆 strengthened them until they arrived at that place. And when they arrived at Gâghûltâ (Golgotha), which is the centre of the earth, the Angel of 𐤀𐤉𐤄𐤆 showed Shem the place [for the body of Adam]. And when Shem had deposited the body of our father Adam upon that place the four quarters [of the earth] separated themselves from each other, and the earth opened itself in the form of a cross, and Shem and Melchisedek deposited the body of Adam there (i.e. in the cavity). And as soon as they had laid it therein, the four quarters [of the earth] drew quickly together, and enclosed the body of our father Adam, and the door of the created world was shut fast. And that place was called "Karkaphtâ " (i.e. "Skull"), because the head of all the children of men was deposited there. And it was called "Gâghûltâ," because it was round [like the head], and "Resîphtâ " (i.e. a trodden-down thing), because the head of the accursed serpent, that is to say, Satan, was crushed there, and "Gefîftâ " (Gabbatha), because all the nations were to be gathered together to it. And Shem said unto Melchisedek, "Thou shalt be the priest of the Most High Elohim, because thou alone hath 𐤀𐤉𐤄𐤆 chosen to minister before Him in this place. And thou shalt sit (i.e. dwell) here continually, and shalt not depart from this place all the days of thy life. Thou shalt not take a wife, thou shalt not shave thy head, and thou shalt not pour out blood in this place. Thou shalt not offer up wild beasts nor feathered fowl, but thou shalt offer up bread and wine always; and thou shalt not build a building in this place. And behold, the Angel of 𐤀𐤉𐤄𐤆 shall come down to thee and visit thee continually." And Shem embraced and kissed Melchisedek, and blessed him, and he returned to his brethren. And Mâlâkh, the father of Melchisedek, and Yôzâdhâk, his mother, said [unto Shem], "Where is the young man?" And he said, "He died on the journey, and I buried him there" (i.e. where he died); and they mourned for him greatly.

Abraham Goes to Beth El!

Genesis 13

²And Abram was very rich in livestock, in silver, and in gold. ³And he went on his journey from the South as far as <u>Beyth El, to the place where his tent had been at the beginning, between Beyth El and Ai</u>, ⁴to the place of the altar which he had made there at first. And there Abram called on the Name of ayaz. ⁵Now Lot, who went with Abram, also had flocks and herds and tents. ⁶And the land was not able to bear them, that they might dwell together, for their possessions were great, so that they could not dwell together. ⁷And there was strife between the herds-men of Abram's livestock and the herds-men of Lot's livestock. And at that time the Kena'anites and the Perizzites dwelt in the land. ⁸Then Abram said to Lot, "Please let there be no strife between you and me, and between my herdsmen and your herdsmen, for we are brothers. ⁹"Is not all the land before you? Please separate from me. If you take the left, then I go to the right; or, if you go to the right, then I go to the left." ¹⁰And Lot lifted his eyes and saw all the plain of the Yarden, that it was well watered everywhere – before ayaz destroyed Sedom and Amorah – like the garden of ayaz, like the land of Mitsrayim as you go toward Tso'ar. ¹¹So Lot chose for himself all the plain of the Yarden, and **Lot moved east**. Thus they separated from each other, ¹²Abram dwelling in the land of Kena'an, and Lot dwelling in the cities of the plain and pitched his tent as far as Sedom. ¹³But the men of Sedom were evil and sinned before ayaz, exceedingly so. ¹⁴And after Lot had separated from him, ayaz said to Abram, "Now lift up your eyes and look from the place where you are, northward and southward and eastward and westward, ¹⁵for all the land which you see I shall give to you and your seed forever.

Abraham Battles the Kings!

Genesis 5

⁵And in the fourteenth year Kedorla'omer and the sovereigns that were with him came and smote the Repha'im in Ashteroth Qarnayim, and the Zuzim in Ham, and the Emites in Shaweh Qiryathayim, ⁶and the Horites in their mountain of Se'ir, as far as El Paran, which is by the wilderness. ⁷And they turned back and came to En Mishpat, that is Qadesh, and smote all the country of the Amaleqites, and also the Amorites who dwelt in Hatsetson Tamar. ⁸And the sovereign of Sedom, and the sovereign of Amorah, and the sovereign of Admah, and the sovereign of Tseboyim, and the sovereign of Bela, that is Tso'ar, went out and joined together in battle in the Valley of Siddim, ⁹against Kedorla'omer sovereign of Eylam, and Tid'al sovereign of Goyim, and Amraphel sovereign of Shin'ar, and Aryok sovereign of Ellasar – four sovereigns against five.

Abraham Battles the Kings!

Genesis 5, cont.
[10] And the Valley of Siddim had many tar pits. And the sovereigns of Sedom and Amorah fled and fell there, and the remainder fled to the mountains. [11] And they took all the goods of Sedom and Amorah, and all their food, and went away. [12] And they took Lot, Abram's brother's son who dwelt in Sedom, and his goods, and left. [13] And one who had escaped came and informed Abram the Hebrew, for he dwelt by the terebinth trees of Mamre the Amorite, brother of Eshkol and brother of Aner, and they had a covenant with Abram. [14] And when Abram heard that his brother was taken captive, he armed his three hundred and eighteen trained servants who were born in his own house, and went in pursuit as far as Dan. [15] And he and his servants divided against them by night, and smote them and pursued them as far as Hobah, which is on the left of Damascus. [16] So he brought back all the goods, and also brought back his brother Lot and his goods, as well as the women and the people. [17] And after his return from the defeat of Kedorla'omer and the sovereigns who were with him, the sovereign of Sedom came out to meet him at the Valley of Shaweh, that is, the Sovereign's Valley. [18] <u>And Melchitsedeq sovereign of Shalem brought out bread and wine. Now he was the priest of the Most High El.</u> [19] And he blessed him and said, "Blessed be Abram of the Most High El, Possessor of the heavens and earth. [20] "And blessed be the Most High El who has delivered your enemies into your hand." And he gave him a tenth of all. [21] And the sovereign of Sedom said to Abram, "Give me the people, and take the goods for yourself." [22] But Abram said to the sovereign of Sedom, "I have lifted my hand to 𐤀𐤉𐤄𐤅, the Most High El, the Possessor of the heavens and earth, [23] not to take a thread or a sandal strap or whatever is yours, lest you should say, 'I have made Abram rich,' [24] except only what the young men have eaten, and the portion of the men who went with me: Aner, Eshkol, and Mamre. Let them take their portion."

One of the most touching stories in Scripture occurs at the sacrifice of Isaac! Abraham **was** willing to sacrifice His beloved son Isaac for 𐤀𐤉𐤄𐤅! Isaac was Abraham's son of the Promise! Isaac had a pure heart and was more than willing to be an offering to 𐤀𐤉𐤄𐤅! In fact that moment in Isaac's life was his defining moment, even though he was only 17 years old! **Of course, it was all a test of Abraham's and Isaac's love for 𐤀𐤉𐤄𐤅!**

Abraham and Isaac Are Tested!

Genesis 22
And it came to be after these events that Elohim tried Abraham, and said to him, "Abraham!" And he said, "Here I am."

Abraham and Isaac Are Tested!

Genesis 22, cont. ²And He said, "Take your son, now, your only son Yitshaq, whom you love, and go to the land of Moriyah, and offer him there as a burnt offering on one of the mountains which I command you." ³And Abraham rose early in the morning and saddled his donkey, and took two of his young men with him, and Yitshaq his son. And he split the wood for the burnt offering, and arose and went to the place which Elohim had commanded him. ⁴And on the third day Abraham lifted his eyes and saw the place from a distance. ⁵So Abraham said to his young men, "Stay here with the donkey while the boy and I go over there and worship, and come back to you." ⁶And Abraham took the wood of the burnt offering and laid it on Yitshaq his son. And he took the fire in his hand, and a knife, and the two of them went together. ⁷And Yitshaq spoke to Abraham his father and said, "My father!" And he said, "Here I am, my son." And he said, "See, the fire and the wood! But where is the lamb for a burnt offering?" ⁸And Abraham said, "My son, Elohim does provide for Himself the lamb for a burnt offering." And the two of them went together. ⁹And they came to the place which Elohim had commanded him, and Abraham built an altar there and placed the wood in order. And he bound Yitshaq his son and laid him on the altar, upon the wood. ¹⁰And Abraham stretched out his hand and took the knife to slay his son, ¹¹but the Messenger of **יהוה** called to him from the heavens and said, "Abraham, Abraham!" And he said, "Here I am." ¹²And He said, "Do not lay your hand on the boy, nor touch him. For now I know that you fear Elohim, seeing you have not withheld your son, your only son, from Me." ¹³And Abraham lifted his eyes and looked and saw behind him a ram caught in a bush by its horns, and Abraham went and took the ram and offered it up for a burnt offering instead of his son. ¹⁴And Abraham called the name of the place, **יהוה** Yireh,' as it is said to this day, "On the mountain **יהוה** provides." ¹⁵And the Messenger of **יהוה** called to Abraham a second time from the heavens, ¹⁶and said, "By Myself I have sworn, declares **יהוה**, because you have done this, and have not withheld your son, your only son, ¹⁷that I shall certainly bless you, and I shall certainly increase your seed as the stars of the heavens and as the sand which is on the seashore, and let your seed possess the gate of their enemies. ¹⁸"And in your seed all the nations of the earth shall be blessed, because you have obeyed My voice."

Book of Yashar
Abraham and Isaac Are Tested!

Chapter 23.

41 And on the 3rd day Abraham lifted up his eyes and saw the place at a distance which The Almighty had told him of. 42 And a pillar of fire appeared to him that reached from the earth to heaven, and a cloud of glory upon the mountain, and the glory of 𐤀𐤉𐤄𐤅 was seen in the cloud. 43 And Abraham said to Isaac, My son, do you see in that mountain, which we perceive at a distance, that which I see upon it? 44 And Isaac answered and said to his father, I see and lo a pillar of fire and a cloud, and the glory of 𐤀𐤉𐤄𐤅 is seen upon the cloud. 45 And Abraham knew that his son Isaac was accepted before 𐤀𐤉𐤄𐤅 for a burnt offering. 46 And Abraham said to Eliezer and to Yismael his son, Do you also see that which we see upon the mountain which is at a distance? 47 And they answered and said, We see nothing more than like the other mountains of the earth. And Abraham knew that they were not accepted before 𐤀𐤉𐤄𐤅 to go with them, and Abraham said to them, Abide ye here with the ass while I and Isaac my son will go to distant mountain and worship there before 𐤀𐤉𐤄𐤅 and then return to you. 48 And Eliezer and Yismael remained in that place, as Abraham had commanded. 49 And Abraham took wood for a burnt offering and placed it upon his son Isaac, and he took the fire and the knife, and they both went to that place. 50 And when they were going along Isaac said to his father, Behold, I see here the fire and wood, and where then is the lamb that is to be the burnt offering before 𐤀𐤉𐤄𐤅? 51 And Abraham answered his son Isaac, saying, The Lord has made choice of you my son, to be a perfect burnt offering instead of the lamb. 52 And Isaac said to his father, I will do all that 𐤀𐤉𐤄𐤅 spoke to you with joy and cheerfulness of heart. 53 And Abraham again said to Isaac his son, Is there in your heart any thought or counsel concerning this, which is not proper? tell me my son, I pray you, O my son conceal it not from me. 54 And Isaac answered his father Abraham and said to him, O my father, as 𐤀𐤉𐤄𐤅 lives and as your soul lives, there is nothing in my heart to cause me to deviate either to the right or to the left from the word that he has spoken to you. 55 Neither limb nor muscle has moved or stirred at this, nor is there in my heart any thought or evil counsel concerning this. 56 But I am of joyful and cheerful heart in this matter, and I say, Blessed is 𐤀𐤉𐤄𐤅 who has this day chosen me to be a burnt offering before Him. 57 And Abraham greatly rejoiced at the words of Isaac, and they went on and came together to that place that 𐤀𐤉𐤄𐤅 had spoken of. 58 And Abraham approached to build the altar in that place, and Abraham was weeping, and Isaac took stones and mortar until they had finished building the altar.

Abraham and Isaac Are Tested!

Genesis 22, cont.
59 And Abraham took the wood and placed it in order upon the altar which he had built. 60 And he took his son Isaac and bound him in order to place him upon the wood which was upon the altar, to kill him for a burnt offering before ᴧYᴧZ. 61 And Isaac said to his father, Bind me securely and then place me upon the altar lest I should turn and move, and break loose from the force of the knife upon my flesh and thereof profane the burnt offering; and Abraham did so. 62 And Isaac still said to his father, O my father, when you will have killed me and burnt me for an offering, take with you that which will remain of my ashes to bring to Sarah my mother, and say to her, This is the sweet smelling savor of Isaac; but do not tell her this if she should sit near a well or upon any high place, lest she should cast her soul after me and die. 63 And Abraham heard the words of Isaac, and he lifted up his voice and wept when Isaac spake those words; and **Abraham's tears gushed down upon Isaac his son, and Isaac wept bitterly, and he said to his father, Hasten you, O my father, and do with me the will of ᴧYᴧZ, our elohim, as He has commanded you. 64 And the hearts of Abraham and Isaac rejoiced at this thing which ᴧYᴧZ had commanded them; but the eye wept bitterly while the heart rejoiced.** 65 And Abraham bound his son Isaac, and placed him on the altar upon the wood, and Isaac stretched forth his neck upon the altar before his father, and Abraham stretched forth his hand to take the knife to kill his son as a burnt offering before ᴧYᴧZ. 66 At that time the angels of mercy came before ᴧYᴧZ and spake to him concerning Isaac, saying, 67 0 Lord, you art a merciful and compassionate King over all that you have created in heaven and in earth, and you support them all; give therefore ransom and redemption instead of your servant Isaac, and pity and have compassion upon Abraham and Isaac his son, who are this day performing your commands. 68 Have you seen, O ᴧYᴧZ, how Isaac the son of Abraham your servant is bound down to the slaughter like an animal? now therefore let your pity be roused for them, O ᴧYᴧZ. 69 At that time ᴧYᴧZ appeared to Abraham, and called to him, from heaven, and said to him, Lay not your hand upon the lad, neither do you any thing for him, for now I know that you fear The Almighty in performing this act, and in not keeping your son, your only son, from me.

Genesis 28 ᴧYᴧZ Calls Jacob!

[6] And Esaw saw that Yitshaq had blessed Ya'aqob and sent him away to Paddan Aram to take himself a wife from there, and that as he blessed him he gave him a command, saying, "Do not take a wife from the daughters of Kena'an," [7] and that Ya'aqob had obeyed his father and his mother and had gone to Paddan Aram.

ᴀYᴀZ Calls Jacob!

Genesis 28, cont.
⁸So Esaw saw that the daughters of Kena'an did not please his father Yitshaq, ⁹and Esaw went to Yishma'el and took Mahalath the daughter of Yishma'el, Abraham's son, the sister of Nebayoth, to be his wife, besides the wives he had. ¹⁰And Ya'aqob went out from Be'ersheba and went toward Haran. ¹¹And he came upon a place and stopped over for the night, for the sun had set.And he took one of the stones of that place and put it at his head, and he lay down in that place to sleep. ¹²And he dreamed and saw a ladder set up on the earth, and its top reached to the heavens, and saw messengers of Elohim going up and coming down on it. ¹³And see, ᴀYᴀZ stood above it and said, "I am ᴀYᴀZ Elohim of Abraham your father and the Elohim of Yitshaq. The land on which you are lying, I give it to you and your seed. ¹⁴"And your seed shall be as the dust of the earth, and you shall break forth to the west and to the east, to the north and the south. And all the clans of the earth shall be blessed in you and in your seed. ¹⁵"And see, I am with you and shall guard you wherever you go, and shall bring you back to this land. For I am not going to leave you until I have done what I have spoken to you." ¹⁶And Ya'aqob awoke from his sleep and said, "Truly, ᴀYᴀZ is in this place, and I did not know it." ¹⁷And he was afraid and said, "How awesome is this place! This is none other than the house of Elohim, and this is the gate of the heavens!"¹⁸And Ya'aqob rose early in the morning, and took the stone that he had put at his head, set it up as a standing column, and poured oil on top of it. **¹⁹And he called the name of that place Beyth El, however, the name of that city had been Luz previously.** ²⁰And Ya'aqob made a vow, saying, "Seeing Elohim is with me, and has kept me in this way that I am going, and has given me bread to eat and a garment to put on– ²¹when I have returned to my father's house in peace, and ᴀYᴀZ has been my Elohim, ²²then this stone which I have set as a standing column shall be Elohim's house, and of all that You give me, I shall certainly give a tenth to You."

Genesis 32
²²And he rose up that night and took his two wives, and his two female servants, and his eleven sons, and passed over the ford of Yabboq. ²³And he took them and sent them over the stream, and sent over what he had. ²⁴And Ya'aqob was left alone. And a Man wrestled with him until the breaking of day. ²⁵And when He saw that He did not overcome him, He touched the socket of his hip. And the socket of Ya'aqob's hip was dislocated as He wrestled with him. ²⁶And He said, "Let Me go, for the day breaks." But he said, "I am not letting You go until You have blessed me!" ²⁷So He asked him, "What is your name?" And he said, "Ya'aqob."

Genesis 32, cont.
²⁸And He said, "Your name is no longer called Ya'aqob, but <u>Yisra'el</u>, because you have striven with Elohim and with men, and have overcome." ²⁹And Ya'aqob asked Him, saying, "Please let me know Your Name." And He said, "Why do you ask about My Name?" And He blessed him there. ³⁰And Ya'aqob called the name of the place Peni'el, "For I have seen Elohim face to face, and my life is preserved."

Jacob Dwells at Beth El!!

Genesis 35
And Elohim said to Ya'aqob, "Arise, go up to Beyth El and dwell there. And make an altar there to El who appeared to you when you fled from the face of Esaw your brother." ²And Ya'aqob said to his household and to all who were with him, "Put away the foreign mighty ones that are among you, and cleanse yourselves, and change your garments. ³"And let us arise and go up to Beyth El, and let me make there an altar to El, who answered me in the day of my distress, and has been with me in the way which I have gone." ⁴So they gave Ya'aqob all the foreign mighty ones which were in their hands, and all their earrings which were in their ears. And Ya'aqob hid them under the terebinth tree which was near Shekem. ⁵And they departed, and the fear of Elohim was upon the cities that were all around them, and they did not pursue the sons of Ya'aqob. ⁶**And Ya'aqob <u>came to Luz, that is Beyth El</u>, which is in the land of Kena'an, he and all the people who were with him.** ⁷**And he built there an altar and called the place <u>El Beyth El, because there Elohim appeared to him when he fled from the face of his brother</u>.** ⁸And Deborah, Ribqah's nurse, died, and she was buried below Beyth El under the terebinth tree. So the name of it was called Allon Bakuth. ⁹And Elohim appeared to Ya'aqob again, when he came from Paddan Aram, and blessed him. ¹⁰And Elohim said to him, "Your name is Ya'aqob, your name is no longer called Ya'aqob, but Yisra'el is your name." So He called his name Yisra'el. ¹¹And Elohim said to him, "I am El Shaddai. Bear fruit and increase, a nation and a company of nations shall be from you, and sovereigns come from your body. ¹²"And the land which I gave Abraham and Yitshaq I give to you. And to your seed after you I give this land." ¹³And Elohim went up from him in the place where He had spoken with him. ¹⁴And Ya'aqob set up a standing column in the place where He had spoken with him, a monument of stone. And he poured a drink offering on it, and he poured oil on it. ¹⁵**And Ya'aqob called the name of the place where Elohim spoke with him, Beyth El.** ¹⁶Then they set out from Beyth El. And it came to be, when there was but a little distance to go to Ephrath, that Rahel began to give birth, and had great difficulty giving birth.

Jacob Dwells at Beth El!!

Genesis 35, cont.
¹⁷And it came to be, as she was having great difficulty giving birth, that the midwife said to her, "Do not fear, for it is another son for you." ¹⁸And it came to be, as her life was going out – for she died – that she called his name Ben-Oni. But his father called him Binyamin. ¹⁹So Rahel died and was buried on the way to Ephrath, that is Beyth Lehem. ²⁰And Ya'aqob set a standing column on her grave, which is the monument of Rahel's grave to this day.

Joseph was sent by his father to Shekem, which was just north of Beth El to check on his brothers. The story of Joseph is sure to evoke strong emotions! It is the story of how Joseph was sold into slavery by his own brothers and later reunited with his family!

Genesis 37
²³So it came to be, when Yoseph had come to his brothers, that they stripped Yoseph of his robe, the long robe which was on him. ²⁴And they took him and threw him into a pit. And the pit was empty, there was no water in it. ²⁵And they sat down to eat a meal. And they lifted their eyes and looked and saw a company of Yishma'elites, coming from Gil'ad with their camels, bearing spices, and balm, and myrrh, going to take them down to Mitsrayim. ²⁶And Yehudah said to his brothers, "What would we gain if we kill our brother and conceal his blood? ²⁷"Come and let us sell him to the Yishma'elites, and let not our hand be upon him, for he is our brother, our flesh." And his brothers listened. ²⁸And men, Midyanite traders passed by, so they pulled Yoseph up and lifted him out of the pit, and sold him to the Yishma'elites for twenty pieces of silver. And they took Yoseph to Mitsrayim. ²⁹And Re'uben returned to the pit, and see, Yoseph was not in the pit. And he tore his garments. ³⁰And he returned to his brothers and said, "The boy is gone! And I, where am I to go?" ³¹So they took Yoseph's robe, killed a male goat, and dipped the robe in the blood, ³²and sent the long robe and brought it to their father and said, "We have found this. Please look, is it the robe of your son or not?" ³³And he recognized it and said, "It is my son's robe. An evil beast has devoured him. Yoseph is torn, torn to pieces." ³⁴And Ya'aqob tore his garments, and put sackcloth on his waist, and mourned for his son many days. ³⁵And all his sons and all his daughters arose to comfort him, but he refused to be comforted, and he said, "Now let me go down into the grave to my son in mourning." So his father wept for him. ³⁶And the Midanites had sold him in Mitsrayim to Potiphar, an officer of Pharaoh and captain of the guard.

What a wonderful moment, when Jacob finds out that his beloved son, Joseph, is still alive!

Genesis 45
^{25}And they went up out of Mitsrayim, and came to the land of Kena'an to Ya'aqob their father. ^{26}And they told him, saying, "Yoseph is still alive, and he is governor over all the land of Mitsrayim." And Ya'aqob's heart ceased, for he did not believe them. ^{27}But when they spoke to him all the words which Yoseph had spoken to them, and when he saw the wagons which Yoseph had sent to transport him, the spirit of Ya'aqob their father revived. ^{28}And Yisra'el said, "Enough! My son Yoseph is still alive. Let me go and see him before I die."

Jacob sets out with his family **for Mitsrayim in northwestern Arabia not in Egypt!** One of the problems that has confounded scholars for centuries is the lack of physical evidence of a large Israelite occupation in Egypt! That's because the Exodus never occurred in Egypt, of course! Many scholars have even doubted that an Exodus ever occurred because of the lack of archeological evidence in Egypt! The evidence just does not support a large Israelite population in Egypt! **The Truth is that the first Exodus never occurred in Egypt because the Israelites were not in bondage in Egypt!** However, the Exodus most certainly did occur! Well, if the first Exodus was not from Egypt, then where was the Exodus from? The Israelites left Mitsrayim! The Hebrew Scriptures have it right! The Scriptures clearly state that the Exodus was from Mitsrayim! English translators replaced Mitsrayim with Egypt! Mitsrayim was the most powerful nation in the world at the time of the first Exodus! It was located in today's northwestern Saudi Arabia! Mitsrayim is sometimes referred to as Misr or Musri by researchers like T.K. Cheyne, Fritz Hommel, and Hugo Winckler! These three world renowned scholars determined the real location of Mitsrayim based on their translations of ancient inscriptions in the Middle East! Even the Catholic Encyclopedia describes their work as thorough, but attempts to trivialize their findings as too radical! Much more will be discussed about this fact in later chapters! But for now just remember that the descendents of Jacob spent 430 years in Mitsrayim in today's northwestern Saudi Arabia, **not Egypt**!

Genesis 46
And Yisra'el set out with all that he had, and came to Be'ersheba, and brought offerings to the Elohim of his father Yitshaq. ^{2}And Elohim spoke to Yisra'el in the visions of the night, and said, "Ya'aqob, Ya'aqob!" And he said, "Here I am." ^{3}And He said, "I am the El, Elohim of your father. Do not be afraid to go down to Mitsrayim, or I shall make you there into a great nation. ^{4}"I Myself am going down with you to Mitsrayim and I Myself shall certainly bring you up again. And let Yoseph put his hand on your eyes."

Genesis 46, cont.
⁵And Ya'aqob rose up from Be'ersheba. And the sons of Yisra'el brought their father Ya'aqob, and their little ones, and their wives, in the wagons which Pharaoh had sent to transport him. ⁶And they took their livestock and their property which they had acquired in the land of Kena'an, and came into Mitsrayim, Ya'aqob and all his seed with him.

Summary

Noah's Ark came to rest in the mountains of northwestern Saudi Arabia not Turkey, after the Flood! Shem's line was chosen by 𐤀𐤉𐤄𐤆 to be the line of the Righteous seed, after the Flood! Abraham was in the line of Shem and proved himself before 𐤀𐤉𐤄𐤆 in Chaldea under the most difficult of circumstances! Abraham was chosen to be Yahuah's Righteous planting in the Promised Land! He was instructed to leave his home in the land of Chaldea and to go to a new land, which was hand-picked by 𐤀𐤉𐤄𐤆! It was the Promised Land! 𐤀𐤉𐤄𐤆 made a covenant with Abraham at Beth El, then reaffirmed that covenant with Isaac and Jacob! Mount Sinai is in today's northwestern Saudi Arabia in the Land of Madyan! Abraham's covenant with 𐤀𐤉𐤄𐤆 is still in effect today! **Anyone on the earth**, who will answer Yahuah's call, and will allow themselves to fall in love with 𐤀𐤉𐤄𐤆 and His son, OWY𐤀𐤆, are <u>accepted</u> under the terms and conditions of Abraham's original covenant! When you fall in love with 𐤀𐤉𐤄𐤆 and OWY𐤀𐤆, <u>**you will want**</u> to please them with all your heart! You'll **want** to guard Yahuah's Torah! Yahuah's set apart Spirit, His Ruach HaQodesh, will teach you Yahuah's ways a little here and a little there! After the Flood, Ham committed a terrible sexual sin, when he uncovered his own father's nakedness! The phrase uncovering his father's nakedness means that Ham actually <u>had sexual relations with his own mother</u>. Cush was one of Ham's sons, who became very wicked! Cush had a son in his old age named Nimrod! Nimrod was Noah's great grandson, but Nimrod rebelled against Noah's teachings and became the most wicked man, after the Flood! Nimrod even studied the ways of Cain and worshiped the sun, moon, and the stars! He became the first mighty conqueror on the earth! Nimrod conquered peoples by military force and put them into subjection to his own desires! Nimrod was the first man to train armies for war and to build military fortifications! The building of the tower of Babel was led by Nimrod and the other sons of Ham! They devised a plan to lay siege to the heavenly Mount Zion because they wanted to become elohim **(mighty ones)** like 𐤀𐤉𐤄𐤆! Nimrod married Semiramis, who was reported to be his own mother! When Nimrod was killed, Semiramis claimed that Nimrod had become one with the sun!

Nimrod has the dubious distinction of being the first man to ever be deified as a god! Nimrod is the root of the false religions of the whole world! He's been worshiped under many names such as Baal, Bacchus, Osiris, etc.! The list goes on and on, but the names are all connected with Sun worship in some way! Nimrod was so wicked that he even wanted to conquer Yahuah's kingdom in the Heavens! That was Nimrod's motivation for building the Tower of Babel! As you will discover as you read *Let My People Go*, Nimrod is the prime candidate for the first beast of Revelation! He will be **raised from the Abyss** on the Day of ᶏYᶏZ! From the time of Nimrod's death, evergreen trees, palms, and oaks have been cut down, decorated, and worshiped in honor of Nimrod's rebirth as the unconquered sun! This pagan tradition was later syncretized by Constantine! Now it has become the most beloved tradition in America, which we all know as Christmas! When Nimrod is raised from the Abyss as the beast on the Day of ᶏYᶏZ, he will be ultimately defeated by OWYᶏZ! The Scriptures teach that at that time **even** the cedar and cypress trees will rejoice because they will no longer be cut down for Christmas celebrations!

Isaiah 14

[5]"ᶏYᶏZ has broken the staff of the wrong, the scepter of the rulers, [6]he who smote the people in wrath with ceaseless blows, he who ruled the gentiles in displeasure, is persecuted and no one restrains. [7]"All the earth is at rest and at peace, they shall break forth into singing. [8]"**Even the cypress trees rejoice over you, and the cedars of Lebanon, saying, 'Since you were cut down, no wood cutter has come up against us.**' [9]"The grave from beneath is excited about you, to meet you at your coming; it stirs up the dead for you, all the chief ones of the earth; it has raised up from their thrones all the sovereigns of the gentiles. [10]"All of them respond and say to you, 'Have you also become as weak as we? Have you become like us? [11]'Your arrogance has been brought down to the grave, and the sound of your stringed instruments; the maggot is spread under you, and worms cover you.' [12]"How you have fallen from the heavens, O Helel, son of the morning! You have been cut down to the ground, you who laid low the gentiles! [13]"For you have said in your heart, '**Let me go up to the heavens, let me raise my throne above the stars of El, and let me sit in the mount of meeting on the sides of the north;** [14]**let me go up above the heights of the clouds, let me be like the Most High.**' [15]"But you are brought down to the grave, to the sides of the Pit. [16]"Those who see you stare at you, and ponder over you, saying, 'Is this the man who made the earth tremble, who shook reigns, [17]who made the world as a wilderness and destroyed its cities, who would **not open the house of his prisoners?**'

The Real Promised Land
Chapter 7

⁷"For ayaz your Elohim is bringing you into a good land, a land of streams of water, of fountains and springs, that flow out of valleys and hills, ⁸a land of wheat and barley, of vines and fig trees and pomegranates, a land of olive oil and honey, ⁹a land in which you eat bread without scarcity, in which you do not lack at all, a land whose stones are iron and out of whose hills you dig copper. ¹⁰"And you shall eat and be satisfied, and shall bless ayaz your Elohim for the good land which He has given you.
Debarim (Deuteronomy) 8

Before the Flood, Noah and his family came down from the Set Apart Mountain, Mount Sinai, and entered the Ark! After the Flood waters receded, the Ark came to rest on a mountain range called Harrat. Where are the mountains of Harrat today? You guessed it! That mountain range is in northwestern Saudi Arabia, not Turkey! After the Flood, the lands of today's Arabia were divided between Shem, Ham, and Yapeth! ayaz chose Shem's line to be the line that would be traceable to OWYaz! Abraham, Isaac, and Jacob were born into the line of Shem! They each had personal encounters with ayaz, after the Flood! These encounters were recorded in Genesis and occurred at a set apart place called Beth El! Beth El means "abode or house of the Mighty One"! Before the 1st Exodus, Abraham, Isaac, and Jacob would sojourn before ayaz at Beth El many times! It was a special place to ayaz! These patriarchs were shepherds! They would move from place to place as ayaz directed! Beth El was located adjacent to the mountain that was first known as the set apart Mountain of El Shaddai and later as Mount Sinai in the 1st Exodus! The book of Genesis records that Beth El was also known as Luz! The word Luz means "almond"! Today there is an abundance of almond trees growing in that area of Madyan (Midian)! Jebel al Lawz is a mountain located in Madyan! Obviously there is a similarity between Luz and Lawz! Madyan is in northwestern Saudi Arabia today just like it was in antiquity! Jebel al Lawz is the very best candidate for Mount Sinai! I personally believe that the evidence clearly indicates that Jebel al Lawz is the very same Mount Sinai, which Moses ascended to receive "The Ten Commandments"! The evidence is overwhelming! Interestingly enough there is an ancient almond tree growing in the most unlikely of places on the very summit of Jebel al Lawz between two **massive** tablet-like granite stones! The blackened peak next to Jebel al Lawz is known as Jebel al Maqla! Paul wrote that Mount Sinai was located in Arabia in Galations!

The blackened peak of Jebel al Maqla is evidence of 𝐚𝐘𝐚𝐙 descending on top of that Mountain with fire, when He spoke the Ten Commandments to Israel! 𝐚𝐘𝐚𝐙 spoke to Israel from the fire and smoke, which engulfed those two mountain peaks! In recent years explorers like Ron Wyatt and the Caldwell family have greatly increased the world's knowledge about the true location of Mount Sinai! Jim and Penny Caldwell and their two children, Lucas and Chelsea, lived in Saudi Arabia over ten years! They had many adventures exploring in the vicinity of Jebel al Lawz! The Caldwell family is responsible for the vast majority of pictures and video footage available of Jebel al Lawz! They have written a book and appear in a video about the Mountain called *The Mountain of Fire!* Jim and Penny also have a very interesting web site, Jimandpenny.com! An abundance of physical evidence is present at Jebel al Lawz, which helps to establish the site's authenticity! Most of the events that we love in the Scriptures actually occurred in the districts of today's northwestern Saudi Arabia, **not Palestine**! So what does all this mean? What it all means is that the Promised Land today is in the wrong place! Today's State of Israel is **not** the true location of the Promised Land! An incredible **switch-r-rue** has occurred! This switch has been cloaked in mystery! I believe the actual switch occurred in the aftermath of the Bar Kochbah revolt against the Romans, after 135 CE! The switch was planned and executed by the Romans! The Romans completely destroyed Yahrushalayim in 135 CE and even plowed it like a field just as the prophets said would happen! After Rome defeated the army of Jewish zealots, the Romans killed over 575,000 Jews with twelve Roman legions! The remaining survivors were exiled away from the Promised Land! The Romans sold surviving Jews as slaves into every Roman province in Rome's empire! This was the beginning of the last exile of the Jews into the nations, which is still in effect today! Surviving Jews in Arabia were prohibited from reentering the ruins of Yahrushalayim under the penalty of death! It was during this chaotic time that the real location of Yahrushalayim was switched by the Romans! The Romans absolutely **hated** the real Yahrushalayim because it was so dear to the heart of every real Jew! They used their vast resources **to reinvent the city in a new location** 200 miles to the north in today's Palestine! After a few generations the last eye witnesses died off and the knowledge of the real Promised Land's where-abouts faded out of the Jews memory! Some Jewish families fled and migrated further south into southern Arabia! Over the years other Jewish families migrated northward into Palestine, where the counterfeit State of Israel is today! Until Mohammed persecuted the Jews, there was a very large Jewish population in the areas around Mecca and Medina in western Arabia!

Jews would have remained in Arabia until this very day, if it had not been for the Islamic persecution and oppression! Jewish families were forced to completely leave Arabia or be terrorized by the Moslems! The last remaining Jews were evacuated out of Arabia in 1949! One legendary rescue operation, was dubbed "Operation Magic Carpet"! It airlifted Jews from Yemen to the State of Israel in 1949. By 1950, nearly 50,000 Yemenite Jews were flown out of Arabia into the State of Israel in Palestine!

Northwestern Saudi Arabia

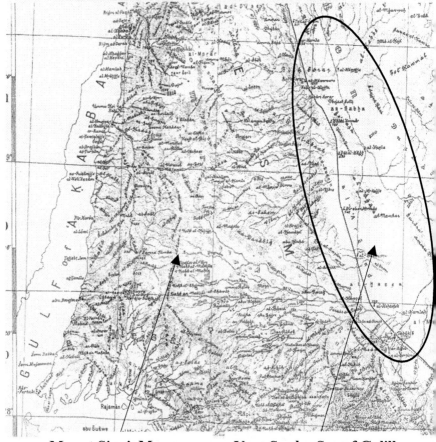

Mount Sinai, Map from *Northern Arabia*, Alois Musil

Yam Suph= Sea of Galillee

And Lot lifted up his eyes, and beheld all the plain of Jordan, that it was well watered every where, before 𐤄𐤅𐤄𐤉 *destroyed Sodom and Gomorrah, even as the garden of* 𐤄𐤅𐤄𐤉, *like the land of Mitsrayim, as thou comest unto Zoar. Then Lot chose him all the plain of Jordan; and Lot journeyed **east**: and they separated themselves the one from the other. Abram dwelled in the land of Canaan, and Lot dwelled in the cities of the plain, and pitched his tent toward Sodom.* **Genesis 13**

If you traveled **east** from anywhere in the Land of Madyan, you would travel **further into today's Saudi Arabia, not Palestine**! Palestine is at least 150 miles to the northwest! Mount Sinai, Jebel al Lawz

The Jordan River valley was **East** of the set apart Mountain of 𐤄𐤅𐤄𐤉, Mount Sinai! Sodom was located in this valley!

The Land of Madyan is in Northwestern Saudi Arabia! Any good map will attest to that fact! Madyan is still located in northwestern Arabia where it's always been! That has **not** changed! In Genesis 13, when Abraham and Lot separated, Lot traveled **east** from Beth El, which was adjacent to the set apart Mountain of ᚨYᚨZ (Mount Sinai) in the Land of Madyan! Traveling east will take you **further and further into Arabia, not Palestine**! Palestine is at least 150 miles to the northwest! Today if you travel east from Mount Sinai in Madyan, you will cross the Jordan River Valley and eventually the ancient location of the Sea of Galilee or Yam Suph! Of course the real Sea of Galilee was dried up many years ago as have all the other rivers of the real Promised Land in northwestern Saudi Arabia! ᚨYᚨZ dried them all up, but when OWYᚨZ returns, these rivers will spring forth again! Remember don't judge by appearances! It's a very small thing for ᚨYᚨZ to change the dried up and desolated places in northwestern Arabia into wonderful lush places that will make the most beautiful garden places of this world look like child's play! ᚨYᚨZ loves to confound the wisdom of this world's intellectuals!

[19] For it has been written, "I shall destroy the wisdom of the wise, and set aside the learning of the learned ones." [20] Where is the wise? Where is the scholar? Where is the debater of this age? Has not Elohim made foolish the wisdom of this world? **1 Corinthians 1**

YeshaYahu 43

Remember ye not the former things, neither consider the things of old. Behold, I will do a new thing; now it shall spring forth; shall ye not know it? I will even make <u>a way in the wilderness</u>, and <u>rivers in the desert</u>. The beast of the field shall honour me, the dragons and the owls: because I give <u>waters in the wilderness, and rivers in the desert</u>, to give drink to my people, my chosen.

YeshaYahu 35

Then shall the lame man leap as an hart, and the tongue of the dumb sing: for in the wilderness shall <u>waters break out</u>, and <u>streams in the desert</u>. And the parched ground shall <u>become a pool</u>, and the <u>thirsty land springs of water</u>: in the habitation of dragons, where each lay, shall be grass with reeds and rushes. And an highway shall be there, and a way, and it shall be called The way of holiness; the unclean shall not pass over it; but it shall be for those: the wayfaring men, though fools, shall not err therein. No lion shall be there, nor any ravenous beast shall go up thereon, it shall not be found there; but the redeemed shall walk there: And the ransomed of ᚨYᚨZ shall return, and come to Zion with songs and everlasting joy upon their heads: they shall obtain joy and gladness, and sorrow and sighing shall flee away.

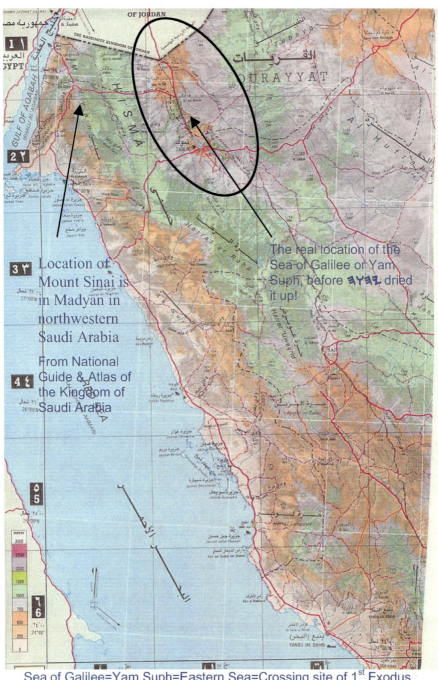

Sea of Galilee=Yam Suph=Eastern Sea=Crossing site of 1st Exodus

Today the Land of Israel is a mirage! It **is a traditional Holy Land set up by men**! But it's definitely **not the real location** of the true Promised Land! Obviously I love the idea of the people of Israel returning to the Promised Land! I have financially supported several organizations that have helped Jews go to the State of Israel from the Soviet Union! My heart was in the right place, but 𐤀𐤉𐤄𐤅 had **not** revealed the counterfeit Promised Land to me at that time! However, over time I have discovered the real truth about the modern State of Israel! It always hurts, when you discover that a cause that you trusted in, is **not** what you thought it was! Now let me make sure you grasp the magnitude of what I am trying to explain to you! What I am trying to say is that Jerusalem in the State of Israel today is **not** the real Yahrushalayim where OWY𐤄𐤅 was hung on a tree as our Passover Lamb! Bethlehem in the State of Israel today is **not** where OWY𐤄𐤅 was borne! Hebron in the State of Israel is **not** where Abraham buried his wife Sarah! Jericho in the State of Israel today is **not** the city where the walls fell down! But now you get the picture, don't you? I am saying to you that all those places in the State of Israel are reproductions and counterfeits of the real set apart cities! Today the real Promised Land lies at least 150 miles to the southeast of Palestine! The set apart places of 𐤀𐤉𐤄𐤅 are in ruins in the sands of northwestern Saudi Arabia just as the prophets said they would be at the time of Yahushua's return! Saudi Arabia is a country locked down to western tourism, but especially to people, who love the Yahuah's Scriptures! What a coincidence! Mecca is located in Saudi Arabia! Mecca is the Holiest place on earth to the servants of Islam! Western tourists just don't go to Saudi Arabia, unless they are invited! The only westerners invited to Saudi Arabia are generally workers, who support the oil industry or other Saudi business interests! However, there is another reason that Saudi Arabia is locked down so tightly! If the real Truth about northwestern Saudi Arabia was known to the masses of people in the world, there would be pressure to open that country up to Jews and Christians! Capitalist would market the real set apart places as "Holy" tourist sites just like they have done in the counterfeit State of Israel today! Tourism is the main industry in the State of Israel!

𐤀𐤉𐤄𐤅 knows that the hearts of men are desperately wicked! Wicked men would defile and exploit Yahuah's real set apart places, **if they could**! They will exploit anything that has the potential for bringing them wealth! 𐤀𐤉𐤄𐤅 never intended for wicked men to use His set apart places as tourist attractions for their financial gain! When you visit the various sites in the State of Israel today, the tour guides will tell you that each site is the "**traditional site**"! The State of Israel today is full of traditional sites created by men, but **the genuine sites are in northwestern Saudi Arabia!**

The real sites are hidden and protected by 𝐚𝐘𝐚𝐙 in northwestern Saudi Arabia from exploitation by greedy men! Like everything else in this world, fees are charged to visit the "holy" sites in today's State of Israel! Now, I want you to think about the one time recorded in the Scriptures, when OWY𝐚𝐙 experienced righteous anger! Do you remember, when OWY𝐚𝐙 ran the merchants out of the Temple area? OWY𝐚𝐙 was angered because these merchants were defiling the Temple by their unethical business practices! On the surface these merchants were selling doves, sheep, and goats to the people, which would be used in their sacrifices! OWY𝐚𝐙 took great offence to what they were doing in that set apart area, which was dedicated to 𝐚𝐘𝐚𝐙! OWY𝐚𝐙 said that these merchants were defiling His Temple! These merchants had turned Yahuah's house into a house of thieves instead of a house of prayer! Now, if OWY𝐚𝐙 got that upset about what the merchants were doing in the Temple back then, why would 𝐚𝐘𝐚𝐙 allow merchants today to exploit Yahushua's real birth place or His real burial place **for money**? Wicked merchants just want to make money at any cost! If greedy men can make money by exploiting the spiritual emotions of sincere sheep, they will do it and have done it in today's State of Israel! There is **no way** that 𝐚𝐘𝐚𝐙 would allow any of His real set apart places to be defiled by the merchants of this world! So even though Saudi Arabia has tough policies about Christians and Jews visiting the country, 𝐚𝐘𝐚𝐙 is really behind the tough Saudi policies in order to protect His set apart places from exploitation by wicked men! 𝐚𝐘𝐚𝐙 will protect His places, until the OWY𝐚𝐙 returns! At that time the Scriptures teach that Yahuah's set apart places will be rebuilt and reinhabited by His First Fruits! If Saudi Arabia would allow archeological digs to take place today, a tremendous amount of physical evidence would be uncovered that would validate that a very large Hebrew occupation existed over many years in northwestern Saudi Arabia! Massive amounts of astounding evidence supporting the Hebrew Scriptures and the 1st Exodus would come to light! Obviously that's **not** on the agenda of the Saudi Arabian government! However, those cities will be rebuilt and reinhabited on Yahuah's Day! You can count on that! Mount Sinai and the real cities of Yahrushalayim, Hebron, Beth Lehem, and Yericho are all located in what is today called the Wadi As Sirhan Quadrangle! The Wadi As Sirhan is located in the northwestern quadrant of Saudi Arabia! Today this area is in the Tabuk region of Saudi Arabia! The beloved cities of the Scriptures remain desolated and in ruins **just as the prophets of the Scriptures said they would remain**, until OWY𝐚𝐙 returns to establish His Kingdom! What does all this mean? It means that the ruins of those cities will remain in the sands of Saudi Arabia, until OWY𝐚𝐙 returns at the opening of the 6th Seal of Revelation! Close study of the Scriptures will testify to that fact!

How do I know that these cities are in today's Saudi Arabia and not in Palestine? Paul testifies himself that Mount Sinai is in Arabia in the book of Galations! In Genesis Mount Sinai was reported to be in the Land of Madyan! Close study of Genesis 10 confirms that Shem, Ham, and Japheth all settled their families in today's Arabia, not in Palestine! Saudi Arabia today is filled with place names derived from those families! **Northwestern Saudi Arabia was the real cradle of civilization**, not Iraq! You may be thinking that this guy has lost it! No, I'm far from crazy, but the **Truth is astounding**! How do I know that all the sacred cities that we love to read about in Scriptures are in Saudi Arabia? Anyone can figure it out! **Just use your own common sense**! If you believe that the Scriptures are true, then it's not hard to prove that the Promised Land is in Saudi Arabia and not in Palestine! To start with identify the real location of a known reference point from the Scriptures! I am positive that Mount Sinai's location is in the land of Madyan in northwestern Saudi Arabia! In this case, I am using Mount Sinai, Jebel al Lawz, as my reference point! But, I could use the whole land of Madyan as my reference point just as well! **Either way the conclusion will be the same**! Follow the directions given in the Scriptures and you will discover the truth! Anyone can determine the approximate locations of other places in the Scriptures by evaluating the direction of travel and the travel time from point A to point B! Remember Lot traveled **east** from Beth El in Madyan to the Jordan River valley to settle, when He separated from Abraham! **If you travel east from anywhere in Madyan, you will just go further and further into Saudi Arabia**! Palestine is 150 miles to the Northwest! **Helloo-oo, I smell a rat**! There are many references in the Scriptures, which give direction and travel time! From the Scriptures I know that Yahrushalayim was in the Mountains north of the Jordan River Valley! In Genesis Sodom was reported to be in the Jordan River Valley due **east** of Beth El, which was adjacent to Mount Sinai! Melchizedek, the king of Yahrushalayim, came out to greet Abraham as did the king of Sodom, after Abraham returned from his defeat of the kings of the nations! Sodom and Yahrushalayim were not very far apart! Beth Lehem was a very short distance from Yahrushalayim probably less than 10 miles to the East! Shekem was located north of Beth El! Shiloh was on the northern side of Mount Sinai!

Summary

The cradle of civilization was <u>not</u> in Iraq or somewhere else in Mesopotamia! To find the earliest origins of man, look no further than today's northwestern Saudi Arabia! Before the Flood, northwestern Saudi Arabia was the habitation of Adam and Hawwah!

Righteous men and their families lived on Yahuah's set apart Mountain, later known as Mount Sinai, until the Flood! After the Flood, the ark landed on a mountain in northwestern Arabia, **not** Turkey! After the Flood, Noah's three sons divided the land and settled in various parts of Arabia! The land called Cainan was supposed to be Shem's portion, but the children of Cainan transgressed Yahuah's instructions and settled there instead! Remember Cainan was the illegitimate son of Ham resulting from Ham's rape of his own mother! That's why it was called the land of Cainan! Later, ayaz rightfully promised the land of Cainan to Abraham and his seed! ayaz confirmed His promise with Isaac and later reaffirmed that same promise with Jacob! The Righteous of Israel are still destined to receive that same Promised Land! I will find my Sabbath rest there as will <u>all</u> the rest of Israel! The Scriptures record that Moses tended Yethro's sheep in the land of Madyan! Moses spoke to OWYAZ in the burning bush on Mount Sinai in the land of Madyan! Today the Promised Land is still in northwestern Saudi Arabia where it has always been! **ayaz has not relocated the Promised Land, men did**! The present State of Israel is an invention of men for their own selfish purposes! It's **not** part of Yahuah's plan for Israel, but it's a diversion and a snare to the sheep! This can easily be proven by a little personal research! Yahuah's plan for the return His people, Israel, to the Promised Land **DOES <u>NOT</u> DEPEND ON THE ACTIONS OF MEN**! Yahuah's plan for the return of Israel will be **even more <u>supernatural</u> than the 1st Exodus**! The events that will occur on the Day of ayaz, when ayaz returns Israel to the real Promised Land, will manifest the greatest spectacles that the world has ever seen! If you prepare yourself, then you will be ready! **If not, woe be it to you!**

The First Exodus From Mitsrayim
Chapter 8

And afterwards Mosheh and Aharon went in and said to Pharaoh, "Thus said ayaz Elohim of Yisra'el, 'Let My People Go, so that they keep a festival to Me in the wilderness.'" **Exodus 5**

If you are like most sheep today, then you have been taught, since your childhood, that Moses led the Israelites out of **Egypt!** Until a few years ago, I believed the very same thing! As I searched the Scriptures for truth, Yahuah's Ruach HaQodesh impressed upon my heart that something was terribly wrong with the Exodus from Egypt scenario! Over time I realized that Egypt was not where the 1st Exodus actually occurred! The actual transliterated Hebrew word that has been mistranslated into English as Egypt is **Mitsrayim**! As I studied Genesis I noticed how the Scriptures consistently referred to Yahuah's people going **down** to Mitsrayim! Going down sounds like going **south** to me! Abraham went **down** to Mitsrayim! Jacob went **down** to Mitsrayim! Today's Egypt was not down or toward the south from the real Promised Land, it was to the west or southwest! Another thing that struck me was that in every account, when ayaz instructed one of His Patriarchs to go **down** to Mitsrayim, nothing at all was ever said about the **necessity** of crossing any sea or large body of water! This is true in every case and even true when Joseph and Mary were instructed to go down to Mitsrayim with the baby, OWYaZ! An obstacle as great as the "Red Sea" would have been at least mentioned in the narratives of a journey, wouldn't it? If you traveled south from the real Promised Land to Mitsrayim like Abraham did, you would go **down**, but you would still be in today's Saudi Arabia! The ancient incense trade route followed today's Red Sea coast and extended all the way down to today's Yemen! Over time I knew in my heart that Mitsrayim had to be in the western or northwestern regions of Saudi Arabia! What I had concluded spiritually in my studies of the Scriptures, other well known scholars had also concluded from their field studies of ancient inscriptions in the Middle East! World renowned researchers like Hugo Winckler, Fritz Hommel, and T.K. Cheyne all realized that there was another very powerful nation in the northwestern area of Saudi Arabia called Mitsrayim! Mitsrayim sometimes was called Misr or Musri! Even the Catholic Encyclopedia **(of all places)** discusses the thoroughness of their conclusions, but of course it was quick to discredit their views as **too radical**! The Catholic Encyclopedia dismissed their conclusions as "premature, ultra radical, and without worldwide acceptance"!

Well today, the name of 𐤀𐤇𐤉𐤄 is regarded as ultra radical and without worldwide acceptance! However, everyone's next breath depends entirely on the mercy of 𐤀𐤇𐤉𐤄. The following is the description given in the Catholic online Encyclopedia of Winckler's, Cheyne's, and Hommel's conclusions:

THE NORTH-ARABIAN MITSRAYIM AND THE OLD TESTAMENT

"The cuneiform inscriptions of Assyria have thrown considerable light on various geographical localities in North Arabia, having important bearing on the history of the ancient Hebrews and on the critical study of the Old Testament. The importance of these new facts and researches has of late assumed very bewildering proportions, the credit for which unmistakably belongs to Winckler, Hommel, and Cheyne. It is needless to say that however ingenious these hypotheses may appear to be they are not as yet entitled to be received without caution and hesitation. Were we to believe, in fact, the elaborate theories of these eminent scholars, a great part of the historical events of the Old Testament should be transferred from **"EGYPT AND CHANAN INTO ARABIA"**; for, according to the latest speculations of these scholars, many of the passages in the Old Testament which, until recently, were supposed to refer to Egypt (in Hebrew, Mitsrayim) and to Ethiopia (in Hebrew, Kush) do not really apply to them, but to two regions of similar names in North Arabia, called in the Assyro-Babylonian inscriptions Mitsrayim, or Mitsrayimm, and Chush, respectively. They hold that partly by means of editorial manipulation and partly by reason of corruption in the text, and in consequence of the faded memory of long-forgotten events and countries, these two archaic North-Arabian geographical names became transformed into names of similar sound, but better known, belonging to a different geographical area namely, the Egyptian Mitsrayim and the African Chush, or Ethiopia. According to this theory, Agar, Sarai's handmaid was not Misrite or Egyptian, but Mitsrayimte, i.e. from Mitsrayim, in Northern Arabia. Abraham did not go down into Mitsrayim, or Egypt, where he is said to have received from the pharaoh a gift of men-servants and handmaids, but into Misrim, or Mitsrayim, in Northern Arabia. Joseph, when bought by the Ismaelites, or Madianites, i.e. arabs, was not brought into Egypt (Mitsrayim), but to Mitsrayim, or Misrim, in North Arabia, which was the home of the Madianites. In 1 Kings we should not read "I am a young man of Egypt [Mitsrayim], slave of an Amalecite," but of Mitsrayim in North Arabia. In Kings, Solomon is said to have married the daughter of an Egyptian king, which is extremely improbable; for Mitsrayim in North Arabia, and not the Egyptian Mitsrayim, is the country whose king's daughter Solomon married.

THE NORTH-ARABIAN MITSRAYIM AND THE OLD TESTAMENT

In 1 Kings the wisdom of Solomon is compared to the "wisdom of all the children of the east country [i.e. the arabians] and all the wisdom of Egypt." but the last-mentioned country, they say, is not Egypt but, as the parallelism requires, Madian, or Mitsrayim, whose proverbial wisdom is frequently alluded to in the Old Testament. Horses are said to have been brought from Egypt, but horses were very scarce in Egypt, while very numerous and famous in Arabia. The same emendation can be made in at least a dozen more Old Testament passages. The most revolutionary result, however, would follow if we applied the same theory to the famous sojourn of the Hebrews in Egypt; for it is self-evident that if the Israelites sojourned not in the Egyptian Mitsrayim, but in the North Arabian Mitsrayim, and from thence fled into Chanaan, which was nearby, the result to ancient Hebrew history and religion would be of the most revolutionary character. Another important geographical name frequently mentioned in the Old Testament, and in all instances referred, till recently, to Assyria, is Assur (abbreviated into Sur). A country of similar name has also been discovered in Arabia. In this last view Winckler and Cheyne are warmly supported by Hommel, by whom it was first suggested. Cheyne, furthermore, has pushed these identifications to such extremities as to transplant the whole historical and religious life of Israel to the Nejeb, the country of Jerameel in northern Arabia. According to him the prophets Elias, Eliseus, Amos, Osee, Ezechiel, Joel, and Abdias are all North Arabians; and all the rest of the prophets either came from that country or have it constantly in view. Isaias was according to him, composed in Northern Arabia; Ezechiel also suffered imprisonment and prophesied there; and hundreds of personal and geographical proper names in the Old Testament are, according to him, intentional or accidental corruptions of Jerameel, Arabia, and Nejeb. However great our appreciation of Winckler's and Cheyne's ingenuity and learning may be, and allowing that their theories are not entirely lacking in plausibility, yet they have received, so far, little support and encouragement from the majority of biblical scholars and critics. It is true that the new theories, in some of their applications, give highly satisfactory results, **but in their extreme form they are, to say the least, premature and ultra-radical.**"

Moses and the Burning Bush
Exodus 3
And Mosheh was shepherding the flock of Yithro his father-in-law, the priest of <u>Madyan</u>. And he led the flock to the back of the wilderness, and came to Horeb, <u>the mountain of Elohim</u>.

Moses and the Burning Bush

Exodus 3, cont.
²And the Messenger of 𐤉𐤄𐤅𐤄 appeared <u>to him in a flame of fire</u> from the midst of a bush. And he looked and saw the bush burning with fire, but the bush was not consumed. ³And Mosheh said, "Let me turn aside now, and see this great sight, why the bush does not burn." ⁴And 𐤉𐤄𐤅𐤄 saw that he turned aside to see, and Elohim called to him from the midst of the bush and said, "Mosheh! Mosheh!" And he said, "Here I am." ⁵And He said, "Do not come near here. Take your sandals off your feet, <u>for the place on which you are standing is set-apart ground</u>." ⁶And He said, "I am the Elohim of your father, the Elohim of Abraham, the Elohim of Yitshaq, and the Elohim of Ya'aqob." And Mosheh hid his face, for he was afraid to look at Elohim. ⁷And 𐤉𐤄𐤅𐤄 said, "I have indeed seen the oppression of My people who are in Mitsrayim, and have heard their cry because of their slave-drivers, for I know their sorrows. ⁸"And I have come down to deliver them from the hand of the Mitsrites, and to bring them up from that land to a good and spacious land, to a land flowing with milk and honey, to the place of the Kena'anites and the Hittites and the Amorites and the Perizzites and the Hiwwites and the Yebusites. ⁹"And now, see, the cry of the children of Yisra'el has come to Me, and I have also seen the oppression with which the Mitsrites oppress them. ¹⁰"And now, come, I am sending you to Pharaoh, to bring My people, the children of Yisra'el, out of Mitsrayim." ¹¹And Mosheh said to Elohim, "Who am I that I should go to Pharaoh, and that I should bring the children of Yisra'el out of <u>Mitsrayim</u>?" ¹²And He said, "Because I am with you. And this is to you the sign that I have sent you: When you have <u>brought the people out of Mitsrayim, you are to serve Elohim on this mountain</u>."
¹³And Mosheh said to Elohim, "See, when I come to the children of Yisra'el and say to them, 'The Elohim of your fathers has sent me to you,' and they say to me, 'What is His Name?' what shall I say to them?" ¹⁴And Elohim said to Mosheh, "I am that which I am." And He said, "Thus you shall say to the children of Yisra'el, 'I am has sent me to you.' " ¹⁵And Elohim said further to Mosheh, "Thus you are to say to the children of Yisra'el, '𐤉𐤄𐤅𐤄 Elohim of your fathers, the Elohim of Abraham, the Elohim of Yitshaq, and the Elohim of Ya'aqob, has sent me to you. This is My Name forever, and this is My remembrance to all generations.'

Today, there is a continuous stream of television programs that focus on Egypt and its pyramids. Our society seems to be obsessed with Egyptology! But it doesn't matter how hard the theologians may try to associate the Exodus with Egypt, they will never find any hard evidence of a large Israelite population in Egypt!

Scholars for many years have experienced great difficulty locating the crossing sight of the Red Sea! Some so-called experts even dismiss the crossing of the Red Sea at all! The problem surrounds the translation of the transliterated Hebrew words "Yam Suph"! "Yam Suph" has been rendered Red Sea in error! The Israelites did cross a large body of water! It was an inland Sea or a large inland Lake! The Israelites went out of their way to cross it as they came up from a place in northwestern Saudi Arabia called Mitsrayim! The Israelites did not cross the Yam Suph because it was an obstacle that **had to be crossed** to arrive at their destination! It was possible to go to Mount Sinai from Mitsrayim without crossing any sea! That's why no mention of crossing any sea is given in the Genesis accounts, when the patriarchs went down to Mitsrayim to sojourn! In the 1st Exodus it was not mandatory that the Yam Suph be crossed to get to Mount Sinai from Mitsrayim! The Israelites could have traveled the whole way from Mitsrayim to Mount Sinai without crossing any sea at all! The Israelites were instructed by ayaz to turn to the coast of the Yam Suph to a special place where ayaz planned to destroy the army of Mitsrayim in order to make His name known to all the nations! ayaz intentionally led the Pharaoh of Mitsrayim and his army into a trap! ayaz planned to demonstrate His power and deliverance on behalf of Israel! How did all this occur? The Israelites left Mitsrayim, which was in the northwestern part of today's Saudi Arabia! The Scriptures say that they traveled by the way or by the road of the "Yam Suph"! Without a doubt in antiquity, a large lake or inland sea existed in northwestern Saudi Arabia! At the time of Moshe it was known as Yam Suph! In the New Testament times, it was known as the Sea of the Galilee! **The Israelites actually crossed the same inland sea that we recognize in the New Testament as the Sea of Galilee!** The Sea of Galilee was also called the Lake of Tiberius or Lake Kinneseret in the New Testament! Today the Sea of Galilee, Yam Suph, is no longer visible **because ayaz has dried it up**! The Sea of Galilee still exists, but ayaz has hidden it underground from our view right now just like He has hidden the real Jordan River and all the other rivers of Saudi Arabia for the moment! When OWYAZ returns ayaz will make His land fruitful again! All of Yahuah's rivers and springs will flow once again! The Yam Suph will become visible again! HalleluYah! HalleluYah! HalleluYah!

YeshaYahu (Isaiah) 35
Let the wilderness and the dry place be glad for them, and let the desert rejoice, and blossom as the rose. [2]*It blossoms much and rejoices, even with joy and singing. The esteem of Lebanon* **(the forest)** *shall be given to it, the excellence of Karmel and Sharon. They shall see the esteem of* ayaz, *the excellency of our Elohim.*

YeshaYahu (Isaiah) 35, cont.

³Strengthen the weak hands, and make firm the weak knees. ⁴Say to those with anxious heart, "Be strong, do not fear! See, your Elohim comes with vengeance, with the recompense of Elohim. He is coming to save you." ⁵Then the eyes of the blind shall be opened, and the ears of the deaf be opened. ⁶Then the lame shall leap like a deer, and the tongue of the dumb sing, <u>because waters shall burst forth in the wilderness</u>, and <u>streams in the desert</u>. ⁷And the parched ground shall become <u>a pool</u>, and the thirsty land <u>springs of water</u> in the home for jackals, where each lay, grass with reeds and rushes. ⁸And there shall be a highway, and a way, and it shall be called "The Way of Set-apartness." The unclean does not pass over it, but it is for those who walk the way, and no fools wander on it. ⁹No lion is there, nor any ravenous beast go up on it, it is not found there. But the redeemed shall walk there. ¹⁰And the ransomed of 𐤀𐤅𐤄𐤉 shall return and enter Tsiyon with singing, with ever lasting joy on their heads. They shall obtain joy and gladness, and sorrow and sighing shall flee away.

YeshaYahu (Isaiah) 41

¹⁷"When the poor and needy seek water, and there is none, and their tongues have failed for thirst, I, 𐤀𐤅𐤄𐤉, do answer them; I, the Elohim of Yisra'el, do not forsake them. ¹⁸"I open rivers on bare hills, and fountains in the midst of valleys; I make a wilderness become a pool of water, and a dry land springs of water. ¹⁹"I set in the wilderness cedar, acacia and myrtle and oil tree; I place in the desert cypress, pine and box tree together.

YeshaYahu (Isaiah) 43

¹⁸"Do not remember the former events, nor consider the events of old. ¹⁹"See, I am doing what is new, let it now spring forth. Do you not know it? I am even making a way in the wilderness and rivers in the desert. ²⁰"The beast of the field esteems Me, the jackals and the ostriches, because I have given waters in the wilderness and rivers in the desert, to give drink to My people, My chosen, ²¹this people I have formed for Myself, let them relate My praise.

Today, Saudi Arabia has no visible rivers and very little surface water at all! However, if you consider the incredible number of very large rivers, streams, lakes, and inland seas that once existed in antiquity in Saudi Arabia, the Scriptural account of the Israelite crossing makes perfect sense! Today very large wadis, which are dried up river beds, are still visible in Saudi Arabia! They testify to the fact that at one time Saudi Arabia was a place with an abundance of flowing water! Scholars have been puzzled for a long time about the location of the Red Sea crossing! The pieces just wouldn't fit!

When you analyze satellite imagery and topographical maps of northwestern Saudi Arabia, the locations of ancient rivers, lakes, and inland seas are clearly visible! These springs, rivers, and lakes are all flowing underground now, but they still exist and they will spring forth, when OWY︎︎︎ send His Word! Remember, **do not** judge by appearances! The Israelites crossed the Sea of Galilee, which was east of the Jordan River in the district called "Galilee of the nations"! There was a road or a way by the Sea of Galilee that was used by the Israelites as they traveled northwest from the land of Mitsrayim! The Scriptures record that ︎Y︎Z did not take them across through the land of the Philistines, even though that way was more direct! Instead they traveled by the wilderness way by the Sea of Galilee and crossed the Sea of Galilee in the south! Based on the Scriptural evidence, the actual crossing site was in the land of Zebulun, as it would have been known, after the conquest of the Promised Land! Remember how OWY︎︎︎ concentrated on the land on both sides of the Sea of Galilee during His ministry! At some point in antiquity, after the time of Yahushua's ascension, ︎Y︎Z determined to dry up the Sea of Galilee as well as all the lakes, rivers, and large streams that were in abundance at one time in Arabia! This is a very important fact that serious students of the Scriptures must understand! ︎Y︎Z **has decreed ruins and desolations for the real Promised Land, until OWY︎︎︎ returns**! Desolations were decreed in the Promised Land by ︎Y︎Z because of Israel's harlotry with the the nations and later Israel's rejection of OWY︎︎︎, when OWY︎︎︎ came as our Passover Lamb! When the set time has come and the Day of ︎Y︎Z is upon us, then the Promised Land's complete desolation will be over! Then Israel's exile will be ended! OWY︎︎︎ will bring us home, no one else! HalleluYah! HalleluYah! HalleluYah!

Exodus 13 The Journey Begins From Mitsrayim

[17] And it came to be, when Pharaoh had let the people go, that Elohim did not lead them by way of the land of the Philistines, though that was nearer, for Elohim said, "Lest the people regret when they see fighting, and return to Mitsrayim." [18] So Elohim led the people around by way of the wilderness of the Sea of Reeds. And the children of Yisra'el went up armed from the land of Mitsrayim. [19] And Mosheh took the bones of Yoseph with him, for he certainly made the children of Yisra'el swear, saying, "Elohim shall certainly visit you, and you shall bring my bones from here with you." [20] And they departed from Sukkoth and camped in Etham at the edge of the wilderness. [21] And ︎Y︎Z went before them by day in a column of cloud to lead the way, and by night in a column of fire to give them light, so as to go by day and night. [22] The column of cloud did not cease by day, nor the column of fire by night, before the people.

Yahuah's Deliverance through the Sea
Exodus 14

And יהוה spoke to Mosheh, saying, [2]"Speak to the children of Yisra'el, that they turn and camp before Pi Hahiroth, between Migdol **(the mountain)** and the sea, opposite Ba'al Tsephon–camp before it by the sea **(Sea of Galillee)**. [3]"For Pharaoh shall say of the children of Yisra'el, 'They are entangled in the land, the wilderness has closed them in.' [4]"And I shall harden the heart of Pharaoh, and he shall pursue them. But am to be esteemed through Pharaoh and over all his army, and the Mitsrites shall know that I am יהוה." And they did so. [5]And it was reported to the sovereign of Mitsrayim that the people had fled, and the heart of Pharaoh and his servants was turned against the people. And they said, "Why have we done this, that we have let Yisra'el go from serving us?" [6]So he made his chariot ready and took his people with him. [7]And he took six hundred choice chariots, and all the chariots of Mitsrayim with officers over all of them. [8]And יהוה hardened the heart of Pharaoh sovereign of Mitsrayim, and he pursued the children of Yisra'el, but the children of Yisra'el went out defiantly. [9]And the Mitsrites pursued them, and all the horses and chariots of Pharaoh, and his horsemen and his army, and overtook them camping by the sea beside Pi Hahiroth, before Ba'al Tsephon. [10]And when Pharaoh drew near, the children of Yisra'el lifted their eyes and saw the Mitsrites coming up after them. And they were greatly afraid, so the children of Yisra'el cried out to יהוה. [11]And they said to Mosheh,"Did you take us away to die in the wilderness because there are no graves in Mitsrayim? What is this you have done to us, to bring us up out of Mitsrayim? [12]"Is this not the word that we spoke to you in Mitsrayim, saying, 'Leave us alone and let us serve the Mitsrites?' For it would have been better for us to serve the Mitsrites than to die in the wilderness." [13]And Mosheh said to the people, "Do not be afraid. Stand still, and see the deliverance of יהוה, which He does for you today. For the Mitsrites whom you see today, you are never, never to see again. [14]"יהוה does fight for you, and you keep still." [15]And יהוה said to Mosheh, "Why do you cry to Me? Speak to the children of Yisra'el, and let them go forward. [16]"And you, lift up your rod, and stretch out your hand over the sea and divide it, and let the children of Yisra'el go on dry ground through the midst of the sea. [17]"And I, see I am hardening the hearts of the Mitsrites, and they shall follow them. And I am to be esteemed through Pharaoh and over all his army, his chariots, and his horsemen. [18]"And the Mitsrites shall know that I am יהוה, when I am esteemed through Pharaoh, his chariots, and his horsemen." [19]And the Messenger of Elohim, who went before the camp of Yisra'el, moved and went behind them.

Yahuah's Deliverance through the Sea
Exodus 14, cont.
And the column of cloud went from before them and stood behind them, [20] and came between the camp of the Mitsrites and the camp of Yisra'el. And it was the cloud and the darkness, and it gave light by night, and the one did not come near the other all the night. [21] And Mosheh stretched out his hand over the sea. And 𐤀𐤉𐤄𐤅 caused the sea to go back by a strong east wind all that night, and made the sea into dry land, and the waters were divided. [22] And the children of Yisra'el went into the midst of the sea on dry ground, and the waters were a wall to them on their right and on their left. [23] And the Mitsrites pursued and went after them into the midst of the sea, all the horses of Pharaoh, his chariots, and his horsemen. [24] And it came to be, in the morning watch, that 𐤀𐤉𐤄𐤅 looked down upon the army of the Mitsrites through the column of fire and cloud, and He brought the army of the Mitsrites into confusion. [25] And He took off their chariot wheels, so that they drove them with difficulty. And the Mitsrites said, "Let us flee from the face of Yisra'el, for 𐤀𐤉𐤄𐤅 fights for them against the Mitsrites." [26] Then 𐤀𐤉𐤄𐤅 said to Mosheh, "Stretch out your hand over the sea, and let the waters come back upon the Mitsrites, on their chariots, and on their horsemen." [27] And Mosheh stretched out his hand over the sea, and the sea returned to its usual flow, at the break of day, with the Mitsrites fleeing into it. Thus 𐤀𐤉𐤄𐤅 over-threw the Mitsrites in the midst of the sea, [28] and the waters returned and covered the chariots, and the horsemen, and all the army of Pharaoh that came into the sea after them, and not even one was left of them. [29] And the children of Yisra'el walked on dry ground in the midst of the sea, and the waters were a wall to them on their right and on their left. [30] Thus 𐤀𐤉𐤄𐤅 saved Yisra'el that day out of the hand of the Mitsrites, and Yisra'el saw the Mitsrites dead on the seashore.

The Song of the Sea
Exodus 15
Then Mosheh and the children of Yisra'el sang this song to 𐤀𐤉𐤄𐤅, and spoke, saying, "I sing to 𐤀𐤉𐤄𐤅, for He is highly exalted! The horse and its rider He has thrown into the sea! [2] "Yah is my strength and song, and He has become my deliverance. He is my El, and I praise Him – Elohim of my father, and I exalt Him. [3] "𐤀𐤉𐤄𐤅 is a man of battle, 𐤀𐤉𐤄𐤅 is His Name. [4] "He has cast Pharaoh's chariots and his army into the sea, and his chosen officers are drowned in the Sea of Reeds. [5] "The depths covered them, they went down to the bottom like a stone. [6] "Your right hand, O 𐤀𐤉𐤄𐤅, has become great in power. Your right hand, O 𐤀𐤉𐤄𐤅, has crushed the enemy.

The Song of the Sea
Exodus 15, cont.
[7] "And in the greatness of Your excellence You pulled down those who rose up against You. You sent forth Your wrath, it consumed them like stubble. [8] "And with the wind of Your nostrils the waters were heaped up, the floods stood like a wall, the depths became stiff in the heart of the sea. [9] "The enemy said, 'I pursue, I overtake, I divide the spoil, my being is satisfied on them. I draw out my sword, my hand destroys them.' [10] "You did blow with Your wind, the sea covered them, they sank like lead in the mighty waters. [11] "Who is like You, O יהוה, among the mighty ones? Who is like You, great in set-apartness, awesome in praises, working wonders? [12] "You stretched out Your right hand, the earth swallowed them. [13] "In Your kindness You led the people whom You have redeemed, in Your strength You guided them to Your set-apart dwelling. [14] "Peoples heard, they trembled, anguish gripped the inhabitants of Philistia. [15] "Then the chiefs of Edom were troubled, the mighty men of Mo'ab, trembling grips them, all the inhabitants of Kena'an melted. [16] "Fear and dread fell on them, by the greatness of Your arm they are as silent as a stone, until Your people pass over, O יהוה, until the people, whom You have bought, pass over. [17] "You bring them in and plant them in the mountain of Your inheritance, in the place, O יהוה, which You have made for Your own dwelling, the set-apart place, O יהוה, which Your hands have prepared. [18] "יהוה reigns forever and ever." [19] For the horses of Pharaoh went with his chariots and his horsemen into the sea, and יהוה brought back the waters of the sea upon them. And the children of Yisra'el went on dry ground in the midst of the sea. [20] And Miryam the prophetess, the sister of Aharon, took the timbrel in her hand. And all the women went out after her with timbrels and with dances. [21] And Miryam answered them, "Sing to יהוה, for He is highly exalted! The horse and its rider He has thrown into the sea!" [22] And Mosheh brought Yisra'el from the Sea of Reeds, and they went out into the Wilderness of Shur. And they went three days in the wilderness and found no water.

יהוה Makes the Bitter Waters Sweet!
Exodus 15
[23] And they came to Marah, and they were unable to drink the waters of Marah, for they were bitter. So the name of it was called Marah. [24] And the people grumbled against Mosheh, saying, "What are we to drink?" [25] Then he cried out to יהוה, and יהוה showed him a tree. And when he threw it into the waters, the waters were made sweet. There He made a law and a right ruling for them, and there He tried them.

Exodus 15, cont.
[26] And He said, "If you diligently obey the voice of 𐤉𐤄𐤅𐤄 your Elohim and do what is right in His eyes, and shall listen to His commands and shall guard all His laws, I shall bring on you none of the diseases I brought on the Mitsrites, for I am 𐤉𐤄𐤅𐤄 who heals you." [27] And they came to Elim, where there were twelve fountains of water and seventy palm trees. And they camped there by the waters.

𐤉𐤄𐤅𐤄 Proposes Marriage to Israel!

Exodus 19
[2] For they set out from Rephidim, and had come to the Wilderness of Sinai, and camped in the wilderness. So Yisra'el camped there before the mountain. [3] And Mosheh went up to Elohim, and 𐤉𐤄𐤅𐤄 called to him from the mountain, saying, "This is what you are to say to the house of Ya'aqob, and declare to the children of Yisra'el: [4] 'You have seen what I did to the Mitsrites, and how I bore you on eagles' wings and brought you to Myself. [5] 'And now, if you diligently obey My voice, and shall guard My covenant, then you shall be My treasured possession above all the peoples – for all the earth is Mine – [6] 'and you shall be to Me a reign of priests and a set-apart nation.' Those are the words which you are to speak to the children of Yisra'el." [7] And Mosheh came and called for the elders of the people, and set before them all these words which 𐤉𐤄𐤅𐤄 commanded him. [8] And all the people answered together and said, "All that 𐤉𐤄𐤅𐤄 has spoken we shall do." So Mosheh brought back the words of the people to 𐤉𐤄𐤅𐤄. [9] And 𐤉𐤄𐤅𐤄 said to Mosheh, "See, I am coming to you in the thick cloud, so that the people hear when I speak with you, and believe you forever." And Mosheh reported the words of the people to 𐤉𐤄𐤅𐤄. [10] And 𐤉𐤄𐤅𐤄 said to Mosheh, "Go to the people and set them apart today and tomorrow. And they shall wash their garments, [11] and shall be prepared by the third day. For on the third day 𐤉𐤄𐤅𐤄 shall come down upon Mount Sinai before the eyes of all the people. [12] "And you shall make a border for the people all around, saying, 'Take heed to yourselves that you do not go up to the mountain or touch the border of it. Whoever touches the mountain shall certainly be put to death. [13] 'Not a hand is to touch it, but he shall certainly be stoned or shot with an arrow, whether man or beast, he shall not live.' When the trumpet sounds long, let them come near the mountain." [14] And Mosheh came down from the mountain to the people and set the people apart, and they washed their garments. [15] And he said to the people, "Be prepared by the third day. Do not come near a wife." [16] And it came to be, on the third day in the morning, that there were thunders and lightnings, and a thick cloud on the mountain. And the sound of the ram's horn was very loud, and all the people who were in the camp trembled.

Exodus 19, cont.
[17] And Mosheh brought the people out of the camp to meet with Elohim, and they stood at the foot of the mountain. [18] And Mount Sinai was in smoke, all of it, because 𐤉𐤄𐤅𐤄 descended upon it in fire. And its smoke went up like the smoke of a furnace, and all the mountain trembled exceedingly. [19] And when the blast of the ram's horn sounded long and became louder and louder, Mosheh spoke, and Elohim answered him by voice. [20] And 𐤉𐤄𐤅𐤄 came down upon Mount Sinai, on the top of the mountain. And 𐤉𐤄𐤅𐤄 called Mosheh to the top of the mountain, and Mosheh went up. [21] And 𐤉𐤄𐤅𐤄 said to Mosheh, "Go down, and warn the people, lest they break through unto 𐤉𐤄𐤅𐤄 to see, and many of them fall. [22] "And let the priests who come near 𐤉𐤄𐤅𐤄 set themselves apart too, lest 𐤉𐤄𐤅𐤄 break out against them." [23] And Mosheh said to 𐤉𐤄𐤅𐤄, "The people are not able to come up to Mount Sinai, for You warned us, saying, 'Make a border around the mountain and set it apart.' " [24] And 𐤉𐤄𐤅𐤄 said to him, "Come, go down and then come up, you and Aharon with you. But do not let the priests and the people break through to come up to 𐤉𐤄𐤅𐤄, lest He break out against them." [25] And Mosheh went down to the people and spoke to them.

The Ten Commandments
Exodus 20
And Elohim spoke all these Words, saying, [2] "I am 𐤉𐤄𐤅𐤄 your Elohim, who brought you out of the land of Mitsrayim, out of the house of slavery. [3] "You have no other mighty ones against My face. [4] "You do not make for yourself a carved image, or any likeness of that which is in the heavens above, or which is in the earth beneath, or which is in the waters under the earth, [5] you do not bow down to them nor serve them. For I, 𐤉𐤄𐤅𐤄 your Elohim am a jealous El, visiting the crookedness of the fathers on the children to the third and fourth generations of those who hate Me, [6] but showing kindness to thousands, to those who love Me and guard My commands. [7] "You do not bring the Name of 𐤉𐤄𐤅𐤄 your Elohim to naught, for 𐤉𐤄𐤅𐤄 does not leave the one unpunished who brings His Name to naught.
[8] "Remember the Sabbath day, to set it apart. [9] "Six days you labor, and shall do all your work, [10] but the seventh day is a Sabbath of 𐤉𐤄𐤅𐤄 your Elohim. You do not do any work–you, nor your son, nor your daughter, nor your male servant, nor your female servant, nor your cattle, nor your stranger who is within your gates. [11] "For in six days 𐤉𐤄𐤅𐤄 made the heavens and the earth, the sea, and all that is in them, and rested the seventh day. Therefore 𐤉𐤄𐤅𐤄 blessed the Sabbath day and set it apart. [12] "Respect your father and your mother, so that your days are prolonged upon the soil which 𐤉𐤄𐤅𐤄 your Elohim is giving you. [13] "You do not murder. [14] "You do not commit adultery. [15] "You do not steal.

The Ten Commandments
Exodus 20, cont.
[16]"You do not bear false witness against your neighbor. [17]"You do not covet your neighbor's house, you do not covet your neighbor's wife, nor his male servant, nor his female servant, nor his ox, nor his donkey, or whatever belongs to your neighbor." [22]And ᚨYᚨZ said to Mosheh, "Say this to the children of Yisra'el: 'You yourselves have seen that I have spoken to you from the heavens. [23]'You do not make besides Me mighty ones of silver, and you do not make mighty ones of gold for yourselves. [24]'Make an altar of earth for Me, and you shall slaughter on it your burnt offerings and your peace offerings, your sheep and your cattle. In every place where I cause My Name to be remembered I shall come to you and bless you. [25]'And if you make Me an altar of stone, do not build it of cut stone, for if you use your chisel on it, you have profaned it. [26]'Nor do you go up by steps to My altar, lest your nakedness be exposed on it.'

Israel Accepts Yahuah's Wedding Proposal!
Exodus 24
And Moses came and told the people all the words of ᚨYᚨZ, and all the judgments: and all the people answered with one voice, and said, <u>All the words which ᚨYᚨZ hath said will we do</u>. And Moses wrote all the words of ᚨYᚨZ, and rose up early in the morning, and builded an altar under the hill, and twelve pillars, according to the twelve tribes of Israel. And he sent young men of the children of Israel, which offered burnt offerings, and sacrificed peace offerings of oxen unto ᚨYᚨZ. And Moses took half of the blood, and put it in basins; and half of the blood he sprinkled on the altar. And he took the book of the covenant, and read in the audience of the people: and they said, All that ᚨYᚨZ hath said will we do, and be obedient. And Moses took the blood, and sprinkled it on the people, and said, Behold the blood of the covenant, which ᚨYᚨZ hath made with you concerning all these words. Then went up Moses, and Aaron, Nadab, and Abihu, and seventy of the elders of Israel: And they saw the Elohim of Israel: and there was under his feet as it were a paved work of a sapphire stone, and as it were the body of heaven in his clearness. And upon the nobles of the children of Israel he laid not his hand: also they saw Elohim, and did eat and drink. And ᚨYᚨZ said unto Moses, Come up to me into the mount, and be there: and I will give thee tables of stone, and a law, and commandments which I have written; that thou mayest teach them. And Moses rose up, and his minister Joshua: and Moses went up into the mount of Elohim. And he said unto the elders, Tarry ye here for us, until we come again unto you: and, behold, Aaron and Hur are with you: if any man have any matters to do, let him come unto them.

Exodus 24, cont.
And Moses went up into the mount, and a cloud covered the mount. And the glory of 𐤀𐤉𐤄𐤆 abode upon mount Sinai, and the cloud covered it six days: and the seventh day he called unto Moses out of the midst of the cloud. And the sight of the glory of 𐤀𐤉𐤄𐤆 was like devouring fire on the top of the mount in the eyes of the children of Israel. And Moses went into the midst of the cloud, and gat him up into the mount: and Moses was in the mount forty days and forty nights.

The Sign of the Sabbath
Exodus 31
And 𐤀𐤉𐤄𐤆 spake unto Moses, saying, Speak thou also unto the children of Israel, saying, Verily my sabbaths ye shall keep: for it is a sign between me and you throughout your generations; that ye may know that I am 𐤀𐤉𐤄𐤆 that doth sanctify you. Ye shall keep the sabbath therefore; for it is holy unto you: every one that defileth it shall surely be put to death: for whosoever doeth any work therein, that soul shall be cut off from among his people. Six days may work be done; but in the seventh is the sabbath of rest, holy to 𐤀𐤉𐤄𐤆: whosoever doeth any work in the sabbath day, he shall surely be put to death. Wherefore the children of Israel shall keep the sabbath, to observe the sabbath throughout their generations, for a perpetual covenant. It is a sign between me and the children of Israel for ever: for in six days 𐤀𐤉𐤄𐤆 made heaven and earth, and on the seventh day he rested, and was refreshed. And he gave unto Moses, when he had made an end of communing with him upon mount Sinai, two tables of testimony, tables of stone, written with the finger of Elohim.

Sadly, while Moses was on the set apart Mountain receiving Yahuah's Torah, Israel rebelled!

Exodus 32
And when the people saw that Moses delayed to come down out of the mount, the people gathered themselves together unto Aaron, and said unto him, Up, make us elohim, which shall go before us; for as for this Moses, the man that brought us up out of the land of Mitsrayim, we wot not what is become of him. And Aaron said unto them, Break off the golden earrings, which are in the ears of your wives, of your sons, and of your daughters, and bring them unto me. And all the people brake off the golden earrings which were in their ears, and brought them unto Aaron. And he received them at their hand, and fashioned it with a graving tool, after he had made it a molten calf: and they said, These be thy elohim, O Israel, which brought thee up out of the land of Mitsrayim.

Exodus 32, cont.
And when Aaron saw it, he built an altar before it; and Aaron made proclamation, and said, To morrow is a feast to 𐤉𐤄𐤅𐤄. And they rose up early on the morrow, and offered burnt offerings, and brought peace offerings; and the people sat down to eat and to drink, and rose up to play. And 𐤉𐤄𐤅𐤄 said unto Moses, Go, get thee down; for thy people, which thou broughtest out of the land of Mitsrayim, have corrupted themselves: They have turned aside quickly out of the way which I commanded them: they have made them a molten calf, and have worshipped it, and have sacrificed thereunto, and said, These be thy elohim, O Israel, which have brought thee up out of the land of Mitsrayim. And 𐤉𐤄𐤅𐤄 said unto Moses, I have seen this people, and, behold, it is a stiffnecked people: Now therefore let me alone, that my wrath may wax hot against them, and that I may consume them: and I will make of thee a great nation. And Moses besought 𐤉𐤄𐤅𐤄 his Elohim, and said, 𐤉𐤄𐤅𐤄, why doth thy wrath wax hot against thy people, which thou hast brought forth out of the land of Mitsrayim with great power, and with a mighty hand? Wherefore should the Mitsrites speak, and say, For mischief did he bring them out, to slay them in the mountains, and to consume them from the face of the earth? Turn from thy fierce wrath, and repent of this evil against thy people. Remember Abraham, Isaac, and Israel, thy servants, to whom thou swarest by thine own self, and saidst unto them, I will multiply your seed as the stars of heaven, and all this land that I have spoken of will I give unto your seed, and they shall inherit it for ever. And 𐤉𐤄𐤅𐤄 repented of the evil which he thought to do unto his people. And Moses turned, and went down from the mount, and the two tables of the testimony were in his hand: the tables were written on both their sides; on the one side and on the other were they written. And the tables were the work of Elohim, and the writing was the writing of Elohim, graven upon the tables. And when Joshua heard the noise of the people as they shouted, he said unto Moses, There is a noise of war in the camp. And he said, It is not the voice of them that shout for mastery, neither is it the voice of them that cry for being overcome: but the noise of them that sing do I hear. And it came to pass, as soon as he came nigh unto the camp, that he saw the calf, and the dancing: and Moses' anger waxed hot, and he cast the tables out of his hands, and brake them beneath the mount. And he took the calf which they had made, and burnt it in the fire, and ground it to powder, and strawed it upon the water, and made the children of Israel drink of it. And Moses said unto Aaron, What did this people unto thee, that thou hast brought so great a sin upon them? And Aaron said, Let not the anger of my master wax hot: thou knowest the people, that they are set on mischief.

Exodus 32, cont.
For they said unto me, Make us elohim, which shall go before us: for as for this Moses, the man that brought us up out of the land of Mitsrayim, we wot not what is become of him. And I said unto them, Whosoever hath any gold, let them break it off. So they gave it me: then I cast it into the fire, and there came out this calf. And when Moses saw that the people were naked; (for Aaron had made them naked unto their shame among their enemies:) Then Moses stood in the gate of the camp, and said, Who is on Yahuah's side? let him come unto me. And all the sons of Levi gathered themselves together unto him. And he said unto them, Thus saith ayaz Elohim of Israel, Put every man his sword by his side, and go in and out from gate to gate throughout the camp, and slay every man his brother, and every man his companion, and every man his neighbor. And the children of Levi did according to the word of Moses: and there fell of the people that day about three thousand men. For Moses had said, Consecrate yourselves to day to ayaz, even every man upon his son, and upon his brother; that he may bestow upon you a blessing this day. And it came to pass on the morrow, that Moses said unto the people, Ye have sinned a great sin: and now I will go up unto ayaz; peradventure I shall make an atonement for your sin. And Moses returned unto ayaz, and said, Oh, this people have sinned a great sin, and have made them elohim of gold. Yet now, if thou wilt forgive their sin; and if not, blot me, I pray thee, out of thy book which thou hast written. And ayaz said unto Moses, Whosoever hath sinned against me, him will I blot out of my book. Therefore now go, lead the people unto the place of which I have spoken unto thee: behold, mine Angel shall go before thee: nevertheless in the day when I visit I will visit their sin upon them. And ayaz plagued the people, because they made the calf, which Aaron made.

After the golden calf incident, ayaz gave Moses the Ten Commandments once again!

One More Time
Chapter 34

And ayaz said to Mosheh, "Cut two tablets of stone like the first ones, and I shall write on these tablets the Words that were on the first tablets which you broke. ²"And be ready in the morning. Then you shall come up in the morning to Mount Sinai, and present yourself to Me there on the top of the mountain. ³"And let no man come up with you, and let no man be seen in all the mountain, and let not even the flock or the herd feed in front of that mountain."

One More Time

Chapter 34, cont.
⁴And he cut two tablets of stone like the first ones. Then Mosheh rose early in the morning and went up Mount Sinai, as 𐤉𐤄𐤅𐤄 had commanded him, and he took two tablets of stone in his hand. ⁵And 𐤉𐤄𐤅𐤄 came down in the cloud and stood with him there, and proclaimed the Name, 𐤉𐤄𐤅𐤄. ⁶And 𐤉𐤄𐤅𐤄 passed before him and proclaimed, 𐤉𐤄𐤅𐤄, 𐤉𐤄𐤅𐤄, an El compassionate and showing favor, patient, and great in kindness and Truth, ⁷watching over kindness for thousands, forgiving crookedness and transgression and sin, but by no means leaving unpunished, visiting the crookedness of the fathers upon the children and the children's children to the third and the fourth generation." ⁸And Mosheh hurried and bowed himself toward the earth, and did obeisance, ⁹and said, "If, now, I have found favor in Your eyes, O 𐤉𐤄𐤅𐤄, I pray, let 𐤉𐤄𐤅𐤄 go on in our midst, even though we are a-stiff-necked people. And forgive our crookedness and our sin, and take us as Your inheritance."

Yahuah's people, Israel, have been exhorted time and time again **not** to adopt the ways of the nations! Israel **must reject** Sunday Sabbath, Christmas, Easter, Valentine's Day, and all the other pagan days, which evolved from the worship of the sun, moon, and stars! Israel **cannot mix**, period! Today, these pagan days are special to multitudes of sheep across the earth, but 𐤉𐤄𐤅𐤄 **hates them with a passion**! Israel belongs to 𐤉𐤄𐤅𐤄! Yahuah's appointed times must be our appointed times **by our own free will because we love** 𐤉𐤄𐤅𐤄 **and** OWY𐤄𐤋 **and want to please them, not men**!

Yahuah's Set Apart Days

Perhaps we won't completely understand Yahuah's set apart Days, until we see OWY𐤄𐤋 face to face, when we are brought back into the Promised Land! Then we will fully understand! Until that time we should observe to the best of our ability what the Scriptures teach about Yahuah's set apart Days! Of course everyone on the planet is commanded to observe the weekly Sabbath Day on the seventh day of the week! And the Seven Feasts of OWY𐤄𐤋 are eternal! We are told in the Scriptures that these Days will be observed by every nation whether they like it or not in Yahushua's Kingdom! Yahushua's Seven Festivals are packed with shadows and symbolism of solemn events in Israel's past as well as solemn events still to come in Israel's future! It's also clear that the New Moons are special set apart Days to Israel! The Scriptures testify that the people called Israel should worship 𐤉𐤄𐤅𐤄 in the morning, in the evening, on the Sabbaths, and during the sighting of the New Moons!

Leviticus 23

And אYאZ spoke to Mosheh, saying, [2]"Speak to the children of Yisra'el, and say to them, 'The appointed times of אYאZ, which you are to proclaim as set-apart gatherings, My appointed times, are these: [3]'Six days work is done, but the **seventh day is a Sabbath of rest**, a set-apart gathering. You do no work, it is a Sabbath to אYאZ in all your dwellings. [4]'These are the appointed times of אYאZ, set-apart gatherings which you are to proclaim at their appointed times. [5]'In the first month, on the fourteenth day of the month, between the evenings, is the **Passover** to אYאZ. [6]'And on the fifteenth day of this month is the Festival of Unleavened Bread to אYאZ– seven days you eat **unleavened bread**. [7]'On the first day you have a set-apart gathering, you do no servile work. [8]'And you shall bring an offering made by fire to אYאZ for seven days. On the seventh day is a set-apart gathering, you do no servile work.' " [9]And אYאZ spoke to Mosheh, saying, [10]"Speak to the children of Yisra'el, and you shall say to them, 'When you come into the land which I give you, and shall reap its harvest, then you shall bring a sheaf of the **first-fruits of your harvest** to the priest. [11]'And he shall wave the sheaf before אYאZ, for your acceptance. On the morrow after the Sabbath the priest waves it. [12]'And on that day when you wave the sheaf, you shall prepare a male lamb a year old, a perfect one, as a burnt offering to אYאZ, [13]and its grain offering: two-tenths of an ephah of fine flour mixed with oil, an offering made by fire to אYאZ, a sweet fragrance, and its drink offering: one-fourth of a hin of wine. [14]'And you do not eat bread or roasted grain or fresh grain until the same day that you have brought an offering to your Elohim – a law forever throughout your generations in all your dwellings. [15]'And from the morrow after the Sabbath, from the day that you brought the sheaf of the wave offering, you shall count for yourselves: seven completed Sabbaths, **Shabuoth.** [16]'Until the morrow after the seventh Sabbath you count fifty days, then you shall bring a new grain offering to אYאZ. [17]'Bring from your dwellings for a wave offering two loaves of bread, of two-tenths of an ephah of fine flour they are, baked with leaven, first-fruits to אYאZ. [18]'And besides the bread, you shall bring seven lambs a year old, perfect ones, and one young bull and two rams. They are a burnt offering to אYאZ, with their grain offering and their drink offerings, an offering made by fire for a sweet fragrance to אYאZ. [19]'And you shall offer one male goat as a sin offering, and two male lambs a year old, as a peace offering. [20]'And the priest shall wave them, besides the bread of the first-fruits, as a wave offering before אYאZ, besides the two lambs. They are set-apart to אYאZ for the priest.

Leviticus 23, cont.
²¹'And on this same day you shall proclaim a set-apart gathering for yourselves, you do no servile work on it – a law forever in all your dwellings throughout your generations. ²²'And when you reap the harvest of your land do not completely reap the corners of your field when you reap, and do not gather any gleaning from your harvest. Leave them for the poor and for the stranger. I am 𐤀𐤉𐤄𐤅 your Elohim.' " ²³And 𐤀𐤉𐤄𐤅 spoke to Mosheh, saying, ²⁴"Speak to the children of Yisra'el, saying, 'In the seventh month, on the first day of the month, you have a rest, **a remembrance of blowing of trumpets, a set-apart gathering.** ²⁵'You do no servile work, and you shall bring an offering made by fire to 𐤀𐤉𐤄𐤅.' " ²⁶And 𐤀𐤉𐤄𐤅 spoke to Mosheh, saying, ²⁷"On the tenth day of this seventh month is the **Day of Atonement**. It shall be a set-apart gathering for you. And you shall afflict your beings, and shall bring an offering made by fire to 𐤀𐤉𐤄𐤅. ²⁸"And you do no work on that same day, for it is the Day of Atonement, to make atonement for you before 𐤀𐤉𐤄𐤅 your Elohim. ²⁹"For any being who is not afflicted on that same day, he shall be cut off from his people. ³⁰"And any being who does any work on that same day, that being I shall destroy from the midst of his people. ³¹"You do no work –a law forever throughout your generations in all your dwellings. ³²'It is a Sabbath of rest to you, and you shall afflict your beings. On the ninth day of the month at evening, from evening to evening, you observe your Sabbath." ³³And 𐤀𐤉𐤄𐤅 spoke to Mosheh, saying, ³⁴"Speak to the children of Yisra'el, saying, 'On the fifteenth day of this **seventh month is the Festival of Booths** for seven days to 𐤀𐤉𐤄𐤅. ³⁵'On the first day is a set-apart gathering, you do no servile work.

2 Chronicles 2
Behold, I build an house to the name of 𐤀𐤉𐤄𐤅 my Elohim, to dedicate it to him, and to burn before him sweet incense, and for the continual showbread, and for the burnt offerings morning and evening, **on the sabbaths, and on the new moons, and on the solemn feasts** of 𐤀𐤉𐤄𐤅 our Elohim. This is an ordinance **forever** to Israel.

2 Chronicles 8
Even after a certain rate every day, offering according to the commandment of Moses, on the **sabbaths**, and on the **new moons**, and on the **solemn feasts**, three times in the year, even in the feast of unleavened bread, and in the feast of weeks, and in the feast of tabernacles.

Summary

𝐚𝐘𝐚𝐙 used Moses to lead His people out of the land of Mitsrayim in northwestern Arabia, **not out of Egypt**! This is why so much confusion has existed among scholars concerning the 1st Exodus! Some people even believe that the first Exodus never occurred! Substantial archeological evidence does **not** exist that proves an Israelite sojourn in Egypt for 430 years! The answer is simple! The Exodus occurred from Mitsrayim in northwestern Saudi Arabia just like Scriptures testify, **not Egypt**! The better literal translations of the Scriptures actually record Mitsrayim instead of Egypt! OWYaZ used Moses to lead the Israelites to Mount Sinai in the land of Madyan, which is still located in northwestern Saudi Arabia today! Logically, if Madyan is in northwestern Saudi Arabia and the real Mount Sinai is in the land of Madyan, then we know that the real Mount Sinai is also in northwestern Saudi Arabia! Moses and the Israelites were actually lead by OWYaZ! They followed a cloud by day and a pillar of fire by night! OWYaZ led Israel to Yahuah's set apart Mountain, Mount Sinai! At this Mountain 𝐚𝐘𝐚𝐙 had originally established His promises with Adam! After the Flood, 𝐚𝐘𝐚𝐙 reaffirmed His promises to Abraham, Isaac, and Jacob at Beth El! At the time of the first Exodus 𝐚𝐘𝐚𝐙 married His people called Israel at Mount Sinai! Yahuah's marriage covenant is still in affect for Israel, today, **even though we all have been unfaithful to 𝐚𝐘𝐚𝐙**! HalleluYah! HalleluYah! HalleluYah! 𝐚𝐘𝐚𝐙 spoke His Ten Commandments directly to Israel from the fire that engulfed the summit of Mount Sinai just like He spoke to Moses from the fire of the burning bush! Israel was given the Torah at Mount Sinai! The Ten Commandments are eternal! The thoughts and actions of all of us will be judged by OWYaZ using the Ten Commandments as "**Yahuah's standard**"! Israel is called to worship 𝐚𝐘𝐚𝐙 by observing His eternal set apart days, not man's counterfeit days! It's needless to say, Israel must **not** observe the contaminated holidays, which have pagan origins! Remember clean is clean and unclean is unclean!

The Real OWYAZ
Chapter 9

²*The Spirit of ayaz shall rest upon Him–the Spirit of wisdom and understanding, the Spirit of counsel and might, the Spirit of knowledge and of the fear of ayaz,* ³*and shall make Him breathe in the fear of ayaz. And He shall not judge by the sight of His eyes, nor decide by the hearing of His ears.* ⁴*But with righteousness He shall judge the poor, and shall decide with straightness for the meek ones of the earth, and shall smite the earth with the rod of His mouth, and slay the wrong with the breath of His lips.* ⁵*And righteousness shall be the girdle of His loins, and trustworthiness the girdle of His waist.* YeshaYahu 11

I consider this chapter of *Let My People Go* the most solemn and the most important words that I will ever write! Very important aspects of the 1ˢᵗ coming of OWYAZ as our Passover Lamb have been greatly misunderstood, twisted, and forgotten! We have all misunderstood the real OWYAZ! We have **not** understood what really happened during the last three years of Yahushua's life! Men have manipulated the Scriptures and twisted their meanings to suit their own selfish agendas! To top it all off, men have even renamed OWYAZ! False shepherds gave OWYAZ a name that is **not** even a Hebrew name! In fact, it is a foreign name and a name that's an **abomination** to ayaz! Many lies and errors have become accepted into the traditional religious beliefs about OWYAZ! Men have created an image of OWYAZ that differs greatly from the real OWYAZ! The way OWYAZ has been portrayed has caused people of this world to become blinded to the Truth! The sheep are spiritually asleep because their shepherds have taught them lies, errors, and half-truths! Most of us are ignorant of the life that OWYAZ actually lived and the magnitude of the sacrifices that OWYAZ actually made for us! After reading this chapter, I hope that you will have a new appreciation of the life that OWYAZ was willing to endure for you! If you already love OWYAZ, this chapter will prick your heart and make your love for OWYAZ reach new levels! After you really understand, then your love for OWYAZ will go off the charts!

What Has Changed?

As we have already discussed, the true geographical locations of the "Holy Land" have long been forgotten in the shifting sands of time, after the Romans did their best to erase all memory of its real location! Significant changes in the Promised Land's geography, landscape, and topography have occurred, just as ayaz planned it! The knowledge of the original locations of the set apart cities of Yahudah and even Yahrushalayim was forgotten over many generations!

Even the calendars have been manipulated many times! Significant blocks of time have been lost! The set apart Scriptures have been translated into many languages, but the Hebraic context of the Scriptures has not been preserved in most translations! The Hebraic heritage of the Scriptures was replaced with the Roman Catholic **spin**, which still looms large to this very day! After the Protestant Reformation, many idolatrous traditions were continued by the Protestant denominations even though most of the sheep sitting in the pews were ignorant of the truth! Tremendous amounts of wisdom and understanding have been lost due to translation errors! I believe most were made intentionally, but some may have been unintentional! Religious men throughout history have hunted down, tortured, raped, and murdered righteous men and women, who resisted the false shepherd's efforts to control the sheep of this world! Many attempts have been made to destroy all the old Hebrew manuscripts as well as anything else that would help people understand the Truth about ayaz and OWYaz! Wicked men have destroyed or perverted everything written that could potentially lead men to a knowledge of the real OWYaz! What these wicked men could not destroy, they have altered, twisted, and contaminated! Even the set apart personal names of the Father and the Son have been suppressed for thousands of years by both the Jews and the Christians! How crazy is that? It makes absolutely no sense at all, does it? The names of ayaz and OWYaz **are the only real names by which men can be saved!** It appalls me to think about how many good people are ignorant of these two wonderful names! The names of ayaz and OWYaz are the keys to eternal life in the world to come! They have been intentionally hidden from the trusting sheep of this world! This same situation existed at the time of Yahushua's first coming! The use of the set apart name had been made into a crime of blasphemy by the religious establishment! Many questions need to be reexamined about Yahushua's life in order for us to fully understand what OWYaz really endured! When did the Israelite people expect the Messiah to come? Where did Yahushua's ministry actually occur? What messages did OWYaz teach? And most importantly, why was OWYaz not recognized by the masses of Israel?

When was Yahushua born?

Modern scholars teach that OWYaz came about 2,000 years ago! Most Christian scholars teach that approximately 6,000 years have elapsed, since Adam was created! The people of antiquity believed that the Messiah would come 5,500 years, after Adam fell from Paradise! The 5,500 year milestone for Yahushua's arrival is stated repeatedly in the *Book of Adam and Eve*! Also, *The Book of Enoch* states that OWYaz would come and later ascend in the 6th week!

In *The Book of Enoch* each week was equal to 1,000 years! Early believers absolutely expected the Messiah at the 5,500 year mark!

Book of Adam and Eve

Chapter 3

Concerning the promise of the great five and a half days. 1 ᎪYᎯZ said to Adam, "I have ordained on this earth days and years, and you and your descendants shall live and walk in them, until the days and years are fulfilled; when I shall send the Word (OWYᎯZ) that created you, and against which you have transgressed, the Word that made you come out of the garden, and that raised you when you were fallen. 2 Yes, the Word that will again save you when the five and a half days are fulfilled." 3 But when Adam heard these words from ᎪYᎯZ, and of the great five and a half days, he did not understand the meaning of them. 4 For Adam was thinking there would be only five and a half days for him until the end of the world. 5 And Adam cried, and prayed to ᎪYᎯZ to explain it to him. 6 Then ᎪYᎯZ in his mercy for Adam who was made after His own image and likeness, explained to him, that these were 5,000 and 500 years; and how One would then come and save him and his descendants.

The Book of Enoch

₈And after that in the sixth week **(5,500 years)** all who live in it shall be blinded, And the hearts of all of them shall godlessly forsake wisdom (OWYᎯZ). And in it a man shall ascend (OWYᎯZ) ascends back to His Father); And at its close the house of dominion shall be burnt with fire, And the whole race of the chosen root shall be dispersed.

I believe that OWYᎯZ did in fact come, at the 5,500 year mark from Adam, but you have to decide for yourself! We are currently living in the 8th period of 1,000 years right now! Enoch described the days of man from Adam to the final Judgment! Enoch broke down the days into ten one thousand year periods, which Enoch calls weeks. The final Judgment of OWYᎯZ will take place in the tenth 1,000 year period! According to *The Book of Enoch,* OWYᎯZ will return in the 8th week to render His righteous judgment on the wicked, to reward the Righteous, and to establish His Kingdom on the Earth! What does all this mean? It means that we are currently living in the 8th 1,000 year week right now! **It means that OWYᎯZ is about to return very, very, very soon!**

Where was OWYᎯZ born?

OWYᎯZ was not born in today's Bethlehem in Palestine! OWYᎯZ was born in Beth Lehem in the land of Yahudah, which today is located in the northwestern region of Saudi Arabia, as I have stated over and over in *Let My People Go*! Today the exact site of the town of Beth Lehem lies in ruins!

It's in the sands of northwestern Saudi Arabia just like Yahuah's other set apart cities! Those ruins are waiting just like the rest of creation for the appointed day and the hour, when OWYAZ returns! The Scriptures teach that then and only then will the authentic old places be rebuilt and reinhabited!

Where did Yahushua Minister?

OWYAZ ministered in the cities of the <u>real</u> Promised Land in northwestern Saudi Arabia, <u>not</u> the counterfeit cities that are in Palestine today! Yahushua's ministry did <u>not</u> occur in today's "Holy Land" at all! After Yahushua ascended, Rome completely destroyed the real Yahrushalayim in 135 CE! After they destroyed and plowed Yahrushalayim, the Romans renamed cities in Palestine, after the authentic set apart places in the real Promised Land! Today these counterfeit cities in Palestine are a diversion and a stumbling block to the sheep, who would put their complete trust in them! These counterfeits have been used by religious authorities for centuries to exploit billions of dollars in revenue from spiritually minded sheep! When good people take Holy Land tours to the State of Israel today they will hear, "This is the traditional site...!" That statement is absolutely true! Those are **not** the real sites! **They are traditional sites and they** are cleverly designed **counterfeits**! OWYAZ was raised by Mary and Yosef in Natsareth in the Galil district! The Galil district is located in northwestern Saudi Arabia <u>northeast</u> of Mount Sinai! The Sea of Galilee was sometimes called Lake Kinnesaret, sometimes called Lake Tiberius, sometimes called the Eastern Sea, and sometimes called Yam Suph **(Sea of Reeds)** in the Scriptures! Much of Yahushua's ministry occurred around the cities and towns that surrounded this inland sea. The Sea of Galilee is where Peter, James, John, and Andrew were recruited by OWYAZ! It was a large inland sea, which has long since dried up in northwestern Saudi Arabia! The Sea of Galilee has dried up at the command of AYAZ as have all the ancient rivers in Saudi Arabia! However, satellite imagery and topographical maps clearly show the ancient location of this Eastern Sea! Much of the ministry of OWYAZ occurred in various cities on each side of the Sea of Galilee! Well, what about Mount Sinai? Have the people of Israel seen the last of that set apart Mountain? The temptation of OWYAZ and His transfiguration occurred in the wilderness area of Mount Sinai! Mount Sinai is the mountain where Adam and Hawwah lived, after their fall from Paradise! It was the mountain where Seth, Enos, Cainan, Mahalael, Yared, Enoch, Methusalah, Lamek, and Noah lived, before the Flood! It's the mountain that Abraham, Isaac, and Jacob recognized as the house of AYAZ, Beth El! It's the mountain where Moses saw OWYAZ in the burning bush!

It's the same mountain where Yahuah's pillar of fire led the children of Israel, when they left from Mitsrayim! Mount Sinai is the same mountain where ᴀYᴀZ married Israel and gave His Commandments! Mount Sinai is the mountain where Elijah fled from Jezebel! And it's the very same mountain where Paul journeyed, after his conversion! **When the 7th Trumpet sounds, Mount Sinai is the place where OWYᴀZ will gather all of Israel from every generation for the greatest wedding celebration of all time!** HalleluYah! HalleluYah! HalleluYah!

Who Do the People Say that I Am?

Why was something that should have been so easy, so hard for the people of Israel to see? Why couldn't Israel recognize OWYᴀZ? Why were so many people unable to discern, who OWYᴀZ really was, even though He performed unprecedented supernatural signs and wonders? What was it about OWYᴀZ that confused the people so much? Why was Yahushua's true identity not readily apparent to the vast majority of Israel's sheep, who He encountered? When Satan tempted OWYᴀZ, why was even satan unsure of Yahushua's identity? Didn't OWYᴀZ consistently perform all kinds of increditable miracles? Didn't OWYᴀZ calm the storm on the Sea of Galilee? Didn't OWYᴀZ overpower all the unclean spirits, who He ever encountered? Didn't OWYᴀZ overcome death, when He raised people from the dead? Even after all those miracles, OWYᴀZ still asked His disciples, "**Who do the people say that I Am?" Shouldn't that have been a no brainer?** What's the answer? Selah! Think about those questions as you read on!

Matthew 4   Temptation of OWYᴀZ

Then was OWYᴀZ led up of the Spirit into the wilderness to be tempted of the devil. And when he had fasted forty days and forty nights, he was afterward an hungered. And when the tempter came to him, he said, <u>If thou be the Son of Elohim</u>, command that these stones be made bread. But he answered and said, It is written, Man shall not live by bread alone, but by every word that proceedeth out of the mouth of ᴀYᴀZ. Then the devil taketh him up into the holy city, and setteth him on a pinnacle of the temple, And saith unto him, <u>If thou be the Son of Elohim</u>, cast thyself down: for it is written, He shall give his angels charge concerning thee: and in their hands they shall bear thee up, lest at any time thou dash thy foot against a stone. OWYᴀZ said unto him, It is written again, Thou shalt not tempt OWYᴀZ thy Elohim.

Why was it so hard to discern, who OWYᴀZ was? Weren't the people of Israel expecting their Mashiach? Yes, of course, they were! What kind of Messiah were they expecting?

They were expecting a mighty warrior, who would be reminiscent of Israel's beloved King David! The people of Israel wanted a warrior king, who would restore Israel to its former glory! Of course, David was a brave warrior from his youth, who is remembered for his defeat of Goliath! David became King of Israel, after Saul! He was the one king of Israel, who did it right! Even though David experienced extreme lows, he never forgot ayaz! He subdued all of Israel's enemies and the land of Israel prospered like never before or since during his reign! When OWYaz came, He was not at all what the people of Israel were expecting! YeshaYahu (Isaiah) reported that OWYaz had no form or comliness that anyone would desire him! **From His birth** OWYaz was not handsome or appealing at all! Yahushua's facial features and His bodily form did not make Him appealing to Israel! OWYaz was **not** tall, dark, and handsome from the very beginning of His life! But as you will discover as you read on, Yahushua's appearance got much worse day by day during His earthly ministry! Even the fact that OWYaz was raised in the Galil district did not meet the expectations of Israel for a suitable place for their Messiah to grow up! The Galil district was obviously on the wrong side of the tracks! The religious teachers of Yahushua's day had established false expectations about the Messiah in the people's minds just like they have done today! When ayaz did come, He did **not** match the people's expectations at all! Yahushua's mission was completely misunderstood by nearly everyone, except His remnant, who **did not judge Him by his physical appearance**! OWYaz did **not** come at that time as a warrior king, who would liberate the Jews from Roman oppression! However, when OWYaz returns, **He** will come back as a mighty warrior king, **who will be far, far more glorious that David ever was**! At that time OWYaz will judge the nations and reward Israel! Since the time of the Roman Emperor, Constantine, false shepherds have portrayed OWYaz and His messages in a context that has obscured the real Truth about **Him**! These false shepherds have twisted and confused the understanding of the sheep about their OWYaz! Instead, they have promoted the doctrines of men for their own personal gain!

Yahushua Suffered During His Life and His Death!

Isaiah wrote of a Messiah, who would experience sicknesses and diseases, many sorrows, incretdible pain, and a multitude of rejections. OWYaz **chose** to completely humble Himself **during** His lifetime and then to lay down His life for His sheep on a tree! OWYaz certainly didn't have a sun nimbus over his head! Nor was OWYaz strikingly handsome as pictured in the movies and portraits today!

ОWYƎZ **was not** a blond haired, blue eyed hunk of a man, who captured the hearts of men and women by His physical appearance or His stature! Isaiah makes it perfectly clear that Yahushua's appearance was the **stumbling block** that caused the vast majority of the sheep of Israel to be completely blinded to Yahushua's true identity! What's a stumbling block anyway? Well, a stumbling block is a deterrent or an obstacle in the way! It's something that will cause someone to fall, if you're not paying very close attention! Yahushua's appearance was **extremely undesirable and not pleasing at all even before ОWYƎZ started His ministry!** There's a fragment in *the Dead Sea Scrolls* that seems to describe some aspects of the Yahushua's physical appearance! This fragment describes the Messiah's hair as red! It also states that He had moles and/or freckles! Our society has never approved of red hair, freckles, or moles, has it? It's very, very likely that society back then did not regard those physical characteristics favorably either! If ОWYƎZ did in fact have red hair, it would explain why a Red Heifer without a spot or a blemish was used as a shadow or type for ОWYƎZ in the Scriptures!

Dead Sea Scroll 4Q534

$_1$[...] *of his hand, two [...] a mark.* <u>His hair will be red and he will have moles on [...]</u> $_1$ *and small marks in his thighs. [And after t]wo years, he will know one thing from another. While he is young, he will be like ...[...like] someone who knows nothing, until he* $_5$*knows the three Books [...] Then he will gain wisdom and learn understanding [...] visions will come to him while he is on his knees.* $_1$ *And with his father and ancestors [...] life and old age. He will have wisdom and discretion and he will know the secrets of man. His wisdom will reach out to everyone and he will know the secrets of all living things. All of their plans against him will fail, and his rule over all things will be great.* $_{10}$[...] *his plans will succeed because he is the one picked by* ƎYƎZ *His birth and the breath of his spirit [...] and his plans will last forever.*

Numbers 19

This is the ordinance of the law which ƎYƎZ *hath commanded, saying, Speak unto the children of Israel, that they bring thee a* <u>red heifer</u> *without spot, wherein is no blemish, and upon which never came yoke: And ye shall give her unto Eleazar the priest, that he may bring her forth without the camp, and one shall slay her before his face: And Eleazar the priest shall take of her blood with his finger, and sprinkle of her blood directly before the tabernacle of the congregation seven times: And one shall burn the heifer in his sight; her skin, and her flesh, and her blood, with her dung, shall he burn: And the priest shall take cedar wood, and hyssop, and scarlet, and cast it into the midst of the burning of the heifer.*

Numbers 19, cont.
Then the priest shall wash his clothes, and he shall bathe his flesh in water, and afterward he shall come into the camp, and the priest shall be unclean until the even. And he that burneth her shall wash his clothes in water, and bathe his flesh in water, and shall be unclean until the even. And a man that is clean shall gather up the <u>ashes of the heifer</u>, and lay them up without the camp in a clean place, and it shall be kept for the congregation of the children of Israel for a water of separation: <u>it is a purification for sin</u>.

In addition to this fragment in the Dead Sea Scrolls, the Scriptures describe Yahushua's appearance in great detail, but people have been blinded to the truth for a very long time! Dear ayaz, I pray in the name of OWYaz that **all** those reading *Let My People Go* will understand the truth, after studying your word! I pray that Israel will really understand how much you love them and how much OWYaz suffered for them, even **before** His death on the Passover tree! YeshaYahu asks this question, **"Who will believe our report?"**. Thanks to the false shepherds, most people have **not** taken YeshaYahu's report seriously! Well, it's clear to me that most people have overlooked YeshaYahu's report altogether or they've chosen to believe the false shepherd's reports about OWYaz instead! YeshaYahu clearly reported that OWYaz was not handsome at all! But YeshaYahu went much, much further! YeshaYahu's writings indicate that Yahushua's appearance was not only imperfect from His childhood, but Yahushua's appearance **rapidly** deteriorated as His earthly ministry progressed! Yahushua's appearance became horrible by human standards! YeshaYahu reported that OWYaz became sick and diseased! In fact YeshaYahu reported that ayaz was pleased to make OWYaz **sick**! Yahushua's appearance was the stumbling block that prevented most people from recognizing OWYaz as their long awaited Mashiach! ayaz was looking then just as He is today for sheep, who do not make judgments by outward physical appearances!

John 7
[24] *"Do not judge according to appearance, but judge with righteous judgment."*

ayaz wanted His people to love OWYaz for what He said and did, **not** how He looked! Yahushua's followers loved OWYaz for His inner self and did not judge OWYaz by His **DREADFUL** physical appearance! Isaiah states that Yahushua's appearance was so bad that people **were appalled** at Him! They **hid their faces** and **the faces of their children** from OWYaz! They hid there faces from OWYaz because **they believed that He was UNCLEAN**! The Scriptures report that this rejection hurt Yahushua's heart immensely!

People were **repulsed** and even **terrified** by Yahushua's vile physical appearance! What does all this mean? It means that Yahushua's appearance was **very, very, very bad by every human standard**! As Yahushua's ministry progressed, Yahushua's facial appearance and the condition of His body **steadily deteriorated**! But why did Yahushua's appearance steadily deteriorate? Keep reading and you will understand! YeshaYahu stated that Yahushua's appearance was **marred more than any man's appearance** (Isaiah Chapter 52)! YeshaYahu reported that Yahushua's physical appearance was so bad that **He didn't even appear to be human**! Do you believe YeshaYahu's report? I certainly do!

YeshaYahu 53
Who has believed our report? And to whom was the arm of 𐤀𐤉𐤄𐤆 *revealed? ²For He grew up before Him as a tender plant, and as a root out of dry ground. He has no form or splendor that we should look upon Him, nor appearance that we should desire Him – ³despised and rejected by men, a man of pains and **knowing sickness**. And as one from whom the face is hidden, being despised, and we did not consider Him.*

Most people were immediately **repulsed** and **appalled** by Yahushua's physical appearance! People would hide there faces from OWYƎZ because they did **not** want to look at Him! They would hide their children from OWYƎZ as He passed by in the streets! Many would **mock, jeer, and wag their heads in disgust at Him**! YeshaYahu says that OWYƎZ looked so bad that people believed that **He was stricken or cursed by** 𐤀𐤉𐤄𐤆! I know that this is shocking, **but the Truth is the Truth!** 𐤀𐤉𐤄𐤆 **determined** that His son, OWYƎZ, would have an extremely humble appearance from His birth! 𐤀𐤉𐤄𐤆 **decreed** that OWYƎZ **would contract sicknesses and diseases**, while He was healing everyone, who came to Him! Day by day Yahushua's physical appearance steadily degraded because of the diseased and emaciated condition of His body! The affects of the sicknesses and diseases that OWYƎZ had contracted combined with the physical toll of His severe fasting, caused Yahushua's physical appearance to rapidly deteriorate! OWYƎZ **was absolutely horrible to look at**! In Psalms 22 OWYƎZ said this about Himself, **"But I am a worm, and no man; a reproach of men, and despised of the people!"** OWYƎZ prayed daily for the strength that He would need to overcome the extreme pain, suffering, and rejection that He would face **that day**! Each and everyday was a tremendous struggle for OWYƎZ! But, OWYƎZ was determined to finish the task that 𐤀𐤉𐤄𐤆 had assigned Him, **no matter what**!

When we are in Yahuah's furnace of affliction, we must overcome the troubles of each and everyday just like OWYAZ did! OWYAZ showed Israel how to overcome!

YeshaYahu 53
¹⁰But AYAZ was pleased to crush Him, He laid sickness on Him, that when He made Himself an offering for guilt, He would see a seed, He would prolong His days and the pleasure of AYAZ prosper in His hand. ¹¹He would see the result of the suffering of His life and be satisfied. Through His knowledge My righteous Servant makes many righteous, and He bears their crookednesses.

Progressively Yahushua's appearance degraded day by day! As OWYAZ healed those people, He literally **took their sins upon Himself!** Study the last two verses of YeshaYahu 52 and all of YeshaYahu 53 for yourself! YeshaYahu taught that OWYAZ would experience extreme rejection, affliction, sorrow, suffering, pain, sickness and disease **by first hand experience during His lifetime!** OWYAZ faced all these afflictions **before** He experienced the pain, suffering, and the humiliation of being hung on the Passover tree! OWYAZ **truly was in a body of flesh like ours**! OWYAZ completely understands our struggles! OWYAZ understands because He has first hand experience with our struggles, our sicknesses, our diseases, and our rejections! Yahushua's body **was** clearly made subject to sickness and disease by His own loving father! The Scriptures teach that OWYAZ experienced sickness and disease first hand, not in some mystical symbolic sense! I know that this is new to most people because it doesn't match the popular religious teachings about Jesus! **It's not a portrayal of Jesus that I'm talking about**, it's OWYAZ! OWYAZ is the anointed one of the Scriptures! He's the one that I'm talking about! OWYAZ is the son of AYAZ, the Mighty One of the Heavens and the Earth! OWYAZ is Yahuah's provision for our salvation and **not** some fabrication of man's imagination, **who never even existed!** The Truth is what it is and it must be told, so that the sheep of this present world can understand the depth of what OWYAZ actually suffered for all of us, even before OWYAZ was hung on the Passover tree! It's very painful for me to think about OWYAZ suffering for us the way that I've just described! The thought of all the possible infirmities that OWYAZ may have taken on Himself as He healed **all** the sheep, who came to Him, **just boggles my mind!** The thought of how much OWYAZ suffered physically and mentally **makes me want to cry**! OWYAZ healed everyone, who came to Him for healing! OWYAZ literally took **their** sins and **their** diseases on Himself **right then**, not sometime in the future! When OWYAZ hung on the tree, He took on Himself the penalty for all the sins of all Israel past and future!

OWYAZ **promised** all Israel complete forgiveness of all their sins and the complete salvation of their spirits and their bodies! **Israel's salvation will be perfected and that promise fulfilled, when we see** OWYAZ **face to face!** At the 7th **Trumpet, all of Israel will be BORN AGAIN into glorious incorruptible bodies! Then Israel will be made perfect!** Then and only then will Israel's salvation be complete! Right now, if you love OWYAZ and obey His Commandments, then you have Yahushua's seed planted inside of you! OWYAZ looked to the future and saw all Israel being made perfect, because of His sufferings and sacrifices! I believe that dream of our future with OWYAZ was the dream that sustained OWYAZ countless times during His ministry! As you can imagine, OWYAZ experienced extreme lows, which were brought on by all the misery, pain, rejection, and suffering that He was enduring each and everyday! Those were the times that OWYAZ would retreat to one of His mountains to be alone with AYAZ! **AYAZ was the only one, who completely understood!** AYAZ would encourage and reassure OWYAZ like a good father would! OWYAZ would regain enough strength to face yet another day! Isn't this the same pattern of behavior that sustains all of Yahushua's overcomers today? Isn't the dream of our future glory with OWYAZ the same Hope that exhorts us on to continue each and everyday instead of just giving up? Selah, stop and meditate on how much OWYAZ suffered for you and then you'll realize that your burdens, however large that they may seem right now, are really light in comparison to Yahushua's sufferings! OWYAZ **counted our future rebirth with Him worth all the shame, worth all the suffering, worth all the pain, and worth all the rejection that He carried!** All the called out ones of Israel, since Yahushua's Passover sacrifice, are exhorted to follow Yahushua's example of **patient endurance**! We are to patiently endure! By our endurance we will overcome all sorts of adversities, afflictions, and oppressions! We are to humbly walk by the Torah before AYAZ! We must quietly endure the pain, the suffering, and the rejection that we will experience in our lives because of Yahuah's call on our lives! As painful as it is to hear today, while we are in the midst of our own struggles and afflictions, we are to bear all the rejections, all the sicknesses, all the diseases, all the humiliation, and even **lay down our lives,** if necessary, in order to attain Yahushua's eternal life in the world to come! Then we will truly share in Yahushua's esteem **because we have also shared in His suffering**!

Matthew 10
[38]*"And he who does not take up his stake and follow after Me is not worthy of Me.* [39]*"He who has found his life shall lose it, and he that has lost his life for My sake shall find it.*

Yahuah's Ruach HaQodesh actively works in the hearts of all the called out ones of Israel today! Physical healing now is not out of the question! Pour out your heart to ᗩYᗩZ! Make you petitions to ᗩYᗩZ in the name of OWYᗩZ! Appeal to the mercy and lovingkindness of ᗩYᗩZ! ᗩYᗩZ has not forgotten how to heal! His arm is not too short to save today! When ᗩYᗩZ determines that healing is in our eternal best interest based on His understanding and not ours, then He can and does grant healing today! ᗩYᗩZ is extremely compassionate and very, very, very merciful! ᗩYᗩZ does heal in miraculous ways, which surpasses our understanding! Remember, OWYᗩZ warned us that His way is very narrow and very afflicted! It is a very, very hard way! Yahushua's Way is very afflicted and full of sorrows! That's why so few will travel it! But if we patiently endure all the afflictions, troubles, and hardships like OWYᗩZ did, then ᗩYᗩZ promises that we will not be sorry in the end! All the sheep of the earth, who have experienced personal sicknesses and diseases in their own bodies or worse yet in their own children, must realize that our OWYᗩZ understands perfectly the suffering that sicknesses and diseases bring! OWYᗩZ knows by first hand experience how it feels to be sick with diseases! He came to abolish sickness, disease, and sin because He loves Israel so much! If you or your children are sick today, then pour out your heart to ᗩYᗩZ and ask ᗩYᗩZ to heal you or your children in the name of OWYᗩZ everyday, until you have your answer! ᗩYᗩZ loves mercy and He knows the optimum time to grant your request for the best eternal good of everyone involved! OWYᗩZ hates disease and endured increditable pain in His own body so that sin, sickness, disease, and death would be destroyed forever! HalleluYah! HalleluYah! HalleluYah! Please take the time to look up and translate for yourself (word by word) the meanings of YeshaYahu's passages! The Strong's numbers are inside the brackets. Online search engines like the Blue Letter Bible can make the lookup easy (http://blueletterbible.org/)!

YeshaYahu (Isaiah) 52

Isa 52:14 As many [07227] were astonied (appalled, astonished, stuned)[08074] at thee; his visage [04758] was so marred (disfigurement of face), [04893] more than any man [0376], and his form (appearance)[08389] more than the sons [01121] of men [0120]:

Isa 52:15 So shall he (startle) sprinkle [05137] many [07227] nations [01471]; the kings [04428] shall shut [07092] their mouths [06310] at him: for [that] which had not been told [05608] them shall they see [07200]; and [that] which they had not heard [08085] shall they consider [0995].

YeshaYahu (Isaiah) 53

Isa 53:1 Who hath believed *(trusted)[0539]* our report *(message, instruction)[08052]*? And to whom is the arm *(mighty helper)[02220]* of ᗅᘔᖇᐃ *(Yahuah)[03068]* revealed *(to make known)[01540]*?

Isa 53:2 For he *(OWYᗅᘔ))* shall grow up [05927] before [06440] him as a tender plant *(suckling, babe)[03126]*, and as a root *(lowest part of a thing)[08328]* out of a dry [06723] *(wilderness)* ground *(country, territory)[0776]*: he hath no form *(appearance, countenance)[08389]* nor comeliness *(honor, splendor, majesty)[01926]*; and when we shall see [07200] him, [there is] no beauty *(fair appearance)[04758]* that we should desire *(delight greatly in)[02530]* him.

Isa 53:3 He is despised *(contemptible, scorned, disdained, considered vile)* [0959] and rejected *(made destitute by men, forsaken)[02310]* of men [0376]; a man [0376] of sorrows *(physical and mental pain)* [04341], and acquainted [03045] with grief *(sickness and diseases by first hand experience)* [02483]: and we hid as it were [04564] [our] faces [06440] from him; he was despised *(contemptible, scorned, disdained, considered vile)* [0959], and we esteemed *(prized, esteemed, to be equal to someone, to be taken for granted)* [02803] him not.

Isa 53:4 Surely [0403] he hath borne *(carried, endured)[05375]* our griefs *(sickness and diseases by first hand experience)[02483]*, and carried [05445] our sorrows *(physical and mental pain)[04341]*: yet we did esteem [02803] him stricken *(stricken with disease, plagued with leprosy)[05060]*, smitten *(send judgment upon, punished, smitten with disease)* [05221] of God [0430], and afflicted *(oppressed, humbled, be afflicted, be bowed down)* [06031].

Isa 53:5 But he [was] wounded *(defiled, profaned, pierced, slain)* [02490] for our transgressions *(rebellion against Yahuah)* [06588], [he was] bruised *(crushed, humbled, made contrite, broken)[01792]* for our iniquities *(depravity, guilt, crimes)* [05771]: the chastisement *(discipline, correction, chastening)[04148]* of our peace *(completeness, soundness, health)[07965]* [was] upon him; and with his stripes *(wounds, hurts)[02250]* we are healed [07495].

Isa 53:6 All we like sheep [06629] have gone astray [08582]; we have turned [06437] every one [0376] to his own way *(way of living, way of worshiping)[01870]*; and ᗅᘔᖇᐃ *(Yahuah)[03068]* hath laid [06293] on him the iniquity [05771] of us all.

Isa 53:7 He was oppressed **(harassed, distressed, hard pressed)**[05065], and he was afflicted **(oppressed, humbled, be afflicted, be bowed down)** [06031], yet he opened [06605] not his mouth [06310]: he is brought [02986] as a lamb [07716] to the slaughter [02874], and as a sheep [07353] before [06440] her shearers [01494] is dumb [0481], so he openeth [06605] not his mouth [06310].

Isa 53:8 He was taken [03947] from prison [06115] and from judgment [04941]: and who shall declare [07878] his generation [01755]? For he was cut off [01504] out of the land [0776] of the living [02416]: for the transgression **(rebellion against Yahuah)** [06588] of my people [05971] was he stricken **("nega" transliterated Hebrew word used to describe the leprosy)** [05061].

Isa 53:9 And he made [05414] his grave [06913] with the wicked [07563], and with the rich [06223] in his death [04194]; because he had done [06213] no violence [02555], neither [was any] deceit [04820] in his mouth [06310].

Isa 53:10 Yet it pleased [02654] ayaz **(Yahuah)** [03068] to bruise [01792] him; he hath put [him] to grief **(made OWYAZ sick)** [02470]: when thou shalt make [07760] his soul [05315] an offering for sin [0817], he shall see [07200] [his] seed [02233], he shall prolong [0748] [his] days [03117], and the pleasure [02656] of ayaz **(Yahuah)**[03068] shall prosper [06743] in his hand [03027].

Isa 53:11 He shall see [07200] of the travail [05999] of his soul [05315], [and] shall be satisfied [07646]: by his knowledge [01847] shall my righteous [06662] servant [05650] justify [06663] many [07227]; for he shall bear [05445] their iniquities [05771].

Isa 53:12 Therefore will I divide [02505] him [a portion] with the great [07227], and he shall divide [02505] the spoil [07998] with the strong [06099]; because he hath poured out [06168] his soul [05315] unto death [04194]: and he was numbered [04487] with the transgressors [06586]; and he bare [05375] the sin [02399] of many [07227], and made intercession for the transgressors.

I hope that you are beginning to understand the magnitude of Yahushua's suffering, even before OWYAZ was hung on the Passover tree! Even though the propaganda machine of the "Church" has tried to hide the truth about Yahushua's physical appearance, since the time of Constantine, the Scriptures give overwhelming testimony to the Truth! **Israel must shout the Truth about the real OWYAZ from the roof tops!** This world is full of suffering and diseased sheep!

These sheep don't understand that they have a kinsman redeemer, who completely understands their plight with sickness, disease, suffering, and rejection by **His own first hand experience**! They don't know because they have never been told by the false shepherds! While in His body of **flesh, OWYAZ did not in any way shun the plight of the poor and needy**, but instead OWYAZ chose to experience our suffering to the absolute fullest extent possible, while remaining absolutely faithful to AYAZ! We all have far, far underestimated, what OWYAZ actually endured for us!

What is Leprosy?

Leprosy is a terrible disease, which causes extreme physical and mental pain as it grossly deteriorates and deforms the human body! In Leviticus 13 and 14 AYAZ gave Moses specific commandments concerning the control and cure for outbreaks of leprosy! Today medical science tells us that leprosy is a disease caused by Mycobacterium bacteria, which affects the body's nervous system! The face, eyes, hands, feet, and skin are affected in terrible, terrible ways! Leprosy is progressive, which means the symptoms get worse and worse and worse as time goes by! People, who contract leprosy, are affected both physically and socially! Lepers are ostracized, shamed, humiliated, and often go into hiding, when forced out of their communities! Leprosy is often called "**A LIVING DEATH**" because of the many horrifying effects that it has on the human body. Unless cured, it can leave people grossly deformed and in despair for the rest of their lives.

Face
Leprosy bacilli can enter the mucous lining of the nose, leading to internal damage and scarring. Eventually the damage causes the nose to collapse.

Eyes
When leprosy affects facial nerves, a person loses the blinking reflex of the eye, which eventually leads to dryness, ulceration, and blindness. The cornea can also become numb, so the person doesn't know when dirt or particles cause irritation.

Hands
Leprosy bacilli attack peripheral nerves, leading to a loss of feeling. Lepers lose the automatic withdrawal reflexes which protect against hot or sharp objects. Burns and other wounds become infected and tissues and bones are eventually eroded.

Feet
When leprosy attacks nerves in the legs, it interrupts the communication of sensation in the feet. The feet then become subject to bone damage and deformity through unnoticed wounds and infection. Serious infections can lead to amputations.

Skin
In early stages of leprosy, white or pale patches develop on the skin! These later mutate into severe festering boils and open lesions!

Please take a look at some of the internet images of leprosy! Our Rabbi OWYAZ experienced leprosy and other sicknesses by first hand experience for you and me!

Some Leprosy Images on Internet
http://health.cdwriter.com/c12/p391/images/leprosy_images.html
http://news.bbc.co.uk/2/hi/in_depth/photo_gallery/3401031.stm

OWYAZ is very humble and very, very compassionate! OWYAZ grieved over the condition of humanity and was **perfectly willing to fulfill His destiny to save His Sheep**!

Luke 4
And he came to Nazareth, where he had been brought up: and, as his custom was, he went into the synagogue on the sabbath day, and stood up for to read. And there was delivered unto him the book of the prophet Isaiah. And when he had opened the book, he found the place where it was written, The Spirit of AYAZ is upon me, because he hath anointed me to preach the gospel to the poor; he hath sent me to heal the brokenhearted, to preach deliverance to the captives, and recovering of sight to the blind, to set at liberty them that are bruised, To preach the acceptable year of AYAZ. And he closed the book, and he gave it again to the minister, and sat down. And the eyes of all them that were in the synagogue were fastened on him. And he began to say unto them, This day is this scripture fulfilled in your ears. And all bare him witness, and wondered at the gracious words which proceeded out of his mouth. And they said, Is not this Joseph's son? **And he said unto them, Ye will surely say unto me this proverb, Physician, heal thyself.**

Why did OWYAZ say in verse 23, "Ye will surely say unto me this proverb, **Physician, heal thyself.**" Why did John the Baptist's disciples have to ask OWYAZ, if He was the one, after John had **just** previously immersed OWYAZ at the Jordan at the beginning of His ministry? After OWYAZ had cleansed the men possessed with unclean spirits in the country of the Gergesenes, why was OWYAZ asked to leave the area, when the town's people **saw** Him? Why were they **terrified**?

Why did the woman weep so profusely as she annointed Yahushua's feet and dried them with her hair? Why was OWYAZ **not** immediately recognized by Mary at the tomb, when she had seen OWYAZ alive just three days earlier? Had Mary forgotten, how OWYAZ looked? Why didn't the two followers of OWYAZ recognize OWYAZ immediately, when they walked together on the road to Emmaus? Why didn't Peter and the other disciples, who were fishing in the boat, recognize OWYAZ on the bank of the Sea, until He spoke to them? Weren't they very familiar with Yahushua's appearance? Yes, that was the problem! **They were very familiar with Yahushua's repulsive leprous appearance,** when He was with them! They were **not** used to seeing OWYAZ **whole!** Yahushua's disciples and friends remembered OWYAZ the way He had looked with them during His ministry! OWYAZ was disfigured, emaciated, marred more than any man, and diseased! It was very difficult to recognize OWYAZ without the marring of the diseases and the emaciation! When OWYAZ was resurrected, He was **not** diseased, ugly, or disfigured anymore!

Matthew 8
And when he was come to the other side into the country of the Gergesenes, there met him two possessed with devils, coming out of the tombs, exceeding fierce, so that no man might pass by that way. And, behold, they cried out, saying, What have we to do with thee, OWYAZ, thou Son of Elohim? Art thou come hither to torment us before the time? And there was a good way off from them an herd of many swine feeding. So the devils besought him, saying, If thou cast us out, suffer us to go away into the herd of swine. And he said unto them, Go. And when they were come out, they went into the herd of swine: and, behold, the whole herd of swine ran violently down a steep place into the sea, and perished in the waters. And they that kept them fled, and went their ways into the city, and told every thing, and what was befallen to the possessed of the devils. And, behold, the whole city came out to meet OWYAZ: **and when they saw him, they besought him that he would depart out of their coasts. they were taken with great fear: and he went up into the ship, and returned back again.**

Luke 24
And, behold, two of them went that same day to a village called Emmaus, which was from Yahrushalayim about threescore furlongs. And they talked together of all these things which had happened. And it came to pass, that, while they communed together and reasoned, OWYAZ himself drew near, and went with them. **But their eyes were holden that they should not know him.** And he said unto them, What manner of communications are these that ye have one to another, as ye walk, and are sad?

Luke 24, cont.
And the one of them, whose name was Cleopas, answering said unto him, Art thou only a stranger in Yahrushalayim, and hast not known the things which are come to pass therein these days? And he said unto them, What things? And they said unto him, Concerning OWYAZ of Nazareth, which was a prophet mighty in deed and word before Elohim and all the people: And how the chief priests and our rulers delivered him to be condemned to death, and have crucified him. But we trusted that it had been he which should have redeemed Israel: and beside all this, to day is the third day since these things were done. Yea, and certain women also of our company made us astonished, which were early at the sepulcher; And when they found not his body, they came, saying, that they had also seen a vision of angels, which said that he was alive. And certain of them which were with us went to the sepulcher, and found it even so as the women had said: but him they saw not. Then he said unto them, O fools, and slow of heart to believe all that the prophets have spoken: Ought not the Messiah to have suffered these things, and to enter into his glory? And beginning at Moses and all the prophets, he expounded unto them in all the scriptures the things concerning himself. And they drew nigh unto the village, whither they went: and he made as though he would have gone further. But they constrained him, saying, Abide with us: for it is toward evening, and the day is far spent. And he went in to tarry with them. And it came to pass, as he sat at meat with them, he took bread, and blessed it, and brake, and gave to them. And their eyes were opened, and they knew him; and he vanished out of their sight. And they said one to another, Did not our heart burn within us, while he talked with us by the way, and while he opened to us the scriptures?

Mary at the Tomb
John 20
Then cometh Simon Kepha following him, and went into the sepulcher, and seeth the linen clothes lie, And the napkin, that was about his head, not lying with the linen clothes, but wrapped together in a place by itself. Then went in also that other disciple, which came first to the sepulcher, and he saw, and believed. For as yet they knew not the scripture, that he must rise again from the dead. Then the disciples went away again unto their own home. But Mary stood without at the sepulcher weeping: and as she wept, she stooped down, and looked into the sepulcher, And seeth two angels in white sitting, the one at the head, and the other at the feet, where the body of OWYAZ had lain. And they say unto her, Woman, why weepest thou? She saith unto them, Because they have taken away my Rabbi, and I know not where they have laid him.

And when she had thus said, she turned herself back, and saw OWYAZ standing, and knew not that it was OWYAZ. OWYAZ saith unto her, Woman, why weepest thou? Whom seekest thou? She, supposing him to be the gardener, saith unto him, Sir, if thou have borne him hence, tell me where thou hast laid him, and I will take him away. OWYAZ saith unto her, Mary. She turned herself, and saith unto him, Rabboni; which is to say, Master. **(Mary recognized Yahushua's voice!)** OWYAZ saith unto her, Touch me not; for I am not yet ascended to my Father: but go to my brethren, and say unto them, I ascend unto my Father, and your Father; and to my Elohim, and your Elohim. Mary Magdalene came and told the disciples that she had seen OWYAZ, and that he had spoken these things unto her.

Yahushua shows Himself to His Disciples!

Then the same day at evening, being the first day of the week, when the doors were shut where the disciples were assembled for fear of the Jews, came OWYAZ and stood in the midst, and saith unto them, Peace be unto you. And when he had so said, **he shewed unto them his hands and his side.** Then were the disciples glad, when they saw OWYAZ. Then said OWYAZ to them again, Peace be unto you: as my Father hath sent me, even so send I you. And when he had said this, he breathed on them, and saith unto them, Receive ye the Holy Spirit: Whose soever sins ye remit, they are remitted unto them; and whose soever sins ye retain, they are retained. But Thomas, one of the twelve, called Didymus, was not with them when OWYAZ came. The other disciples therefore said unto him, We have seen OWYAZ. But he said unto them, Except I shall see in his hands the print of the nails, and put my finger into the print of the nails, and thrust my hand into his side, I will not believe. And after eight days again his disciples were within, and Thomas with them: then came OWYAZ, the doors being shut, and stood in the midst, and said, Peace be unto you. Then saith he to Thomas, reach hither thy finger, and behold my hands; and reach hither thy hand, and thrust it into my side: and be not faithless, but believing. And Thomas answered and said unto him, My Master and my Mighty One.

Yahushua's Message

OWYAZ loved and obeyed all of Yahuah's commandments because He loved His Father and desired to please Him! OWYAZ observed the eternal Sabbaths and Festivals, which AYAZ set apart at Mount Sinai! OWYAZ **never advocated**, **condoned**, or **participated** in the mixing of Truth with pagan practices and traditions of men! OWYAZ ate **clean foods** and **did not** submit to the sensual desires of the flesh! OWYAZ **was not** a Greek boy and His name **was not** Jesus! The letter "J" **did not** even exist in any language until hundreds of years later! And of course, OWYAZ **did not** worship the sun, the moon, or the stars!

OWYAZ **did not** observe the Sabbath on Sunday! OWYAZ **did not** observe Christmas, Easter, or Valentine's Day! He **did not** accumulate wealth, nor did He advocate the accumulation of wealth in this **present** world! In fact OWYAZ stated that it is impossible outside of Yahuah's purposes for a person with great wealth to enter His Kingdom! OWYAZ **did not** want to be the king of this present world! OWYAZ flatly rejected that offer, when it was made to Him by satan! OWYAZ **hates** this present world system with all its lustful desires, lies, materialism, and lawlessness! What were the real messages taught by OWYAZ? Yahushua's very **first** recorded teaching is called the Sermon on the Mount! This teaching is extremely important, so we should pay particular attention to what OWYAZ taught **first**! It must **be very, very important**! OWYAZ starts His message by **encouraging** His called out ones **(Israel)**, not only of that time, but for all future generations! OWYAZ knew that all Israel in every generation would need encouragement from Him in order to overcome this world as He did! OWYAZ was well aware of all the afflictions, rejections, and struggles that all His overcomers would face in their future lives as they traveled His narrow Way! The lives of all Yahushua's followers from then to now are destined to be extremely difficult and afflicted! Our lives **will follow the same general pattern as Yahushua's own life**! OWYAZ demonstrated to all of Israel how to **overcome** the struggles and afflictions Israel will face in this present world!

The Sermon on the Mount
Matthew 5

³"Blessed are the <u>poor in spirit</u>, because theirs is the reign of the heavens. ⁴"Blessed are <u>those who mourn</u>, because they shall be comforted. ⁵"Blessed are the <u>meek</u>, because they shall inherit the earth. ⁶"Blessed are those who <u>hunger</u> and <u>thirst</u> for <u>righteousness</u>, because they shall be filled. ⁷"Blessed are the <u>compassionate</u>, because they shall obtain compassion. ⁸"Blessed are the <u>clean in heart</u> because they shall see Elohim. ⁹"Blessed are the <u>peacemakers</u>, because they shall be called sons of Elohim. ¹⁰"Blessed are those <u>persecuted for righteousness</u>' sake, because theirs is the reign of the heavens.

The first eleven verses are very interesting because these verses actually describe the characteristics of the Righteous called out ones, Israel! OWYAZ knew that His sheep would experience a great amount of affliction, rejection, persecution, reproach, sadness, and sorrow in this present world! OWYAZ also knew that His sheep would become very humble, meek, and compassionate! OWYAZ looks for the pure in heart and the peace makers! OWYAZ knew that His sheep would mourn **(cry a lot)** in this present world! Why would the Righteous mourn?

Because we are living in a fallen world in which the Prince of darkness reigns supreme! Error is taught and believed instead of truth! Right is called wrong and wrong is called right! When you think of the millions of good people, who are dying of all kinds of diseases and violence everyday, we should all be drawn to tears! Murder, lust, materialism, deceit, and sexual sin are rampant in this world! Violence is everywhere! The rulers and judges of this world are deceitful, crooked, and have no regard for ᚨYᚨZ or OWYᚨZ and certainly not the people of ᚨYᚨZ! The religious institutions have done everything possible to suppress the **real Truth** in order to perpetuate their religious money making machines! False shepherds have no mercy on their own sheep! Many sheep would listen, if they had a good shepherd! People **are** hungry and thirsty, but are **not** being **feed** the **Truth**! Even the set apart names of ᚨYᚨZ and OWYᚨZ have been replaced, forgotten, and completely disrespected in this present world system! It should greatly sadden you to see the instructions and teachings of ᚨYᚨZ ignored and rejected! We should all cry out for justice and right ruling in this **present world**! We should desire with all our heart for OWYᚨZ to return and set up His Kingdom! Remember, our redemption will not be complete until OWYᚨZ returns with our reward!

Let Your Light Shine!
[12]"Rejoice and be glad, because your <u>reward</u> in the heavens is great. For in this way they <u>persecuted</u> the prophets who were before you. [13]"You are the salt of the earth, but if the salt becomes tasteless, how shall it be seasoned? For it is no longer of any use but to be thrown out and to be trodden down by men. [14]"You are <u>the light of the world</u>. It is impossible for a city to be hidden on a mountain. [15]"Nor do they light a lamp and put it under a basket, but on a lamp stand, and it shines to all those in the house. [16]<u>"Let your light so shine before men, so that they see your good works and praise your Father who is in the heavens</u>.

Yahuah's Instructions, the "Torah"
*[17]"Do not think that I came to destroy the Torah or the Prophets. <u>**I did not come to destroy but to complete**</u>. [18]"For truly, I say to you, till the heaven and the earth pass away, one jot or one tittle shall by no means pass from the Torah till all be done. [19]"Whoever, then, breaks one of the least of these commands, and teaches men so, shall be called least in the reign of the heavens; **but whoever does and teaches them, he shall be called great in the reign of the heavens.** [20]<u>"For I say to you, that unless your righteousness exceeds that of the scribes and Pharisee ,you shall by no means enter into the reign of the heavens</u>.*

Lust and Adultery

²⁵"Be well-minded with your opponent, promptly, while you are on the way with him, lest your opponent deliver you to the judge, and the judge to the officer, and you be thrown into prison. ²⁶"Truly, I say to you, you shall by no means get out of there till you have paid the last penny. ²⁷"You heard that it was said to those of old, 'You shall not commit adultery.' ²⁸"But I say to you that everyone looking at a woman to lust for her has already committed adultery with her in his heart. ²⁹"And if your right eye causes you to stumble, pluck it out and throw it away from you. For it is better for you that one of your members perish, than for your entire body to be thrown into Gehenna. ³⁰"And if your right hand causes you to stumble, cut it off and throw it away from you. For it is better for you that one of your members perish, than for your entire body to be thrown into Gehenna. ³¹"And it has been said, 'Whoever puts away his wife, let him give her a certificate of divorce.' ³²"But I say to you that whoever puts away his wife, except for the matter of whoring, makes her commit adultery. And whoever marries a woman who has been put away commits adultery. ³³"Again, you heard that it was said to those of old, 'You shall not swear falsely, but shall perform your oaths to 𐤀𐤉𐤄𐤅.'

Love your Enemies!

³⁴"But I say to you, do not swear at all, neither by the heaven, because it is Elohim's throne; ³⁵nor by the earth, for it is His footstool; nor by Yahrushalayim, for it is the city of the great Sovereign; ³⁶nor swear by your head, because you are not able to make one hair white or black. ³⁷"But let your word 'Yea' be 'Yea,' and your 'No' be 'No.' And what goes beyond these is from the wicked one. ³⁸"You heard that it was said, 'An eye for an eye and a tooth for a tooth,' ³⁹but I say to you, <u>do not resist the wicked</u>. But whoever slaps you on your right cheek, turn the other to him also. ⁴⁰"And he who wishes to sue you and take away your inner garment, let him have your outer garment as well. ⁴¹"And whoever compels you to go one mile, go with him two. ⁴²"Give to him who asks of you, and from him who wishes to borrow from you, do not turn away. ⁴³"You heard that it was said, 'You shall love your neighbor and hate your enemy.' ⁴⁴"But I say to you, love your enemies, bless those cursing you, do good to those hating you, and pray for those insulting you and persecuting you, ⁴⁵so that you become sons of your Father in the heavens. Because He makes His sun rise on the wicked and on the good, and sends rain on the righteous and on the unrighteous. ⁴⁶"For if you love those loving you, what reward have you? Are the tax collectors not doing the same too? ⁴⁷"And if you greet your brothers only, what do you do more than others? Are the tax collectors not doing so too? ⁴⁸"Therefore, be perfect, as your Father in the heavens is perfect.

Right Motives
Matthew 6
²"Thus, when you do a kind deed, do not sound a trumpet before you as the hypocrites do, in the congregations and in the streets, to be praised by men. Truly, I say to you, they have their reward. ³"But when you do a kind deed, do not let your left hand know what your right hand is doing, ⁴so that your kind deed shall be in secret. And your Father who sees in secret shall Himself reward you openly.

How to Pray
⁵"And when you pray, you shall not be like the hypocrites. For they love to pray standing in the congregations and on the corners of the streets, to be seen by men. Truly, I say to you, they have their reward. ⁶"But you, when you pray, go into your room, and having shut your door, pray to your Father who is in the secret place. And your Father who sees in secret shall reward you openly. ⁷"And when praying, do not keep on babbling like the gentiles. For they think that they shall be heard for their many words. ⁸"Therefore do not be like them, for your Father knows what you need before you ask Him. ⁹"This, then, is the way you should pray: 'Our Father who is in the heavens, **let Your Name be set-apart,** ¹⁰**let Your reign come**, let Your desire be done on earth as it is in heaven. ¹¹'Give us today our daily bread. ¹²'And forgive us our debts, as we for give our debtors. ¹³'And do not lead us into trial, but deliver us from the wicked one – because Yours is the reign and the power and the esteem, forever. Amen.'

Do Not Lay Up Treasures!
¹⁹"**Do not lay up for yourselves treasures on earth**, where moth and rust destroy and where thieves break in and steal, ²⁰but **lay up for yourselves treasures in heaven**, where neither moth nor rust destroys and where thieves do not break in and steal. ²¹"For where your treasure is, there your heart shall be also. ²²"The lamp of the body is the eye. If therefore your eye is good, all your body shall be enlightened. ²³"But if your eye is evil, all your body shall be darkened. If, then, the light that is within you is darkness, how great is that darkness! ²⁴"No one is able to serve two masters, for either he shall hate the one and love the other, or else he shall cleave to the one and despise the other. You are not able to serve Elohim and mammon.

Do Not Worry About Your Life!
²⁵"Because of this I say to you, do not worry about your life, what you shall eat or drink, or about your body, what you shall put on. Is not life more than the food and the body more than the clothing? ²⁶"Look at the birds of the heaven, for they neither sow nor reap nor gather into storehouses, yet your heavenly Father does feed them.

Do Not Worry About Your Life!

Are you not worth more than they? ^{27}"And which of you by worrying is able to add one cubit to his life's span? ^{28}"So why do you worry about clothing? Note well the lilies of the field, how they grow. They neither toil nor spin, ^{29}and I say to you that even Shelomoh in all his esteem was not dressed like one of these. ^{30}"But if Elohim so clothes the grass of the field, which exists today, and tomorrow is thrown into the furnace, how much more you, O you of little belief? ^{31}"Do not worry then, saying, What shall we eat?' or 'What shall we drink?' or 'What shall we wear? ^{32}"For all these the gentiles seek for. And your heavenly Father knows that you need all these. ^{33}"But seek first the reign of Elohim, and His righteousness, and all these matters shall be added to you. ^{34}"Do not, then, worry about tomorrow, for tomorrow shall have its own worries. Each day has enough evil of itself.

The Narrow Gate

^{12}"Therefore, whatever you wish men to do to you, do also to them, for this is the Torah and the Prophets. ^{13}"**Enter in through the narrow gate! Because the gate is wide – and the way is broad–that leads to destruction, and there are many who enter in through it.**
^{14}"**Because the gate is narrow and the way is <u>hard pressed</u> which leads to life, and <u>there are few who find it</u>.** ^{15}"But beware of the false prophets, who come to you in sheep's clothing, but inwardly they are savage wolves.

Why did OWY37 say that the narrow Way is hard pressed or afflicted? In fact, it's so hard that OWY37 said that **<u>few</u>** people will **<u>ever</u>** find it! Sadly most people will travel <u>**the broad way, which appears to be the right way,**</u> but is really a lie, which leads to total destruction! **The wide way is easy, but it leads to sure and complete destruction! Yahushua's messages do <u>not</u> match the messages of prosperity that thousands of false shepherds are teaching their flocks today, do they?** So, who's telling the truth? **Is OWY37 telling the truth or are the false shepherds telling the truth?** Da-a, think about that very carefully! Thousands of false shepherds teach doctrines like, "If you have faith for a break through, then speak it with your mouth and you **<u>will</u>** receive what you desire!" May AYAZ rebuke them! They teach, "If you have **<u>real faith,</u>** then you should never be sick, never be diseased, and that you should be financially prosperous!" These wolf shepherds teach these things even though OWY37 experienced sickness, disease, and lots of struggles in His life! OWY37 **<u>absolutely</u>** taught **<u>against</u>** the accumulation of wealth in this world! **Our lives are supposed to be patterned, after Yahushua's life, aren't they?** Do you know what? <u>**I believe it's the false wolf shepherds, who are lieing**</u>!

False shepherds teach that the life of a Christian should be financially prosperous and healthy at all times! Thousands of false shepherds teach that you can speak into existence blessings **regardless of Yahuah's desires and plans for your life**! Remember ayaz uses struggles to humble us and set us apart to His Way of thinking! All these doctrines are false and **180° out of alignment with Yahushua's real messages**! So, **who's telling the Truth**, OWYaz or those greedy **wolf shepherds**? On the authority of the Yahuah's Scriptures, I say OWYaz is **telling the Truth and the false shepherds are lieing**! OWYaz said that the Way to Eternal life is **hard pressed and afflicted with many troubles**! Many are the afflictions of the Righteous, but ayaz carries them through them all! I have **never** read anything in the Scriptures relating seed time and harvest to financial giving! These wolves in sheep's clothing take the Scriptures and twist them to feed their ravenous appetites for more and more stuff! They never have enough! Where do the Scriptures instruct you to give your money to a preacher's ministry as a seed? Where do the Scriptures say that you will receive a great financial harvest in this world or a financial breakthrough for a planted seed in any preacher's ministry? **These men and women, who are collecting your money, are prime examples of ravenous wolves dressed in sheep's clothing!** They are making **their fortunes** in this present world system by fleecing their sheep! People like me trusted them for years! **I believed they were legitimate, until I really studied the Scriptures for myself because of the hard struggles that I was in! If the false shepherds were really serving OWYaz, then they would be following Yahushua's lead too**! But they don't! **So what does that tell you?** Selah, **you shall know them by their fruit!** These wolves are no better than the wicked Pharisees living during Yahushua's ministry! Please use your common sense and **stay far away from them and their teachings**! They are a trap and a snare for you, **no matter how kind** and **gentle they appear**! **Remember, do not judge by outward appearances!** OWYaz clearly exhorts us **not to accumulate** wealth in his world! So why are these false prophets wealthy? Why are they flying around the world in private multi-million dollar jets, driving luxury cars, and riding $50,000 motorcycles? They are deceiving more and more innocent people to follow the way of Balaam! They are greedy and ravenous wolves, who have **sold out** for fame and fortune! They have gone the way of Balaam! Are these preachers exempt from the instructions of OWYaz? No, they serve a **different** Messiah than OWYaz of the Scriptures! They don't love the names of ayaz and OWYaz! They teach lawlessness from their pulpits! They are imposters! **Where are the good shepherds?**

Good Fruit vs. Bad Fruit

[16]"By their fruits you shall know them. Are grapes gathered from thorn bushes or figs from thistles? [17]"So every good tree yields good fruit, but a rotten tree yields wicked fruit. [18]"A good tree is unable to yield wicked fruit, and a rotten tree to yield good fruit. [19]"**Every tree that does not bear good fruit is cut down and thrown into the fire**. [20]"So then, **by their fruits you shall know them**– [21]"Not everyone who says to Me, 'Master, Master,' shall enter into the reign of the heavens, but he who is doing the desire of My Father in the heavens.

"I Never Knew You, You Who Work Lawlessness!"

[22]"Many shall say to Me in that day, 'Master, Master, have we not prophesied in Your Name, and cast out demons in Your Name, and done many mighty works in Your Name?' [23]"And then I shall declare to them, 'I never knew you, depart from Me, **you who work lawlessness**!' [24]"Therefore everyone who hears these words of Mine, and does them, shall be like a wise man who built his house on the rock, [25]and the rain came down, and the floods came, and the winds blew and beat on that house, and it did not fall, for it was founded on the rock. [26]"And everyone who hears these words of Mine, and does not do them, shall be like a foolish man who built his house on the sand, [27]and the rain came down, and the floods came, and the winds blew, and they beat on that house, and it fell, and great was its fall."

Yahushua's Suffering

Psalms 22 was completely fulfilled concerning Yahushua's life and death! If you have ever experienced rejection and betrayal from a wife, a husband, or even a close friend, then you know it's very, very, very painful! It hurts very, very deeply! The following passage in Psalms gives a good first person description of how OWYAZ felt during His ministry and how He felt as He hung on the tree! However, I don't believe that we have the capability in our hearts and minds **now** to fully grasp the depth of Yahushua's suffering on this earth! Yes, all of Israel will be put into Yahuah's furnace of affliction sometime in their lives, but none of Israel will ever undergo as much rejection, humiliation, affliction, and severe pain as OWYAZ did! OWYAZ was truly the consummate suffering servant! **Does anybody really care? Does anybody really care what OWYAZ endured! Does anybody at all care how OWYAZ felt during His suffering**? It hurts me so much to think about what OWYAZ really endured for me! I can't change, what I've already done! However, I want to finish this life well! Yahushua's physical suffering on the tree was incredible, but when I think about the mental and physical suffering that OWYAZ suffered during His life **before** the tree, it brings me to tears!

Psalms 22

My El, my El, why hast thou forsaken me? Why art thou so far from helping me, and from the words of my roaring? O my Elohim, <u>I cry in the daytime</u>, but <u>thou hearest not</u>; and in the night season, and am not silent. But thou art holy, O thou that inhabitest the praises of Israel. Our fathers trusted in thee: they trusted, and thou didst deliver them. They cried unto thee, and were delivered: they trusted in thee, and were not confounded. But **I am a worm**, and **no man; a reproach of men**, and **despised of the people.** All **they that see me laugh me to scorn**: they shoot out the lip, they shake the head saying, He trusted on **ayaz** that he would deliver him: let him deliver him, seeing he delighted in him. But thou art he that took me out of the womb: thou didst make me hope when I was upon my mother's breasts. I was cast upon thee from the womb: thou art my El from my mother's belly. Be not far from me; **for trouble is near; for there is none to help**. Many bulls have compassed me: strong bulls of Bashan have beset me round. They gaped upon me with their mouths, as a ravening and a roaring lion. **I am poured out like water, and all my bones are out of joint: my heart is like wax; it is melted in the midst of my bowels.** My strength is dried up like a potsherd; **and my tongue cleaveth to my jaws**; and thou hast brought me into the dust of death. For dogs have compassed me: the assembly of the wicked have enclosed me: **they pierced my hands and my feet**. I may tell all my bones: **they look and stare upon me**. They part my garments among them, and cast lots upon my vesture. But be not thou far from me, O **ayaz**: O my strength, haste thee to help me. Deliver my soul from the sword; my darling from the power of the dog. Save me from the lion's mouth: for thou hast heard me from the horns of the unicorns. <u>I will declare thy name unto my brethren</u>: in the midst of the congregation will I praise thee. Ye that fear **ayaz**, praise him; all ye the seed of Jacob, glorify him; and fear him, all ye the seed of Israel. For he hath not <u>despised nor abhorred the affliction of the afflicted</u>; neither hath he hid his face from him; but when he cried unto him, he heard. My praise shall be of thee in the great congregation: I will pay my vows before them that fear him. The meek shall eat and be satisfied: they shall praise **ayaz** that seek him: your heart shall live for ever. All the ends of the world shall remember and turn unto **ayaz** and all the kindreds of the nations shall worship before thee. For the kingdom is **Yahuah's** and he is the governor among the nations.

Matthew 27

He trusted in Elohim; let him deliver him now, if he will have him: for he said, I am the Son of Elohim. The thieves also, which were crucified with him, cast the same in his teeth. Now from the sixth hour there was darkness over all the land unto the ninth hour.

Matthew 27, cont.
And about the ninth hour OWY3Z cried with a loud voice, saying, Eli, Eli, lama sabachthani? that is to say, My Elohim, my Elohim, why hast thou forsaken me? Some of them that stood there, when they heard that, said, This man calleth for EliYah. And straightway one of them ran, and took a sponge, and filled it with vinegar, and put it on a reed, and gave him to drink. The rest said, Let be, let us see whether EliYah will come to save him. OWY3Z, when he had cried again with a loud voice, yielded up the Spirit. And, behold, the veil of the temple was rent in twain from the top to the bottom; and the earth did quake, and the rocks rent; And the <u>graves were opened</u>; and <u>many bodies of the saints which slept arose</u>, And came out of the graves after his resurrection, and <u>went into the holy city</u>, and appeared unto many. Now when the centurion, and they that were with him, watching OWY3Z, **saw the earthquake, and those things that were done, they feared greatly, saying, Truly this was the Son of the Almighty.** And many women were there beholding afar off, which followed OWY3Z from Galilee, ministering unto him:

Mark 15
<u>Save thyself, and come down from the tree</u>. Likewise also the chief priests mocking said among themselves with the scribes, He saved others; himself he cannot save. Let the Messiah the King of Israel descend now from the tree, that we may see and believe. And they that were crucified with him reviled him. And when the sixth hour was come, there was darkness over the whole land until the ninth hour. And at the ninth hour OWY3Z cried with a loud voice, saying, Eloi, Eloi, lama sabachthani? which is, being interpreted, My Elohim, my Elohim, why hast thou forsaken me? And some of them that stood by, when they heard it, said, Behold, he calleth <u>EliYah</u>! (Mighty One 3Y3Z)

The Righteous will Mourn!
Zach. 12
And I will pour upon the house of David, and upon the inhabitants of Yahrushalayim, the spirit of favor and of supplications: and they shall look upon me whom they have pierced, and they shall mourn for him, as one mourneth for his only son, and she will be in bitterness for him, as one that is in bitterness for his firstborn. In that day shall there be a great mourning in Yahrushalayim, as the mourning of Hadadrimmon in the valley of Megiddon. And the land shall mourn, every family apart; the family of the house of David apart, and their wives apart; the family of the house of Nathan apart, and their wives apart; The family of the house of Levi apart, and their wives apart; the family of Shimei apart, and their wives apart; All the families that remain, every family apart, and their wives apart.

Luke 23
Then said **OWYAZ**, *Father, forgive them; for they know not what they do. And they parted his raiment, and cast lots. And the people stood beholding. And the rulers also with them derided him, saying, He saved others; let him save himself, if he be the Messiah, the chosen of Elohim. And the soldiers also mocked him, coming to him, and offering him vinegar, And saying, If thou be the king of the Jews, save thyself. And a superscription also was written over him in letters of Greek, and Latin, and Hebrew, THIS IS THE KING OF THE JEWS. And one of the malefactors which were hanged railed on him, saying, If thou be the Messiah, save thyself and us. But the other answering rebuked him, saying, Dost not thou fear Elohim, seeing thou art in the same condemnation? And we indeed justly; for we receive the due reward of our deeds: but this man hath done nothing amiss. And he said unto* **OWYAZ**, *Rabbi, remember me when thou comest into thy kingdom. And* **OWYAZ** *said unto him, verily I say unto thee, Today shalt thou be with me in paradise. And it was about the sixth hour, and there was a darkness over all the earth until the ninth hour. And the sun was darkened, and the veil of the temple was rent in the midst. And when* **OWYAZ** *had cried with a loud voice, he said, Father, into thy hands I commend my spirit: and having said thus, he gave up the Spirit. Now when the centurion saw what was done, he glorified Elohim, saying, Certainly this was a righteous man. And all the people that came together to that sight, beholding the things which were done, smote their breasts, and returned.*

John 19
And he bearing his stake went forth into a place called the place of a skull, which is called in the Hebrew Golgotha: Where they crucified him, and two other with him, on either side one, and **OWYAZ** *in the midst. And Pilate wrote a title, and put it on the stake. And the writing was,* **OWYAZ** *OF NAZARETH THE KING OF THE JEWS. This title then read many of the Jews: for the place where* **OWYAZ** *was crucified was nigh to the city: and it was written in Hebrew, and Greek, and Latin. Then said the chief priests of the Jews to Pilate, Write not, The King of the Jews; but that he said, I am King of the Jews. Pilate answered, What I have written I have written.*

Summary
One of the harshest realities that **OWYAZ** experienced was the rejection, the disdain, and the contempt that He received from the very people that He came to save! Yahushua's rejection was so extreme that **many people hid their faces from Him**! Why did they hide their faces? **They hid their faces because of Yahushua's repulsive physical appearance!**

The appearance of Yahushua's face and body were marred more than any man's even to the point that OWYAZ **no longer looked human**! Yahushua's severe disfigurement was caused by the diseases, which He had assimilated as He became the **sin bearer** for Israel! Most assuredly those diseases included **leprosy**! As His ministry progressed OWYAZ suffered the penalty for those sheep's sins in His own **flesh**! OWYAZ forgave those sheep's sins and took them on Himself because of His great **chesed** (loving-kindness) and compassion towards humanity!

YeshaYahu 53:4 [4]*Truly, He has borne our sicknesses and carried our pains. Yet we reckoned Him stricken, **smitten** by Elohim, and afflicted.*

Jerome's Latin Vulgate Isaiah 53:4 *vere languores nostros ipse tulit et dolores nostros ipse portavit et nos putavimus eum quasi **leprosum** et percussum a Deo et humiliatum.*

We did esteem him stricken--judicially [LOWTH], namely, for *His* sins; whereas it was for *ours*. "We thought Him to be a **leper**" [JEROME, *Vulgate*], **leprosy** being the direct divine judgment for guilt.

Douay Rheims Bible Isaiah *53:4 Surely he hath borne our infirmities and carried our sorrows: and we have thought him as it were a **leper**, and as one struck by god (**should be** AYAZ) and afflicted.*

Amplified Bible Isaiah *53:4 Surely He has borne our griefs (sicknesses, weaknesses, and distresses) and carried our sorrows and pains [of punishment], yet we [ignorantly] considered Him stricken, smitten, and afflicted by god (**should be** AYAZ) [as if with **leprosy**].*[(]

The transliterated Hebrew words "naga" used in Isaiah 53:4 and "nega", used in Isaiah 53:8 are used almost exclusively in the Scriptures to describe the plague of leprosy! Nega (Neh'-gah, Strong's #5161) and naga (Na-gah', Strongs # 5060) are used repeatedly in the Scriptures in connection with being stricken or plagued with the marks of leprosy! Initially leprosy manifests itself as light spots or marks on the skin, which later evolve into severe festering boils! Leprosy causes the hands and feet to become severely clawed, knurled, and disfigured! Fingers and toes get shorter because of the bone loss and appear **pitifully** distorted! The face and the eyes are severely deformed as the nose sinks into distorted facial muscles, which eventually leads to blindness! **Before the time of Constantine**, the followers of Yahushua's narrow Way were well aware that the appearance of OWYAZ was extremely repulsive, even to the point that OWYAZ did not look human, just as YeshaYahu prophesied! However, after Constantine, OWYAZ was pictured by the "Church" as having the ideal or perfect **Greek** physical beauty! Of course, **that image is completely opposite of the TRUTH**, but the image of ideal Greek beauty is still how "Jesus" is typically pictured today!

Well, there's the old **switch-r-rue** again and, if you notice, Constantine always seems to be a **ring leader**! What a wicked man Constantine was! The Scriptures tell us that ayaz was pleased to lay sickness on His only begotten Son, OWYaZ! Even though OWYaZ knew that people were judging Him by His awful outward appearance, the reality of that **rejection still pierced His heart**! **Israel's rejection literally broke His heart**! The times recorded in the Scriptures, when OWYaZ retreated to one of His Mountains to pray to His Father, were the very times, when OWYaZ Himself needed to be embraced and strengthened by ayaz! OWYaZ knew that ayaz would <u>not</u> reject **Him and would <u>not</u> hide His face from Him**! I don't have the words to describe so great a deliverer and so great a salvation as we have in our OWYaZ! HalleluYah! HalleluYah! HalleluYah! Thank you OWYaZ so, so much! Many people hid their faces from OWYaZ during His earthly ministry! Since then it's been Yahuah's turn to hide His face from us! OWYaZ, the face of ayaz, has been hidden from all of Israel, since He ascened back up to the heavenly Mount Zion! OWYaZ will remain hidden from us until He returns to reward Israel and to judge the wicked! This is all very soon to come! Get ready!

Tribulation of the Righteous
Chapter 10

²⁸*And we know that all matters work together for good to those who love Elohim, to those who are called according to His purpose. ²⁹Because those whom He knew before-hand, He also ordained beforehand to be conformed to the likeness of His Son, for Him to be the first-born among many brothers.* (Romans) 8

From the time of Yahushua's death on the tree until the sounding of the 7th Trumpet, all the overcomers of Israel will suffer a lot of troubles, afflictions, sicknesses, persecution, oppression, trials, and hardships in this present world! Believe it or not that is what the Scriptures teach! OWYƎZ warned that His narrow way is very hard pressed and very afflicted. Since the time of the Messiah's death on the tree, all His called out ones have suffered affliction, oppression, persecution, rejection, sickness, disease, testing, and all kinds of troubles! It's not a question of whether we will suffer in Yahuah's furnace of affliction! The question is how we will react to the heat, when we are in Yahuah's furnace! We are to follow Yahushua's model for righteous living even in the midst of struggles and afflictions! The "tribulation of the Righteous" has been going on for a very long time! The tribulation of the Righteous will become more and more intense! It will peak in the last 3½ years before the 7th Trumpet is sounded! When the 7th Trumpet sounds, the suffering will be over! The Scriptures teach that the tribulation of the Righteous will end, when OWYƎZ returns to judge the world and reward the Righteous at the 7th Trumpet! The Scriptures instruct the Righteous not to envy the wicked, but to continue doing well, even when unjustly persecuted and afflicted! The wicked appear to have wonderful lives full of this world's material pleasures! They seem to experience very little sickness, affliction, and trouble! However, the tribulation of the sinners will come on the Day of ƎYƎZ and the tables will turn! When OWYƎZ comes back at the sounding of the 7th Trumpet, then He will reward the Righteous and judge the wicked! That's when the wicked will experience the "Tribulation of the Sinners"! The seven Trumpet judgments are progressive and are designed to evoke repentance from sheep still ensnared in apostasy! ƎYƎZ is so merciful! But why must the called out ones of Israel suffer so much now? Why do so many bad things seem to happen to such very good people? There **is a curse attached to sin!** Yahuah's judgment **starts** with the people, who ƎYƎZ calls Israel! Yahuah's reasoning and His ways are **exponentially** higher than ours! Israel will overcome by patient endurance, while remaining faithful and true to ƎYƎZ!

Sometimes we cannot see an answer, but in the end, if we endure, then all our questions will be answered! We will not be sorry for following OWYAZ! AYAZ uses struggles and extreme hardships in this life to make huge improvements in our character! They are the catalysts that AYAZ uses to humble Israel and to draw Israel to Himself!

Romans 8

The Spirit itself beareth witness with our spirit, that we are the children of AYAZ: And if children, then heirs; heirs of AYAZ, and joint-heirs with the Messiah; if so be that we suffer with him, that we may be also glorified together. For I reckon that the sufferings of this present time are not worthy to be compared with the glory which shall be revealed in us. For the earnest expectation of the creature waiteth for the manifestation of the sons of AYAZ. For the creature was made subject to vanity, not willingly, but by reason of him who hath subjected the same in hope, Because the creature itself also shall be delivered from the bondage of corruption into the glorious liberty of the children of AYAZ. For we know that the whole creation groaneth and travaileth in pain together until now. And not only they, but ourselves also, which have the first fruits of the Spirit, even we ourselves groan within ourselves, waiting for the adoption, to wit, the redemption of our body. For we are saved by hope: but hope that is seen is not hope: for what a man seeth, why doth he yet hope for? But if we hope for that we see not, then do we with patience wait for it. Likewise the Spirit also helpeth our infirmities: for we know not what we should pray for as we ought: but the Spirit itself maketh intercession for us with groanings which cannot be uttered. And he that searcheth the hearts knoweth what is the mind of the Spirit, because he maketh intercession for the saints according to the will of AYAZ. And we know that all things work together for good to them that love AYAZ, to them who are the called according to his purpose. For whom he did foreknow, he also did predestinate to be conformed to the image of his Son, that he might be the firstborn among many brethren. Moreover whom he did predestinate, them he also called: and whom he called, them he also justified: and whom he justified, them he also glorified. What shall we then say to these things? If AYAZ be for us, who can be against us? He that spared not his own Son, but delivered him up for us all, how shall he not with him also freely give us all things? Who shall lay any thing to the charge of AYAZ's elect? It is AYAZ that justifieth. Who is he that condemneth? It is the Messiah that died, yea rather, that is risen again, who is even at the right hand of AYAZ, who also maketh intercession for us.

Romans 8, cont.
Who shall separate us from the love of the Messiah? <u>shall tribulation, or distress, or persecution, or famine, or nakedness, or peril, or sword</u>? As it is written, For thy sake we are killed all the day long; we are accounted as sheep for the slaughter. Nay, in all these things **we are more than conquerors through him that loved us.** For I am persuaded, that neither death, nor life, nor angels, nor principalities, nor powers, nor things present, nor things to come, Nor height, nor depth, nor any other creature, shall be able to separate us from the love of ᴀYᴀZ, which is in Messiah OWYᴀZ our Savior.

Once a person, who ᴀYᴀZ calls is totally humbled, then they become <u>really</u> hungry to learn the Truth! To Israel the pursuit of wisdom and understanding is a matter of life and death! These people are beginning a quest to discover Yahuah's Truth! The people of ᴀYᴀZ develop an extreme love for the truth as well as a complete disgust for the lies that previously enslaved them! Some of the people of ᴀYᴀZ go from denomination to denomination still trying to find the Truth in churches! Many sheep become complacent in churches! The sheep depend on the preacher to teach them all they need to know in 25 minutes every Sunday! The sheep's learning capacity is stifled with only a 25 minute sermon on Sunday morning! However, there is a small remnant of people, who will <u>finally</u> realize that the complete Truth does <u>not</u> lie in traditional churches! These people have <u>great</u> courage! They are being lead by the Yahuah's Ruach HaQodesh to go back to the old ways and to discover things that have been lost and hidden in the religious systems of man for a very long time! These people will discover that they have a great love for the Torah! They will begin to understand what righteousness is really all about! These Righteous overcomers, who ᴀYᴀZ calls Israel, will make a lot of changes in their lives over time in order to align themselves with Yahuah's Torah! Very early in their journey, these called out ones will begin to experience troubles, hardships, and afflictions! These troubles will escalate at an alarming rate! Israel will experience rejection and usually some form of persecution from close family members, friends, as well as constant oppression from the outright wicked! Israel will feel great sorrow for the condition of this world and the deception that has trapped so many good people! That sorrow will make the people of Israel mourn! Israel's chief desire will be the return of OWYᴀZ and the establishment of His kingdom!

Hebrews 10
But call to remembrance the former days, in which, <u>after ye were illuminated, ye endured a great fight of afflictions</u>; Partly, whilst ye were made a gazing stock both by <u>reproaches</u> and <u>afflictions</u>; and partly, whilst ye became companions of them that were so used.

Hebrews 10, cont.

For ye had compassion of me in my bonds, and took joyfully the spoiling of your goods, knowing in yourselves that ye have in heaven a better and an enduring substance. Cast not away therefore your confidence, which hath great recompense of reward. For ye have need of <u>patience</u>, that, after ye have done the will of **ayaz**, ye might receive the promise. For yet a little while, and he that shall come will come, and will not tarry. Now the just shall live by faith: but if any man draw back, my soul shall have no pleasure in him. But we are not of them who draw back unto perdition; but of them that believe to the saving of the soul.

ayaz has ordained that His called out ones **will** follow in the footsteps of **OWYaZ**! They will experience the same types of struggles that **OWYaZ** experienced, but in much smaller doses! **OWYaZ** experienced incredible struggles, afflictions, and rejections, while He was on the earth and the called out ones of Israel will experience those types of things too! **OWYaZ** overcame them all by the power of **ayaz** and the remnant of Israel will do the same thing! **OWYaZ** suffered all these troubles without complaining or turning away from His assigned mission! **OWYaZ** was the consummate suffering servant of **ayaz** and He was a <u>model</u> son! **OWYaZ** is our savior and our example for patient endurance! If you truly love **OWYaZ** and want to enter into His narrow gate, then you <u>must follow Yahushua's lead</u>! You must be willing to suffer and endure all types of hardships for Yahushua's name! You must ask **OWYaZ** to give you His wisdom and understanding in the midst of your struggles! If you are sincere, **OWYaZ** will do it! When you determine to follow **OWYaZ**, it will take great courage! It will involve many personal sacrifices in the short term! **Yahushua's Way is very hard and afflicted and it involves many troubles and afflictions**! <u>Few</u> will find it because <u>few</u> <u>choose</u> to travel that Way!

2 Corinthians

We are **troubled on every side**, yet not distressed; we are **perplexed**, but not in despair; **Persecuted**, but not forsaken; **cast down**, but not destroyed; Always bearing about in the body the dying of the Master **OWYaZ**, that the life also of **OWYaZ** might be made manifest in our body. For we which live are always delivered unto death for **OWYaZ** sake, that the life also of **OWYaZ** might be made manifest in our mortal flesh. So then death worketh in us, but life in you. We having the same spirit of faith, according as it is written, I believed, and therefore have I spoken; we also believe, and therefore speak; Knowing that he which raised up the Master **OWYaZ** shall raise up us also by **OWYaZ**, and shall present us with you.

2 Corinthians, cont.

For all things are for your sakes, that the abundant favor might through the thanksgiving of many redound to the glory of **ayaz**. *For which cause we faint not; but though our outward man perish, yet the inward man is renewed day by day. For our light <u>affliction</u>, which is but <u>for a moment</u>, worketh for us a <u>far more exceeding and eternal weight of glory</u>; While we look not at the things which are seen, but at the things which are not seen: for the things which are seen are temporal; but the things which are not seen are eternal.*

I know that everything that I have said <u>is very hard to swallow</u>! Suffering is not popular or pleasant! However, while not pleasant or popular, study will reveal it to be an important part of Yahushua's Narrow Way! If we want to be found perfect, when **OWYaZ** comes, then we must go where **OWYaZ** went! We must experience a little of the suffering that He experienced! We must endure it, while still living righteously in the midst of it! We must be willing to lose our life in this present world in order to gain Yahushua's eternal life! Keep your mind set on Yahushua's rewards, which are coming to the Righteous, when **OWYaZ** returns! At that time you will experience Yahuah's Sabbath Day's rest! Then all your pain and suffering will no longer come to your mind! You won't be sorry! Act now and don't be double minded! Be a valiant man, woman, or young person for **OWYaZ**! Make your life count now before **OWYaZ** returns, while there is still time! If you can grasp the Truth, wash your garments now! Then you may be set apart as a First Fruit of **OWYaZ**! Most of the preachers today don't like to talk about suffering with **OWYaZ**, do they? These false shepherds teach <u>smooth</u> things! They teach prosperity, prosperity, and more prosperity because prosperity messages are popular with their sheep! Some things never change, do they? The more people there are in a congregation, the more material rewards there will be for the false shepherds! The sheep will pack the pews to hear smooth talk that will tickle their ears! The false shepherds say that this suffering business is "silly and just plain stupid"! They say that teaching about suffering with **OWYaZ** is "<u>gloom</u> and <u>doom</u>" teaching! These preachers will exhort you to choose to be prosperous and to practice their doctrines of "seedtime and harvest"! What a crock that is! They want you to partner with them by giving your hard earned money to <u>their</u> ministry, so that they can live their rich and famous lifestyles <u>at your expense</u>! These preachers will promise you a <u>breakthrough</u>, but it never comes! They can't support their doctrines in the Scripture without twisting the Truth! Those preachers have traded the Truth of the Scriptures for a lie! It's the same lie that Balaam traded his soul for and it's the same lie that Nimrod taught, after the flood! Balaam got his breakthrough, but it cost him eternal life!

Yahushua Warned Us!
Chapter 11

And my cry was in His ears. ⁸"And the earth shook and trembled, The foundations of the heavens were troubled, Because He was wroth. ⁹"Smoke went up from His nostrils, And devouring fire from His mouth; Coals were kindled by it. ¹⁰"And He bowed the heavens and came down, And thick darkness was under His feet. ¹¹"And He rode upon a kerub, and flew, And was seen upon the wings of the wind. ¹²"And He put darkness around Him as booths, Darkness of waters, thick clouds. ¹³"From the brightness before Him Coals of fire were kindled. ¹⁴"ayaz thundered from the heavens, And the Most High sent forth His voice. ¹⁵"And He sent out arrows and scattered them, Lightning, and confused them.
2 Shemu'El (Samuel) 22

The first time OWYAZ came, He came to offer Himself for the people of this world as Israel's Passover Lamb! On the Day of AYAZ, OWYAZ will return at the sounding of the 7th Trumpet to gather all Israel and to judge the wicked and the unrepentant! The First Fruits of Israel will be trapped in the real Yahrushalayim, which will be sacked by the armies of the resurrected Nimrod! The beast and his monstrous army are ready to destroy the First Fruits of Israel! However, at the 7th Trumpet blast, OWYAZ will come riding on the clouds to judge the wicked, to reward Israel, and to establish His kingdom! At that time OWYAZ will officially establish His Kingdom on the Earth! OWYAZ told His disciples that He will gather all His people to Himself, when He returns to deliver Yahrushalayim at the 7th Trumpet! There are many, many Scripture passages that focus on the end time regathering of Yahushua's people! OWYAZ discussed His return and the signs that would precede His coming! He gave an overview of these events to His disciples on the Mount of Olives! Yahushua's conversation was documented in Matthew 24, Mark 13, and Luke 21! Two or three witnesses prove a thing! Study Yahushua's answers to his disciples questions! It's a great place to begin your study about Israel's Final Exodus!

Matthew 24
Verily I say unto you, There shall not be left here one stone upon another, that shall not be thrown down. And as he sat upon the mount of Olives, the disciples came unto him privately, saying, Tell us, when shall these things be? And what shall be the sign of thy coming, and of the end of the world? And OWYAZ answered and said unto them, Take heed that no man deceive you. For many shall come in my name, saying, I am the Messiah; and shall deceive many.

Matthew 24, cont.
And ye shall hear of wars and rumors of wars: see that ye be not troubled: for all these things must come to pass, but the end is not yet. For nation shall rise against nation, and kingdom against kingdom: and there shall be famines, and pestilences, and earthquakes, in divers places. All these are the beginning of sorrows. Then shall they deliver you up to be afflicted, and shall kill you: and ye shall be hated of all nations for my name's sake. And then shall many be offended, and shall betray one another, and shall hate one another. And many false prophets shall rise, and shall deceive many. And because iniquity shall abound, the love of many shall wax cold. But he that shall endure unto the end, the same shall be saved. And this gospel of the kingdom shall be preached in all the world for a witness unto all nations; and then shall the end come. When ye therefore shall see the abomination of desolation, spoken of by Daniel the prophet, stand in the holy place, (whoso readeth, let him understand:) Then let them which be in Judaea flee into the mountains: Let him which is on the housetop not come down to take any thing out of his house: Neither let him which is in the field return back to take his clothes. And woe unto them that are with child, and to them that give suck in those days! But pray ye that your flight be not in the winter, neither on the sabbath day: For then shall be great tribulation, such as was not since the beginning of the world to this time, no, nor ever shall be. And except those days should be shortened, there should no flesh be saved: but for the elect's sake those days shall be shortened. Then if any man shall say unto you, Lo, here is the Messiah, or there; believe it not. For there shall arise false messiahs, and false prophets, and shall shew great signs and wonders; insomuch that, if it were possible, they shall deceive the very elect. Behold, I have told you before. Wherefore if they shall say unto you, Behold, he is in the desert; go not forth: behold, he is in the secret chambers; believe it not. For as the lightning cometh out of the east, and shineth even unto the west; so shall also the coming of the Son of man be. For wheresoever the carcass is, there will the eagles be gathered together. Immediately after the tribulation **(of the Righteous)** of those days shall the <u>sun be darkened</u>, and the <u>moon shall not give her light</u>, and the <u>stars shall fall from heaven</u>, and the powers of the <u>heavens shall be shaken</u>: And then shall appear the <u>sign</u> of the Son of man in heaven: and then shall <u>all the tribes of the earth mourn</u>, and they <u>shall see the Son of man coming in the clouds</u> of heaven with power and great glory. And he shall send his angels **(messengers, emissaries)** with a great sound of a <u>trumpet</u> **(the 7th Trumpet)** and they <u>shall gather together his elect</u> from the <u>four winds</u>, from one end of heaven to the other.

Mark 13
And as he went out of the temple, one of his disciples saith unto him, Rabbi, see what manner of stones and what buildings are here! And **OWYƎZ** *answering said unto him, Seest thou these great buildings?* <u>there shall not be left one stone upon another</u>, *that shall not be thrown down.* **(What does this statement by Yahushua tell you about the Wailing Wall?)** *And as he sat upon the mount of Olives over against the temple, Kepha and James and John and Andrew asked him privately, Tell us, when shall these things be? And what shall be the sign when all these things shall be fulfilled? And* **OWYƎZ** *answering them began to say, Take heed lest any man deceive you: For many shall come in my name, saying, I am the Messiah; and shall deceive many.* **(apostasy, false shepherds)** *And when ye shall hear of wars and rumors of wars, be ye not troubled: for such things must needs be; but the end shall not be yet. For nation shall rise against nation, and kingdom against kingdom: and there shall be earthquakes in divers places, and there shall be famines and troubles: these are the beginnings of sorrows.* **(Birth pangs of the Messiah)** *But take heed to yourselves: for they shall deliver you up to councils; and in the synagogues ye shall be beaten: and ye shall be brought before rulers and kings for my sake, for a testimony against them. And the gospel must first be published among all nations. But when they shall lead you, and deliver you up, take no thought beforehand what ye shall speak, neither do ye premeditate: but whatsoever shall be given you in that hour, that speak ye: for it is not ye that speak, but the Holy Spirit. Now the brother shall betray the brother to death, and the father the son; and children shall rise up against their parents, and shall cause them to be put to death. And ye shall be hated of all men for my name's sake: but he that shall endure unto the end, the same shall be saved. But when ye shall see the abomination of desolation, spoken of by Daniel the prophet, standing where it ought not,* **(Nimrod and His army of winged abominations standing in the conquered Yahrushalayim)** *then let them that be in Judaea flee to the mountains: And let him that is on the housetop not go down into the house, neither enter therein, to take any thing out of his house: And let him that is in the field not turn back again for to take up his garment. But woe to them that are with child, and to them that give suck in those days! And pray ye that your flight be not in the winter. For in those days shall be affliction, such as was not from the beginning of the creation which* **ƎYƎZ** *created unto this time, neither shall be. And except that* **ƎYƎZ** *had shortened those days, no flesh should be saved: but for the elect's sake, whom he hath chosen, he hath shortened the days. And then if any man shall say to you, Lo, here is the Messiah; or, lo, he is there; believe him not:*

Mark 13, cont.
For false Messiahs and <u>false prophets</u> shall rise, and shall shew signs and wonders, to seduce, if it were possible, <u>even</u> <u>the</u> <u>elect</u>. But take ye heed: behold, I have foretold you all things. But in those days, after that tribulation **(of the Righteous)**, the <u>sun</u> <u>shall be darkened</u>, and the <u>moon</u> shall <u>not</u> <u>give her light</u>, And the <u>stars</u> of heaven <u>shall fall</u>, and the powers that are in <u>heaven</u> shall be <u>shaken</u>. And then **(at the sound of the 7th Trumpet)** shall they see the Son of man coming in the clouds with great power and glory. And then shall he send his angels **(messengers, emissaries)**, and shall <u>gather</u> <u>together his elect</u> from <u>the four winds</u>, from the uttermost part of the earth to the uttermost part of heaven.

Luke 21
And he looked up, and saw the rich men casting their gifts into the treasury. And he saw also a certain poor widow casting in thither two mites. And he said, Of a Truth I say unto you, that this poor widow hath cast in more than they all: For all these have of their abundance cast in unto the offerings to Elohim: but she of her penury hath cast in all the living that she had. And as some spake of the temple, how it was adorned with goodly stones and gifts, he said, As for these things which ye behold, the days will come, in the which there shall <u>not be left one stone upon another</u>, that shall not be thrown down. And they asked him, saying, Master, but when shall these things be? And what sign will there be when these things shall come to pass? And he said, Take heed that ye be not deceived: for many shall come in my name, saying, I am the Messiah; and the time draweth near: go ye not therefore after them. But when ye shall hear of wars and commotions, be not terrified: for these things must first come to pass; but the end is not by and by. Then said he unto them, Nation shall rise against nation, and kingdom against kingdom: And great earthquakes shall be in divers places, and famines, and pestilences; and fearful sights and great signs shall there be from heaven. But before all these, they shall lay their hands on you, and persecute you, delivering you up to the synagogues, and into prisons, being brought before kings and rulers for my name's sake. And it shall turn to you for a testimony. Settle it therefore in your hearts, not to meditate before what ye shall answer: For I will give you a mouth and wisdom, which all your adversaries shall not be able to gainsay nor resist. And ye shall be betrayed both by parents, and brethren, and kinsfolk, and friends; and some of you shall they cause to be put to death. And ye shall be hated of all men for my name's sake. But there shall not an hair of your head perish. In your patience possess ye your souls.

Luke 21, cont.
And when ye shall see Yahrushalayim **(the rebuilt Yahrushalayim surrounded by Nimrod's armies)** compassed with armies, then know that the desolation thereof is nigh. Then let them which are in Judaea flee to the mountains; and let them which are in the midst of it depart out; and let not them that are in the countries enter thereinto. For these be the days of vengeance, that all things which are written may be fulfilled. But woe unto them that are with child, and to them that give suck, in those days! for there shall be great distress in the land, and wrath upon this people. And they shall fall by the edge of the sword, and shall be led away captive into all nations: and Yahrushalayim shall be trodden down of the Gentiles, **(Yahrushalayim is sacked by Nimrod and his armies of abominable flying horsemen!)** until the times of the Gentiles be fulfilled. And there shall be <u>signs in the sun</u>, and in the <u>moon</u>, and in the <u>stars</u>; and upon the earth distress of nations, with perplexity; the sea and the <u>waves roaring</u>; Men's hearts failing them for fear, and for looking after those things which are coming on the earth: for the <u>powers of heaven</u> shall be <u>shaken</u>. And then shall they see the Son of man coming in a cloud with power and great glory. And when these things begin to come to pass, then <u>look up</u>, and <u>lift up your heads</u>; for <u>your redemption draweth nigh</u>. And he spake to them a parable; Behold the fig tree, and all the trees;

The setting was on the Mount of Olives in the real Yahrushalayim! Today Yahrushalayim lies in ruins in northwestern Saudi Arabia as I've stated over and over! Peter, James, John, and Andrew were speaking privately with OWYAZ! OWYAZ starts by telling His four beloved disciples that a day will come in which <u>not</u> one stone would be left standing in the massive temple complex built by Herod! OWYAZ said that <u>every</u> stone would be thrown down from that massive structure! That statement was hard for Yahushua's disciples to comprehend because those stones were huge! Yahushua's prophecy about the future of that temple should raise questions about the <u>validity</u> of the Wailing Wall in today's Jerusalem in the State of Israel! Millions of well meaning Jews and other spiritually minded people have traveled to Jerusalem **for a fee** of course to place their prayer requests in the slits between the stones of <u>that</u> Wailing Wall for many years! The Wailing Wall is supposed to be an original section of the Temple complex dating back to the time of OWYAZ and before! So obviously there is a real contradiction there! We know that OWYAZ did <u>not</u> lie! If a person honestly evaluates the evidence, he should have a strong suspicion that the Wailing Wall in Jerusalem is <u>not</u> a part of the real Temple in the real Yahrushalayim **or it wouldn't still be standing**!

Over the centuries many false shepherds have led the majority of the morally good people of the earth into great apostasy! OWYAZ warned His disciples that they would experience a time of great affliction and persecution! OWYAZ spoke of a destruction of Yahrushalayim in which the temple would be leveled, but He also spoke of the destruction of the rebuilt Yahrushalayim by the armies of Nimrod, the Beast! As I have said over and over, the <u>real</u> Yahrushalayim was <u>completely</u> destroyed by the Romans in 135 CE! And it's still lying in ruins in the dust of northwestern Saudi Arabia today! Yahrushalayim will stay in ruins until OWYAZ returns to gather His First Fruits <u>at the opening of the 6th Seal of Revelation</u>! Yahushua's First Fruits will rebuild Yahrushalayim without walls! They will reinhabit it once again! The beloved cities of the Promised Land like Beth Lehem, and Yericho as well as many others will remain in ruins until the opening of the 6th Seal! These set apart cities will be rebuilt and reinhabited by Israel, when OWYAZ returns to gather His First Fruits at the opening of the 6th Seal! However, after 486½ years, Yahrushalayim will be sacked and desolated <u>one final time</u> by the Beast (Nimrod) of Revelation and his armies! OWYAZ told His disciples that <u>Yahrushalayim</u> would be desolated by the beast and remain <u>desolated</u> until "the Times of the Nations" ended! The "Times of the Nations" will end at the sound of the 7th Trumpet, when OWYAZ returns once again to gather all Israel! Today's State of Israel is a snare and a stumbling block to trusting sheep all over the earth! That counterfeit must be detected, understood, and overcome! Billions of dollars have flowed to the wealthy, who have funded and propped up the State of Israel for their own selfish reasons! Tourists in the so-called Holy Land have been exploited for material gain! Billions of well meaning people over the centuries have come to Jerusalem to visit this counterfeit Holy Land! How sad that is!

OWYAZ allowed the Romans to completely destroy the Temple in 70 AD to its foundations! Then in 135 CE the Romans killed 575,000 Yahudim and exiled many more into slavery in the nations! To top it all off, the Romans reinvented Yahrushalayim in Palestine! But of course the Romans <u>changed the name</u> of Yahrushalayim to "Jerusalem" to further disrespect the set apart name of AYAZ! In 135 CE the descendents of Abraham went into a final worldwide exile at the hands of the Romans! While the Romans carried it out, **the exile was decreed by AYAZ!** The people of Israel were dispersed into all the nations! The people of Israel are still scattered and will remain in exile far away from the <u>real</u> Promised Land until Israel's final Exodus begins! Many Yahudim had previously migrated into the midwestern part of Arabia near Mecca and Medina, when the Babylonians destroyed Yahrushalayim hundreds of years earlier.

Many moved even further south into southern Arabia near today's Yemen! Over time Hebrew exiles traveled north into the area that is known as Palestine today! Palestine is the area where the modern State of Israel was reestablished in 1947 by the Zionists! Palestine is at least 150 miles northwest of the real Promised Land, which is located in northwestern Saudi Arabia! The Romans used their vast military and economic resources to send the Hebrews into exile in every known part of the earth! They were sold as slaves and servants! The bloodlines of Hebrews have become completely mingled with peoples from every nation and ethnic group in the world!

I personally believe that many of the sincere people reading this book, will find that somewhere in their own bloodlines they have Hebrew ancestors! However, having Hebrew bloodlines is not a prerequisite to becoming a member of the commonwealth of Israel! What really matters is that you love ayaz and His face, OWYaz! Israel will have circumcised hearts! A person with a circumcised heart will <u>desire more than anything else</u> to please ayaz! Obedience to the instructions of ayaz is pleasing to ayaz and OWYaz! If you find out that you have some Hebrew ancestors, then that will be just icing on the cake! Stir yourself up! Get real hungry for the Truth, while there is still time! Become zealous for OWYaz! Determine to follow Yahushua's example for righteous living! It's documented in the Scriptures! But <u>be prepared </u>to suffer rejection by friends and family! You <u>will be different</u> from the mainstream of society! You will experience sicknesses, diseases, trials, and pressures in this present world in order for ayaz to try the reins of your heart! Trials and testings will surely come, when you make up your mind to follow OWYaz, no matter what! ayaz tries the reins of our hearts and minds to determine, <u>if our love for Him is genuine or counterfeit</u>! When everything seems to be falling apart and your family is suffering, will you still love ayaz and OWYaz? That's the question!

Tribulation of the Righteous

OWYaz describes the destruction of the rebuilt Yahrushalayim as a time of great distress for Israel! Remember the real Yahrushalayim will be rebuilt by the First Fruits of OWYaz, when He returns at the 6th Seal! From the time that OWYaz gave the teaching on the Mount of Olives, until He returns to deliver His First Fruits, is a time period called the "Tribulation of the Righteous"! This time period will last until OWYaz returns at the sounding of the 7th Trumpet! When OWYaz returns the tribulation of the Righteous **is over** and the "**Tribulation of the Sinners" will begin**! Tribulations and afflictions in my own life have been **the catalysts** that prompted me to really search for ayaz and His Ways! So, from an eternal perspective, our hard struggles and afflictions have been the tools that ayaz used to **save** our lives! All our struggles have worked together for our good!

Yahushua's Ruach HaQodesh comforts me in the midst of all my tribulations and afflictions! Without the tribulations, I would have **never** been humbled and never discovered the Truth in the Scriptures or the apostasy that I was a part of! This is a very important fact that every member of Israel should understand! Don't be surprised, if your life seems to get **increasingly difficult** as you fall **more and more in love** with OWYAZ! Yahuah's Ruach HaQodesh will set you apart step by step in order to refine you in Yahuah's furnace of affliction! AYAZ allowed OWYAZ to experience afflictions and rejections that were off the scale and impossible to calculate! Our afflictions however large they may seem to us now in the middle of the fight, are only light and momentary, when compared with the afflictions that OWYAZ experienced for you and me! This affliction is not designed to destroy or consume us, but to **perfect us**! Remember the Burning Bush at Mount Sinai! The bush was on fire, but it was **not** consumed! Israel will be put in the fiery furnace of AYAZ, but Israel **will not** be burned up! AYAZ uses afflictions, rejections, and pressures to **conform us** into the **image** of His son, OWYAZ!

Behold, I have refined thee, but not with silver; I have chosen thee in the furnace of affliction. **Isaiah 48:10**

And I will bring the third part through the fire, and will *refine them as silver is refined, and will try them as gold is tried: they shall call on my name, and I will hear them: I will say, It is my people: and they shall say,* AYAZ *is my Elohim.* **Zechariah 13:9**

As you will pass through Yahuah's furnace of affliction you will become more and more like OWYAZ! Your life will become more and more conformed to the life that OWYAZ lived here! OWYAZ experienced great rejection, disease, sickness, sorrow, pain, and pressures from every side, all at once! However, through it all, OWYAZ was our our model for patient endurance, courage, kindness, gentleness, compassion, love, and victory! OWYAZ warned us that following His Way would be extremely difficult in His sermon on the Mount! **This is not the prosperity message that today's preachers teach, is it?** But the Truth is the Truth! A fundamental Truth that we must learn is that AYAZ actually uses troubles, afflictions, and pressures to conform us to the image of OWYAZ! That's the primary reason that OWYAZ sent His Comforter to indwell in our hearts! OWYAZ knew that we would **need** His Comforter! And that's also why AYAZ gave us Scriptures like Romans 8:28! They are recorded to comfort us because OWYAZ knew that we would need comforting in the midst of our own afflictions!

Romans 8
Likewise the <u>Spirit also helpeth our infirmities</u>: for we know not what we should pray for as we ought: but the Spirit itself maketh intercession for us with groanings which cannot be uttered. And he that searcheth the hearts knoweth what is the mind of the Spirit, because he maketh intercession for the saints according to the will of ayaz*. And we know that <u>all</u> <u>things</u> <u>work</u> <u>together</u> <u>for</u> <u>good</u> to them that love* ayaz*, to them who are the called according to his purpose. For whom he did foreknow, <u>he also did predestinate to be conformed to the image of his Son, that he might be the firstborn among many brethren</u>. Moreover whom he did predestinate, them he also called: and whom he called, them he also justified: and whom he justified, them he also glorified. What shall we then say to these things? If* ayaz *be for us, who can be against us? He that spared not his own Son, but delivered him up for us all, how shall he not with him also freely give us all things? Who shall lay any thing to the charge of* ayaz*'s elect? It is* ayaz *that justifieth. Who is he that condemneth? It is the Messiah that died, yea rather, that is risen again, who is even at the right hand of* ayaz*, who also maketh intercession for us. Who shall separate us from the love of the Messiah? Shall tribulation, or distress, or persecution, or famine, or nakedness, or peril, or sword? As it is written, For thy sake we are killed all the day long; we are accounted as sheep for the slaughter. Nay, in all these things we are more than conquerors through him that loved us. For I am persuaded, that neither death, nor life, nor angels, nor principalities, nor powers, nor things present, nor things to come, Nor height, nor depth, nor any other creature, shall be able to separate us from the love of* ayaz*, which is in Messiah* owyaz *our Savior.*

1 Peter
Beloved, think it not strange concerning the fiery trial which is to try you, as though some strange thing happened unto you: **But rejoice, inasmuch as <u>ye are partakers of Messiah's sufferings</u>; that, when his glory shall be revealed, ye may be glad also with exceeding joy.** *If ye be reproached for the name of Messiah, happy are ye; for the spirit of glory and of* ayaz *resteth upon you: on their part he is evil spoken of, but on your part he is glorified.*

We must understand that all these troubles and afflictions are <u>only temporary</u>! There will come a time, when Israel will enter into <u>her</u> <u>rest</u>! Then owyaz will reward Israel for being faithful and true to Him! At that time Israel's reward will be so overwhelming that we will forget about all the tears that we have shed in our struggle to follow our owyaz! The Scriptures teach that ayaz has captured all our tears in His bottle! None of our tears has been wasted!

The Prophets Told Us!
Chapter 12

²⁵*"And I shall sprinkle clean water on you, and you shall be clean – from all your filthiness and from all your idols I cleanse you.* ²⁶*"And I shall give you a new heart and put a new spirit within you. And I shall take the heart of stone out of your flesh, and I shall give you a heart of flesh,* ²⁷*and put My Spirit within you. And I shall cause you to walk in My laws and guard My right-rulings and shall do them.* ²⁸*"And you shall dwell in the land that I gave to your fathers. And you shall be My people, and I shall be your Elohim.* **Ezekiel 36**

The prophets looked forward to Israel's final Exodus! The messages of the prophets were filled with great anticipation and hope for that Day! Those same messages are the messages of *Let My People Go*! I hope that *Let My People Go* stirs up your spirit and that you will determine to finish your life well, no matter what! Before the Day of ᴀYᴀZ, we must all wash our spiritual garments because the Day of ᴀYᴀZ is fast approaching and in fact it's almost here! OWYᴀZ is about to return! OWYᴀZ will give everyone his just reward! Hurry there's not much time! Teshuba **(turn around)**, teshuba, teshuba! Israel will be gathered to OWYᴀZ and rewarded with eternal life! They will be given incorruptible bodies, which will shine like the stars of the shamayim **(heavens)**! Israel will live in the very presence of OWYᴀZ in the **New Yahrushalayim** for ages without end! HalleluYah! HalleluYah! HalleluYah! However, the wicked and unrepentant will be gathered for destruction in the winepress of Yahuah's fury! And ultimately the wicked will have to face the second death, which is eternal annihilation in Yahuah's Lake of Fire! ᴀYᴀZ will reward the **wicked** and **unrepentant** with the ultimate punishment in the Lake of Fire! This Lake of Fire has flames that burn <u>hotter</u> than fire! That's a pretty simple message, isn't it? The messages of the prophets were very unpopular then just like they are today! History repeats itself, doesn't it? Most people choose the false prophets lies rather than the Commandments of ᴀYᴀZ! Why is that? Don't they understand what righteous judgment means? Do they think that OWYᴀZ will ignore their apostasy against ᴀYᴀZ?

Matthew 7
"Enter in through the narrow gate! Because the gate is wide and the way is broad that leads to destruction, and there are many who enter in through it.

Matthew 7, cont.
¹⁴"Because **the gate is narrow and the way is hard pressed which leads to life**, and there are <u>few</u> who find it. ¹⁵"But beware of the false prophets, who come to you in sheep's clothing, but inwardly they are savage wolves. ¹⁶"By their fruits you shall know them. Are grapes gathered from thorn bushes or figs from thistles? ¹⁷"So every good tree yields good fruit, but a rotten tree yields wicked fruit. ¹⁸"A good tree is unable to yield wicked fruit, and a rotten tree to yield good fruit. ¹⁹"Every tree that does not bear good fruit is cut down and thrown into the fire. ²⁰"So then, by their fruits you shall know the – ²¹"Not everyone who says to Me, 'Master, Master,' shall enter into the reign of the heavens, but he who is doing the desire of My Father in the heavens. ²²"Many shall say to Me in that day, 'Master, Master, have we not prophesied in Your Name, and cast out demons in Your Name, and done many mighty works in Your Name?' ²³"And then I shall declare to them, 'I never knew you, depart from Me, you who work lawlessness!' ²⁴"Therefore everyone who hears these words of Mine, and does them, shall be like a wise man who built his house on the rock, ²⁵and the rain came down, and the floods came, and the winds blew and beat on that house, and it did not fall, for it was founded on the rock. ²⁶"And everyone who hears these words of Mine, and does not do them, shall be like a foolish man who built his house on the sand, ²⁷and the rain came down, and the floods came, and the winds blew, and they beat on that house, and it fell, and great was its fall."

The warnings of Yahuah's prophets were largely ignored by the masses of the sheep then, just like they are today! People always choose to go the **easy way**! They seem to always choose to listen to the false prophets, who are really wolves in sheep's clothing! These false prophets tickled the ears of the people in antiquity with messages of prosperity, prosperity, and more prosperity just like the preachers, bishops, cardinals, and Popes do today! However, today these wolves in sheep's clothing have added a few enhancements to their smooth talk! Thousands of false shepherds today teach a doctrine called "seed time and harvest"! This doctrine is a tool that the wolves cleverly use to fleece their own sheep! Yes, the false shepherds fleece their own sheep and they have **no mercy**! How cruel these false shepherds are! If they truly loved their own sheep, they would teach the truth of the Scriptures to their sheep no matter what the cost to themselves! A tree is judged by its fruit, isn't it? Woe, Woe, Woe be it to these false shepherds! It would be better for them, if they had never been born! If you are teaching apostasy against ayaz, then teshuba, teshuba, while there is still time to repent!

1 Kings 18

²¹And Eliyahu came to all the people, and said, "How long would you keep hopping between two opinions? If 𐤉𐤄𐤅𐤄 is Elohim, follow Him; and if Ba'al, follow him."

We must all separate ourselves from the contamination associated with apostasy! We must worship 𐤉𐤄𐤅𐤄 His Way! Accept no compromise <u>at all</u>, if you want to be found perfect, when OWYAL returns! Come out of the apostate religious systems of man, which have been contaminated with the practices and icons of Babel! 𐤉𐤄𐤅𐤄 and OWYAL <u>hate</u> all those contaminated systems!

II Peter 2

¹²But these, like natural unreasoning beasts, having been born to be caught and destroyed, blaspheme that which they do not know, shall be destroyed in their destruction, ¹³being about to receive the wages of unrighteousness, deeming indulgence in the day a pleasure, spots and blemishes, reveling in their own deceptions while they feast with you, ¹⁴having eyes filled with an adulteress, and unable to cease from sin, enticing unstable beings, having a heart trained in greed, children of a curse, ¹⁵having left the right way they went astray, having followed the way of Bil'am the son of Be'or, who loved the wages of unrighteousness, ¹⁶but he was rebuked for his transgression: a dumb donkey speaking with the voice of a man restrained the madness of the prophet. ¹⁷These are fountains without water, clouds driven by a storm, to whom the blackest darkness is kept forever. ¹⁸For speaking arrogant nonsense, they entice – through the lusts of the flesh, through indecencies – the ones who have indeed escaped from those living in delusion, ¹⁹promising them freedom, though themselves being slaves of corruption – for one is a slave to whatever overcomes him. ²⁰For if, after they have escaped the defilements of the world through the knowledge of the Master and Savior OWYAL Messiah, they are again entangled in them and overcome, the latter end is worse for them than the first. ²¹For it would have been better for them not to have known the way of righteousness, than having known it, to turn from the set-apart command delivered unto them. ²²For them the proverb has proved true, "A dog returns to his own vomit," and, "A washed sow returns to her rolling in the mud."

In antiquity the sheep of Israel persecuted the prophets of 𐤉𐤄𐤅𐤄! Many, if not most, were tortured or put to death! Most people back then, just like today, loved the messages of the false prophets, who spoke **smooth** things, more than the truth of 𐤉𐤄𐤅𐤄! Remember the Way of 𐤉𐤄𐤅𐤄 was narrow and hard pressed back then too! False prophets spoke messages of peace, safety, and prosperity to Israel then just like they do today!

Yahuah's prophets were incredibly brave men, who displayed great courage and served 𝕬𝖄𝕬𝖅 no matter what the consequences to themselves! They faced oppression, torture, and death because the sheep of Israel did **not** like Yahuah's messages just like the people today don't like Yahuah's messages! Only a very small remnant **(a few)** have eyes to really see and ears to really hear! Do you have eyes that really see and ears that really hear? Yahuah's prophets consistently spoke about the Day of 𝕬𝖄𝕬𝖅 and the final Exodus of Israel! These prophets spoke of a **supernatural** ingathering of Yahuah's people from all the nations, where they are scattered to this very day! Over thousands of years these prophet's messages have given the people of Israel hope and great expectations for that Day! In spite of all the rejection, torture, rape, murder, sickness, disease, and exile, Yahuah's overcomers have held on to the promises of Yahuah's Good News! They have continued to love righteousness! They guard the Commandments of 𝕬𝖄𝕬𝖅, and they love their brothers! The messages that the early prophets delivered were the same "Good News" that OWY𝕬𝖅 and his disciples taught later! The prophets described a time in the last days, when Yahuah's remnant people would be scattered in exile among the nations! The prophets spoke of the oppression and bondage that the people of Israel would experience, while in bondage in the Babylonian world system! At the appointed time, when Israel searches for 𝕬𝖄𝕬𝖅 with all their hearts, 𝕬𝖄𝕬𝖅 will bring Israel out of the land of her captivity! Israel will come into her Shabbat Rest on the Day of 𝕬𝖄𝕬𝖅! 𝕬𝖄𝕬𝖅 will **supernaturally** bring Israel out of all the nations! They will come from the north, the south, the east, and the west! Israel will return to the original Promised Land! When 𝕬𝖄𝕬𝖅 returns Israel to her Promised Land in northwestern Arabia, **no** airplanes will be needed, **no** care packages will be needed, **no** financing from banks will be needed, **no** deals between nations will be needed, **no** propaganda campaign will be needed, **no** votes will be needed, and all protestors will be eliminated! Let the heavens and the earth be my witnesses, Israel will return, when the Day of 𝕬𝖄𝕬𝖅 begins! 𝕬𝖄𝕬𝖅 **doesn't need help from anybody!** Is Yahuah's hand too short to save? No, No, No, 𝕬𝖄𝕬𝖅 is the same mighty one yesterday, the same mighty one today, and the same mighty one forever! Israel's final Exodus will be **supernatural**! OWY𝕬𝖅 will harvest His people from the nations on the Day of 𝕬𝖄𝕬𝖅, not before! Today's State of Israel does not fit the Scriptural acceptance criteria for the real Promised Land! It's a cleverly designed fake, a fraud, a lie, a counterfeit, and a deceptive bear trap! Today's State of Israel is very, very thin ice! Be careful or you'll fall through!

Everyone must objectively evaluate the State of Israel's existence against the criteria given in the Scriptures for the final Exodus of Israel! What did Yahuah's prophets say about the harvests of ayaz? Yahuah's harvest will follow the pattern and the time frame given in Daniel 9! The Day of ayaz will be fulfilled in its appointed order! What is Yahuah's pattern for Israel's final Exodus? What's the order? First, Yahushua's **Barley, His First Fruits** will be harvested from the nations! Then many years later, Yahushua's **Wheat** will be harvested! Both Yahuah's Barley and His Wheat will return to the Promised Land! But wait; there is also a third harvest, a third ingathering! ayaz will gather the <u>bad grapes</u> of the wicked and the unrepentant to be **crushed** in the winepress of Yahuah's fury in the valley of Yahushofet **(valley of Yahuah's Judgment)**! If that wasn't enough, later these thorns and thistles will be thrown into the Lake of Fire to be completely consumed in the second death! Yahushua's First Fruits, His Barley, will be led by Yahushua back to the Promised Land <u>**first**</u>!

Revelation 14
⁴*They are those who were not defiled with women, for they are maidens. They are those following the Lamb wherever He leads them on. They were redeemed from among men, being first-fruits to Elohim and to the Lamb. ⁵And in their mouth was found no false-hood, for they are blameless before the throne of Elohim.*

Here is great wisdom! If you are reading this book and it applies to you, hear the message of the prophets! Come out of Babel! Come out of Babel! Come out of Babel! Touch no unclean thing! Come out of Babel completely! Come out of the Babylonian religious systems of man! Come out now! Come out now and you may be gathered with Yahushua's Barley! The First Fruits, Yahushua's Barley, will be rewarded with the highest honors of OWYAZ for all **ETERNITY**! The Barley will have the privilege of rebuilding the old waste places, Yahrushalayim and the real cities of Yahudah, which today are <u>still in ruins</u> in the sands of northwestern Arabia! The First Fruits will rebuild and reinhabit the real Yahrushalayim for 434 years **(62 weeks of years)** during <u>tough</u> times, but in **safety!** Those will be 483 years of being happy and protected **with the very best people in the world**! During those 434 years OWYAZ will <u>cut a covenant</u> with His First Fruits! After those 434 years have expired, there will be wars and rumors of wars against Yahrushalayim and the cities of Yahudah! The people of Yahrushalayim and the cities of Yahudah will fight to defend themselves until the 7ᵗʰ Trumpet sounds! Will the Yahushua's First Fruits remain alive for those 434 years? Yes, OWYAZ alluded to that fact in His Olivet discourse! But most people don't pay any attention to His statement because they don't understand the big picture!

Matthew 24
So likewise ye, when ye shall see all these things, know that it is near, even at the doors. Verily I say unto you, This generation <u>shall not pass</u>, till all these things be fulfilled.

Mark 13
So ye in like manner, when ye shall see these things come to pass, know that it is nigh, even at the doors. Verily I say unto you, that this generation <u>shall not pass</u>, till all these things be done.

Luke 21
So likewise ye, when ye see these things come to pass, know ye that the kingdom of 𐤀𐤉𐤄𐤅𐤄 is nigh at hand. Verily I say unto you, This generation <u>shall not pass away</u>, till all be fulfilled.

Can you imagine the wonderful times that these First Fruits will enjoy! I dream about being there! How about you? HalleluYah! HalleluYah! HalleluYah! After the 6th Seal is opened the beast, Nimrod, will be resurrected from the Abyss and will rise to power as the fourth horseman of Revelation 6! When the 5th Trumpet of Revelation is sounded, Nimrod's army of Kittim, abominable winged horsemen, will be freed from the Abyss by satan, who is called Belial (The Liar)! They will serve Nimrod! The Kittim will be the **abominations or monstrous warriors, who cause desolations on the earth on the Day of 𐤀𐤉𐤄𐤅𐤄!**

Joel 2
Blow a ram's horn in Tsiyon, and sound an alarm in My set-apart mountain! Let all the inhabitants of the earth tremble, for the day of 𐤀𐤉𐤄𐤅𐤄 is coming, for it is near: ^{2}a day of darkness and gloom, a day of clouds and thick darkness, like the morning clouds spread over the mountains – a people many and strong, the <u>like of whom has never been</u>, nor shall there ever be again after them, to the years of many generations. ^{3}<u>**Ahead of them a fire has consumed, and behind them a flame burns. Before them the land is like the Garden of Eden, and behind them a desert waste**</u>. And from them there is no escape. **(These are the Abominations that cause Desolation!)** ^{4}Their appearance is like the <u>appearance of horses</u>, and they run like steeds. ^{5}As the noise of chariots they leap over mountaintops, as the noise of a flaming fire consuming stubble, as a mighty people set in battle array. ^{6}Before them <u>peoples are in anguish, all faces become flushed</u>. ^{7}They run like mighty men, they climb the wall like men of battle, every one goes on his way, and they do not break ranks. ^{8}And they do not press one another, every one goes in his path. <u>They fall among the weapons, but they do not stop</u>. ^{9}They rush on the city, they run on the wall. They climb into the houses, they enter at the windows like a thief.

Joel 2, cont.

¹⁰The earth shall tremble before them, the heavens shall shake. Sun and moon shall be darkened, and the stars withdraw their brightness. ¹¹And איהי shall give forth His voice before His army, for His camp is very great, for mighty is the doer of His word. For the day of איהי is great and very awesome, and who does bear it?

Revelation 9

And the fifth messenger sounded, and I saw a star **(satan)** from the heaven which had fallen to the earth. And the key to the pit of the deep was given to it. ²And he opened the pit of the deep **(the Abyss)**, and smoke went up out of the pit like the smoke of a great furnace. And the sun was darkened, also the air, because of the smoke of the pit. ³And out of the smoke locusts **(The Abominations that cause Desolation!)** came upon the earth, and authority was given to them as the scorpions of the earth possess authority. ⁴And it was said to them that they shall not harm the grass of the earth, or any green matter, or any tree, <u>but only those men who do not have the seal of Elohim upon their foreheads.</u> ⁵And it was given to them that they should not kill them, but to torture them for five months. And their torture was like the torture of a scorpion when it stings a man. ⁶And in those days men shall seek death and shall not find it. And they shall long to die, but death shall flee from them. ⁷And the locusts <u>looked like horses</u> prepared for battle, and on their heads were crowns like gold, and their faces were like the faces of men. ⁸And they had hair like women's hair, and their teeth were like lions' teeth. ⁹And they had breastplates like breastplates of iron, and the <u>sound of their wings</u> was like the sound of chariots of many horses running into battle. ¹⁰And they have tails like scorpions, and stings. And in their tails is their authority to harm men five months. ¹¹And they have over them a sovereign, the messenger of the pit of the deep, whose name in Hebrew is <u>Abaddon, but in Greek he has the name Apolluon.</u> ¹²The first woe is past. See, two woes are still coming after this. ¹³And the sixth messenger sounded, and I heard a voice from the four horns of the golden altar which is before Elohim, ¹⁴saying to the sixth messenger who had the trumpet, "Release the four messengers, those having been bound at the great river Euphrates." ¹⁵And the four messengers, those having been prepared for the hour and day and month and year, were released to kill a third of mankind. ¹⁶And the number of the armies of the horsemen was two hundred million, and I heard the number of them. ¹⁷And this is how I saw the horses in the vision and those who sat on them, having breastplates of fiery red, and hyacinth blue, and sulphur yellow. And the heads of the horses were like the heads of lions, and out of their mouths came fire, and smoke, and sulphur.

Revelation 9, cont.

¹⁸A third of mankind was killed by these three plagues, by the fire and the smoke and the sulphur which came out of their mouths. ¹⁹For the authority of the horses is in their mouth and in their tails, for their tails are like serpents, having heads. And with them they do harm.

First Nimrod and this army will be permitted by 𐤀𐤉𐤄𐤆 to torture the people in the nations for **five months**, and then Nimrod's army will be **permitted to kill**! They will kill millions of people during their conquest of the nations! 𐤀𐤉𐤄𐤆 designed the tribulation of the sinners to humble the morally good sheep in the nations to repentance, but also to torture the wicked! Nimrod and his army will bring the whole world into subjection! **He will rebuild his cities in their places**! That's why in Revelation 18 the destruction of the city of Babylon is discussed in detail! Babylon will be rebuilt by Nimrod! Just as OWYAZ instructs His First Fruits to rebuild the real Yahrushalayim and the ruined places of Yahudah, Nimrod will rebuild Babel and his places!

Isaiah 10

¹²"And it shall be, when 𐤀𐤉𐤄𐤆 has performed all His work on Mount Tsiyon and on Yahrushalayim, that I shall punish the fruit of the greatness of the heart of the sovereign of Ashshur, **(Nimrod)** and the boasting of his haughty looks. ¹³"For he has said, 'By the power of my hand I have done it, and by my wisdom, for I have been clever. And I remove the boundaries of the people, and have robbed their treasuries. And I put down the inhabitants like a strong one. ¹⁴**'And my hand finds the riches of the people like a nest. And I have gathered all the earth like forsaken eggs are gathered. And there was no one who moved his wing, nor opened his mouth with even a peep.'**" ¹⁵Would the axe boast itself over him who chops with it, or the saw exalt itself over him who saws with it? As a rod waving those who lift it up! As a staff lifting up that which is not wood! ¹⁶Therefore the Master, 𐤀𐤉𐤄𐤆 of hosts, sends leanness among his fat ones. And under his esteem he kindles a burning like the burning of a fire. ¹⁷And the Light of Yisra'el shall be for a fire, and his Set-apart One for a flame. And it shall burn and devour his weeds and his thorn bushes in one day, ¹⁸and consume the esteem of his forest and of his fertile field, both life and flesh. And they shall be as when a sick man wastes away, ¹⁹and the remaining trees of his forest shall be so few in number that a child records them. ²⁰And in that day it shall be that the remnant of Yisra'el, and those who have escaped of the house of Ya'aqob, never again lean upon him who defeated them, **(Nimrod)** but shall lean upon 𐤀𐤉𐤄𐤆, the Set-apart One of Yisra'el, in truth. ²¹A remnant shall return, the remnant of Ya'aqob, to the Mighty El.

Isaiah 10, cont.
²²For though your people, O Yisra'el, be as the sand of the sea, yet a remnant of them shall return – a decisive end, overflowing with righteousness. ²³For the Master 𝐚𝐘𝐚𝐙 of hosts is making a complete end, as decided, in the midst of all the earth. ²⁴Therefore thus said the Master 𝐚𝐘𝐚𝐙 of hosts, "My people, who dwell in Tsiyon, be not afraid of Ashshur, who beats you with a rod and lifts up his staff against you, in the way of Mitsrayim. ²⁵"For yet a little while and the displeasure shall be completed, and My displeasure be to their destruction." ²⁶And 𝐚𝐘𝐚𝐙 of hosts stirs up a lash for him as the smiting of Midyan at the rock of Oreb. And as His rod was on the sea, so shall He lift it up in the way of Mitsrayim. ²⁷And in that day it shall be that his burden is removed from your shoulder, and his yoke from your neck, and the yoke shall be destroyed because of the anointing oil. ²⁸He has come upon Ayath, he has passed Migron. At Mikmash he stored his supplies. ²⁹They have gone through the pass, they have taken up lodging at Geba. Ramah is afraid, Gib'ah of Sha'ul has fled. ³⁰Lift up your voice, O daughter of Galliym! Listen, Layishah – O poor Anathoth! ³¹Madmenah has fled, the inhabitants of Gebim sought refuge. ³²Yet he remains at Nob that day; he shakes his fist at the mountain of the daughter of Tsiyon, the hill of Yahrushalayim. ³³Look, the Master, 𝐚𝐘𝐚𝐙 of hosts, is lopping off a branch with an awesome crash, and the tall ones are cut down, and the lofty ones are laid low. ³⁴And He shall cut down the thickets of the forest with iron, and Lebanon shall fall as a mighty one!

At the beginning of the last seven years, 𝐚𝐘𝐚𝐙 will dispatch His two witnesses to prophecy to the nations of the earth and their kings once again! For 1260 days these two witnesses will proclaim the Good News of Yahushua's Kingdom to the nations! They will warn people trapped in the nations in apostasy to repent and to "**Come Out of Babylon**"! These two witnesses of 𝐚𝐘𝐚𝐙 are His two olive trees! They will deliver Yahuah's messages to Nimrod and the kings of the earth! The message, "**Let My People Go!**", will be the primary message **to Nimrod just like it was in the 1ˢᵗ Exodus**! However, Nimrod's heart will be hardened just like the Pharaoh's heart was hardened in the first Exodus! Nimrod will not let Yahuah's **Wheat** Go! Nimrod will stir up the nations to surround and attack the rebuilt Yahrushalayim!

ZekarYah 12
The message of the word of 𝐚𝐘𝐚𝐙 against Yisra'el. 𝐚𝐘𝐚𝐙, stretching out the heavens, and laying the foundation of the earth, and forming the spirit of man within him, declares, ²"See, I am making Yahrushalayim a cup of reeling to all the people all around, and also against Yehudah it is in the siege against Yahrushalayim.

ZekarYah 12, cont.

³"And in that day it shall be that I make Yahrushalayim a very heavy stone for all peoples – all lifting it are severely injured. And all the nations of the earth shall be gathered against it. ⁴"In that day," declares ayaz, "I smite every horse with bewilderment and its rider with madness. And on the house of Yehudah I open My eyes, but every horse of the peoples I smite with blindness.

Nimrod and the wicked armies of the nations will attack and sack Yahrushalayim! Most of Yahrushalayim is captured!

ZekarYah 14

See, a day shall come for ayaz, and your spoil shall be divided in your midst. ²And I shall gather all the gentiles to battle against Yahrushalayim. And the city shall be taken, the houses plundered, and the women ravished. Half of the city shall go into exile, but the remnant of the people shall not be cut off from the city.

At that time, after their witness is complete, Yahuah's two witnesses will be slaughtered in the streets of Yahrushalayim! Yahuah's Barley will be held up on Mount Moriah and the Mount of Olives, but the situation looks hopeless for the First Fruits! However, after 3½ days, ayaz breathes life into His two witnesses! They stand up on their own two feet and are caught up into the heavens in front of their enemies! This is the **pivotal point in world history**! Just in time, OWYaz returns at the sound of the 7th Trumpet, to defend His remnant, who are surrounded in Yahrushalayim! OWYaz and His army from the heavenly Mount Zion, return in the air in fantastic power, esteem, and glory! OWYaz returns to JUDGE the nations! OWYaz will return as a mighty warrior! He's the Lion of Yahudah! Everyone will see Yahushua's return at the sound of the 7th Trumpet!

ZekarYah 14

³And ayaz shall go forth, and He shall fight against those gentiles, as He fights in the day of battle. ⁴And in that day His feet shall stand upon the Mount of Olives, which faces Yahrushalayim on the east. And the Mount of Olives shall be split in two, from east to west, a very great valley, and half of the mountain shall move toward the north and half of it toward the south. ⁵And you shall flee to the valley of My mountain – for the valley of the mountains reaches to Atsal **(Mount Sinai)**. And you shall flee as you fled from the earthquake in the days of Uzziyah sovereign of Yehudah. And ayaz my Elohim shall come – all the set-apart ones with You. ⁶And in that day it shall be: there is no light, it is dark. ⁷And it shall be one day which is known to ayaz neither day nor night, but at evening time there shall be light.

ZekarYah 14, cont.

⁸And in that day it shall be that living waters flow from Yahrushalayim half of them toward the eastern sea and half of them toward the western sea, in summer as well as in winter. ⁹And ayaz shall be Sovereign over all the earth. In that day there shall be one ayaz, and His Name one. ¹⁰All the land shall be changed into a desert plain from Geba to Rimmon south of Yahrushalayim, and she shall be raised up and inhabited in her place from Binyamin's Gate to the place of the First Gate and the Corner Gate, and from the Tower of Hanan'el to the winepresses of the sovereign. ¹¹And they shall dwell in her, and there shall be no more utter destruction, but Yahrushalayim shall be safely inhabited. ¹²And this is the plague with which ayaz plagues all the people who fought against Yahrushalayim: their flesh shall decay while they stand on their feet, **(This plague is assuredly leprosy, not an atomic blast because that would be too quick!)** and their eyes decay in their sockets, and their tongues decay in their mouths. ¹³And it shall be in that day that a great confusion from ayaz is among them, and everyone of them shall seize the hand of his neighbor, and his hand rise up against his neighbor's hand. ¹⁴And Yehudah shall fight at Yahrushalayim as well. And the wealth of all the gentiles round about shall be gathered together: gold, and silver, and garments in great quantities. ¹⁵So also is the plague on the horse and the mule, on the camel and the donkey, and on all the cattle that are in those camps – as this plague.

MattiYahu 24

²⁹"And immediately after the distress of those days the sun shall be darkened, and the moon shall not give its light, and the stars shall fall from the heaven, and the powers of the heavens shall be shaken. ³⁰"And then the sign of the Son of Adam shall appear in the heaven, and then all the tribes of the earth shall mourn, and they shall see the Son of Adam coming on the clouds of the heaven with power and much esteem.

Luke 21

²⁰"And when you see Yahrushalayim surrounded by armies, then know that its laying waste is near. ²¹"Then let those in Yehudah flee to the mountains, and let those who are in the midst of her go out, and let not those who are in the fields enter her. ²²"Because these are days of vengeance, to fill all that have been written. ²³"And woe to those who are pregnant and to those who are nursing children in those days! For there shall be great distress in the earth and wrath upon this people. ²⁴"And they shall fall by the edge of the sword, and be led away captive into all nations.

Luke 21, cont.
And Yahrushalayim shall be trampled underfoot by the gentiles until the times of the gentiles are filled. "And there shall be signs in the sun, and moon, and stars, and on the earth anxiety of nations, in bewilderment at the roaring of the sea, and agitation, [26]men fainting from fear and the expectation of what is coming on the earth, for the powers of the heavens shall be shaken. [27]"And then they shall see the Son of Adam coming in a cloud with power and much esteem. [28]"And when these matters begin to take place, look up and lift up your heads, because your redemption draws near."

Mark 13
But when ye shall see the abomination of desolation, **(Nimrod's flying abominations cause desolations on the earth!)** spoken of by Daniel the prophet, standing where it ought not, (let him that readeth understand,) then let them that be in Judaea flee to the mountains: And let him that is on the housetop not go down into the house, neither enter therein, to take any thing out of his house: And let him that is in the field not turn back again for to take up his garment. But woe to them that are with child, and to them that give suck in those days! And pray ye that your flight be not in the winter. For in those days shall be affliction, such as was not from the beginning of the creation which ayaz created unto this time, neither shall be. And except that ayaz had shortened those days, no flesh should be saved: but for the elect's sake, whom he hath chosen, he hath shortened the days. And then if any man shall say to you, Lo, here is the Messiah; or, lo, he is there; believe him not: For false Messiahs and false prophets shall rise, and shall shew signs and wonders, to seduce, if it were possible, even the elect But take ye heed: behold, I have foretold you all things.
But in those days, after that tribulation, the sun shall be darkened, and the moon shall not give her light, And the stars of heaven shall fall, and the powers that are in heaven shall be shaken. And then shall they see the Son of man coming in the clouds with great power and glory.

The earth and the heavens shake violently! The sun turns black, the moon turns red, and stars fall out of the heavens! The heavens reveal OWYAZ riding the clouds surrounded by fire, darkness, and thick storm clouds!

Habakkuk 3
[3]Eloah comes from Teman, And the Set-apart One from Mount Paran. Selah. His splendor shall cover the heavens, And His praise shall fill the earth. [4]And the brightness is as the light, He has rays from His hand, And there His power is hidden. [5]Before Him goes pestilence, And a burning flame goes forth at His feet.

Habakkuk 3, cont.
⁶He shall stand and measure the earth. He shall look and shake the nations. And the ancient mountains are shattered, The age-old hills shall bow. His ways are everlasting. ⁷I saw the tents of Kushan under sorrow, The curtains of the land of Midyan tremble. ⁸Shall ayaz burn against the rivers? Is Your displeasure against the rivers, Is Your wrath against the sea, That You ride on Your horses, Your chariots of deliverance? ⁹You uncover Your bow, The oaths of the rod of the Word. Selah. You cut through the earth with rivers. ¹⁰The mountains shall see You, they tremble. The storm of water shall pass over. The deep shall give forth its voice, It shall lift up its hands. ¹¹Sun and moon shall stand still in their places. Like light Your arrows fly, Like lightning is Your glittering spear. ¹²You step through the earth in rage, You thresh the gentiles in wrath. ¹³You shall go forth to save Your people, **(Rescue at the 7ᵗʰ Trumpet)** to save Your Anointed.

2 Samuel 22
⁸"And the earth shook and trembled, The foundations of the heavens were troubled, Because He was wroth. ⁹"Smoke went up from His nostrils, And devouring fire from His mouth; Coals were kindled by it. ¹⁰"And He bowed the heavens and came down, And thick darkness was under His feet. ¹¹"And He rode upon a kerub, and flew, And was seen upon the wings of the wind. ¹²"And He put darkness around Him as booths, Darkness of waters, thick clouds. ¹³"From the brightness before Him Coals of fire were kindled. ¹⁴" ayaz thundered from the heavens, And the Most High sent forth His voice. ¹⁵"And He sent out arrows and scattered them, Lightning, and confused them. ¹⁶"And the channels of the sea were seen, The foundations of the world were uncovered At the rebuke of ayaz, At the blast of the breath of His nostrils. ¹⁷"He sent from above, He took me, He drew me out of many waters. ¹⁸"He delivered me from my strong enemy, From those hating me, For they were stronger than I. ¹⁹"They confronted me in the day of my calamity, But ayaz was my support. ²⁰"And He brought me out into a large place, He delivered me for He delighted in me.

At the sound of the 7ᵗʰ Trumpet, the resurrection of the Righteous dead will occur! These are those, who have died loving ayaz from the time of Yahushua's death until the Day the 7ᵗʰ Trumpet is blown! The Righteous dead from Adam to Yahushua's death were resurrected <u>at the time of Yahushua's death</u>! <u>They will return with owyaz</u> from Mount Zion where they have been waiting in Paradise!

MattiYahu 27
⁵⁰And OWYAZ cried out again with a loud voice, and gave up His spirit. ⁵¹And see, the veil of the Dwelling Place was torn in two from top to bottom *(The veil that was torn was the veil that hid Yahuah's heavenly city from view, not the veil of the earthly temple as popularly believed!)*, and the earth was shaken, and the rocks were split, ⁵²and the tombs were opened, and many bodies of the set-apart ones who had fallen asleep *(Adam through Yahushua's death)* were raised, ⁵³and coming out of the tombs after His resurrection, they went into the set-apart city *(New Yahrushalayim)* and appeared to many. ⁵⁴And when the captain and those with him, who were guarding OWYAZ, saw the earthquake and all that took place, they feared exceedingly, saying, "Truly this was the Son of Elohim!"

The moment, when the 7th Trumpet is sounded, is the exact moment in time that Yahushua's people have waited, since Adam fell from Paradise! Even the earth mourns and quakes like a woman in travail because of the curses brought on it by the sins of its inhabitants! Yahushua's reign of the earth officially begins at the 7th Trumpet blast! When OWYAZ returns, His feet will land on the Mount of Olives! The Mount of Olives will split to form a valley of escape through the Mountains of Israel back to Mount Sinai! This great escape is similar to how AYAZ split the Sea (Yam Suph) during the first Exodus, except this time AYAZ splits the Mountains of Israel rather than the Yam Suph! Yahushua's First Fruits escape from Yahrushalayim! They travel through the valley formed by the splitting of the Mount of Olives! They return to Atsal! Where is Atsal anyway? Atsal is none other than the real Mount Sinai in northwestern Saudi Arabia! Mount Sinai of course is the place, where AYAZ originally proposed to Israel! Remember how AYAZ took His people to Mount Sinai during the first Exodus from Mitsrayim! Married couples today often return to the original place where they first exchanged their marriage vows! Couples return to renew their marriage vows on their 50th marriage anniversary, don't they? They reaffirm their love for each other! AYAZ brings Israel back to Mount Sinai to do the very same thing! OWYAZ will be the rear guard for Israel as they escape to Mount Sinai where they will participate in Yahushua's wedding banquet! Then OWYAZ will gather his **Wheat** harvest from the nations to Mount Sinai! But OWYAZ will also gather a third harvest! That harvest is the harvest of the wicked of **all the generations**! They are all gathered to the Valley of Yahushofet to be crushed in the fury of Yahuah's winepress! After OWYAZ has put down all opposition, He will present the Kingdom to AYAZ! At Mount Sinai Yahushua's people will once again live in tents for at least the last 3½ years of Daniel's prophecy!

This is why, when the Feast of Tabernacles is celebrated today, the people of Israel remember it by staying in booths! It will be a wonderful, wonderful time for Yahuah's people! OWYAZ will tabernacle with us! Meanwhile, Nimrod is permitted to continue to create havoc in the nations during the last 3½ years of Daniel's 490 period! Nimrod, who was resurrected from the Abyss, declares Himself to be **"God"** on the Temple Mount! Nimrod will blaspheme the name of AYAZ, Yahuah's people, and the New Yahrushalayim for those final 3½ years! When the 7th Trumpet is blown, OWYAZ will gather His Wheat from all the nations back to the real Promised Land! Remember OWYAZ previously gathered His **Barley,** now it's time for OWYAZ to gather His **Wheat!** Over the last 3½ years of Daniel's 490 year prophecy, OWYAZ will gather His Wheat into His barn at Mount Sinai! At the finale of the last 3½ years, OWYAZ will raise and gather **all** the wicked of **all** the generations for their destruction at the valley of Yahushofet (Yah's Judgment)! They will experience the full recompense of Yahuah's wrath! OWYAZ will gather the wicked into the winepress of His fury for their physical destruction! Then later, at the final judgment, all the wicked will be judged and will face total annihilation in Yahuah's Lake of Fire! OWYAZ will bring judgment on all the nations where Israel was exiled and oppressed! The full measure of Yahuah's wrath will fall on these nations! Woe be it to them! Woe be it to them! Woe be it to them! In the end all rebellion against AYAZ will be put down by OWYAZ!

Daniel 12
"Now at that time Mika'el shall stand up, the great head who is standing over the sons of your people. And there shall be a time of distress, such as never was since there was a nation, until that time. And at that time your people shall be delivered **(from Yahrushalayim)**, *every one who is found written in the book,* [2]*and many of those who sleep in the dust of the earth wake up, some to everlasting life, and some to reproaches, everlasting abhorrence.* **(The wicked from many generations will be resurrected during the 3**[rd] **harvest and brought to the valley of Yahushofet!)**

This great valley is destined by AYAZ to be the place for the destruction of Nimrod and his false prophet as well as all their wicked armies! During this battle, the armies of the wicked are thrown into sheer panic! They kill each other in the terror of the battle!

Isaiah 46 (YeshaYahu)
Bel **(Nimrod)** *has bowed down, Nebo* **(Cush)** *is stooping, their idols were on the beasts and on the cattle. That which is carried is burdensome, a burden to the weary.* [2]*They have stooped, they have bowed down together, they were unable to deliver the burden, but they themselves went into captivity.*

Jeremiah 50 (YirmeYahu)

²²"There is a sound of battle in the land, and of great destruction. ²³"How the <u>hammer</u> **(Cush father of Nimrod and false prophet)** of all the earth has been cut off and broken! How Babel has become a ruin among the nations! ²⁴"I have laid a snare for you, and you were captured, O Babel, and you yourself did not know! You have been found and also caught, because you strove against 𐤀𐤉𐤄𐤆." ²⁵ 𐤀𐤉𐤄𐤆 has opened His armory, and has brought out the weapons of His displeasure, for the Master Elohim of hosts has a work to do in the land of the Chaldeans. ²⁶Come against her from every quarter, open her storehouses, pile her up as heaps of ruins, and put her under the ban. Let her have no remnant. ²⁷Slay all her bulls, let them go down to the slaughter. Woe to them! For their day has come, the time of their punishment. ²⁸Listen! They flee and escape from the land of Babel, to declare in Tsiyon the vengeance of 𐤀𐤉𐤄𐤆 our Elohim, the vengeance of His Hekal. ²⁹"Summon archers against Babel. All you who bend the bow, encamp against it all around, let no one escape. Repay her according to her work, do to her according to all she has done. For she has been proud against 𐤀𐤉𐤄𐤆, against the Set-apart One of Yisra'el. ³⁰"Therefore her young men shall fall in the streets, and all her men of battle shall perish in that day," declares 𐤀𐤉𐤄𐤆. ³¹"See, I am against you, O proud one **(Nimrod)**!" declares the Master 𐤀𐤉𐤄𐤆 of hosts, "for your day has come, the time for your punishment. ³²"And the proud one shall stumble, and he shall fall, with no one to raise him up. And I shall kindle a fire in his cities, and it shall devour all around him." ³³Thus said 𐤀𐤉𐤄𐤆 of hosts, "The children of Yisra'el were oppressed, along with the children of Yehudah. And all who took them captive have held them fast, they refused to let them go. ³⁴"Their Redeemer is strong, 𐤀𐤉𐤄𐤆 of hosts is His Name. He shall strongly plead their case, so as to give rest to the land, but unrest to the inhabitants of Babel. ³⁵"A sword is upon the Chaldeans," declares 𐤀𐤉𐤄𐤆, "and it is upon the inhabitants of Babel, and upon her heads and upon her wise men. ³⁶"A sword is upon the liars, and they shall be fools. A sword is upon her mighty men, and they shall be broken down. ³⁷"A sword is upon their horses, and upon their chariots, and upon all the mixed peoples who are in her midst, and they shall become like women. A sword is upon her treasures, and they shall be plundered.

They kill each other! The wicked families of many generations slaughter each other! The blood of the wicked rises up to the height of a horses bridle! Nimrod, the beast and his false prophet, who were raised from the Abyss, are captured and thrown in Topheth, the Lake of Fire, **alive**! Satan is chained in the Abyss for 1,000 years, while OWY𐤄𐤆 rules the earth from the New Yahrushalayim with a rod of iron!

During that time OWYAZ will rule the nations and His rule of Law will be the Torah of AYAZ! HalleluYah! HalleluYah! HalleluYah! After 1,000 years has expired, satan must be released again to fulfill the Scriptures and to test the rest of the earth's inhabitants! For the final time, Satan stirs up rebellion in the nations! <u>Satan again surrounds the</u> <u>New</u> <u>Yahrushalayim</u> **(big mistake)** with his armies, but his army is quickly consumed by fire from the heavens! In the tenth 1,000 year period, satan, his hoist, the imprisoned watchers, and all the wicked and idolatrous people from <u>all</u> the generations, are raised to stand before Yahushua's Judgment seat for their final judgment! All those <u>not</u> found written in the Book of Life are condemned to the second death in the Lake of Fire! The Lake of Fire burns hotter than fire! The second death is a complete destruction of the body and the spirit! It is the worst form of punishment that AYAZ could create for His enemies! I can't even conceive of how terrible that Lake of Fire must be! Israel's final Exodus from the nations, the establishment of Yahushua's Kingdom, the resurrection of the Righteous, and the punishment of the wicked are the messages of Yahuah's Good News! This Good News was taught by the Prophets from Adam to John! Let's look at some of the writings of Yahuah's great prophets about Israel's final Exodus!

Moses, of course, is remembered as the servant of AYAZ, who led Yahuah's people out of bondage in Mitsrayim during the 1st Exodus! Moses is a very, very special man, who spoke to OWYAZ face to face! He spoke of Israel's final Exodus in Deuteronomy! Moses prophesied that Israel would continue to rebel time and time again! He knew that Israel would be exiled into the nations! But, Moses also knew that a remnant of Israel would repent on the Day of AYAZ and that AYAZ would bring that remnant of Israel back to the real Promised Land!

Deuteronomy 30
And it shall be, when all these words come upon you, the blessing and the curse which I have set before you, and you shall bring them back to your heart among all the gentiles where AYAZ your Elohim drives you, ^{2}and shall turn back to AYAZ your Elohim and obey His voice, according to all that I command you today, with all your heart and with all your being, you and your children, ^{3}then AYAZ your Elohim <u>shall turn back your captivity</u>, and <u>shall have compassion on you</u>, and He shall turn back and <u>gather you from all the peoples where</u> <u>AYAZ your Elohim has scattered you</u>. ^{4}"If any of you are driven out to the farthest parts under the heavens, from there AYAZ your Elohim does gather you, and from there He does take you. ^{5}"And AYAZ your Elohim shall bring you to the land which your fathers possessed, and you shall possess it. And He shall do good to you, and increase you more than your fathers.

Deuteronomy 30, cont.
⁶"And 𐤀𐤉𐤄𐤅 your Elohim shall circumcise your heart and the heart of your seed, to love 𐤀𐤉𐤄𐤅 your Elohim with all your heart and with all your being, so that you might live, ⁷and 𐤀𐤉𐤄𐤅 your Elohim shall put all these curses on your enemies and on those who hate you, who persecuted you. ⁸"And you shall turn back and obey the voice of 𐤀𐤉𐤄𐤅 and do all His commands which I command you today. ⁹"And 𐤀𐤉𐤄𐤅 your Elohim shall make you have excess in all the work of your hand, in the fruit of your body, and in the fruit of your livestock, and in the fruit of your ground for good. For 𐤀𐤉𐤄𐤅 turns back to rejoice over you for good as He rejoiced over your fathers, ¹⁰if you obey the voice of 𐤀𐤉𐤄𐤅 your Elohim, to guard His commands and His laws which are written in this Book of the Torah, if you turn back to 𐤀𐤉𐤄𐤅 your Elohim with all your heart and with all your being.

Samuel was the son of Hannah! He was another great prophet that lived during the reigns of King Saul and King David! Samuel is remembered for the messages of 𐤀𐤉𐤄𐤅 that he delivered to King Saul, Israel's first King and the anointing of King David as King of Israel! Samuel prophesies about Yahushua's return at the 7th Trumpet blast to rescue His people and to establish His kingdom!

2 Samuel 22
And my cry was in His ears. ⁸"And the earth shook and trembled, The foundations of the heavens were troubled, Because He was wroth. ⁹"Smoke went up from His nostrils, And devouring fire from His mouth; Coals were kindled by it. ¹⁰"And He bowed the heavens and came down, And thick darkness was under His feet. ¹¹"And He rode upon a kerub, and flew, And was seen upon the wings of the wind. ¹²"And He put darkness around Him as booths, Darkness of waters, thick clouds. ¹³"From the brightness before Him coals of fire were kindled. ¹⁴"𐤀𐤉𐤄𐤅 thundered from the heavens, And the Most High sent forth His voice. ¹⁵"And He sent out arrows and scattered them, Lightning, and confused them. ¹⁶"And the channels of the sea were seen, The foundations of the world were uncovered At the rebuke of 𐤀𐤉𐤄𐤅, At the blast of the breath of His nostrils. ¹⁷"He sent from above, He took me, He drew me out of many waters. ¹⁸"He delivered me from my strong enemy, From those hating me, For they were stronger than I. ¹⁹"They confronted me in the day of my calamity, But 𐤀𐤉𐤄𐤅 was my support. ²⁰"And He brought me out into a large place, He delivered me for He delighted in me.

Isaiah is one of my favorite prophets! His Hebrew name is YeshaYahu! I believe that YeshaYahu is one of the two witnesses of 𐤀𐤉𐤄𐤅! YeshaYahu was a leader among the prophets of 𐤀𐤉𐤄𐤅!

The book of YeshaYahu provides more detailed information about Israel's final Exodus than any other book in the Scriptures! The book of YeshaYahu and John's Revelation are like book ends, when it comes to Prophecy! The book of YeshaYahu has always been a very popular book! OWYᵃZ quoted from it often! YeshaYahu was martyred for ᵃYᵃZ! YeshaYahu was sawn in half with a jagged wood saw! Below are some of the great Scriptures that YeshaYahu wrote concerning the final Exodus of Israel! It's possible to understand Yahuah's final Exodus by studying the book of YeshaYahu alone!

Isaiah 10 (YeshaYahu)
[20] And in that day it shall be that the remnant of Yisra'el, and those who have escaped of the house of Ya'aqob, never again lean upon him who defeated them, but shall lean upon ᵃYᵃZ, the Set-apart One of Yisra'el, in Truth. [21] A <u>remnant shall return</u>, the remnant of Ya'aqob, <u>to the Mighty El</u>. [22] For though your people, O Yisra'el, be as the sand of the sea, yet a remnant of them shall return – <u>a decisive end, overflowing with righteousness</u>. [23] For the Master ᵃYᵃZ of hosts is <u>making a complete end, as decided, in the midst of all the earth</u>. [24] Therefore thus said the Master ᵃYᵃZ of hosts, "My people, who dwell in Tsiyon, be not afraid of Ashshur **(Nimrod, the beast of Revelation)**, who beats you with a rod and lifts up his staff against you, in the way of Mitsrayim. [25] "For yet a little while and the displeasure shall be completed, and My displeasure be to their destruction." [26] And ᵃYᵃZ of hosts stirs up a lash for him as the smiting of Midyan at the rock of Oreb. And as His rod was on the sea, so shall He lift it up in the way of Mitsrayim **(Yahuah will destroy Asshur as he did the Pharaoh!)**. [27] And in that day it shall be that his burden is removed from your shoulder, and his yoke from your neck, and the yoke shall be destroyed because of the anointing oil.

Isaiah 11 (YeshaYahu)
[10] And in that day there shall be a Root of Yishai **(Yahushua)**, standing as a banner to the people. Unto <u>Him the gentiles shall seek</u>, and His rest shall be esteem. [11] And it shall be in that day that ᵃYᵃZ sets His hand again a second time to recover the remnant of His people who are left, from Ashshur and from Mitsrayim, from Pathros and from Kush, from Eylam and from Shin'ar, from Hamath and from the islands of the sea. [12] <u>And He shall raise a banner for the nations, and gather the outcasts of Yisra'el, and assemble the dispersed of Yehudah from the four corners of the earth</u>. [13] And the envy of Ephrayim shall turn aside, and the adversaries of Yehudah be cut off. Ephrayim shall not envy Yehudah, and Yehudah not trouble Ephrayim.

Isaiah 11(YeshaYahu), cont.

14 But they shall fly down upon the shoulder of the Philistines toward the west; together they plunder the people of the east, their hand stretching forth on Edom and Mo'ab, and the children of Ammon shall be subject to them. **15** And יהוה shall put under the ban the tongue of the Sea of Mitsrayim, and He shall wave His hand over the River with the might of His Spirit, and shall smite it in the seven streams, and shall cause men to tread it in sandals. **16** <u>And there shall be a highway for the remnant of His people, those left from Ashshur, as it was for Yisra'el in the day when he came up from the land of Mitsrayim.</u>

Isaiah 14 (YeshaYahu)

Because יהוה has compassion on Ya'aqob, and <u>shall again choose Yisra'el</u>, and <u>give them rest in their own land</u>. And the <u>strangers shall join them</u>, and they shall cling to the house of Ya'aqob. **2** And <u>peoples shall take them and bring them to their own place</u>. And the house of Yisra'el shall possess them for servants and female servants in the land of יהוה. And they shall make captives of their captors, and rule over their oppressors. **3** And it shall be, in the day יהוה gives you rest from your sorrow, and from your trouble and the hard service in which you were made to serve,

Isaiah 27 (YeshaYahu)

12 And in that day it shall be that יהוה threshes, from the channel of the River to the wadi of Mitsrayim. And you shall be gathered one by one, O children of Yisra'el. **13** And in that day it shall be that a great horn is blown **(the 7th Triumph),** and those who were perishing in the land of Ashshur **(Nimrod)** and the outcasts in the land of Mitsrayim shall come, and shall worship יהוה on the set-apart mountain, in Yahrushalayim.

Isaiah 30 (YeshaYahu)

18 And therefore יהוה shall wait, to show you favor. And therefore He shall be exalted, to have compassion on you. For יהוה is an Elohim of right-ruling. Blessed are all those who wait for Him. **19** For the people shall dwell in Tsiyon at Yahrushalayim, you shall weep no more. He shall show much favor to you at the sound of your cry; when He hears, He shall answer you. **20** Though יהוה <u>gave you bread of adversity</u> and <u>water of affliction</u>, your <u>Teacher shall no longer be hidden</u>. But <u>your eyes shall see your Teacher</u>, **21** and your ears hear a word behind you, saying, "This is the Way, walk in it," whenever you turn to the right, or whenever you turn to the left. **22** And you shall defile the covering of your graven images of silver, and the plating of your molded images of gold. You shall throw them away as a menstrual cloth and say to them, "Be gone!" **23** And He shall give the rain for your seed with which you sow the ground, and bread of the increase of the earth.

Isaiah 30 (YeshaYahu), cont.

And it shall be fat and rich, your cattle grazing in an enlarged pasture in that day, ^{24}and the oxen and the young donkeys that work the ground eat seasoned fodder winnowed with shovel and fan. ^{25}<u>And on every high mountain and on every high hill there shall be rivers and streams of waters, in the day of great slaughter, when the towers fall.</u> ^{26}And the light of the moon shall be as the light of the sun, and the light of the <u>sun be sevenfold</u>, as the light of seven days, in the day that **ayaz** binds up the breach of His people, and heals the wound of His blows. ^{27}See, the <u>Name of</u> **ayaz** <u>is coming from afar</u>, <u>burning with His wrath</u>, and heavy smoke. His lips shall be filled with rage, and His <u>tongue be as a devouring fire</u>; ^{28}and His breath shall be as an overflowing stream, which reaches up to the neck, to sift the nations with a sieve of falsehood, and a misleading bridle on the jaws of the peoples. ^{29}Let the song be to you as in a night set apart for a festival, and gladness of heart as he who is going with a flute, <u>to come into the mountain of</u> **ayaz**, to the Rock of Yisra'el. ^{30}And **ayaz** shall <u>cause His excellent voice to be heard</u>, and <u>show the coming down of His arm</u>(Yahushua), with raging wrath and the flame of a <u>consuming fire, with scattering, downpour and hailstones</u>. ^{31}For through the voice of **ayaz** Ashshur **(Nimrod)** is broken down, with a rod He smites. ^{32}And every passage of the ordained staff which **ayaz** lays on him, <u>shall be with tambourines and lyres, when He shall fight with it, battling with a brandishing arm</u>. ^{33}For Topheth **(Lake of Fire for Asshur, Nimrod)** was ordained of old, even for the sovereign it has been prepared. He has made it deep and large, its fire pit with much wood; the breath of **ayaz**, as a stream of <u>burning sulphur</u>, is burning in it!

Isaiah 35 (YeshaYahu)

Let the <u>wilderness and the dry place be glad for them,</u> and let the <u>desert rejoice</u>, and <u>blossom as the rose</u>. ^{2}It blossoms much and rejoices, even with <u>joy</u> and <u>singing</u>. The esteem of Lebanon shall be given to it, the excellence of Karmel and Sharon. They <u>shall see the esteem of</u> **ayaz**, the excellency of our Elohim. ^{3}<u>Strengthen the weak hands, and make firm the weak knees</u>. ^{4}Say to those with anxious heart, "<u>Be strong, do not fear! See, your Elohim comes with vengeance, with the recompense of Elohim. He is coming to save you.</u>" ^{5}Then the <u>eyes of the blind shall be opened</u>, and the <u>ears of the deaf be opened</u>. ^{6}Then <u>the lame shall leap like a deer</u>, and the <u>tongue of the dumb sing</u>, because <u>waters shall burst forth in the wilderness</u>, and <u>streams in the desert</u>. ^{7}And the parched ground shall become a pool, and <u>the thirsty land springs of water</u> – in the home for jackals, where each lay, grass with reeds and rushes. ^{8}And there shall be a <u>highway, and a way, and it shall be called "The Way of Set-apartness</u>."

Isaiah 35 (YeshaYahu), cont.

The unclean does not pass over it, but it is for those who walk the way, and no fools wander on it. [9]No lion is there, nor any ravenous beast go up on it, it is not found there. <u>But the redeemed shall walk there.</u> [10]And the ransomed of 𐤀𐤅𐤄𐤉 shall return and enter Tsiyon with singing, with everlasting joy on their heads. They shall obtain joy and gladness, and sorrow and sighing shall flee away.

Isaiah 41 (YeshaYahu)

[8]"But you, Yisra'el, are My servant, Ya'aqob, whom I have chosen, the descendants of Abraham My friend, [9]<u>whom I have taken from the ends of the earth, and called from its farthest parts</u>, and said to You, 'You are My servant, I have chosen you and have not rejected you. [10]'Do not fear, for I am with you. Do not look around, for I am your Elohim. I shall strengthen you, I shall also help you, I shall also uphold you with the right hand of My righteousness.' [11]"See, all those who raged against you are ashamed and blush, they are as non-existent. And the men who strive with you perish. [12]"You seek them but do not find them, those who struggle with you. Those who fight you are as non-existent, as naught. [13]"For I, 𐤀𐤅𐤄𐤉 your Elohim, am holding your right hand, saying to you, 'Do not fear, I shall help you.'

Isaiah 43 (YeshaYahu)

[15]"I am 𐤀𐤅𐤄𐤉, your Set-apart One, Creator of Yisra'el, your Sovereign." [16]Thus said 𐤀𐤅𐤄𐤉, who makes a way in the sea and a path through the mighty waters, [17]who brings forth the chariot and horse, the army and the power (they lie down together, they do not rise, they have been extinguished, they have been quenched like a wick): [18]"Do not remember the former events, nor consider the events of old. [19]"See, I am doing what is new, let it now spring forth. Do you not know it? <u>I am even making a way in the wilderness and rivers in the desert.</u> [20]"The beast of the field esteems Me, the jackals and the ostriches, because <u>I have given waters in the wilderness and rivers in the desert, to give drink to My people, My chosen,</u> [21]this people I have formed for Myself, let them relate My praise.

Isaiah 48 (YeshaYahu)

[20]"<u>Come out of Babel! Flee from the Chaldeans! Declare this with a voice of singing, proclaim it, send it out to the end of the earth!</u> Say, '𐤀𐤅𐤄𐤉 has redeemed His servant Ya'aqob!' " [21]And they did not thirst when <u>He led them through the deserts</u>; He caused waters from a rock to flow for them; He split the rock, and waters gushed out.

Isaiah 49 (YeshaYahu)

⁸Thus said 𐤀𐤄𐤅𐤄, "In a favorable time I shall answer You, and in the day of deliverance I shall help You – and I guard You and give You for a covenant of the people, to restore the earth, to cause them <u>to inherit the ruined inheritances,</u> ⁹to say to the prisoners, '<u>Go out,</u>' <u>to those who are in darkness,</u>' Show yourselves.' "Let them feed on the ways, and let their pasture be on all bare hills. ¹⁰"<u>They shall not hunger nor thirst, neither heat or sun strike them,</u> for He who has compassion on them <u>shall lead them, even by fountains of water guide them.</u> ¹¹"<u>And I shall make all My mountains a way, and My highways raised up.</u> ¹²"See, these come from far away, and see, those from the north and the west, and these from the land of Sinim." ¹³<u>Sing, O heavens, rejoice, O earth! And break out in singing, O mountains! For</u> 𐤀𐤄𐤅𐤄 <u>shall comfort His people and have compassion on His afflicted ones.</u> ¹⁴But Tsiyon says, 𐤀𐤄𐤅𐤄 has forsaken me, and 𐤀𐤄𐤅𐤄 has forgotten me." ¹⁵"Would a woman forget her nursing child, and not have compassion on the son of her womb? Though they forget, I never forget you. ¹⁶"See, I have inscribed you on the palms of My hands; your walls are always before Me. ¹⁷"Your sons shall hurry, your destroyers and those who laid you waste depart from you. ¹⁸"<u>Lift up your eyes round about and see, all of them gather together and come to you.</u> As I live," declares 𐤀𐤄𐤅𐤄, "you shall put on all of them as an ornament, and bind them on you as a bride does. ¹⁹"For your wastes, and your deserted places, and the land of your destruction, shall soon be too narrow for the inhabitants, while those who swallowed you up are far away. ²⁰"The sons of your bereavement shall yet say in your ears, 'The place is too narrow for me, make room for me to live.' ²¹"And you shall say in your heart, 'Who has brought forth these for me, since I am bereaved and barren, an exile, and wandering to and fro? And who reared them? See, I was left alone – from where did these come?' " ²²Thus said the Master 𐤀𐤄𐤅𐤄, "See, I lift My hand up to the gentiles, and set up My banner for the peoples; and they shall bring your sons in their arms, and your daughters carried on their shoulders; ²³"And sovereigns shall be your foster fathers, and their sovereignesses your nursing mothers. They bow down to you with their faces to the earth, and lick up the dust of your feet. And you shall know that I am 𐤀𐤄𐤅𐤄 – <u>those who wait for Me shall not be ashamed.</u>"

Isaiah 56 (YeshaYahu)

⁶"Also the sons of the foreigner who join themselves to 𐤀𐤄𐤅𐤄, to serve Him, and to love the Name of 𐤀𐤄𐤅𐤄, to be His servants, all who guard the Sabbath, and not profane it, and hold fast to My covenant – ⁷them I shall bring to My set-apart mountain, and let them rejoice in My house of prayer.

Isaiah 56 (YeshaYahu), cont.
Their burnt offerings and their slaughterings are accepted on My altar, for My house is called a house of prayer for all the peoples." ⁸The Master 𐤀𐤄𐤅𐤄, who gathers the outcasts of Yisra'el, declares, "I gather still others to him besides those who are gathered to him."

Isaiah 60 (YeshaYahu)
"Arise, shine, for your light has come! And the esteem of 𐤀𐤄𐤅𐤄 has risen upon you. ²"For look, darkness covers the earth, and thick darkness the peoples. But 𐤀𐤄𐤅𐤄 arises over you, and His esteem is seen upon you. ³"And the gentiles shall come to your light, and sovereigns to the brightness of your rising. ⁴"Lift up your eyes all around and see: all of them have gathered, they have come to you; your sons come from afar, and your daughters are supported on the side. ⁵"Then you shall see and be bright, and your heart shall throb and swell, for the wealth of the sea is turned to you, the riches of the gentiles come to you. ⁶"A stream of camels cover your land, the dromedaries of Midyan **(in northwestern Arabia)** and Ephah; all those from Sheba come, bearing gold and incense, and proclaiming the praises of 𐤀𐤄𐤅𐤄. ⁷"All the flocks of Qedar are gathered to you, the rams of Nebayoth serve you; they come up for acceptance on My altar, and I embellish My esteemed House. ⁸"Who are these who fly like a cloud, and like doves to their windows? ⁹"Because the coastlands wait for Me, and the ships of Tarshish first, to bring your sons from afar, their silver and their gold with them, to the Name of 𐤀𐤄𐤅𐤄 your Elohim, and to the Set-apart One of Yisra'el, because He has adorned you. ¹⁰"And the sons of foreigners shall build your walls, and their sovereigns serve you. For in My wrath I have smitten you, but in My delight I shall have compassion on you. ¹¹"And your gates shall be open continually, they are not shut day or night, to bring to you the wealth of the gentiles, and their sovereigns in procession. ¹²"For the nation and the reign that do not serve you shall perish, and those gentiles shall be utterly laid waste. ¹³"The esteem of Lebanon shall come to you, cypress, pine, and the box tree together, to embellish the place of My set-apart place. And I shall make the place of My feet esteemed. ¹⁴"And the sons of those who afflicted you come bowing to you, and all those who despised you shall bow themselves at the soles of your feet. And they shall call you: City of 𐤀𐤄𐤅𐤄, Tsiyon of the Set-apart One of Yisra'el. ¹⁵"Instead of you being forsaken and hated, so that no one passes through you, I shall make you an everlasting excellence, a joy of many generations. ¹⁶"And you shall drink dry the milk of the gentiles, and shall milk the breast of sovereigns. And you shall know that I, 𐤀𐤄𐤅𐤄, your Savior and your Redeemer, am the Elohim of Ya'aqob.

Isaiah 66 (YeshaYahu)
[19]"And I shall set a sign among them, and shall send some of those who escape to the nations – Tarshish and Pul and Lud, who draw the bow, and Tubal and Yawan, the coastlands afar off, who have not heard My report nor seen My esteem. And they shall declare My esteem among the gentiles. [20]"And they shall bring all your brothers as an offering to 𐤀𐤉𐤄𐤅 out of all the gentiles, on horses and in chariots and in litters, on mules and on camels, to My set-apart mountain Yahrushalayim," declares 𐤀𐤉𐤄𐤅, "as the children of Yisra'el bring an offering in a clean vessel into the House of 𐤀𐤉𐤄𐤅. [21]"And from them too I shall take for priests – for Lewites," declares 𐤀𐤉𐤄𐤅.

YirmeYahu is another wonderful messenger of 𐤀𐤉𐤄𐤅! YirmeYahu warned the people of Yahrushalayim during his time to repent before the first Babylonian exile! YirmeYahu also warned the people living in the last days to repent as well! YirmeYahu warned Yahuah's people in the last days to repent from their apostasy so that they could be found worthy to live before 𐤀𐤉𐤄𐤅 in the Promised Land! YirmeYahu was told what to write by the Word of Yahuah, OWY𐤀𐤅! YirmeYahu loved Israel! It grieved him terribly, when He saw Yahuah's people in apostasy! YirmeYahu had tremendous compassion for his people! YirmeYahu wept because He understood the oppressions and misery that would accompany the exile of Yahuah's people into the nations!

Jeremiah 23 (YirmeYahu)
[3]"Therefore I shall gather the remnant of My flock out of all the lands where I have driven them, and shall bring them back to their fold. And they shall bear and increase. [4]"And I shall raise up shepherds over them, and they shall feed them. And they shall fear no more, nor be discouraged, nor shall they be lacking," declares 𐤀𐤉𐤄𐤅. [5]"See, the days are coming," declares 𐤀𐤉𐤄𐤅, when I shall raise for Dawid a Branch of righteousness, and a Sovereign shall reign and act wisely, and shall do right-ruling and righteousness in the earth. [6]"In His days Yehudah shall be saved, and Yisra'el dwell safely. And this is His Name whereby He shall be called: 𐤀𐤉𐤄𐤅 our Righteousness.' [7]"Therefore, see, the days are coming," declares 𐤀𐤉𐤄𐤅, when they shall say no more, 'As 𐤀𐤉𐤄𐤅 lives who brought up the children of Yisra'el out of the land of Mitsrayim, [8]but, 'As 𐤀𐤉𐤄𐤅 lives who brought up and led the seed of the house of Yisra'el out of the land of the north and from all the lands where I had driven them.' And they shall dwell on their own soil."

Jeremiah 29 (YirmeYahu)

¹³'And you shall seek Me, and shall find Me, when you search for Me with all your heart. ¹⁴'And I shall be found by you,' declares יהוה, 'and I shall turn back your captivity, and shall gather you from all the gentiles and from all the places where I have driven you, declares יהוה. And I shall bring you back to the place from which I have exiled you.'

Jeremiah 30 (YirmeYahu)

²"Thus spoke יהוה Elohim of Yisra'el, saying, 'Write in a book for yourself all the words that I have spoken to you. ³'For look, the days are coming,' declares יהוה, 'when I shall turn back the captivity of My people Yisra'el and Yehudah,' declares יהוה, 'and I shall bring them back to the land that I gave to their fathers, and let them possess it.'"

Jeremiah 30 (YirmeYahu)

¹⁰'And you, do not fear, O Ya'aqob My servant,' declares יהוה, 'nor be discouraged, O Yisra'el. For look, I am saving you from afar, and your seed from the land of their captivity. And Ya'aqob shall return, and have rest and be at ease, with no one to trouble him. ¹¹'For I am with you,' declares יהוה, 'to save you. Though I make a complete end of all gentiles where I have scattered you, yet I do not make a complete end of you. But I shall reprove you in judgment, and by no means leave you unpunished.'

Jeremiah 31 (YirmeYahu)

"At that time," declares יהוה, "I shall be the Elohim of all the clans of Yisra'el, and they shall be My people." ²Thus said יהוה, A people escaped from the sword found favor in the wilderness, Yisra'el, when it went to find rest." ³ יהוה appeared to me from afar, saying, "I have loved you with an everlasting love, therefore I shall draw you with kindness. ⁴"I am going to build you again. And you shall be rebuilt, O maiden of Yisra'el! Again you shall take up your tambourines, and go forth in the dances of those who rejoice. ⁵"Again you shall plant vines on the mountains of Shomeron. The planters shall plant and treat them as common. ⁶"For there shall be a day when the watchmen cry on Mount Ephrayim, 'Arise, and let us go up to Tsiyon, to יהוה our Elohim.'" ⁷For thus said יהוה, "Sing with gladness for Ya'aqob, and shout among the chief of the nations. Cry out, give praise, and say, 'O יהוה, save Your people, the remnant of Yisra'el!' ⁸"See, I am bringing them from the land of the north, and shall gather them from the ends of the earth, among them the blind and the lame, those with child and those in labor, together a great assembly returning here. ⁹"With weeping they shall come, and with their prayers I bring them. I shall make them walk by rivers of waters, in a straight way in which they do not stumble.

Jeremiah 31 (YirmeYahu), cont.

For I shall be a Father to Yisra'el, and Ephrayim – he is My first-born. ⁱ⁰"Hear the word of 𐤀𐤄𐤅𐤄, O gentiles, and declare it in the isles afar off, and say, 'He who scattered Yisra'el gathers him, and shall guard him as a shepherd his flock.' ¹¹"For 𐤀𐤄𐤅𐤄 shall ransom Ya'aqob, and redeem him from the hand of one stronger than he. ¹²"And they <u>shall come in and shall sing on the height of Tsiyon</u>, and stream to the goodness of 𐤀𐤄𐤅𐤄, for grain and for new wine and for oil, and for the young of the flock and the herd. And their being shall be like a well-watered garden, and never languish again. ¹⁶Thus said 𐤀𐤄𐤅𐤄, "Hold back your voice from weeping, and your eyes from tears, for there is a reward for your work," declares 𐤀𐤄𐤅𐤄, "and <u>they shall return from the land of the enemy</u>. ¹⁷"And there is expectancy for your latter end," declares 𐤀𐤄𐤅𐤄, "<u>and your children shall return to their own country</u>. ¹⁸"I have clearly heard Ephrayim lamenting, 'You have chastised me, and I was chastised, like an untrained calf. Turn me back, and I shall turn back, for You are 𐤀𐤄𐤅𐤄 my Elohim. ¹⁹'For after my turning back, I repented. And <u>after I was instructed, I struck myself on the thigh. I was ashamed, even humiliated, for I bore the reproach of my youth.</u>' ²⁰"Is Ephrayim a precious son to Me, a child of delights? For though I spoke against him, I still remembered him. That is why My affections were deeply moved for him. I have great compassion for him," declares 𐤀𐤄𐤅𐤄. ²¹"Set up signposts, make landmarks; set your heart toward the highway, the way in which you went. Turn back, O maiden of Yisra'el, turn back to these cities of yours! ²²"Till when would you turn here and there, O backsliding daughter? For 𐤀𐤄𐤅𐤄 <u>has created what is new on earth: a woman encompasses a man</u>!" ²³Thus said 𐤀𐤄𐤅𐤄 of hosts, the Elohim of Yisra'el, "Let them once again say this word in the land of Yehudah and in its cities, when I turn back their captivity, '<u>𐤀𐤄𐤅𐤄 bless you</u>, O home of righteousness, mountain of set-apartness!' ²⁴"And in Yehudah and all its cities farmers and those who journey with flocks, shall dwell together. ²⁵"For I shall fill the weary being, and I shall replenish every grieved being." ²⁶At this I awoke and looked around, and my sleep was sweet to me. ²⁷"See, the days are coming," declares 𐤀𐤄𐤅𐤄, "that I shall sow the house of Yisra'el and the house of Yehudah with the seed of man and the seed of beast. ²⁸"And it shall be, that as I have watched over them to pluck up, and to break down, and to throw down, and to destroy, and to afflict, <u>so I shall watch over them to build and to plant</u>," declares 𐤀𐤄𐤅𐤄. ²⁹"In those days they shall no longer say, 'The fathers ate sour grapes, and the children's teeth are blunted.' ³⁰"But each one shall die for his own crookedness – whoever eats sour grapes, his teeth shall be blunted.

Jeremiah 31 (YirmeYahu), cont.

³¹"See, the days are coming," declares יהוה, "when I shall make a new covenant with the house of Yisra'el and with the house of Yehudah, ³²not like the covenant I made with their fathers in the day when I took them by the hand to bring them out of the land of Mitsrayim, My covenant which they broke, though I was a husband to them," declares יהוה. ³³"For this is the covenant I shall make with the house of Yisra'el after those days, declares יהוה: I shall put My Torah in their inward parts, and write it on their hearts. And I shall be their Elohim, and they shall be My people. ³⁴"And no longer shall they teach, each one his neighbor, and each one his brother, saying, 'Know יהוה,' for they shall all know Me, from the least of them to the greatest of them," declares יהוה. "For I shall forgive their crookedness, and remember their sin no more." ³⁵Thus said יהוה, who gives the sun for a light by day, and the laws of the moon and the stars for a light by night, who stirs up the sea, and its waves roar – יהוה of hosts is His Name: ³⁶"If these laws vanish from before Me," declares יהוה, "then the seed of Yisra'el shall also cease from being a nation before Me forever." ³⁷Thus said יהוה, "If the heavens above could be measured, and the foundations of the earth searched out beneath, I would also cast off all the seed of Yisra'el for all that they have done," declares יהוה. ³⁸"See, the days are coming," declares יהוה, "that the city shall be built for יהוה from the Tower of Hanan'el to the Corner Gate. ³⁹"And the measuring line shall again extend straight ahead to the hill Gareb, then it shall turn toward Go'ah. ⁴⁰"And all the valley of the dead bodies and of the ashes, and all the fields as far as the wadi Qidron, to the corner of the Horse Gate toward the east, is to be set-apart to יהוה. It shall not be plucked up or thrown down any more forever."

Jeremiah 32 (YirmeYahu)

³⁶"And now, thus said יהוה, the Elohim of Yisra'el, concerning this city of which you say, 'It shall be given into the hand of the sovereign of Babel by the sword, and by scarcity of food, and by pestilence': ³⁷'See, I am gathering them out of all the lands where I have driven them in My displeasure, and in My wrath, and in great rage. And I shall bring them back to this place, and shall let them dwell in safety. ³⁸'And they shall be My people, and I shall be their Elohim. ³⁹'And I shall give them one heart and one way, to fear Me all the days, for the good of them and of their children after them. ⁴⁰'And I shall make an everlasting covenant with them, that I do not turn back from doing good to them. And I shall put My fear in their hearts so as not to turn aside from Me. ⁴¹'And I shall rejoice over them to do good to them, and shall plant them in this land in Truth, with all My heart and with all My being.'

Jeremiah 33 (YirmeYahu)

⁶'See, I am bringing to it relief and healing. And I shall heal them and reveal to them the riches of peace and Truth. ⁷'And I shall turn back the captivity of Yehudah and the captivity of Yisra'el, and shall build them as at the first, ⁸and shall cleanse them from all their crookedness that they have sinned against Me. And I shall pardon all their crookednesses that they have sinned and by which they have transgressed against Me. ⁹'And it shall be to Me a name of joy, a praise, and a pride before all nations of the earth, who hear all the good I am doing to them, and they shall fear and tremble for all the goodness and all the peace I am doing to it.' ¹⁰"Thus said יהוה, 'In this place of which you say, "It is dried up, without man and without beast," in the cities of Yehudah, in the streets of Yahrushalayim that are deserted, without man and without inhabitant and without beast, there shall once again be heard ¹¹the voice of joy and the voice of gladness, the voice of the bridegroom and the voice of the bride, the voice of those who are saying, "Praise יהוה of hosts, for יהוה is good, for His kindness is forever," of those who are bringing the offering of praise into the House of יהוה. For I shall turn back the captivity of the land, as at the first,' declares יהוה. ¹²"Thus said יהוה of hosts, 'In this place which is dried up, without man and without beast, and in all its cities, there shall once again be a home of shepherds causing their flocks to lie down. ¹³'In the cities of the mountains, in the cities of the low country, and in the cities of the South, and in the land of Binyamin, and in the places around Yahrushalayim, and in the cities of Yehudah, the flocks once again pass under the hands of him who counts them,' declares יהוה.
¹⁴'See, the days are coming,' declares יהוה, 'when I shall establish the good word which I have promised to the house of Yisra'el and to the house of Yehudah: ¹⁵'In those days and at that time I cause a Branch of righteousness to spring forth for Dawid. And He shall do right-ruling and righteousness in the earth. ¹⁶'In those days Yehudah shall be saved, and Yahrushalayim dwell in safety. And this is that which shall be proclaimed to her: 'יהוה our Righteousness.'

Jeremiah 50 (YirmeYahu)

⁴"In those days and at that time," declares יהוה, "the children of Yisra'el shall come, they and the children of Yehudah together, weeping as they come, and seek יהוה their Elohim. ⁵"They shall ask the way to Tsiyon, their faces toward it, 'Come and let us join ourselves to יהוה, in an everlasting covenant, never to be forgotten.'
⁶"My people have been wandering sheep. Their shepherds have led them astray, turning them away on the mountains. They have gone from mountain to hill, they have forgotten their resting place.

Jeremiah 50 (YirmeYahu), cont.

⁷"All who found them have devoured them. And their adversaries have said, 'We are not guilty, because they have sinned against ayaz, the Home of righteousness, and the Expectation of their fathers: ayaz. ⁸"Flee from the midst of Babel, come out of the land of the Chaldeans. And be as rams before a flock.

Jeremiah 51 (YirmeYahu)

⁶Flee from the midst of Babel, and let each one save his life! Do not be cut off in her crookedness, for this is the time of the vengeance of ayaz, the recompense He is repaying her. ⁷Babel was a golden cup in the hand of ayaz, making drunk all the earth. The nations drank her wine, that is why the nations went mad! ⁸Babel shall suddenly fall and be broken. Howl for her!

Yoel is a great servant of ayaz! He is considered one of the Minor prophets because the book he wrote is short! He spoke of the final Exodus and the judgment of the wicked! The book of Yoel describes the Day of ayaz! Remember the Day of ayaz is 1,000 years long! Joel 2 describes the army of horsemen, who are the abominations that cause desolations in the earth! His description of the horsemen parallels the descriptions given in Revelation of the 5th and 6th Trumpets! This army of resurrected horsemen inflict pain, desolation, and death on the wicked and unrepentant souls across the earth! Nimrod is permitted to act for a specified time period within the boundaries that ayaz has preestablished! Yoel describes the gathering of the wicked into the valley of Yahuah's judgment where they will be destroyed in the greatest battle of all time! Nimrod and his army of 200,000,000 will match up against OWYAZ and His army of Israel!

Joel 2 (Yo'el)

Blow a ram's horn in Tsiyon, and sound an alarm in My set-apart mountain! Let all the inhabitants of the earth tremble, for the day of ayaz is coming, for it is near: ²a day of darkness and gloom, a day of clouds and thick darkness, like the morning clouds spread over the mountains – a people many and strong, the like of whom has never been, nor shall there ever be again after them, to the years of many generations. ³Ahead of them a fire has consumed, and behind them a flame burns. Before them the land is like the Garden of Eden, and behind them a desert waste. And from them there is no escape. ⁴Their appearance is like the appearance of horses, and they run like steeds. ⁵As the noise of chariots they leap over mountain tops, as the noise of a flaming fire consuming stubble, as a mighty people set in battle array. ⁶Before them peoples are in anguish, all faces become flushed.

Joel 2 (Yo'el), cont.

⁷They run like mighty men, they climb the wall like men of battle, every one goes on his way, and they do not break ranks. ⁸And they do not press one another, every one goes in his path. They fall among the weapons, but they do not stop. ⁹They rush on the city, they run on the wall. They climb into the houses, they enter at the windows like a thief. ¹⁰The earth shall tremble before them, the heavens shall shake. Sun and moon shall be darkened, and the stars withdraw their brightness. ¹¹And 𐤉𐤄𐤅𐤄 shall give forth His voice before His army, for His camp is very great, for mighty is the doer of His word. For the day of 𐤉𐤄𐤅𐤄 is great and very awesome, and who does bear it? ¹²"Yet even now," declares 𐤉𐤄𐤅𐤄, "turn to Me with all your heart, and with fasting, and with weeping, and with mourning." ¹³And tear your heart and not your garments, and turn back to 𐤉𐤄𐤅𐤄 your Elohim, for He shows favor and is compassionate, patient, and of great kindness, and He shall relent concerning the evil. ¹⁴Who knows – He might turn and relent, and leave a blessing behind Him, a grain offering and a drink offering for 𐤉𐤄𐤅𐤄 your Elohim? ¹⁵Blow a ram's horn in Tsiyon, set apart a fast, call an assembly. ¹⁶Gather the people, set the assembly apart, assemble the elders, gather the children and nursing babes. Let a bridegroom come out from his room, and a bride from her dressing room. ¹⁷Let the priests, servants of 𐤉𐤄𐤅𐤄, weep between the porch and the altar. And let them say, "Spare Your people, O 𐤉𐤄𐤅𐤄, and do not give Your inheritance to reproach, for the gentiles to rule over them. Why should they say among the peoples, 'Where is their Elohim?' ¹⁸And let 𐤉𐤄𐤅𐤄 be jealous for His land, and spare His people. ¹⁹And let 𐤉𐤄𐤅𐤄 answer and say to His people, "See, I am sending you the grain and the new wine and the oil, and you shall be satisfied by them. And no longer do I make you a reproach among the gentiles. ²⁰"And the Northerner I shall remove far from you, and drive him away into a dry and deserted land, with his face toward the eastern sea and his rear toward the western sea. And his stench shall come up and his smell rise, for he has done greatly."

Joel 3 (Yo'el)

"For look, in those days and at that time, when I turn back the captivity of Yehudah and Yahrushalayim, ²then I shall gather all gentiles, and bring them down to the Valley of Yehoshaphat. And I shall enter into judgment with them there for My people, My inheritance Yisra'el, whom they have scattered among the gentiles, and they have divided up My land. ³"And they have cast lots for My people, and have given a young man for a whore, and sold a girl for wine, and drank it. ⁴"And also, what are you to Me, O Tsor and Tsidon, and all the coasts of Philistia? Are you repaying Me? And if you are repaying Me, I would swiftly and speedily return your reward on your own head.

Joel 3 (Yo'el), cont.

⁵"For you have taken My silver and My gold, and brought My treasures into your temples, ⁶and the people of Yehudah and the people of Yahrushalayim you have sold to the sons of Yawan, to remove them far from their borders. ⁷"See, I am stirring them up out of the place to which you have sold them, and I shall return on your own head what you have done, ⁸and shall sell your sons and your daughters into the hand of the people of Yehudah, and they shall sell them to the Shebaites, to a nation far off. For 𐤀𐤉𐤄𐤅 has spoken." ⁹Proclaim this among the gentiles, "Prepare for battle! Wake up the mighty men, let all the men of battle draw near, let them come up. ¹⁰"Beat your plough-shares into swords and your pruning-hooks into spears, let the weak say, 'I am strong.' " ¹¹Hasten and come, all you gentiles, and gather together all around. O 𐤀𐤉𐤄𐤅, let Your mighty men come down here. ¹²"Let the gentiles be aroused, and come up to the Valley of Yehoshaphat. For there I shall sit to judge all the gentiles on every side. ¹³"<u>Put in the sickle, for the harvest has grown ripe</u>. Come, go down, for the winepress is filled, the vats overflow, for their evil is great." ¹⁴Crowds, crowds in the valley of decision! For the day of 𐤀𐤉𐤄𐤅 is near in the valley of decision. ¹⁵Sun and moon shall become dark, and stars shall withdraw their brightness. ¹⁶And 𐤀𐤉𐤄𐤅 <u>shall roar from Tsiyon, and give forth His voice from Yahrushalayim</u>. And <u>the heavens and earth shall shake</u>, but 𐤀𐤉𐤄𐤅 shall be a refuge for His people, and a stronghold for the children of Yisra'el. ¹⁷"Then you shall know that I am 𐤀𐤉𐤄𐤅 your Elohim, dwelling in Tsiyon, My set-apart mountain. And Yahrushalayim shall be set-apart, and foreigners shall not pass through her again. ¹⁸"And it shall be in that day that the mountains drip with new wine, and the hills flow with milk. And all the streams of Yehudah shall be flooded with water, and a fountain flow from the House of 𐤀𐤉𐤄𐤅 and water the wadi Shittim. ¹⁹"Mitsrayim shall become a ruin, and Edom a ruin, a wilderness, because of violence done to the people of Yehudah, whose innocent blood they shed in their land. ²⁰"But Yehudah shall dwell forever, and Yahrushalayim to all generations. ²¹"And I shall avenge their blood, which I have not avenged. And 𐤀𐤉𐤄𐤅 shall be dwelling in Tsiyon!"

The most striking passage in Hoshea in regards to the final Exodus of Israel is contained in Hoshea 2! Hoshea had first hand experience with the restoration of an unfaithful wife! 𐤀𐤉𐤄𐤅 used Hoshea to describe His continued love for His wife, Israel, even though Israel had previously been unfaithful to 𐤀𐤉𐤄𐤅 many times! Hoshea speaks from Yahuah's heart as he relates the desire of 𐤀𐤉𐤄𐤅 to draw His bride back to the wilderness of Mount Sinai for restoration! Israel returns to the wilderness where 𐤀𐤉𐤄𐤅 first married Israel at Mount Sinai!

Hoshea describes the new relationship between 𐤀𐤉𐤄𐤅 and His bride, when 𐤀𐤉𐤄𐤅 leads them back to the wilderness in the real Promised Land!

Hosea 2 (Hoshea)
[14]"Therefore, see, I am alluring her, and shall lead her into the wilderness, and shall speak to her heart, [15]and give to her vineyards from there, and the Valley of Akor as a door of expectation. And there she shall respond as in the days of her youth, as in the day when she came up from the land of Mitsrayim. [16]"And it shall be, in that day," declares 𐤀𐤉𐤄𐤅, "that you call Me 'My Husband,' and no longer call Me 'My Ba'al.' [17]"And I shall remove the names of the Ba'als from her mouth, and they shall no more be remembered by their name. [18]"And in that day I shall make a covenant for them with the beasts of the field, and with the birds of the heavens, and with the creeping creatures of the ground, when bow, and sword, and battle I break from the earth. And I shall make them lie down in safety. [19]"And I shall take you as a bride unto Me forever, and take you as a bride unto Me in righteousness, and in right-ruling, and kindness and compassion. [20]"And I shall take you as a bride unto Me in trustworthiness, and you shall know 𐤀𐤉𐤄𐤅. [21]"And it shall be in that day that I answer," declares 𐤀𐤉𐤄𐤅, "that I answer the heavens, and they answer the earth, [22]and the earth answer the grain and the new wine and the oil, and they answer Yizre'el. [23]"And I shall sow her for Myself in the earth, and I shall have compassion on her who had not obtained compassion. And I shall say to those who were not My people, 'You are My people,' while they say, 'My Elohim!' "

Hosea 6 (Hoshea)
Come, and let us turn back to 𐤀𐤉𐤄𐤅. For He has torn but He does heal us, He has stricken but He binds us up. [2]'<u>After two days He shall revive us, on the third day He shall raise us up, so that we live before Him</u>. [3]'So let us know, let us pursue to know 𐤀𐤉𐤄𐤅. His going forth is as certain as the morning.

Amos was a servant of 𐤀𐤉𐤄𐤅, who prophesied to the Northern Kingdom of Israel! Amos loved the people of Israel and tried to warn the people to repent! Amos gives a lot of insight concerning the final Exodus of Yahuah's people back to the Promised Land! He explains that the exiles, who return will rebuild the ancient ruins of Yahuah's cities! Amos saw Zion and the New Yahrushalayim established above the Mountains of Israel! The land itself will change and yield her bounty to Yahuah's people! Amos also speaks of the gathering of the wicked for the great judgment of 𐤀𐤉𐤄𐤅 in the Mountains of Israel!

Amos 9
¹¹"In that day I shall raise up the booth of Dawid which has fallen down. And I shall repair its breaches and raise up its ruins. And I shall build it as in the days of old, ¹²so that they possess the remnant of Edom, and all the gentiles on whom My Name is called," declares **איהוה** *who does this. ¹³"Look, the days are coming," declares* **איהוה**, *"that the ploughman shall overtake the reaper, and the treader of grapes him who sows seed. And the mountains shall drip new wine, and all the hills melt. ¹⁴"And I shall turn back the captivity of My people Yisra'el. And they shall build the waste cities and inhabit them. And they shall plant vineyards and drink wine from them, and shall make gardens and eat their fruit. ¹⁵"And I shall plant them on their own soil, and not uproot them any more from their own soil I have given them," said* **איהוה** *your Elohim!*

Mikah was a great prophet of **איהוה**! He warned Yahudah and Samaria to repent or face destruction in his time! But Mikah also gives great insight into the events of the Day of **איהוה**! The book of Mikah is full of explicit information about the final Exodus back to the Land that **איהוה** promised to Israel! Mikah discusses the emergence of Asshur, the beast of Revelation, who I believe the Scriptures teach is none other than the resurrected Nimrod! Nimrod, Cush, and Semiramis are largely responsible for the syncretized religious systems that have spawned apostasy against **איהוה** all over the world today!

Micah 1 (Mikah)
³For look, **איהוה** *is coming* **(OWYAZ returns at the 7ᵗʰ Trumpet of Revelation to rescue His people and set up His Kingdom!)** *out of His place, and He shall come down and shall tread on the high places of the earth. ⁴And the mountains shall melt under Him, and the valleys be cleft as wax before the fire, as waters poured down a steep place.*

Micah 4 (Mikah)
And in the latter days it shall be that the mountain of the House of **איהוה** *is established on the top of the mountains, and shall be exalted above the hills. And peoples shall flow to it. ²And many nations shall come and say, "Come, and let us go up to the mountain of* **איהוה**, *to the House of the Elohim of Ya'aqob, and let Him teach us His ways, and let us walk in His paths. For out of Tsiyon comes forth the Torah, and the word of* **איהוה** *from Yahrushalayim. ³And He shall judge among many peoples, and reprove strong nations afar off. They shall beat their swords into plough-shares, and their spears into pruning hooks – nation shall not lift up sword against nation, neither teach battle any more.*

Micah 4 (Mikah)

⁴But each one shall sit under his vine and under his fig tree, with no one to make them afraid, for the mouth of 𐤉𐤄𐤅𐤄 of hosts has spoken. ⁵For all the peoples walk, each one in the name of his mighty one, but we walk in the Name of 𐤉𐤄𐤅𐤄 our Elohim forever and ever. ⁶"In that day," declares 𐤉𐤄𐤅𐤄, "<u>I gather the lame, and I bring together the outcast and those whom I have afflicted.</u> ⁷"And I shall make the lame a remnant, and the outcast a strong nation. And <u>𐤉𐤄𐤅𐤄 shall reign over them in Mount Tsiyon, from now on and forever.</u> ⁹Now why do you cry aloud? Is there no sovereign in you? Has your counselor perished? For pain has gripped you like a woman in labor. <u>¹⁰Be in pain, and deliver, O daughter of Tsiyon, like a woman in labor. For now you are to leave the city, and you shall dwell in the field</u>. And you shall go to Babel, there you shall be delivered, <u>there 𐤉𐤄𐤅𐤄 shall redeem you from the hand of your enemies.</u> ¹¹And now, many gentiles shall be gathered against you, who are saying, "Let her be defiled, and let our eyes look upon Tsiyon!" ¹²But they do not know the thoughts of 𐤉𐤄𐤅𐤄, nor do they understand His counsel. For He has gathered them like sheaves to the threshing-floor. ¹³"Arise and thresh, O daughter of Tsiyon, for I make your horn iron and your hooves bronze. And you shall beat many peoples into pieces, and I shall seclude their gain to 𐤉𐤄𐤅𐤄, and their wealth to the Master of all the earth."

Micah 5 (Mikah)

"But you, Beyth Lehem Ephrathah, you who are little among the clans of Yehudah, out of you shall come forth to Me the One to become Ruler in Yisra'el. And His comings forth are of old, from everlasting." ³Therefore <u>He shall give them up, until the time that she who is in labor has given birth, and the remnant of His brothers return to the children of Yisra'el.</u> ⁴And He shall stand and shepherd in the strength of 𐤉𐤄𐤅𐤄, in the excellency of the Name of 𐤉𐤄𐤅𐤄 His Elohim. And they shall dwell, for at that time He shall be great, to the ends of the earth. ⁵And this shall be peace. When Ashshur **(Nimrod)** comes into our land, and when he treads in our palaces, we shall raise against him seven shepherds **(seven messengers, who blow the Trumpets in Revelation)** and eight leaders of men. ⁶And they shall shepherd the land of Ashshur with the sword, and the land of **Nimrod** at its entrances. And He shall deliver us from Ashshur **(Nimrod)**, when he comes into our land and when he treads within our borders. ⁷And the remnant of Ya'aqob shall be in the midst of many peoples, as dew from 𐤉𐤄𐤅𐤄, as showers on the grass, which do not wait for man nor delay for the sons of men.

Micah 5 (Mikah), cont.

⁸And the remnant of Ya'aqob shall be among the gentiles, in the midst of many peoples, like a lion among the beasts of a forest, like a young lion among flocks of sheep, who, if he passes through, shall both tread down and shall tear, and there is no one to deliver. ⁹Let your hand be lifted up against your adversaries, and all your enemies be cut off. ¹⁰"And it shall be in that day," declares 𐤉𐤄𐤅𐤄, "that I shall cut off your horses out of your midst, and I shall destroy your chariots. ¹¹"And I shall cut off the cities of your land, and I shall pull down all your strongholds. ¹²"And I shall cut off witchcrafts out of your hand, and let you have no magicians. ¹³"And I shall cut off your carved images, and your pillars from your midst, so that you no longer bow down to the work of your hands. ¹⁴"And I shall pluck your Asherim out of your midst, and I shall destroy your cities. ¹⁵"And I shall take vengeance in wrath and rage on the gentiles who did not obey."

Micah 7 (Mikah)

¹⁴Shepherd Your people with Your rod, the flock of Your inheritance, who dwell alone in a forest, in the midst of Karmel. <u>Let them feed in Bashan and Gil'ad, as in days of old.</u> ¹⁵<u>"As in the days when you came out of the land of Mitsrayim, I shall let him see wonders."</u> ¹⁶Let the gentiles see and be ashamed of all their might, let them put their hand over their mouth, let their ears be deaf. ¹⁷Let them lick the dust like a serpent, let them come trembling from their strongholds like snakes of the earth, let them be afraid of 𐤉𐤄𐤅𐤄 our Elohim and fear because of You. ¹⁸Who is an El like You – taking away crookedness and passing over the transgression of the remnant of His inheritance? He shall not retain His wrath forever, for He Himself delights in kindness. ¹⁹He shall turn back, He shall have compassion on us, He shall trample upon our crookednesses! And You throw all our sins into the depths of the sea! ²⁰You give Truth to Ya'aqob, kindness to Abraham, which You swore to our fathers from the days of old!

TsephanYah was a wonderful prophet, who gave us great insight about the coming day of 𐤉𐤄𐤅𐤄! TsephanYah wrote much of his book during the time of Yosiah, Josiah! At that time, Yosiah did everything that he could to lead the people of Israel to repentance, but it was too late to ward off the judgment of 𐤉𐤄𐤅𐤄! I hope with all my heart that this book can help the good people of the earth today, who are unknowingly involved in religious apostasy, to see apostasy for what it is and to repent, before it's too late! When I read the accounts of TsephanYah about the day of 𐤉𐤄𐤅𐤄, it makes me <u>shudder</u>! Read his book for yourself and see just how devastating the future judgment of 𐤉𐤄𐤅𐤄 will be for the wicked and unrepentant! **Prepare yourself! Prepare yourself! Prepare yourself!**

Zephaniah 1 (TsephanYah)

⁷Hush! in the presence of the Master 𐤀𐤉𐤄𐤅. For the day of 𐤀𐤉𐤄𐤅 is near, for 𐤀𐤉𐤄𐤅 has prepared a slaughter, He has set apart His invited ones. ⁸"And it shall be, in the day of the slaughter of 𐤀𐤉𐤄𐤅, that I shall punish the rulers and the sons of the sovereign, and all such as are clad in foreign garments. ⁹"And I shall punish on that day all who leap over the threshold, who fill their masters' houses with violence and deceit. ¹⁰"And on that day there shall be," declares 𐤀𐤉𐤄𐤅, "the sound of a cry from the Fish Gate, and of a howling from the Second Quarter, and of a great crashing from the hills. ¹¹"Howl, you inhabitants of Maktesh, for all the merchant people shall be silenced, all those weighing out silver shall be cut off. ¹²"And at that time it shall be, that I search Yahrushalayim with lamps and punish the men who are settled on their dregs, who say in their heart, '𐤀𐤉𐤄𐤅 does no good, nor does He evil.' ¹³"And their wealth shall become plunder, and their houses laid waste. And they shall build houses but not inhabit them, and they shall plant vineyards but not drink their wine." ¹⁴Near is the great day of 𐤀𐤉𐤄𐤅, near and hurrying greatly, the noise of the day of 𐤀𐤉𐤄𐤅. Let the mighty man then bitterly cry out! ¹⁵That day is a day of wrath, a day of distress and trouble, a day of waste and ruin, a day of darkness and gloominess, a day of clouds and thick darkness, ¹⁶a day of ram's horn and alarm against the walled cities and against the corner towers.
¹⁷"And I shall bring distress on men, and they shall walk like blind men – because they have sinned against 𐤀𐤉𐤄𐤅, and their blood shall be poured out like dust and their flesh like dung." ¹⁸Neither their silver nor their gold shall be able to deliver them in the day of the wrath of 𐤀𐤉𐤄𐤅. And by the fire of His jealousy all the earth shall be consumed, for He makes a sudden end of all those who dwell in the earth.

Zephaniah 3 (TsephanYah)

⁹"For then I shall turn unto the peoples a clean lip, so that they all call on the Name of 𐤀𐤉𐤄𐤅, to serve Him with one shoulder. ¹⁰"From beyond the rivers of Kush my worshippers, the daughter of My dispersed ones, shall bring My offering. ¹¹"In that day you shall not be put to shame for any of your deeds in which you have transgressed against Me, for then I shall remove from your midst your proud exulting ones, and you shall no more be haughty in My set-apart mountain. ¹²"But I shall leave in your midst an oppressed and poor people, and they <u>shall trust in the Name of</u> 𐤀𐤉𐤄𐤅. ¹³"The remnant of Yisra'el shall do no unrighteousness and speak no falsehood, nor is a tongue of deceit found in their mouth. For they shall feed their flocks and lie down, with none to frighten them." ¹⁴Shout for joy, O daughter of Tsiyon! Shout, O Yisra'el! Be glad and rejoice with all your heart, O daughter of Yahrushalayim!

Zephaniah 3 (TsephanYah)
[15] 𐤉𐤄𐤅𐤄 has turned aside your judgments. He has faced your enemy. The Sovereign of Yisra'el, 𐤉𐤄𐤅𐤄, is in your midst. No longer need you fear evil. [16] In that day it shall be said to Yahrushalayim, "Do not fear, Tsiyon, do not let your hands be weak. [17] "𐤉𐤄𐤅𐤄 your Elohim in your midst, is mighty to save. He rejoices over you with joy, He is silent in His love, He rejoices over you with singing." [18] "I shall gather those who grieve about the appointed place, who are among you, to whom its reproach is a burden. [19] "See, I am dealing with all those afflicting you at that time. And I shall save the lame, and gather those who were cast out. And I shall give them for a praise and for a name in all the earth where they were put to shame. [20] "At that time I shall bring you in, even at the time I gather you, for I shall give you for a name, and for a praise, among all the peoples of the earth, when I turn back your captivity before your eyes," said 𐤉𐤄𐤅𐤄.

ZekarYah is one of my personal favorite prophets! I study this book over and over! If you want to understand the last days, then study ZekarYah especially chapters 9-14! ZekarYah extensively covers the final Exodus, the rebuilding of the real Yahrushalayim, Yahrushalayim's destruction by Asshur **(Nimrod)**, the rescue of the inhabitants of Yahrushalayim by OWY𐤄𐤅 at the 7th Trumpet, the journey through the Mountains to Mount Sinai, and the establishment of Yahushua's kingdom! The book of ZekarYah is a treasure trove of information, if you are a serious student of the Scriptures!

Zachariah 1 (ZekarYah)
[14] And the messenger who spoke with me said to me, "Proclaim, saying, 'Thus said 𐤉𐤄𐤅𐤄 of hosts, I have been jealous for Yahrushalayim and for Tsiyon with great jealousy. [15] "And I am very wroth with the nations who are at ease, for when I was a little wroth, they furthered the evil!" [16] 'Therefore thus said 𐤉𐤄𐤅𐤄, "I shall return to Yahrushalayim with compassion. My house shall be built in it," declares 𐤉𐤄𐤅𐤄 of hosts, "and a surveyor's line be stretched out over Yahrushalayim." ' [17] "Again proclaim, saying, 'Thus said 𐤉𐤄𐤅𐤄 of hosts, "Again My cities shall overflow with goodness. And 𐤉𐤄𐤅𐤄 shall again comfort Tsiyon, and shall again choose Yahrushalayim." ' "

Zachariah 8 (ZekarYah)
[3] "Thus said 𐤉𐤄𐤅𐤄, 'I shall return to Tsiyon, and I shall dwell in the midst of Yahrushalayim. And Yahrushalayim shall be called: City of the Truth, and the Mountain of 𐤉𐤄𐤅𐤄 of hosts, the Set-apart Mountain.'

Zachariah 8 (ZekarYah), cont.

⁴"Thus said 𐤉𐤄𐤅𐤄 of hosts, 'Again old men and old women shall dwell in the streets of Yahrushalayim, each one with his staff in his hand because of great age, ⁵and the streets of the city shall be filled with boys and girls playing in its streets.' ⁶"Thus said 𐤉𐤄𐤅𐤄 of hosts, If it is marvelous in the eyes of the remnant of this people in these days, should it also be marvelous in My eyes?' declares 𐤉𐤄𐤅𐤄 of hosts. ⁷"Thus said 𐤉𐤄𐤅𐤄 of hosts, <u>'See, I am saving My people from the land of the sunrise and from the land of the sunset.</u> ⁸<u>'And I shall bring them back, and they shall dwell in the midst of Yahrushalayim.</u> And they shall be My people, and I shall be their Elohim, in Truth and in righteousness.' ⁹"Thus said 𐤉𐤄𐤅𐤄 of hosts, 'Let your hands be strong, you who are listening in these days to these words, from the mouth of the prophets, of the day the foundation was laid for the House of 𐤉𐤄𐤅𐤄 of hosts, the Hekal that was to be rebuilt. ¹⁰'For before these days there was not a wage for a man, nor a hire for beast, and there was no peace for him who went out or came in, because of his enemies, and I set all men one against another. ¹¹'But now I am not as in the former days to the remnant of this people,' declares 𐤉𐤄𐤅𐤄 of hosts. ¹²'Because of the sowing of peace the vine does give its fruit, the ground does give her increase, and the heavens do give their dew. And I shall cause the remnant of this people to inherit all these.' ¹³'And it shall be, as you were a curse among the gentiles, O house of Yehudah and house of Yisra'el, so I shall save you, and you shall be a blessing. Do not fear, let your hands be strong.' ¹⁴"For thus said 𐤉𐤄𐤅𐤄 of hosts, 'As I purposed to do evil to you when your fathers provoked Me,' declares 𐤉𐤄𐤅𐤄 of hosts, 'and I did not relent, ¹⁵<u>so again in these days I have purposed to do good to Yahrushalayim and to the house of Yehudah.</u> Do not fear! ¹⁶'These are the words you should do: speak the Truth to one another, judge with Truth and right-ruling for peace in your gates. ¹⁷'And do not plot evil in your heart against another, and do not love a false oath. For all these I hate,' declares 𐤉𐤄𐤅𐤄." ¹⁸And the word of 𐤉𐤄𐤅𐤄 of hosts came to me, saying, ¹⁹"Thus said 𐤉𐤄𐤅𐤄 of hosts, 'The fast of the fourth, and the fast of the fifth, and the fast of the seventh, and the fast of the tenth months, are to be joy and gladness, and pleasant appointed times for the house of Yehudah – and they shall love the Truth and the peace. ²⁰"Thus said 𐤉𐤄𐤅𐤄 of hosts, <u>'Peoples shall yet come, inhabitants of many cities,</u> ²¹<u>and the inhabitants of the one go to another, saying, "Let us earnestly go and pray before 𐤉𐤄𐤅𐤄, and seek 𐤉𐤄𐤅𐤄 of hosts. myself am going."</u> ²²'And many peoples and strong nations shall come to seek 𐤉𐤄𐤅𐤄 of hosts in Yahrushalayim, and to pray before 𐤉𐤄𐤅𐤄.'

Zachariah 8 (ZekarYah), cont.

²³"Thus said 𐤉𐤄𐤅𐤄 of hosts, 'In those days ten men from all languages of the nations take hold, yea, they shall take hold of the edge of the garment of a man, a Yehudite, saying, "Let us go with you, for we have heard that Elohim is with you."

Zachariah 9 (ZekarYah)

"Rejoice greatly, O daughter of Tsiyon! Shout, O daughter of Yahrushalayim! See, your Sovereign is coming to you, He is righteous and endowed with deliverance, humble and riding on a donkey, a colt, the foal of a donkey. ¹⁰"And I shall cut off the chariot from Ephrayim and the horse from Yahrushalayim. And the battle bow shall be cut off. And He shall speak peace to the nations, and His rule is from sea to sea, and from the River to the ends of the earth. ¹¹"Also you, because of the blood of your covenant, I shall send your prisoners out of the pit. ¹²"Return to the stronghold, you prisoners of the expectation. Even today I declare that I return double to you. ¹³"For I shall bend Yehudah for Me, I shall fill the bow with Ephrayim, and I shall stir up your sons, O Tsiyon, against your sons, O Greece **(mistranslated, should be Yawan)**, and I shall make you like the sword of a mighty man." ¹⁴And 𐤉𐤄𐤅𐤄 shall appear for them, and His arrow go forth like lightning, and the Master 𐤉𐤄𐤅𐤄 sound the ram's horn. And He shall go with whirlwinds from the south, ¹⁵ 𐤉𐤄𐤅𐤄 of hosts shall shield them. And they shall devour and trample on sling stones. And they shall drink, roar as if with wine, and they shall be filled like basins, like the corners of the altar. ¹⁶And 𐤉𐤄𐤅𐤄 their Elohim shall save them in that day, as the flock of His people, for the stones of a diadem, sparkling over His land.

Zachariah 10 (ZekarYah)

⁸"<u>I shall whistle for them and gather them, for I shall ransom them</u>. And they shall increase as they once increased. ⁹"<u>Though I sow them among peoples, they shall remember Me in places far away. And they shall live, together with their children, and they shall return.</u> ¹⁰"And I shall bring them back from the land of Mitsrayim, and gather them from Ashshur, and bring them into the land of Gil'ad and Lebanon, until no more room is found for them. ¹¹"And He shall pass through the sea of distress, and strike the waves of the sea, and all the depths of the River shall dry up. And the pride of Ashshur **(King of the North)** shall be brought down, and the scepter of Mitsrayim **(King of the South)** be taken away. ¹²"And I shall make them mighty in 𐤉𐤄𐤅𐤄, so that they walk up and down in His Name," declares 𐤉𐤄𐤅𐤄.

Zachariah 12 (ZekarYah)

The message of the word of 𐤉𐤄𐤅𐤄 against Yisra'el. 𐤉𐤄𐤅𐤄, stretching out the heavens, and laying the foundation of the earth, and forming the spirit of man within him, declares, ²"See, I am making Yahrushalayim a cup of reeling to all the people all around, and also against Yehudah it is in the siege against Yahrushalayim. ³"And in that day it shall be that I make Yahrushalayim a very heavy stone for all peoples – all lifting it are severely injured. And all the nations of the earth shall be gathered against it. ⁴"In that day," declares 𐤉𐤄𐤅𐤄, "I smite every horse with bewilderment and its rider with madness. And on the house of Yehudah I open My eyes, but every horse of the peoples I smite with blindness. ⁵"And the leaders of Yehudah shall say in their heart, 'The inhabitants of Yahrushalayim are a strength to me, through 𐤉𐤄𐤅𐤄 of hosts, their Elohim.' ⁶"In that day I make the leaders of Yehudah like a fire pot among trees, and like a torch of fire in the sheaves. And they shall consume all the peoples all around, on the right and on the left. And Yahrushalayim shall dwell again in her own place, in Yahrushalayim. ⁷"And 𐤉𐤄𐤅𐤄 shall save the tents of Yehudah first, so that the comeliness of the house of Dawid and the comeliness of the inhabitants of Yahrushalayim would not become greater than that of Yehudah. ⁸"In that day 𐤉𐤄𐤅𐤄 shall shield the inhabitants of Yahrushalayim. And the feeble among them in that day shall be like Dawid, and the house of Dawid like Elohim, like the Messenger of 𐤉𐤄𐤅𐤄 before them! ⁹"And it shall be in that day that I seek to destroy all the gentiles that come against Yahrushalayim. ¹⁰"And I shall pour on the house of Dawid and on the inhabitants of Yahrushalayim a spirit of favor and prayers. And they shall look on Me whom they pierced, and they shall mourn for Him as one mourns for his only son. And they shall be in bitterness over Him as a bitterness over the first-born. ¹¹"In that day the mourning in Yahrushalayim is going to be great, like the mourning at Hadad Rimmon in the valley of Megiddo. ¹²"And the land shall mourn, every clan by itself: the clan of the house of Dawid by itself, and their women by themselves; the clan of the house of Nathan by itself, and their women by themselves; ¹³the clan of the house of Lewi by itself, and their women by themselves; the clan of Shim'i by itself, and their women by themselves; ¹⁴all the rest of the clans, every clan by itself, and their women by themselves.

Zachariah 13 (ZekarYah)

"In that day a fountain shall be opened for the house of Dawid and for the inhabitants of Yahrushalayim, for sin and for uncleanness. ²"And it shall be in that day," declares 𐤉𐤄𐤅𐤄 of hosts, "that I cut off the names of the idols from the earth, and they shall be remembered no more, and I shall also remove the prophets and the unclean spirit from the earth.

Zachariah 13 (ZekarYah), cont.

³"And it shall be, when one prophesies again, then his father and mother who brought him forth shall say to him, 'You shall not to live, because you have spoken falsehood in the Name of יהוה.' And his father and mother who brought him forth shall pierce him through when he prophesies. ⁴"And it shall be in that day that the prophets shall be ashamed, everyone of his vision when he prophesies, and not put a hairy robe on in order to deceive, ⁵but shall say, 'I am no prophet, I am a farmer, for a man sold me as a slave in my youth.' ⁶"And one shall say to him, 'What are these wounds in your hands?' And he shall say, 'Because I was wounded at home by those who love me.' ⁷"O sword, awake against My Shepherd, against the Man who is My Companion," declares יהוה of hosts. "Smite the Shepherd, and let the sheep be scattered. But I shall turn My hand upon the little ones. ⁸And it shall be throughout all the soil," declares יהוה, "that two thirds therein are cut off and die, and one third is left therein. ⁹"And I shall bring the third into fire, and refine them as silver is refined, and try them as gold is tried. They shall call on My Name, and I shall answer them. I shall say, 'This is My people,' while they say, 'יהוה is my Elohim.' "

Zachariah 14 (ZekarYah)

See, a day shall come for יהוה, and your spoil shall be divided in your midst. ²And I shall gather all the gentiles to battle against Yahrushalayim. And the city shall be taken, the houses plundered, and the women ravished. Half of the city shall go into exile, but the remnant of the people shall not be cut off from the city. ³And יהוה shall go forth, and He shall fight against those gentiles, as He fights in the day of battle. ⁴And in that day His feet shall stand upon the Mount of Olives, which faces Yahrushalayim on the east. And the Mount of Olives shall be split in two, from east to west, a very great valley, and half of the mountain shall move toward the north and half of it toward the south. ⁵And you shall flee to the valley of My mountain – for the valley of the mountains reaches to Atsal. And you shall flee as you fled from the earthquake in the days of Uzziyah sovereign of Yehudah. And יהוה my Elohim shall come – all the set-apart ones with You. ⁶And in that day it shall be: there is no light, it is dark. ⁷And it shall be one day which is known to יהוה, neither day nor night, but at evening time there shall be light. ⁸And in that day it shall be that living waters flow from Yahrushalayim, half of them toward the eastern sea and half of them toward the western sea, in summer as well as in winter. ⁹And יהוה shall be Sovereign over all the earth. In that day there shall be one יהוה, and His Name one.

Zachariah 14 (ZekarYah), cont.

¹⁰All the land shall be changed into a desert plain from Geba to Rimmon south of Yahrushalayim, and she shall be raised up and inhabited in her place from Binyamin's Gate to the place of the First Gate and the Corner Gate, and from the Tower of Hanan'el to the winepresses of the sovereign. ¹¹And they shall dwell in her, and there shall be no more utter destruction, but Yahrushalayim shall be safely inhabited. ¹²And this is the plague with which 𐤀𐤉𐤄𐤅 plagues all the people who fought against Yahrushalayim: their flesh shall decay while they stand on their feet, and their eyes decay in their sockets, and their tongues decay in their mouths. ¹³And it shall be in that day that a great confusion from 𐤀𐤉𐤄𐤅 is among them, and everyone of them shall seize the hand of his neighbor, and his hand rise up against his neighbor's hand. ¹⁴And Yehudah shall fight at Yahrushalayim as well. And the wealth of all the gentiles round about shall be gathered together: gold, and silver, and garments in great quantities. ¹⁵So also is the plague on the horse and the mule, on the camel and the donkey, and on all the cattle that are in those camps – as this plague. ¹⁶And it shall be that all who are left from all the gentiles which came up against Yahrushalayim, shall go up from year to year to bow themselves to the Sovereign, 𐤀𐤉𐤄𐤅 of hosts, and to observe the Festival of Booths.

Yehezkel was a great priest and prophet of 𐤀𐤉𐤄𐤅! Yehezkel wrote about the Day of 𐤀𐤉𐤄𐤅, while he was in exile in the Land of the Chaldeans! The writings of Yehezkel give Israel great insight about the final Exodus! This Good News is found throughout the book of Yehezkel! Yehezkel discusses the regathering of Yahuah's people back to the Promised Land, the rebuilding of Yahuah's ruined cities, the resurrection of the righteous dead, the restoration of both houses of Israel, the destruction of Nimrod and His armies in the valley of Yahuah's judgment, and the design of the future Temple of OWYAZ!

Ezekiel 11 (Yehezkel)

¹⁷"Therefore say, 'Thus said the Master 𐤀𐤉𐤄𐤅, "And I shall gather you from the peoples, and I shall assemble you from the lands where you have been scattered, and I shall give you the land of Yisra'el."' ¹⁸"And they shall go there, and shall take away all its disgusting matters and all its abominations from there. ¹⁹"And I shall give them one heart, and put a new spirit within you. And I shall take the stony heart out of their flesh, and give them a heart of flesh, ²⁰so that they walk in My laws, and guard My right-rulings, and they shall do them. And they shall be My people and I shall be their Elohim. ²¹"But to those whose hearts walk after the heart of their disgusting matters and their abominations, I shall recompense their deeds on their own heads," declares the Master 𐤀𐤉𐤄𐤅.

Ezekiel 34 (Yehezkel)

¹⁰'Thus said the Master יהוה, "See, I am against the shepherds, and shall require My flock at their hand, and shall make them cease feeding the sheep, and the shepherds shall feed themselves no more. And I shall deliver My flock from their mouths, and they shall no longer be food for them." ¹¹'For thus said the Master יהוה, "See, I Myself shall search for My sheep and seek them out. ¹²"As a shepherd seeks out his flock on the day he is among his scattered sheep, so I shall seek out My sheep and deliver them from all the places where they were scattered in a day of cloud and thick darkness. ¹³"And I shall bring them out from the peoples and gather them from the lands, and shall bring them to their own land. And I shall feed them on the mountains of Yisra'el, in the valleys, and in all the dwellings of the land. ¹⁴"In good pasture I shall feed them, and their fold shall be on the high mountains of Yisra'el. They shall lie there in a good fold and feed in rich pasture on the mountains of Yisra'el. ¹⁵"I shall feed My flock and make them lie down," declares the Master יהוה. ¹⁶"I shall seek out the lost and bring back the strayed. And I shall bind up the broken and strengthen what was sick, but the fat and the strong I shall destroy. I shall feed them with right-ruling." ¹⁷'And as for you, O My flock, thus said the Master יהוה, "See, I am judging between sheep and sheep, between rams and goats. ¹⁸"Is it not enough for you to have eaten up the good pasture, and the rest of your pasture you trample with your feet. Or that you should drink of the clear waters, and the rest you muddy with your feet? ¹⁹"And as for My flock, they eat what you have trampled with your feet, and they drink what you have muddied with your feet." ²⁰'Therefore thus said the Master יהוה to them, "See, I Myself shall judge between fat and lean sheep. ²¹"Because you have pushed with flank and shoulder, and thrust at all the weak ones with your horns, and scattered them abroad, ²²therefore I shall save My flock, and let them no longer be a prey. And I shall judge between sheep and sheep. ²³"And I shall raise up over them one shepherd, My servant Dawid, and he shall feed them. He shall feed them and be their shepherd. ²⁴"And I, יהוה, shall be their Elohim, and My servant Dawid a prince in their midst. I, יהוה, have spoken. ²⁵"And I shall make a covenant of peace with them, and make evil beasts cease from the land. And they shall dwell safely in the wilderness and sleep in the forest. ²⁶"And I shall make them and the places all around My hill a blessing, and shall cause showers to come down in their season – showers of blessing they are. ²⁷"And the trees of the field shall yield their fruit and the earth yield her increase, and they shall be safe in their land.

Ezekiel 34 (Yehezkel), cont.

And they shall know that I am 𐤉𐤄𐤅𐤄, when I have broken the bars of their yoke. And <u>I shall deliver them from the hand of those who enslaved them,</u> [28]and they shall no longer be a prey for the gentiles, and the beast of the earth shall not devour them. And they shall dwell safely, with no one to make them afraid. [29]"And I shall raise up for them a planting place of name, and they shall no longer be consumed by hunger in the land, nor bear the shame of the gentiles any more. [30]"And they shall know that I, 𐤉𐤄𐤅𐤄 their Elohim, am with them, and that they, the house of Yisra'el, are My people," declares the Master 𐤉𐤄𐤅𐤄.' " [31]"And you, My flock, the flock of My pasture, are men, and I am your Elohim," declares the Master 𐤉𐤄𐤅𐤄.' "

Ezekiel 36 (Yehezkel)

[6]"Therefore prophesy concerning the land of Yisra'el, and you shall say to mountains, and to hills, to rivers, and to valleys, 'Thus said the Master 𐤉𐤄𐤅𐤄, "See, I have spoken in My jealousy and My wrath, because you have borne the shame of the gentiles." [7]'Therefore thus said the Master 𐤉𐤄𐤅𐤄, "I have lifted My hand in an oath that the gentiles that are around you shall bear their own shame. [8]"But you, O <u>mountains of Yisra'el, put forth your branches and bear your fruit to My people Yisra'el, for they are about to come!</u> [9]"For look, I am for you, and I shall turn to you, and you shall be tilled and sown. [10]<u>"And I shall increase men upon you, all the house of Yisra'el, all of it. And the cities shall be inhabited and the ruins rebuilt.</u> [11]"And I shall increase upon you man and beast, and they shall increase and bear young. And I shall make you inhabited as of old, and do better for you than at your beginnings. And you shall know that I am 𐤉𐤄𐤅𐤄. [12]"And I shall let men, My people Yisra'el, walk upon you, and let them possess you, and you shall be their inheritance, and no longer let you add to their bereavement." [13]'Thus said the Master 𐤉𐤄𐤅𐤄, "Because they say to you, 'You devour men and have bereaved your nation,' [14]therefore you shall no longer devour men, and no longer bereave your nation," declares the Master 𐤉𐤄𐤅𐤄. [15]"And no longer shall I let you hear the insults of the gentiles. And the reproach of the peoples you shall bear no more, and no longer cause your nations to stumble," declares the Master 𐤉𐤄𐤅𐤄.' " [16]And the word of 𐤉𐤄𐤅𐤄 came to me, saying, [17]"Son of man, when the house of Yisra'el dwelt in their own land, they defiled it by their own ways and deeds. To Me their way was like the uncleanness of a woman in her monthly period. [18]"So I poured out My wrath on them for the blood they had shed on the land, and for their idols they defiled it. [19]"And I scattered them among the gentiles, and they were dispersed throughout the lands. I have judged them according to their ways and their deeds.

Ezekiel 36 (Yehezkel), cont.

²⁰"And when they came to the gentiles, wherever they went, they profaned My set-apart Name for it was said of them, 'These are the people of 𐤉𐤄𐤅𐤄, and yet they have gone out of His land.' ²¹"But I had compassion on My set-apart Name, which the house of Yisra'el had profaned among the gentiles wherever they went. ²²"Therefore say to the house of Yisra'el, 'Thus said the Master 𐤉𐤄𐤅𐤄, I do not do this for your sake, O house of Yisra'el, but for My set-apart Name's sake, which you have profaned among the gentiles wherever you went. ²³"<u>And I shall set apart My great Name</u>, which has been profaned among the gentiles, which you have profaned in their midst. And the gentiles shall know that I am 𐤉𐤄𐤅𐤄," declares the Master 𐤉𐤄𐤅𐤄, "when I am set-apart in you before their eyes. ²⁴"And I shall take you from among the gentiles, and I shall gather you out of all lands, and I shall bring you into your own land. ²⁵"And I shall sprinkle clean water on you, and you shall be clean – from all your filthiness and from all your idols I cleanse you. ²⁶"And **I shall give you a new heart and put a new spirit within you**. And I shall take the heart of stone out of your flesh, and I shall give you a heart of flesh, ²⁷ and put My Spirit within you. And I shall cause you to walk in My laws and guard My right-rulings and shall do them. ²⁸"And you shall dwell in the land that I gave to your fathers. And you shall be My people, and I shall be your Elohim. ²⁹"And I shall save you from all your uncleannesses. And I shall call for the grain and increase it, and I shall bring no scarcity of food upon you. ³⁰"And I shall increase the fruit of your trees and the increase of your fields, so that you need never again bear the reproach of scarcity of food among the gentiles. ³¹"And you shall remember your evil ways and your deeds that were not good. And you shall loathe yourselves in your own eyes, for your crookednesses and your abominations. ³²"Not for your sake am I acting," declares the Master 𐤉𐤄𐤅𐤄, "let it be known to you. Be ashamed and blush for your ways, O house of Yisra'el!" ³³'Thus said the Master 𐤉𐤄𐤅𐤄, "On the day that I cleanse you from all your crookednesses, I shall cause the cities to be inhabited, and the ruined places shall be rebuilt, ³⁴ and the land that was laid waste tilled instead of being a ruin before the eyes of all who pass by. ³⁵"And they shall say, 'This land that was laid waste has become like the garden of Eden. <u>And the wasted, the deserted, and the destroyed cities are now walled and inhabited.</u>' ³⁶"Then the gentiles which are left all around you shall know that I, 𐤉𐤄𐤅𐤄, <u>have rebuilt the destroyed places and planted what was laid waste</u>. I, 𐤉𐤄𐤅𐤄, have spoken it, and I shall do it." ³⁷'Thus said the Master 𐤉𐤄𐤅𐤄, "Once again I shall let the house of Yisra'el inquire of Me to do for them: I shall increase their men like a flock. ³⁸"As a set-apart flock, as the flock at Yahrushalayim at her appointed times, so shall the wasted cities be filled with flocks of men. And they shall know that I am 𐤉𐤄𐤅𐤄."

Ezekiel 37 (Yehezkel)

²¹"And speak to them, 'Thus said the Master אYaZ, "See, I am taking the children of Yisra'el from among the gentiles, wherever they have gone, and shall <u>gather them from all around</u>, and I shall bring them into <u>their land</u>. ²²"And I shall make them one nation in the land, <u>on the mountains of Yisra'el</u>. And one sovereign shall be sovereign over them all, and let them no longer be two nations, and let them no longer be divided into two reigns. ²³"And they shall no longer defile themselves with their idols, nor with their disgusting matters, nor with any of their transgressions. And I shall save them from all their dwelling places in which they have sinned, and I shall cleanse them. And they shall be My people, and I be their Elohim, ²⁴while Dawid My servant is sovereign over them. And they shall all have one shepherd and walk in My right-rulings and guard My laws, and shall do them. ²⁵"And they shall dwell in the land that I have given to Ya'aqob My servant, where your fathers dwelt. And they shall dwell in it, they and their children and their children's children, forever, and My servant Dawid be their prince forever. ²⁶"And I shall make a covenant of peace with them – an everlasting covenant it is with them. And I shall place them and increase them, and shall place My set-apart place in their midst, forever. ²⁷"And <u>My Dwelling Place shall be over them.</u> And I shall be their Elohim, and they shall be My people. ²⁸"And the gentiles shall know that I, אYaZ, am setting Yisra'el apart, when My set-apart place is in their midst – forever."

Ezekiel 39 (Yehezkel)

²³"And the gentiles shall know that the house of Yisra'el went into exile for their crookedness, because they have trespassed against Me, so that <u>I hid My face from them, and I gave them into the hand of their adversaries</u>, and they all fell by the sword. ²⁴"According to their uncleanness and according to their transgressions I have dealt with them, and hidden My face from them." ' ²⁵"Therefore thus said the Master אYaZ, 'Now I am going to bring back the captives of Ya'aqob. And I shall have compassion on all the house of Yisra'el, and shall be jealous for My set-apart Name. ²⁶'And they shall have borne their shame, and all their trespass they committed against Me, when they dwell safely in their own land, with none to make them afraid, ²⁷when I have brought them back from the peoples and gathered them out of the lands of their enemies. And I shall be set apart in them before the eyes of many gentiles. ²⁸'And they shall know that I am אYaZ their Elohim, who sent them into exile among the gentiles, and then <u>gathered them back to their own land, and left none of them behind.</u>

Ezekiel 39 (Yehezkel), cont.

²⁹'And no longer do I hide My face from them, for I shall have poured out My Spirit on the house of Yisra'el,' declares the Master ayaz."

Daniel **(Dani'El)** is another wonderful prophet of ayaz. We all love to listen to the story of Daniel in the Lion's den! I love the story of how **(Hananyah)** Shadrak, and **(Misha'el)** Meyshak, and **(AzarYah)**, Abed-Nego, survived the fiery furnace! Daniel gives Israel specific information about the timing of Israel's final Exodus in Daniel 9, the rise to power of the beast **(Nimrod)** of Revelation, and the resurrection of the dead **(both the righteous and unrighteous)**!

Dani'El 8

And from one of them came a little horn which became exceedingly great toward the south, and toward the east, and toward the Splendid Land. ¹⁰And it became great, up to the host of the heavens. And it caused some of the host and some of the stars to fall to the earth, and trampled them down. ¹¹It even exalted itself as high as the Prince of the host. And it took that which is continual away from Him, and threw down the foundation of His set-apart place. ¹²And because of transgression, an army was given over to the horn to oppose that which is continual. And it threw the truth down to the ground, and it acted and prospered. ¹³Then I heard a certain set-apart one speaking. And another set-apart one said to that certain one who was speaking, "Till when is the vision, concerning that which is continual, and the transgression that lays waste, to make both the set-apart place and the host to be trampled under foot? ¹⁴And he said to me, "For two thousand three hundred days, then that which is set- apart shall be made right."

Dani'El 11

²¹"And in his place shall arise a despised one, to whom they shall not give the excellency of the rule. But he shall come in peaceably, and seize the rule by flatteries. ²²"And the arms of the flood shall be swept away from before him and be broken, and also the prince of the covenant. ²³"And after they joined him, he shall work deceit, and shall come up and become strong with a small nation. ²⁴"He shall enter peaceably, even into the richest places of the province, and do what his fathers have not done, nor his forefathers: distribute among them plunder and spoil and supplies, and devise his plots against the strongholds, but only for a time. ²⁵"And he shall stir up his power and his heart against the sovereign of the South with a great army, and the sovereign of the South shall be stirred up to battle with a very great and mighty army, but not stand, for they shall devise plots against him. ²⁶"And those who have been eating his food shall destroy him, and his army be swept away, and many fall down slain.

Dani'El 11, cont.

²⁷"And both these sovereigns' hearts are to do evil, and speak lies at the same table, but not prosper, for the end is still for an appointed time. ²⁸"Then he shall return to his land with much supplies, and his heart be against the set-apart covenant. And he shall act, and shall return to his land. ²⁹"At the appointed time he shall return and go toward the south, but it shall not be like the former or the latter. ³⁰"For ships from Kittim shall come against him, and he shall lose heart, and shall return in rage against the set-apart covenant, and shall act, and shall return and consider those who forsake the set-apart covenant. ³¹"And strong ones shall arise from him and profane the set-apart place, the strong-hold, and shall take away that which is continual, and set up the abomination that lays waste. ³²"And by flatteries he shall profane those who do wrong against the covenant, but the people who know their Elohim shall be strong, and shall act. ³³"And those of the people who have insight shall give understanding to many. And they shall stumble by sword and flame, by captivity and plundering, for days. ³⁴"And when they stumble, they shall be helped, a little help, but many shall join them, by flatteries. ³⁵"And some of those who have insight shall stumble, to refine them, and to cleanse them, and to make them white, until the time of the end, for it is still for an appointed time. ³⁶"And the sovereign shall do as he pleases, and exalt himself and show himself to be great above every mighty one, and speak incredible matters against the El of mighty ones, and shall prosper until the wrath has been accomplished – for what has been decreed shall be done – ³⁷and have no regard for the mighty ones of his fathers nor for the desire of women, nor have regard for any mighty one, but exalt himself above them all. ³⁸"But in his place he shall give esteem to a mighty one of strongholds. And to a mighty one which his fathers did not know he shall give esteem with gold and silver, with precious stones and costly gifts. ³⁹"And he shall act against the strongest strongholds with a foreign mighty one, which he shall acknowledge. He shall increase in esteem and cause them to rule over many, and divide the land for gain. ⁴⁰"At the time of the end the sovereign of the South shall push at him, and the sovereign of the North rush against him like a whirlwind, with chariots, and with horsemen, and with many ships. And he shall enter the lands, and shall overflow and pass over, ⁴¹and shall enter the Splendid Land, and many shall stumble, but these escape from his hand: Edom, and Mo'ab, and the chief of the sons of Ammon. ⁴²"And he shall stretch out his hand against the lands, and the land of Mitsrayim shall not escape. ⁴³"And he shall rule over the treasures of gold and silver, and over all the riches of Mitsrayim, and Libyans and Kushites shall be at his steps.

Dani'El 11, cont.
⁴⁴"Then reports from the east and the north shall disturb him, and he shall go out with great wrath to destroy and put many under the ban, ⁴⁵and he shall pitch the tents of his palace between the seas and the splendid set-apart mountain, but shall come to his end with none to help him.

Dani'El 12
"Now at that time Mika'el shall stand up, the great head who is standing over the sons of your people. And there shall be a time of distress, such as never was since there was a nation, until that time. And at that time your people shall be delivered, every one who is found written in the book, ²and many of those who sleep in the dust of the earth wake up, some to everlasting life, and some to reproaches, everlasting abhorrence. ³"And those who have insight shall shine like the brightness of the expanse, and those who lead many to righteousness like the stars forever and ever.

Enoch was one of the greatest prophets, who ever lived! This prophet lived **before the Flood**! He was the seventh patriarch born in the Righteous line of Adam! He was called the Scribe of Righteousness by 𐤀𐤉𐤄𐤅 His name in Hebrew is Hanok, but we know him as Enoch! Even though men have suppressed his writings for thousands of years, *The Book Enoch* gives more insight into the **big picture** about the Day of 𐤀𐤉𐤄𐤅 than any other prophet! Hanok answers hard questions! He provides the bedrock for Israel's understanding of events that occurred long ago, before the Flood! Hanok explains the offense and the punishment of the "**Watchers**"! Remember the "Watchers" were sons of Elohim (not angels) from the Righteous line of Adam and Seth! But these sons of Elohim were seduced by the daughters of Cain! These watchers were lead by Azazel and they descended from their lofty abode on Mount Sinai! They took wives from the daughters of Cain below the Mountain against the will of 𐤀𐤉𐤄𐤅 These offenses were in direct defiance of Yahuah's instructions! 𐤀𐤉𐤄𐤅 was so disgusted and infuriated with the watchers that He decreed that no forgiveness would be available to them, **ever**! The punishment decreed on the watchers was severe! It included; watching their offspring destroyed before their own eyes, torture and imprisonment in the darkness of the Abyss for several thousand years, and last, but not least, a total annihilation in the Lake of Fire with the other adversaries of 𐤀𐤉𐤄𐤅 These Watchers spurned their inheritance as sons of Elohim, which amounted to exchanging eternal **life** with OWY𐤀𐤋 for eternal damnation in the Lake of Fire! Hanok pleased 𐤀𐤉𐤄𐤅 so much that 𐤀𐤉𐤄𐤅 translated Hanok straight into Paradise!

𝕒𝕐𝕒𝕫 had his heavenly messengers teach Hanok knowledge about the heavens and the earth! Hanok was shown everything about the future Day of 𝕒𝕐𝕒𝕫! He wrote it down for the future generations, especially the generation chosen to live in the Day of 𝕒𝕐𝕒𝕫! **I believe that's us**! All the writings of the other prophets provide additional detail to the template that Hanok already laid out concerning the Day of 𝕒𝕐𝕒𝕫! The Book Enoch is full of exhortations for the Righteous and warnings for the wicked and unrepentant! If you are called out by 𝕒𝕐𝕒𝕫 to be a member of the commonwealth of Israel, then *The Book Enoch* will provide a source of inspiration and comfort to you! *The Book Enoch* will help you understand why so <u>many</u> afflictions happen to the people of 𝕒𝕐𝕒𝕫 in comparison to those that happen to the wicked! From the very first chapter the Good News is Hanok's central theme!

*Enoch 1 (*Hanok)

The words of the blessing of Enoch, wherewith he blessed the elect and righteous, <u>who will be living in the day of tribulation,</u> <u>when all the wicked and godless are to be removed</u> **(the Day of Yahuah)**. *And he took up his parable and said Enoch a righteous man, whose eyes were opened by* 𝕒𝕐𝕒𝕫*, saw the vision of the Holy One in the heavens, which the angels showed me, and from them <u>I heard everything</u>, and from them I understood as I saw, but <u>not for this generation, but for a remote one which is for to come</u>.* **(That's us!)** *Concerning the elect I said, and took up my parable concerning them: The Holy Great One will come forth from His dwelling(***Yahushua's Return at the 7*th* Trumpet Blast)***, And the eternal* 𝕒𝕐𝕒𝕫 *will tread upon the earth, (even)* <u>on Mount Sinai</u>*, [And appear from His camp] and appear in the strength of His might from the heaven of heavens. And all shall be smitten with fear And the Watchers shall quake, And great fear and trembling shall seize them unto the ends of the earth. And the high mountains shall be shaken, And the high hills shall be made low, And shall melt like wax before the flame. And the earth shall be wholly rent in sunder, And all that is upon the earth shall perish, And there shall be a judgment upon all (men).*

The Day of ᎠᎩᎮᏃ
Chapter 13

⁴¹'And I shall rejoice over them to do good to them, and shall plant them in this land in truth, with all My heart and with all My being.' *YirmeYahu 32*

The Day of ᎠᎩᎮᏃ will be the culmination of every hope and every dream that the Righteous of Israel have trusted in, since the day Adam and Hawwah came out of the Garden of Eden! Contrary to popular opinion, the Day of ᎠᎩᎮᏃ is **not** a twenty-four hour day as most people assume. The Day of ᎠᎩᎮᏃ is actually a 1,000 year period of time. On the Day of ᎠᎩᎮᏃ all the milestones listed in Daniel's 490 year prophecy will be accomplished.

Daniel 9
²⁴"<u>Seventy weeks</u> **(of years)** are decreed for your people and for your set-apart city, to <u>put an end</u> to the <u>transgression</u>, and to seal up sins, and to cover crookedness, and <u>to bring in everlasting righteousness</u>, and to seal up vision and prophet, and to anoint the Most Set-apart. ²⁵"Know, then, and understand: from the going forth of the <u>command to restore</u> and build Yahrushalayim until Messiah the Prince is <u>seven weeks</u> and <u>sixty-two weeks</u>. It shall be built again, with streets and a trench, but in times of **affliction**. ²⁶"And after the sixty-two weeks Messiah shall be cut off **(mistranslated; should be "Cut a covenant with many, but not for Himself!")** and have naught. And the people of a coming prince **(Nimrod, the resurrected beast)** shall destroy the city and the set-apart place **(the rebuilt Yahrushalayim, see ZekarYah:14)**. And the end of it is with a flood. And wastes are decreed, and fighting until the end. ²⁷"And he **(the resurrected beast)** shall confirm a covenant with many for one week. And in the middle of the week he **(Nimrod, the resurrected beast)** shall put an end to slaughtering and meal offering **(ZekarYah 14)**. And on the wings of abominations **(flying horsemen and riders resurrected from the Abyss at the 5ᵗʰ Trumpet-Kittim)** he **(Nimrod)** shall lay waste **(the nations)**, even until the complete end and that which is decreed is poured out on the one **(Nimrod)**, who lays waste."

The Day of ᎠᎩᎮᏃ is **not** a matter of one literal 24 hour day as most sheep assume. Yahuah's reckoning of time is **not** at all like man's reckoning of time. For example, do you remember Yahuah's promise to Adam concerning the Tree of Knowledge of Good and Evil?

Genesis 2 (Berishith)
¹⁵And 𐤀𐤉𐤄𐤅 Elohim took the man and put him in the garden of Eden to work it and to guard it. ¹⁶And 𐤀𐤉𐤄𐤅 Elohim commanded the man, saying, "Eat of every tree of the garden, ¹⁷but do <u>not</u> eat of the tree of the knowledge of good and evil, <u>for in the day that you eat of it you shall certainly die</u>."

Of course Adam did eat of the Tree of the Knowledge and the Scriptures record that Adam **did die** at the ripe old age of 930 years. **Remember one day to 𐤀𐤉𐤄𐤅 is like 1,000 of our years**. If you consider that fact, Adam did die on the very same day that he ate of the Tree of Knowledge of Good and Evil. In the Psalms it is recorded that 1,000 years to 𐤀𐤉𐤄𐤅 is like a watch in the night.

Psalms 90 (Tehillim)
²Before the mountains were born, Or You had brought forth the earth and the world, Even from everlasting to everlasting You are El. ³You turn man back to dust, And say, "Return, O children of men." **⁴For a thousand years in Your eyes are like yesterday that has past, or like a watch in the night.**

Peter discussed the Day of 𐤀𐤉𐤄𐤅 and gave us a very important clue or reminder about Yahuah's time scale!

2 Peter 2 (Kepha)
This is now, beloved ones, the second letter I write to you, in which I stir up your sincere mind, to remember ²the words previously <u>spoken by the set-apart prophets</u>, and of the <u>command of the Master and Savior, spoken by your emissaries</u>, ³knowing this first: that mockers shall come in the last days with mocking, walking according to their own lusts, ⁴and saying, "Where is the promise of His coming? For since the fathers fell asleep, all continues as from the beginning of creation." ⁵For they choose to have this hidden from them: that the heavens were of old, and the earth standing out of water and in the water, by the Word of Elohim, ⁶through which the world at that time was destroyed, being flooded with water. ⁷And the present heavens and the earth are treasured up by the same Word, being kept for fire, to a day of judgment and destruction of wicked men. ⁸But, beloved ones, <u>let not this one matter be hidden from you: that with 𐤀𐤉𐤄𐤅 one day is as a thousand years, and a thousand years as one day</u>. ⁹𐤀𐤉𐤄𐤅 is not slow in regard to the promise, as some count slowness, but is patient toward us, not wishing that any should perish but that all should come to repentance ¹⁰But the day of 𐤀𐤉𐤄𐤅 shall come as a thief in the night, in which the heavens shall pass away with a great noise, and the elements shall melt with intense heat, and the earth and the works that are in it shall be burned up.

2 Peter 2 (Kepha), cont.

[11] Seeing all these are to be destroyed in this way, what kind of people ought you to be in set-apart behavior and reverence, [12] looking for and hastening the coming of the day of Elohim, through which the heavens shall be destroyed, being set on fire, and the elements melt with intense heat! [13] But according to His promise we wait for a renewed heavens and a renewed earth in which righteousness dwells. [14] So then, beloved ones, looking forward to this, do your utmost to be found by Him in peace, spotless, and blameless, [15] and reckon the patience of our Master as deliverance, as also our beloved brother Shaul wrote to you, according to the wisdom given to him, [16] as also in all his letters, speaking in them concerning these matters, in which some are hard to understand, which those who are untaught and unstable twist to their own destruction, as they do also the other Scriptures. [17] You, then, beloved ones, being forewarned, watch, lest you also fall from your own steadfastness, being led away with the delusion of the lawless, [18] but grow in the favor and knowledge of our Master and Savior OWYAZ Messiah.

Daniel records the fact that 490 years will be required to accomplish **several milestones** on the Day of ayaz. Contrary to popular opinion those milestones have **not** already been accomplished. Many intelligent people point to certain past historical events as the fulfillment of Daniel's prophecy. However, the events of Daniel's 490 year prophecy are all still to come **in the future**! Daniel said that a decree would be given to rebuild Yahrushalayim. Koresh king of Paras mistranslated in English as Cyrus king of Persia gave a decree to rebuild Yahrushalayim at the end of the first Babylonian exile, but that decree should **not** be confused with the **future** decree of OWYAZ to rebuild Yahrushalayim! The key to understanding the difference between Koresh's decree and **Yahushua's** future decree is to look at the milestones that Daniel said would be accomplished by the end of the **future** 490 year period. None of these milestones have been accomplished as I write *Let My People Go*. So we should know that the decree to rebuild Yahrushalayim is an event that will happen in the **future**. Let's examine the milestones that Daniel said would be accomplished during the 490 year period. **(1) Rebellion and sin against ayaz will be completely put down by OWYAZ! (2) Injustice will be righteously recompensed! (3) Visions and prophecy about the Day of ayaz will end! (4) Everlasting righteousness will arrive with Yahushua's kingdom! (5) The New Yahrushalayim will be anointed!** Daniel's future decree to rebuild Yahrushalayim should **not** to be confused with any past decree to rebuild Yahrushalayim because these milestones have definitely not occurred.

As I stated before, King Koresh of Paras, gave a decree to rebuild Yahrushalayim, after the first Babylonian exile. This is recorded in the book of Ezra. Most prophecy scholars today identify that decree as the fulfillment of Daniel 9, but that is a major error. Today a city called Jerusalem is a thriving tourist city in the State of Israel. Jerusalem is **touted** to be the very same city that we read about in the Scriptures! That Jerusalem in the State of Israel doesn't need to be rebuilt, does it? Because today's Jerusalem is a thriving tourist city, many scholars conclude that Daniel's prophecy **must** have already been fulfilled. So the decree to rebuild Yahrushalayim issued by Koresh seems to be a logical choice, doesn't it? It may seem logical, but it's a big error! Read the verse to remember again! Don't judge things by their appearances! Take a close look at how the State of Israel came into existence! Today's State of Israel was concocted and established by **powerful Zionist**, **not supernaturally** by ायेशू as the Scriptures clearly record will happen! Study the Zionist movement and the creation of today's State of Israel for yourself. You will be surprised and disappointed. The present day State of Israel is a huge stumbling block for serious students of the Scriptures. Zionist supporters of the State of Israel have touted modern Jerusalem as the set apart city of the Scriptures! **That's a big, big lie!** Daniel's decree to rebuild Yahrushalayim specifically applies to a great **future** event. Jerusalem in the State of Israel today is **not** the Yahrushalayim that was spoken of by the prophet Daniel! The Jerusalem in Zionist Israel today is a **counterfeit and a deceptive snare, just like traditional religions of men are counterfeits for the true worship of** ायेशू! Deceptive traditions of men have caused the sheep of this world to be blinded to the real truth. The Jerusalem in Palestine is actually about 150 miles northwest of the ruins of the real Yahrushalayim! Today the real Yahrushalayim is located in the desolated wilderness areas of northwestern Saudi Arabia. Yes, the real Yahrushalayim lies in ruins in the wilderness regions of northwestern Saudi Arabia far away from those, **who would exploit it for money and power**. The prophets wrote that Yahrushalayim and the set apart cities of Yahudah would **remain** desolate and in ruins, until OWYAZ returns at the opening of 6th Seal on the Day of ायेशू to gather His First Fruits! Many will **not** believe my report on this, but those, who have eyes to see and ears to hear will seek out the truth. It is hard to believe that the State of Israel is a big counterfeit because of all the news, propaganda, and hoopla that surrounds it! However, complete neutrality is paramount, when reading *Let My People Go*. **Remember do not judge anything solely by its outward appearances!** A love for the truth is a vital characteristic for acceptance into the commonwealth of Israel!

I've found that Yahuah's truth is **not** found with popular apostate religious opinions. The false shepherds jumped on the counterfeit State of Israel's bandwagon just like they jumped on Nimrod's sun worship band wagon. The shepherds have succeeded in convincing their sheep that today's State of Israel is the genuine Holy Land of the Scriptures. These shepherds organize tours to the State of Israel for their congregations. They get free vacations, which would be fine **except** the "Holy Land" in today's State of Israel is **not** the real Holy Land at all! It's all a sinister lie! That Holy Land is an imposter! It is **not** set apart to ayaz! **It was set apart in 1947 by powerful men to satisfy their own greed and lusts**! Many spiritual Jews have chosen not to relocate to the State of Israel. They believe that it would be **rebellion** against ayaz to take it upon themselves to end their own exile. Those sheep are very, very wise. Those spiritual Jews choose **to wait** for ayaz to bring them home as the Scriptures clearly declare that He will. I know that many reading this book have taken "Holy Land" tours and experienced special times in Palestine. I can understand that perfectly. However, I can say based on the words of the Prophets of ayaz, that the Holy Land of Palestine is **not** the real Promised Land! That's **not** to say that the **stirring**, which you felt in your heart, when you visited that Holy Land, was not real! On the contrary, I believe the stirring, which you may have experienced, was real! ayaz has built into all His called out ones a passionate desire to return to the real Promised Land and a compassionate love for His people, who He calls Israel. Yahuah's people, Israel, have soft compassionate hearts, they love the Torah, they love the name of ayaz, and they have an **insatiable drive to go back to the real Promised Land**! As you fall more and more in love with ayaz and owyaz, you will feel the stirring of ayaz regardless of where you are! When I feel that stirring, it will often bring me to **tears** no matter where I am! ayaz lovingly draws all His called out ones to Himself step by step. If you feel an overpowering love for ayaz, which sometimes brings you to tears, then that would explain to me why you are reading this humble book.

John 6 (Yohanan)
"No one is able to come to Me unless the Father who sent Me draws him. And I shall raise him up in the last day. [45]*"It has been written in the prophets, 'And they shall all be taught by* ayaz*. Everyone, then, who has heard from the Father, and learned, comes to Me.*

ayaz has a definite set order for the unfolding of the events on the Day of ayaz. It was recorded by Paul in the Scriptures, but it has been widely misunderstood.

1 Corinthians 15
23 *But each in his own order:* **OWY𐤄𐤉** **(the first of the First Fruits)**, *the firstfruits* ***(First Fruits is plural);*** *then, when he comes* ***(at the sound of the 7th Trumpet),*** *those who belong to him* ***(His Wheat).***

The order, which Paul and the prophets laid out, has been greatly misunderstood and misinterpreted by the false shepherds over many generations. Here is the order as stated in the Scriptures! First **OWY𐤄𐤉** comes at the opening of the 6th Seal! When **OWY𐤄𐤉** comes at the opening of the 6th Seal of Revelation, He gathers His First Fruits to Himself in the real Promised Land! This will occur amidst great world chaos and confusion, which will result from Yahushua's coming! When Yahushua's First Fruits are gathered, then **OWY𐤄𐤉 will give the decree** to His First Fruits to rebuild and reinhabit the real Yahrushalayim, which lies in ruins today! **The ruins of Yahrushalayim are rebuilt and reinhabited safely by His First Fruits and their families for 434 years (62 weeks of years)**! From year 434 until year 486½ there will be wars, rumors of wars, and desolations against the people of the Covenant! By year 486½ most of the real Yahrushalayim will be sacked by the beast and his army! Many people In Yahrushalem will be killed, raped, imprisoned, or exiled! When Yahuah's two witnesses' assignment is completed, they will also be slaughtered by the forces of Nimrod in the streets of the city! Their bodies will lie in the streets of Yahrushalayim for 3½ days without a decent burial! However, before the 7th Trumpet sounds, the two witnesses will be resurrected up into the heavens in front of their enemies! When the 7th Trumpet sounds, **OWY𐤄𐤉** will return in great power to rescue His First Fruits from Yahrushalayim, where they will be trapped on the Mount of Olives and on the Temple Mount! Everyone on the planet **will see** **OWY𐤄𐤉** return! At the 7th Trumpet **OWY𐤄𐤉** will resurrect the Righteous of Israel, who have died, since His death! They wait patiently in Sheol for the 7th Trumpet to sound! The First Fruits will be reborn in the twinkling of an eye into incorruptible spiritual bodies like Yahushua's! From those rescued from Yahrushalayim, **OWY𐤄𐤉** will hand select fishermen to fish His Wheat out of the nations! These fishermen will gather all Yahushua's **Wheat**, who will be severly oppressed in the nations! **OWY𐤄𐤉** will gather all Israel to His wedding banquet at Mount Sinai, where the heavenly Mount Zion is now clearly visible above Mount Sinai just like it was during the life of Adam! Over the final 3½ years of Daniel's 490 year prophecy, **OWY𐤄𐤉** will establish His undisputed reign over the entire earth and gather all the wicked from **every** generation for their torture and destruction in the wine press of His fury at the valley of Yahushofet! Let's set the stage for Yahushua's **first** reappearance, which will occur at the opening of the 6th Seal of Revelation.

The first four Seals that OWYAZ will open set in motion the world dynamics that will be in operation, when OWYAZ returns to gather His First Fruits. When the first four Seals of Revelation are opened, four wicked kings will be set loose one after the other in their appointed order in the regions occupied by today's Saudi Arabia, Jordan, Palestine, Iran, Iraq, and Yemen. These wicked conquering kings will establish the world dynamics that will be in operation, when OWYAZ returns at the opening of the 6th seal to gather His First Fruits. What was John seeing, when He recorded the events of the first four Seals? Daniel saw the same events and recorded them in Daniel 11.

Revelations 5
And I saw when the Lamb opened one of the seals, and I heard one of the four living creatures saying, like a sound of thunder, "Come and see **(Mistranslated, Should be "Go!")**." *(1st Seal)* ^{2}And I looked and saw a white horse, and he, who sat on it holding a bow. And a crown was given to him, and he went out overcoming and to overcome. ^{3}And when He opened the *(2nd Seal)* second seal, I heard the second living creature saying, "Come and see **(Should be "Go!")**." ^{4}And another horse, fiery red, went out. And it was given to the one who sat on it to take peace from the earth, and that they should slay one another. And a great sword was given to him. ^{5}And when He opened the *(3rd Seal)* third seal, I heard the third living creature say, "Come and see **(Should be "Go!")**." And I looked and saw a black horse, and he who sat on it holding a pair of scales in his hand. ^{6}And I heard a voice in the midst of the four living creatures saying, "A quart of wheat for a day's wage, and three quarts of barley for a day's wage. And do not harm the oil and the wine." ^{7}And when He opened the *(4th Seal)* fourth seal, I heard the voice of the fourth living creature saying, "Come and see **(Should be "Go!")**." ^{8}And I looked and saw a pale horse. And he who sat on it had the name Death **(The beast, The destroyer, Asshur, Nimrod)**, and the grave followed with him. **(the Kittim, Nimrod's wicked winged warriors , who are presently prisoners in the underworld, but will be let loose at the sound of the 5th Trumpet!)** And authority was given to them over a fourth of the earth, to kill with sword, and with hunger, and with death, and by the beasts of the earth. ^{9}And when He opened the *(5th Seal)* fifth seal, I saw under the altar the beings of those having been slain for the Word of Elohim and for the witness which they held, ^{10}and they cried with a loud voice, saying, "How long, O Master, set-apart and true, until You judge and avenge our blood on those who dwell on the earth?"

The first four seals that John saw are four horsemen that will be loosed at the command of OWYAZ to fulfill Yahuah's plans.

These horsemen are to be loosed at their appointed times and will be commanded to "Go" to their appointed places to fulfill their role in Yahuah's plan. Where do we look for the identity of these four horsemen? We look in the book of Daniel. The first three horsemen are three wicked kings, who will stir up the nations to war! The 1st horseman is called the King of the North. He will be a king from the land of ancient Babel in northern Arabia. The 2nd horseman is called the King of the South. He will be a king from the land of ancient Mitsrayim in today's northwestern Saudi Arabia. The first King of the North will disappear from the scene, but he will be replaced by the 3rd horseman. This second King of the North will impose taxes, but his rule will only last a short time. He will be replaced by the 4th horseman, who will be a **vile** man, who will acquire his rule by the use of intrigue and deception!

The 4th Horseman

But woe, woe, woe there is a 4th horseman! He will be a vile and deceitful person, who will be **resurrected from the Abyss**! He will be called the "Destroyer" of the earth! This 4th horseman has been appointed to subjugate all the nations of the earth to him just like he did in his first life. He and his wicked armies will desolate the earth during Daniel's 490 year prophecy! The 4th horseman will be the third king of the North, after the first two have left the scene. There is no doubt whatsoever that this 4th horseman will be a person from the distant past, who will be **resurrected** from the Abyss (Sheol, or the underworld)! This 4th horseman has already lived in the ancient past! He was the very first king of mankind, after the Flood! He once built a tower to storm the heavens in order to make a name for himself! This 4th horseman is the consummate rebel! When he lived before, He was a **mighty hunter** in the face of 𐤀𐤉𐤀𐤆!

^{9}He was a mighty hunter before 𐤀𐤉𐤀𐤆, therefore it is said, Like Nimrod the mighty hunter before 𐤀𐤉𐤀𐤆." ^{10}And the beginning of his reign was Babel, and Erek, and Akkad, and Kalneh, in the land of Shin'ar. ^{11}From that land he went to Ashshur and built Nineweh, and Rehoboth Ir, and Kelah, ^{12}and Resen between Nineweh and Kelah, the great city.
Genesis 10

𐤀𐤉𐤀𐤆 long ago designated this 4th horseman as the Destroyer, who will be resurrected on the Day of 𐤀𐤉𐤀𐤆. Throughout the Scriptures you can find a lot of references to this 4th horseman, his name is Nimrod!

Daniel 11
^{2}"And now I declare the truth to you: See, three more sovereigns are to arise in Persia and the fourth is to become far richer than them all.

Daniel 11, cont.
*And by his power, through his riches, he stirs up all against the rulership of Greece **(Mistranslated as Greece, but should be Yawan)** ³"And a mighty sovereign shall arise, and he shall rule with great authority, and do as he pleases. ⁴"But when he has arisen, his rule shall be broken **(the beast's rule, not Alexander the Great's)** up and divided toward the four winds of the heavens, but not among his descendants nor according to his authority with which he ruled, because his rule shall be uprooted, even for others **(Israel)** besides these. ⁵"And a sovereign of the South shall become strong, along with one of his princes who gains power over him and shall rule – his rule being a great rule. ⁶"And at the end of years they shall join themselves together, and a daughter of the sovereign of the South shall come to the sovereign of the North **(Rider of the 1ˢᵗ Seal)** to make an alliance. But she shall not retain the strength of her power, nor would he or his power stand. And she shall be given up, with those who brought her, and he who brought her forth, and he who supported her in those times.⁷"But from a branch of her roots one **(Rider of the 2ⁿᵈ Seal)** shall arise in his place, and he shall come into the defense and come into a stronghold of the sovereign of the North, and shall act against them, and shall prevail, ⁸and also their mighty ones, with their princes and their precious utensils of silver and gold he shall seize and bring to Mitsrayim. And he shall stand more years than the sovereign of the North. ⁹"Then he shall enter the reign of the sovereign of the South, but shall return to his own land. ¹⁰"But his sons shall stir themselves up, and assemble a great army. And he shall certainly come and overflow and pass through, then return to his stronghold, and be stirred up. ¹¹"Then the sovereign of the South shall be enraged and go out to fight with him, with the sovereign of the North, who shall raise a large army. But the army shall be given into the hand of his enemy, ¹²and he shall capture the army, his heart being exalted. And he shall cause tens of thousands to fall, but not prevail. ¹³"And the sovereign of the North shall return and raise an army greater than the former, and certainly come at the end of some years with a great army and much supplies. ¹⁴"And in those times many shall rise up against the sovereign of the South, while some violent ones among your people exalt themselves to establish the vision, but they shall stumble. ¹⁵"Then the sovereign of the North shall come in and build a siege mound, and capture a city of strongholds. And the arms of the South shall not stand, nor his choice people, for there is no strength to stand. ¹⁶"So his opponent shall do as he pleases – with no one standing against him – and stand in the Splendid Land with destruction in his hand.*

Daniel 11, cont.
[17]"And he shall set his face to enter with the strength of his entire rule, and make an alliance with him. And he shall do so, and give him the daughter of women to corrupt her. But she shall not stand, neither be for him. [18]"Then he shall turn his face to the coastlands and capture many. But a ruler shall bring the reproach against them to an end. And with the reproach removed, he shall turn back on him. [19]"Then he shall turn his face toward the strongholds of his own land, but shall stumble and fall, and not be found. [20]"And in his place one shall stand up who imposes taxes **(Rider of the 3rd Seal)** on the adorned city of the rule, but within a few days he is destroyed, but not in wrath or in battle. [21]"And in his place shall arise a despised one **(Rider of the 4th Seal)**, to whom they shall not give the excellency of the rule. But he shall come in peaceably, and seize the rule by flatteries. [22]"And the arms of the flood shall be swept away from before him and be broken, and also the prince of the covenant. [23]"And after they joined him, he shall work deceit, and shall come up and become strong with a small nation. [24]"He shall enter peaceably, even into the richest places of the province, and do what his fathers have not done, nor his forefathers: distribute among them plunder and spoil and supplies, and devise his plots against the strongholds, but only for a time. [25]"And he shall stir up his power and his heart against the sovereign of the South with a great army, and the sovereign of the South shall be stirred up to battle with a very great and mighty army, but not stand, for they shall devise plots against him. [26]"And those who have been eating his food shall destroy him, and his army be swept away, and many fall down slain. [27]"And both these sovereigns' hearts are to do evil, and speak lies at the same table, but not prosper, for the end is still for an appointed time. [28]"Then he shall return to his land with much supplies, and his heart be against the set-apart covenant. And he shall act, and shall return to his land. [29]"At the appointed time he shall return and go toward the south, but it shall not be like the former or the latter. [30]"For ships from Kittim shall come against him, and he shall lose heart, and shall return in rage against the set-apart covenant, and shall act, and shall return and consider those who forsake the set-apart covenant. [31]"And strong ones shall arise from him and profane the set-apart place, the stronghold, and shall take away that which is continual, and set up the abomination that lays waste. [32]"And by flatteries he shall profane those who do wrong against the covenant, but the people who know their Elohim shall be strong, and shall act. [33]"And those of the people who have insight shall give understanding to many. And they shall stumble by sword and flame, by captivity and plundering, for days. [34]"And when they stumble, they shall be helped, a little help, but many shall join them, by flatteries.

Daniel 11, cont.

[35]"And some of those who have insight shall stumble, to refine them, and to cleanse them, and to make them white, until the time of the end, for it is still for an appointed time. [36]"And the sovereign shall do as he pleases, and exalt himself and show himself to be great above every mighty one, and speak incredible matters against the Ěl of mighty ones, and shall prosper until the wrath has been accomplished – for what has been decreed shall be done – [37]and have no regard for the mighty ones of his fathers nor for the desire of women, nor have regard for any mighty one, but exalt himself above them all. [38]"But in his place he shall give esteem to a mighty one of strongholds. And to a mighty one which his fathers did not know he shall give esteem with gold and silver, with precious stones and costly gifts. [39]"And he shall act against the strongest strongholds with a foreign mighty one, which he shall acknowledge. He shall increase in esteem and cause them to rule over many, and divide the land for gain. [40]"At the time of the end the sovereign of the South shall push at him, and the sovereign of the North rush against him like a whirlwind, with chariots, and with horsemen, and with many ships. And he shall enter the lands, and shall overflow and pass over, [41]and shall enter the Splendid Land, and many shall stumble, but these escape from his hand: Edom, and Mo'ab, and the chief of the sons of Ammon. [42]"And he shall stretch out his hand against the lands, and the land of Mitsrayim shall not escape. [43]"And he shall rule over the treasures of gold and silver, and over all the riches of Mitsrayim, and Libyans and Kushites shall be at his steps. [44]"Then reports from the east and the north shall disturb him, and he shall go out with great wrath to destroy and put many under the ban, [45]and he shall pitch the tents of his palace between the seas **(Gulf of Aqaba in the west and the Sea of Galilee in the east)** and the splendid set-apart mountain, but shall come to his end with none to help him.

YeshaYahu (Isaiah) 10

[5]"Woe to Ashshur **(Nimrod)**, the rod of My displeasure and the staff in whose hand is My displeasure. [6]"Against a defiled nation I send him, and against the people of My wrath I command him to seize the spoil, to take the prey, and to tread them down like the mud of the streets. [7]"But he does not intend so, nor does his heart think so, or it is in his heart to destroy, and cut off not a few nations. [8]"For he says, Are not my princes sovereigns? [9]'Is not Kalno like Karkemish? Is not Hamath like Arpad? Is not Shomeron like Damascus? [10]'As my hand has found the reigns of the idols, whose carved images excelled those of Yahrushalayim and Shomeron, [11]as I have done to Shomeron and her idols, do I not do also to Yahrushalayim and her idols?'

YeshaYahu (Isaiah) 10, cont.

[12] "And it shall be, when אYהZ has performed all His work on Mount Tsiyon and on Yahrushalayim, that I shall punish the fruit of the greatness of the heart of the sovereign of Ashshur, and the boasting of his haughty looks. [13] "For he has said, 'By the power of my hand I have done it, and by my wisdom, for I have been clever. And I remove the boundaries of the people, and have robbed their treasuries. And I put down the inhabitants like a strong one. [14] 'And my hand finds the riches of the people like a nest. And I have gathered all the earth like forsaken eggs are gathered. And there was no one who moved his wing, nor opened his mouth with even a peep.' " [15] Would the axe boast itself over him who chops with it, or the saw exalt itself over him who saws with it? As a rod waving those who lift it up! As a staff lifting up that which is not wood! [16] Therefore the Master, אYהZ of hosts, sends leanness among his fat ones. And under his esteem he kindles a burning like the burning of a fire. [17] And the Light of Yisra'el shall be for a fire, and his Set-apart One for a flame. And it shall burn and devour his weeds and his thorn bushes in one day, [18] and consume the esteem of his forest and of his fertile field, both life and flesh. And they shall be as when a sick man wastes away, [19] and the remaining trees of his forest shall be so few in number that a child records them.
[20] And in that day it shall be that the remnant of Yisra'el, and those who have escaped of the house of Ya'aqob, never again lean upon him who defeated them, but shall lean upon אYהZ, the Set-apart One of Yisra'el, in truth. [21] A remnant shall return, the remnant of Ya'aqob, to the Mighty El. [22] For though your people, O Yisra'el, be as the sand of the sea, yet a remnant of them shall return – a decisive end, overflowing with righteousness. [23] For the Master אYהZ of hosts is making a complete end, as decided, in the midst of all the earth. [24] Therefore thus said the Master אYהZ of hosts, "My people, who dwell in Tsiyon, be not afraid of Ashshur, who beats you with a rod and lifts up his staff against you, in the way of Mitsrayim. [25] "For yet a little while and the displeasure shall be completed, and My displeasure be to their destruction." [26] And אYהZ of hosts stirs up a lash for him as the smiting of Midyan at the rock of Oreb. And as His rod was on the sea, so shall He lift it up in the way of Mitsrayim.

Ezekiel 38

[2] "Son of man, set your face against Gog, of the land of Magog, the prince of Rosh, Meshek, and Tubal, and prophesy against him. [3] "And you shall say, 'Thus says the Master אYהZ, "See, I am against you, O Gog, the prince of Rosh, Meshek, and Tubal. [4] "And I shall turn you around, and I shall put hooks into your jaws, and shall lead you out, with all your army, horses and horsemen, clad perfectly, a great assembly with armour and shields, all of them handling swords.

Ezekiel 38, cont.

⁵"Persia (Paran), Kush, and Put are with them, all of them with shield and helmet, ⁶"Gomer and all its bands, the house of Togarmah from the far north and all its bands, many peoples with you. ⁷"Be ready, prepare yourself, you and all your assemblies that are assembled unto you. And you shall be a guard for them. ⁸"After many days you shall be **called up** *(Nimrod resurrected from the Abyss)*. In the latter years you shall come into the land of those brought back from the sword and gathered from many people on the mountains of Yisra'el **(Barley Harvest, the First Fruits)**, which had been a **continual waste**. But they were brought out of the gentiles, and all of them shall dwell safely. ⁹"And you shall go up, coming like a storm, covering the land like a cloud, you and all your bands and many peoples with you." ¹⁰'Thus said the Master 𐤀𐤅𐤄𐤉, "And it shall be in that day that words arise in your heart, and you shall devise an evil plan: ¹¹"And you shall say, 'Let me go up against a land of unwalled villages, let me go to those at rest who dwell safely, all of them dwelling without walls, and having neither bars nor gates,' ¹²to take plunder and to take booty, to stretch out your hand against the waste places that are **again inhabited**, and **against a people gathered from the gentiles**, acquiring livestock and goods, who dwell in the middle of the land. ¹³"Sheba, and Dedan, and the merchants of Tarshish, and all their young lions shall say to you, 'Have you come to take plunder? Have you gathered your army to take booty, to bear away silver and gold, to take away livestock and goods, to take great plunder?' ¹⁴"Therefore, son of man, prophesy, and you shall say to Gog, 'Thus said the Master 𐤀𐤅𐤄𐤉, "In that day when My people Yisra'el dwell safely, would you not know? ¹⁵"And you shall come from your place out of the far north, you and many peoples with you, all of them riding on horses, a great assembly and a mighty army. ¹⁶"And you shall come up against My people Yisra'el like a cloud, to cover the land – in the latter days it shall be. And I shall bring you against My land, in order that the gentiles know Me, when I am set apart in you, **(just like 𐤀𐤅𐤄𐤉 used Pharaoh)** O Gog, before their eyes." ¹⁷'Thus said the Master 𐤀𐤅𐤄𐤉, "Are you the one I spoke of in former days by My servants the prophets of Yisra'el, who prophesied for years in those days, to bring you against them? ¹⁸"And it shall be on that day, on the day when Gog comes against the land of Yisra'el," declares the Master 𐤀𐤅𐤄𐤉, "that My wrath shall come up in My face. ¹⁹"For in My jealousy and in the fire of My wrath I have spoken, 'On that day there shall be a great **shaking in the land** of Yisra'el, ²⁰so that the fish of the sea, and the birds of the heavens, and the beasts of the field, and all creeping creatures that creep on the earth, and all men who are on the face of the earth shall shake at My presence. And the mountains shall be thrown down, and the steep places shall fall, and every wall fall to the ground.'

Ezekiel 38, cont.

²¹"And I shall call for a sword against Gog on all My mountains," declares the Master ⟨YHWH⟩, "the sword of each one being against his brother. ²²"And I shall judge him with pestilence and blood, and rain down flooding rain and hailstones, fire and sulphur, on him and on his bands and on the many peoples who are with him.

What happens, when OWYAZ opens the 5ᵗʰ Seal? When ⟨YHWH⟩ opens the 5ᵗʰ Seal, the spirits of the Righteous dead under the altar in Sheol ask OWYAZ a question! "How much longer?" The earth has always been the altar for Israel! Yahuah's people have given their lives for the name of ⟨YHWH⟩ for thousands of years! Sheol is the underworld; the place **under** the earth prepared for the departed spirits of the dead. The spirits of the Righteous dead in Sheol, **since** Yahuah's death on the Passover tree, will be anxious, but they must wait patiently for the 7ᵗʰ Trumpet to sound. When they hear that sound, they will be resurrected and gathered with the rest of Israel to Mount Sinai and the heavenly Mount Zion! When the 6ᵗʰ Seal is opened, ⟨YHWH⟩ will no longer hide His face from His people! Yahuah's face is OWYAZ. During Yahushua's 1260 day ministry on earth, the Scriptures report that most of the people at that time hid their faces from OWYAZ because of His **grotesque** physical appearance, which resulted from His leprosy and other afflictions! Because of their blindness, ⟨YHWH⟩ has hidden OWYAZ, His face, from us! When the 6ᵗʰ Seal is opened, OWYAZ will **gather** His First Fruits to the real Promised Land in today's northwestern Saudi Arabia! The final Exodus of Israel will begin! This Exodus will begin amidst great world chaos, which will be caused by the incredible shaking that will accompany Yahushua's return! After His First Fruits are gathered, then OWYAZ will instruct them to rebuild Yahrushalayim! The First Fruits will safely inhabit Yahrushalayim for 434 years, but in times of great affliction! During that time, OWYAZ will cut a very special covenant with His First Fruits! From year 434 to the end of Daniel's 486½ year prophecy the people of the Covenant in Yahrushalayim and Yahudah will fight valiantly against the beast and his wicked armies!

Dead Sea Scrolls-The War Scroll

*During the remaining **thirty-three** years of the war the men of renown, those called of the Congregation, and all the heads of the congregation's clans shall choose for themselves men of war for all the lands of the nations. From all tribes of Israel they shall prepare capable men for themselves to go out for battle according to the summons of the war, year by year. But during the years of remission they shall not ready men to go out for battle, for it is a Sabbath of rest for Israel. During the thirty-five years of service the war shall be waged.*

Dead Sea Scrolls-The War Scroll

For six years the whole congregation shall wage it together, and a war of divisions shall be waged during the twenty-nine remaining years. In the first year they shall fight against Mesopotamia, in the second against the sons of Lud, in the third they shall fight against the rest of the sons of Aram: Uz, Hul, Togar, and Mesha, who are beyond the Euphrates. In the fourth and fifth they shall fight against the sons of Arpachshad, in the sixth and seventh they shall fight against all the sons of Assyria and Persia and the easterners up to the Great Desert. In the eighth year they shall fight against the sons of Elam, in the ninth year they shall fight against the sons of Ishmael and Keturah, and during the following ten years the war shall be divided against all the sons of Ham according to [their] c[lans and] their [terri]tories. During the remaining ten years the war shall be divided against all [sons of Japhe]th according to their territories.

By year 486½ most of Yahrushalayim will be sacked **(See ZekarYah, Zachariah 14!)**, but the remnant of ayaz will still possess the Mount of Olives and the Temple Mount! From year 483 until year 486½, Yahuah's two witnesses will measure the Mount of Olives and the Temple Mount and those worshipping there. They must prophesy to the nations once again! At the appointed time, after the two witness have completed their witness at about year 486½, Nimrod will slaughter Yahuah's two witness in the streets of Yahrushalayim! The remnant of Yahushua's First Fruits will hold on, but they will be completely surrounded by Nimrod's armies! The situation looks very, very bad! But at the appointed time, the 7th Trumpet will sound very, very loudly! At that moment, the next stage of Israel's worldwide Exodus will begin! All the called out ones of Israel from all the ages, since Adam, will be gathered together at the same place at the same time for a **mega** wedding celebration! All the called out ones will be given incorruptible bodies like Yahushua's! The Righteous dead of Israel, who have died since Yahushua's death, will be resurrected at the 7th Trumpet! Those, who will be alive at Yahushua's coming, will be reborn into incorruptible bodies! They will be united with OWYaz and the rest of Israel, who have been waiting in Paradise on the heavenly Mount Zion! Then OWYaz will lead all the tribes of Israel to Mount Zion, which has descended to her place in the wilderness, in the most joyous procession ever! The heavenly Mount Zion will be suspended over Mount Sinai as Yahushua's wedding canopy **(Yahushua's Chuppah)**! OWYaz shouts like a mighty man, when He returns as the Lion of Yahudah! OWYaz returns with awesome power to rescue His First Fruits in Yahrushalayim from the fowler's **(Nimrod's)** snare! OWYaz will split the Mount of Olives from east to west!

When the Mount of Olives splits, a set apart highway will be formed for all the called out ones of 𝐘𝐇𝐖𝐇 to travel to Yahushua's fabulous wedding banquet! Yahushua's highway of set-apartness will allow Israel to travel across the mountain heights of Israel in great glory and esteem! They will go back to Mount Sinai, where all the people of Israel will be gathered to renew their wedding vows with 𝐘𝐇𝐖𝐇! And at the appointed time, the Righteous will enter the gates of the New Yahrushalayim! At the 7th Trumpet the Righteous dead from the time of Yahushua's death until the 7th Trumpet sounds, will be resurrected and united with the Righteous dead, who lived from Adam until Yahushua's death! The Righteous dead, who lived from Adam until Yahushua's death, were resurrected at the moment of Yahushua's death! **See Matthew 27! Israel's final worldwide Exodus is all about a fabulous gathering of all the Righteous of Israel, who have ever lived!** All of Israel will be gathered from **Paradise** on Mount Zion, from **Sheol** under the earth, and from **those** still **alive on the earth at Yahushua's coming**! How exciting that will be! Absolutely nothing else in this world can compare to the joy and the happiness that's in store for **Israel**! That's Yahuah's Good News! OWYAZ returns **first** at the opening of the 6th Seal in the midst of total world chaos caused by the devastating earthquakes and tsunami's, which will occur at His coming! **Every mountain will be moved out of its place!** OWYAZ seals His First Fruits with the name of 𝐘𝐇𝐖𝐇 and gathers them back to northwestern Saudi Arabia, where OWYAZ instructs them to rebuild the **real Yahrushalayim in its right place**! Meanwhile, the nations are totally preoccupied with their own survival and with the rebuilding of their devastated infrastructures! The First Fruits will rebuild and then live in Yahrushalayim for a total of 486½ years, before the 7th Trumpet sounds. At that time OWYAZ will return to rescue His First Fruits from Yahrushalayim, after most of the city is sacked by Nimrod's armies! OWYAZ will come to rescue His Barley and to gather all Israel to His fabulous wedding banquet underneath His Chuppah, Mount Zion! OWYAZ will select fishermen and hunters from those He rescues from Yahrushalayim. These hunters and fishermen will go out to the nations and gather all of Yahushua's Wheat harvest. The Wheat will still be in the nations because of Nimrod's refusal to let them go. During the last 3½ years of Daniel's 490 year prophecy, OWYAZ will put down all the rebellion of the nations and completely destroy Nimrod's hideous Kittim army of winged horsemen, who will cause desolations across the whole earth! Nimrod will be captured in the final great battle at the valley of Yahushofet! He and his wicked prophet will be thrown alive into Abbadon in the deepest recesses of the Abyss, which is called the Lake of Fire!

Until the appointed time for Yahushua's Barley harvest, 𐤀𐤉𐤄𐤅 **will not allow the real Yahrushalayim to be rebuilt!** Of course, that means that Jerusalem in Palestine today is a fraud and a counterfeit! What is a **First Fruit** anyway? When the people of Israel were in the real Promised Land, there were two harvests of good grain each year. The first crop that ripened in northwestern Saudi Arabia at that time was the Barley crop. The first sheaf of Barley was harvested in the spring and was waived by the Priest as the First Fruit offering to 𐤀𐤉𐤄𐤅. Israel has been commanded in the Scriptures to remember the Feast of First Fruits because it is a shadow of the future gathering of Yahushua's First Fruits on the Day of 𐤀𐤉𐤄𐤅. Over the next seven weeks all the Barley was harvested and stored in the barns. The second crop of grain harvested in the Promised Land was the Wheat. It was harvested in the Fall! Yahuah's appointed times are shadows of events in store for Israel on the Day of 𐤀𐤉𐤄𐤅. All seven of Yahuah's Feasts, the Shabbat, and the New Moons are reminders to Israel of Yahushua's return and His future harvests. I hope that you understand that OWY𐤀𐤋 has two good harvests on the Day of 𐤀𐤉𐤄𐤅! First the Barley will be harvested at the opening of the 6th Seal, then 486½ years later at the 7th Trumpet, the Wheat will be harvested. Before we examine the Barley Harvest in greater detail, there is **one** more harvest! It's a harvest of **bad** fruit. That harvest is the harvest of the wicked and unrepentant to face Yahuah's undiluted wrath! The wicked and unrepentant are often referred to as thorns and thistles in the Scriptures! They will be harvested and burned in the fire of the Abyss! The wicked are sometimes spoken of as ripened grapes ready to be crushed in Yahuah's winepress in the Valley of Yahuah's judgment called Yahushofet! These gatherings are as easy as one, two, three! There will be **three** harvests on the Day of 𐤀𐤉𐤄𐤅. There will be two harvests of good grain and one harvest of bad grain. Now, let's examine the Barley Harvest in a lot more detail.

The Final Exodus Begins with Yahushua's Barley Harvest!
First OWY𐤀𐤋 will return to gather His **First** Fruits, His Barley Harvest. The Barley will be gathered to the real Promised Land in northwestern Saudi Arabia, not to be confused with today's counterfeit State of Israel! The Barley Harvest will be comprised of 144,000 hand picked sons of Israel. The bloodlines of the Barley will be traceable by 𐤀𐤉𐤄𐤅 to each of the twelve tribes of Israel. Willing family members of the 144,000 will return to the Promised Land too! So the actual number of the assembly will be much larger than 144,000. These 144,000 First Fruits are Yahushua's faithful and true. They will be called servants of 𐤀𐤉𐤄𐤅 because they will cling to His name and follow OWY𐤀𐤋, wherever He leads!

Today, some of these First Fruits **are** no doubt in Christian churches, Jewish synagogues, Messianic Jewish congregations, or in some other place, but they are destined to become the First Fruits of OWYAZ. The First Fruits are being set apart to AYAZ by His Ruach HaQodesh, even as I write this book. They will be ready for their service to AYAZ, when it's time. When the Barley crop has ripened, OWYAZ will gather them back to the real Promised Land in northwestern Saudi Arabia. They will have the **privilege** of rebuilding the real Yahrushalayim and to live there for 486½ years! These First Fruits were described by John, when he spoke about the Philadelphia assembly.

Revelation 7
[7]"And to the messenger of the assembly in Philadelphia write, 'He OWYAZ who is set-apart, He who is true, He who has the key of Dawid, He who opens and no one shuts, and shuts and no one opens, says this **(Yahushua)**: [8]"I know your works – see, I have set before you an open door, and no one is able to shut it – that you have little power, yet have **guarded My Word, and have not denied My Name**. [9]"See, I am giving up those of the congregation of Satan, who say they are Yehudim and are not, but lie. See, I am making them come and worship before your feet, and to know that I have loved you. [10]"Because you have guarded My Word of endurance, I also shall guard you from the hour of trial which shall come upon all the world, to try those who dwell on the earth. [11]"See, I am coming speedily! Hold what you have that no one take your crown. [12]"He who overcomes **(Israel)**, I shall make him a supporting post in the Dwelling Place of My Elohim, and he shall by no means go out. And I shall write on him the Name of My Elohim **(Sealed)** and the name of the city of My Elohim, the renewed Yahrushalayim, which comes down out of the heaven from My Elohim, and My renewed Name. John spoke about the events of Yahushua's Barley Harvest in Revelation Chapters 6 and 7!

Revelation 6
*And I beheld when he had opened the sixth seal, and, lo, there was a great earthquake; and the sun became black as sackcloth of hair, and the moon became as blood; And the stars of heaven fell unto the earth, even as a fig tree casteth her untimely figs, when she is shaken of a mighty wind. **(Devastation of the world's infrastructure occurs!)** And the heaven departed as a scroll when it is rolled together; and every mountain and island were moved out of their places. **(Great Shaking)***

Revelation 6, cont.
And the kings of the earth, and the great men, and the rich men, and the chief captains, and the mighty men, and every bondman, and every free man, <u>hid</u> themselves in the <u>dens</u> and in the <u>rocks</u> of the <u>mountains</u>; And said to the mountains and rocks, <u>Fall on us</u>, and <u>hide us</u> from the face of him that sitteth on the throne, and from the <u>wrath of the Lamb</u>: For the great day **(the Day of ᐊYᗐZ Begins)** of his wrath is come; and who shall be able to stand?

What will happen, when **OWYᗐZ** opens the 6th Seal? The sun will turn really, really black! The moon will turn blood red and stars will fall out of the heavens! The earth will quake **so violently** that **every mountain and every island will be moved out of their places**! I believe that this movement of every island will restore the continents of the earth back to their original configuration. That will be the configuration that existed, before ᐊYᗐZ separated the continents at the time of Peleg. If ᐊYᗐZ can separate the continents at the time of Peleg, then ᐊYᗐZ can certainly move the continents back at will. ᐊYᗐZ divided the earth and ᐊYᗐZ can restore the earth! That's a very small thing for ᐊYᗐZ. When **OWYᗐZ** returns at the 6th Seal for His First Fruits, then Yahuah's Israel's Final Exodus will begin in its appointed order.

Genesis 10
²⁵And to Eber were born two sons, the name of one was Peleg, <u>for in his days the earth was divided</u>, and his brother's name was Yoqtan.

Shaking the Heavens and the Earth
When ᐊYᗐZ spoke the Ten Commandments to the Israelites at Mount Sinai, He caused Mount Sinai to shake violently! When **OWYᗐZ** returns on the Day of ᐊYᗐZ, not only does **OWYᗐZ** shake the earth, but **OWYᗐZ shakes both the Heavens and the Earth violently**! Has anyone ever heard of the heavens shaking before? Of course the answer is no-o-o.

Hebrews 12
²²But you have drawn near to Mount Tsiyon and to the city of the living Elohim, to the heavenly Yahrushalayim, to myriads of messengers, ²³to the entire <u>gathering and assembly</u> of the first-born **(Israel)** having been enrolled in heaven, and to Elohim the Judge of all, and to the spirits of righteous men made perfect, ²⁴and to **OWYᗐZ** the Mediator of a new covenant, and to the blood of sprinkling which speaks better than the blood of Hebel. ²⁵Take heed not to refuse the One speaking. For if those did not escape who refused the warning on earth, much less we who turn away from Him from heaven, ²⁶whose voice <u>shook the earth then</u>, but now He has promised, saying, **"Yet once more I shake not only the earth, but also the heaven."**

Shaking of the earth is called an earthquake. Scientists have even developed a scale to measure an earthquake's magnitude called the Ritcher Scale. However, the Ritcher Scale will be **absolutely useless** on the Day of ायaz because the Ritcher Scale will be **too small**! The magnitude of the earthquakes at that time will be far too large to be measured on the Ritcher Scale! The earthquakes will be increditable, but then there's the matter of the shaking of the heavens too! It's very hard for us to imagine what shaking of the heavens will be like, since no one has ever experienced it before. The Scriptures teach that this shaking of the heavens will be so violent that it will cause stars to fall from the heavens. The sun will turn very black and the moon will turn blood red! What happens, when there is no light from the sun, the moon, or the stars? The earth and its inhabitants will experience extreme darkness! That will be really terrifying!

Confusion and Chaos

Can you imagine the damage that this kind of shaking will do to the earth's infrastructure? Power lines will be down everywhere! Water, gas, and oil lines will rupture! Fires will be uncontrollable! Buildings and bridges will fall! Masses of people will be killed or trapped in the rubble! Roads will split apart and become undrivable! Airplanes on the ground will be destroyed! Airplanes in the air will fall! The oceans will be so violent that submarines and ships of all kinds will be destroyed! Missiles and weapons will be useless **because they can't fly**! Satellites will fall out of their orbits, which will **disable** everything that depends on satellite transmissions! Nothing can stay in the air, when the heavens are shaking violently! Buildings will be flattened everywhere! Power plants **will not** be able to generate power! Ladies the toilets will **not** flush on that day! Dams will burst! Huge waves will form in the seas, which will devastate all the coastlands! Flooding will be worldwide! Industrial production will come to a complete halt! Water plants and sewage plants will **not** operate! The transportation industry won't be able to move people or products! Food and supplies will stop moving! Grocery stores will run out of food! Hospitals will be overrun and useless! The dead and wounded will be everywhere! Disease will be rampant across the earth! Violence, robbery, murder, rape, and every kind of crime will be uncontrollable! Remember how it was in New Orleans! The New Orleans crisis will amount to a drop in the bucket in comparison with the complete worldwide devastation and chaos that will occur, when OWYaz returns at the 6th Seal! Man's technological infrastructure will be completely paralyzed! It certainly will not be business as usual on the earth! **The bell won't ring on Wall Street**! The bull won't be running! There will be no more interest in sporting events like the Super Bowl or the World Series because **nobody will be playing ball**!

There will be no more Wall Street, no more interest in houses, no more interest in fashion, no more interest in TV, movies, or any of the Hollywood celebrities! Yahushua's judgments have begun! The Barley Harvest will come like a <u>thief</u> in the night! It will occur in the midst of this world crisis. The wicked **will not know or even care** what has happened to the First Fruits! It will be **"everyman for himself"**. Yahushua's First Fruits will be gathered from the nations during this time of utter chaos. Of course the rich and famous will be scurrying into their holes, caves, and bunkers trying to ensure their own survival!

Revelation 6

¹⁴*And heaven departed like a scroll being rolled up, and every mountain and island was <u>moved out of its place</u>. ¹⁵And the sovereigns of the earth, and the great ones, and the rich ones, and the commanders, and the mighty, and every slave and every free one, hid themselves in the caves and in the rocks of the mountains, ¹⁶and said to the mountains and rocks, "Fall on us and hide us from the face of Him sitting on the throne and from the wrath of the Lamb, ¹⁷because the <u>great day of His wrath has come</u>, and who is able to stand?"*

The wicked will be terrified, when they see the great signs in the heavens, on the land, and in the seas. The leaders of this world will try to hide from ayaz and the face of His Lamb! **They will not know or even care that the First Fruits have left the nations bound for the Promised Land.** OWYaz rises from the East and commands four heavenly messengers **not** to harm the earth, **until** His First Fruits are sealed with the name of ayaz. Those, who are alive and have completely answered the call of ayaz, **before** OWYaz returns, are candidates for Yahushua's First Fruits. The First Fruits will be brought out of the nations by OWYaz. They will follow OWYaz, **wherever He leads**! They will be led to the ruins of the real Yahrushalayim in the Promised Land.

Revelation 7 (Paleo Name Version by Todd Effren)
1) And afterwards saw I four malachim (messengers) standing upon four corners of the earth and holding upon four winds so that not will wind blow strongly-upon the earth and not upon any tree. 2) And saw I another malak (messenger) ascend from the east and bearing a seal of El Chai, and will call out he with a great voice to the four malachim (messengers) for it was appointed by their hand to destroy the earth and the sea. 3) And said he, " Not will destroy you the earth and the sea and the trees until seal we servants of Eloheinu upon their foreheads."4) And I heard the number of the (ones) to be sealed: One hundred thousand and four and forty thousand that will be sealed from among all b'nei (sons) Yisrael (Israel) according to their tribes:

Revelation 7 (Paleo Name Version by Todd Effren), cont.
5) of tribe of b'nei (sons) Yahudah will be sealed twelve thousand, of tribe b'nei (sons) Reuben twelve thousand, of tribe of b'nei (sons) Gad twelve thousand, 6) of tribe b'nei (sons) Asher twelve thousand, of tribe b'nei (sons) Naphtali twelve thousand, of tribe b'nei (sons) Menasheh twelve thousand, 6) of tribe of b'nei (sons) Shimon twelve thousand, of tribe b'nei (sons) Lewi twelve thousand, of tribe b'nei (sons) Yisaschar twelve thousand, 8) of tribe of b'nei (sons) Zebulun twelve thousand, of tribe b'nei (sons) Yoseph twelve thousand, of tribe b'nei (sons) Binyamin twelve thousand. 9) Afterwards saw I a very great multitude that not was able a man to number from among all ha'goyim (nations) and the families and the peoples and the languages. **Came in they and will stand before haKisei (throne) and before haSeh (Lamb) dressed of garments of white and palm branches in their hands.**

Revelation 14
And I looked and saw a Lamb standing on Mount Tsiyon, and with Him one hundred and forty-four thousand, **having His Father's Name written upon their foreheads**. ²And I heard a voice out of the heaven, like the voice of many waters, and like the voice of loud thunder, and I heard the sound of harpists playing their harps. ³And they sang a renewed song before the throne, and before the four living creatures, and the elders. And no one was able to learn that song except the hundred and forty-four thousand who were redeemed from the earth. ⁴They are those who were not defiled with women **(false religions originating from the worship of the sun, moon, and stars)**, for they are **(spiritual)** maidens. **They are those following the Lamb wherever He leads them on**. They were redeemed from among men, being **First-Fruits** to Elohim and to the Lamb. ⁵And in their mouth was found no falsehood, for they are blameless before the throne of Elohim.

OWYAZ will lead the First Fruits back to the Promised Land. The First Fruits will be like the five wise virgins, who were prepared and waiting for their Bridegroom. They **will not** be caught spiritually naked. The First Fruits will have already washed their spiritual garments, before OWYAZ comes. Today these First Fruits are scattered all over the earth. When they are gathered, their number will be 144,000 sons of Israel, but there will also be a very large number of family members, who will return with them. The Barley will be from all the 12 tribes of Israel. The 144,000 First Fruits and their families will be led into the wilderness of northwestern Saudi Arabia, **not Palestine**! They will follow OWYAZ and look for a city to settle in. Today the area of northwestern Saudi Arabia where the real Promised Land is located, is very desolate and nearly uninhabitable.

Psalms 107

Give thanks to **ᴬYᴬZ**! For He is good, For His kindness is everlasting. ²Let the redeemed of **ᴬYᴬZ** say so, Whom He has redeemed from the hand of the adversary, ³And gathered out of the lands, From east and from west, From north and from south. ⁴They wandered in a wilderness, in a desert way; They found no city to dwell in. ⁵Hungry and thirsty, Their being in them grew faint. ⁶Then they cried out to **ᴬYᴬZ** in their distress, He delivered them out of their troubles. ⁷And He guided them by the right way, To go to a city to settle. ⁸Let them give thanks to **ᴬYᴬZ** for His kindness, And His wonders to the children of men! ⁹For He has satisfied a longing being, And has filled the hungry being with goodness.

ᴬYᴬZ has told us through the writings of the Prophets that the area will remain desolate, until **OWYᴬZ** returns. Today there are **no visible** rivers and virtually no surface water in all of northwestern Saudi Arabia. The temperature in the summer time is typically 125° F or greater. Northwestern Saudi Arabia is nearly uninhabitable, only a few local Bedouins live there. However, something wonderful happens, when Yahushua's First Fruits get to the wilderness of northwestern Saudi Arabia! They are looking for a city to rest with **OWYᴬZ**. They are tired! They are thirsty! They are hungry! They are fleeing from the nations! They have left everything that was familiar to them at home just like Abraham did long ago, when he left Chaldea! The First Fruits will cry out to **OWYᴬZ** and **He will answer them**! **OWYᴬZ** will lead His Barley back to the land of Yahudah and to the ruins of the real Yahrushalayim. When **OWYᴬZ** returns to Yahudah, the land itself comes back to life. The King is home! HalleluYah! HalleluYah! HalleluYah! The King is home! The King is home! The area around Yahrushalayim in northwestern Saudi Arabia becomes fruitful again because **OWYᴬZ** has returned! **OWYᴬZ** is back in His Land with His people. HalleluYah! HalleluYah! HalleluYah!

Revelation 7

And after this I saw four messengers standing at the four corners of the earth, holding the four winds of the earth, that the wind should not blow on the earth, nor on the sea, nor on any tree. ²And I saw another messenger coming up from the rising of the sun, holding the seal of the living Elohim. And he cried with a loud voice to the four messengers to whom it was given to harm the earth and the sea, ³saying, "Do not harm the earth, nor the sea, nor the trees until we have sealed the servants of our Elohim upon their foreheads."

Revelation 7, cont.
⁴And I heard the number of those who were sealed, one hundred and forty-four thousand, sealed out of all the tribes of the children of Yisra'el: ⁵of the tribe of Yehudah twelve thousand were sealed, of the tribe of Re'uben twelve thousand were sealed, of the tribe of Gad twelve thousand were sealed, ⁶of the tribe of Asher twelve thousand were sealed, of the tribe of Naphtali twelve thousand were sealed, of the tribe of Menashsheh twelve thousand were sealed, ⁷of the tribe of Shim'on twelve thousand were sealed, of the tribe of Lewi twelve thousand were sealed, of the tribe of Yissaskar twelve thousand were sealed, ⁸of the tribe of Zebulun twelve thousand were sealed, of the tribe of Yoseph twelve thousand were sealed, of the tribe of Binyamin twelve thousand were sealed. ⁹After this I looked and saw a great crowd which no one was able to count, out of all nations and tribes and peoples and tongues, standing before the throne and before the Lamb, dressed in white robes, and <u>palm branches in their hands</u>, ¹⁰and crying out with a loud voice, saying, "Deliverance belongs to our Elohim who sits on the throne, and to the Lamb!" ¹¹And all the messengers stood around the throne and the elders and the four living creatures, and fell on their faces before the throne and worshipped Elohim, ¹²saying, "Amen! The blessing, and the esteem, and the wisdom, and the thanks- giving, and the respect, and the power, and the might, to our Elohim forever and ever. Amen." ¹³And one of the elders responded, saying to me, "Who are these dressed in white robes, and where did they come from?" ¹⁴And I said to him, "Master, you know." And he said to me, "These are those coming out of the great distress, having washed their robes and made them white in the blood of the Lamb. ¹⁵"Because of this they are before the throne of Elohim, and serve Him day and night in His Dwelling Place. And He who sits on the throne shall spread His Tent over them. ¹⁶"They shall hunger no more, neither thirst any more, neither shall the sun strike them, nor any heat, ¹⁷because the Lamb who is in the midst of the throne shall shepherd them and lead them to fountains of waters of life. And Elohim shall wipe away every tear from their eyes."

Allured to The Wilderness
Hoshea 2
¹⁴**"Therefore, see, <u>I am alluring her</u>, and shall lead her into the <u>wilderness</u>, and shall speak to her heart, ¹⁵and give to her vineyards from there, and the Valley of Akor as a door of expectation. And there she shall respond as in the days of her youth, as in the day when <u>she came up from the land of Mitsrayim</u>.**

Allured to The Wilderness
Hoshea 2, cont.
[16]"And it shall be, in that day," declares יהוה, "that you call Me 'My Husband,' and no longer call Me 'My Ba'al.' [17]"And I shall remove the names of the Ba'als from her mouth, and they shall no more be remembered by their name. [18]"And in that day I shall make a covenant for them with the beasts of the field, and with the birds of the heavens, and with the creeping creatures of the ground, when bow, and sword, and battle I break from the earth. And I shall make them lie down in safety. [19]"And I shall take you as a bride unto Me forever, and take you as a bride unto Me in righteousness, and in right-ruling, and kindness and compassion. [20]"And I shall take you as a bride unto Me in trustworthiness, and you shall know יהוה. [21]"And it shall be in that day that I answer," declares יהוה, "that I answer the heavens, and they answer the earth, [22]and the earth answer the grain and the new wine and the oil, and they answer Yizre'el. [23]"And I shall sow her for Myself in the earth, and I shall have compassion on her who had not obtained compassion.

Rebuilding the Ruined Cities!
After יהושע gathers His Barley to the real Promised Land in northwestern Saudi Arabia, He will lead them to the site of the ancient Yahrushalayim! The city will be without inhabitant and will be in ruins just as the prophets told us. יהושע will instruct His First Fruits to rebuild the real Yahrushalayim. What an honor that will be! The First Fruits will rebuild and reinhabit the real Yahrushalayim on its own mound for 486½ years. HalleluYah! HalleluYah! HalleluYah! I can't wait!

Jeremiah 30
[18]"Thus said יהוה, 'See, I turn back the captivity of Ya'aqob's tents, and have compassion on his dwelling places. And **the city shall be built upon its own mound, and the palace stand on its right place**. [19]'And out of them shall arise thanksgiving and the voice of those who are laughing. And I shall increase them, and they shall not diminish. And I shall esteem them, and they shall not be small. [20]'And his children shall be as before, and his congregation shall be established before Me. And I shall punish all who oppress them. [21]'And his Prince shall be from him, and his Ruler shall come from among him. And I shall bring him near, and he shall approach Me, for who is this who pledged his heart to approach Me?' declares יהוה. [22]'And you shall be My people, and I shall be your Elohim.' " [23]See, the storm of יהוה shall go forth in a rage, a whirling storm! It bursts upon the head of the wrong. [24]The burning displeasure of יהוה shall not turn back until He has done and established the purposes of His heart. In the latter days you shall understand it.

Amos 9

For look, I am commanding, and I shall sift the house of Yisra'el among all the gentiles, as one sifts with a sieve, yet not a grain falls to the ground. ¹⁰"All the sinners of My people are going to die by the sword, those who are saying, 'Evil does not overtake us nor meet us **(Remember the rapture teaching!).**' ¹¹"In that day I shall raise up the booth of Dawid which has fallen down. **And I shall repair its breaches and raise up its ruins. And I shall build it as in the days of old,** ¹²so that they possess the remnant of Edom, and all the gentiles on whom My Name is called, declares 𐤀𐤉𐤄𐤆 who does this. ¹³"Look, the days are coming," declares 𐤀𐤉𐤄𐤆, "that the ploughman shall overtake the reaper, and the treader of grapes him who sows seed. And the mountains shall drip new wine, and all the hills melt. ¹⁴"And I shall turn back the captivity of My people Yisra'el. **And they shall build the waste cities and inhabit them.** And they shall plant vineyards and drink wine from them, and shall make gardens and eat their fruit. ¹⁵"And I shall plant them on their own soil, and not uproot them any more from their own soil I have given them," said 𐤀𐤉𐤄𐤆 your Elohim.

Isaiah 61

And they shall rebuild the old ruins, raise up the former wastes. And they shall restore the ruined cities, the wastes of many generations. ⁵And strangers shall stand and feed your flocks, and the sons of the foreigner be your ploughmen and your vinedressers. ⁶But you shall be called, Priests of 𐤀𐤉𐤄𐤆,' 'Servants of our Elohim' shall be said of you. You shall consume the strength of the gentiles, and boast in their esteem.

Isaiah 49

"Lift up your eyes round about and see, all of them gather together and come to you. As I live," declares 𐤀𐤉𐤄𐤆, "you shall put on all of them as an ornament, and bind them on you as a bride does. ¹⁹**"For your wastes, and your deserted places, and the land of your destruction, shall soon be too narrow for the inhabitants, while those who swallowed you up are far away.** ²⁰"The sons of your bereavement shall yet say in your ears, 'The place is too narrow for me, make room for me to live.' ²¹"And you shall say in your heart, 'Who has brought forth these for me, since I am bereaved and barren, an exile, and wandering to and fro? And who reared them? See, I was left alone – from where did these come?' " ²²Thus said the Master 𐤀𐤉𐤄𐤆, "See, I lift My hand up to the gentiles, and set up My banner for the peoples; and they shall bring your sons in their arms, and your daughters carried on their shoulders;

Isaiah 51

"Listen to Me, you who pursue righteousness, seeking יהוה: Look to the rock you were hewn from, and to the hole of the pit you were dug from. ²"Look to Abraham your father, and to Sarah who bore you. For he was alone when I called him, and I blessed him and increased him. ³"For יהוה shall comfort Tsiyon, **He shall comfort all her waste places. For He makes her wilderness like Eden, and her desert like the garden of** יהוה. Joy and gladness are found in it, thanksgiving and the voice of song. ⁴"Listen to Me, My people, and give ear to Me, O My nation, for the Torah goes forth from Me, and My right-ruling I set as a light to peoples.

Isaiah 52

Awake, awake! Put on your strength, O Tsiyon, put on your garments of splendor, **O Yahrushalayim, the set-apart city! For no more do the uncircumcised and the unclean come into you.** ²<u>Shake yourself from the dust, arise, and sit down, O Yahrushalayim.</u> Loose yourself from the bonds of your neck, O captive daughter of Tsiyon! ³For thus said יהוה, "You have been sold for naught, and you are redeemed not with silver." ⁴For thus said the Master יהוה, "At first My people went down into Mitsrayim to sojourn there, and Ashshur oppressed them without cause. ⁵"And now, what have I here," declares יהוה, "that My people are taken away for naught? Those who rule over them make them wail," declares יהוה, "and My Name is despised all day continually.⁶"Therefore **My people shall know My Name**, in that day, for I am the One who is speaking. See, it is I." ⁷How pleasant upon the mountains are the feet of him who brings good news, who proclaims peace, who brings good news, who proclaims deliverance, who says to Tsiyon, "Your Elohim reigns!" ⁸The voice of your watchmen! They shall lift up their voices, together they shout for joy, because eye to eye they see the return of יהוה to Tsiyon. ⁹**Break forth into joy, sing together, you waste places of Yahrushalayim!** For יהוה shall comfort His people, He shall redeem Yahrushalayim. ¹⁰ יהוה shall lay bare His set-apart arm in the eyes of all the nations. And all the ends of the earth shall see the deliverance of our Elohim. ¹¹Turn aside! Turn aside! Come out from there, touch not the unclean. Come out of her midst, be clean, you who bear the vessels of יהוה. ¹²For you shall not come out in haste, nor go in flight.

Isaiah 58

Then your light would break forth like the morning, your healing spring forth speedily. And your righteousness shall go before you, the esteem of יהוה would be your rear guard.

Isaiah 58, cont.

⁹"Then, when you call, 𐤀𐤉𐤄𐤅 would answer; when you cry, He would say, 'Here I am.' "If you take away the yoke from your midst, the pointing of the finger, and the speaking of unrighteousness, ¹⁰if you extend your being to the hungry and satisfy the afflicted being, then your light shall dawn in the darkness, and your darkness be as noon. ¹¹"Then 𐤀𐤉𐤄𐤅 would guide you continually, and satisfy your being in drought, and strengthen your bones. And you shall be like a watered garden, and like a spring of water, whose waters do not fail. ¹²"**And those from among you shall build the old waste places. You shall raise up the foundations of many generations.** And you would be called the Repairer of the Breach, **the Restorer of Streets to Dwell In**."

The First Fruits will rebuild Yahrushalayim **during times of affliction**! During those 62 weeks of years (434 years), OWY𐤀𐤆 will cut a Covenant with His First Fruits. What kind of covenant? Yahushua's Covenant is a marriage covenant reminiscent of His first marriage Covenant with Israel at Mount Sinai, after the 1st Exodus only much better! This marriage covenant will be perfect and both parties will remain completely faithful to it forever. Yahushua's marriage Covenant with Israel will be the most wonderful position of kinship that anyone will ever experience. How wonderful it is to belong to 𐤀𐤉𐤄𐤅 and OWY𐤀𐤆! I am so very thankful. Remember Yahuah's first marriage Covenant to Israel was cut at Mount Sinai, immediately after the 1st Exodus from Mitsrayim. Let's flash back to Mount Sinai.

Exodus 19

³And Mosheh went up to Elohim, and 𐤀𐤉𐤄𐤅 called to him from the mountain, saying, "This is what you are to say to the house of Ya'aqob, and declare to the children of Yisra'el: ⁴'You have seen what I did to the Mitsrites, and how I bore you on eagles' wings and brought you to Myself. ⁵'**And now, if you diligently obey My voice, and shall guard My covenant, then you shall be My treasured possession above all the peoples – for all the earth is Mine –** ⁶'**and you shall be to Me a reign of priests and a set-apart nation.**' **(YAHUAH'S marriage proposal, HALLELUYAH!)** Those are the words which you are to speak to the children of Yisra'el." ⁷And Mosheh came and called for the elders of the people, and set before them all these words which 𐤀𐤉𐤄𐤅 commanded him. ⁸And all the people answered together and said, **"All that 𐤀𐤉𐤄𐤅 has spoken we shall do."(Israel's acceptance)** So Mosheh brought back the words of the people to 𐤀𐤉𐤄𐤅. ⁹And 𐤀𐤉𐤄𐤅 said to Mosheh, "See, I am coming to you in the thick cloud, so that the people hear when I speak with you, and believe you forever."

Exodus 19, cont.
And Mosheh reported the words of the people to 𐤉𐤄𐤅𐤄. [10]And 𐤉𐤄𐤅𐤄 said to Mosheh, "Go to the people and set them apart today and tomorrow. And they shall wash their garments, [11]and shall be prepared by the third day. For on the third day 𐤉𐤄𐤅𐤄 shall come down upon Mount Sinai before the eyes of all the people. [12]"And you shall make a border for the people all around, saying, 'Take heed to yourselves that you do not go up to the mountain or touch the border of it. Whoever touches the mountain shall certainly be put to death. [13]'Not a hand is to touch it, but he shall certainly be stoned or shot with an arrow, whether man or beast, he shall not live.' When the trumpet sounds long, let them come near the mountain." [14]And Mosheh came down from the mountain to the people and set the people apart, and they washed their garments. [15]And he said to the people, "Be prepared by the third day. Do not come near a wife." [16]And it came to be, on the third day in the morning, that there were thunders and lightnings, and a thick cloud on the mountain. And the sound of the ram's horn was very loud, and all the people who were in the camp trembled. [17]And Mosheh brought the people out of the camp to meet with Elohim, and they stood at the foot of the mountain. [18]And Mount Sinai was in smoke, all of it, because 𐤉𐤄𐤅𐤄 descended upon it in fire. And its smoke went up like the smoke of a furnace, and all the mountain trembled exceedingly. [19]And when the blast of the ram's horn sounded long and became louder and louder, Mosheh spoke, and Elohim answered him by voice. [20]And 𐤉𐤄𐤅𐤄 came down upon Mount Sinai, on the top of the mountain. And 𐤉𐤄𐤅𐤄 called Mosheh to the top of the mountain, and Mosheh went up. [21]And 𐤉𐤄𐤅𐤄 said to Mosheh, "Go down, and warn the people, lest they break through unto 𐤉𐤄𐤅𐤄 to see, and many of them fall. [22]"And let the priests who come near 𐤉𐤄𐤅𐤄 set themselves apart too, lest 𐤉𐤄𐤅𐤄 break out against them." [23]And Mosheh said to 𐤉𐤄𐤅𐤄, "The people are not able to come up to Mount Sinai, for You warned us, saying, Make a border around the mountain and set it apart.' " [24]And 𐤉𐤄𐤅𐤄 said to him, "Come, go down and then come up, you and Aharon with you. But do not let the priests and the people break through to come up to 𐤉𐤄𐤅𐤄, lest He break out against them." [25]And Mosheh went down to the people and spoke to them.

The Ten Commandments
Exodus 20
And Elohim spoke all these Words, saying, [2]"I am 𐤉𐤄𐤅𐤄 your Elohim, who brought you out of the land of Mitsrayim, out of the house of slavery. [3]"You have no other mighty ones against My face.

Exodus 20, cont.
[4]"You do not make for yourself a carved image, or any likeness of that which is in the heavens above, or which is in the earth beneath, or which is in the waters under the earth, [5]you do not bow down to them nor serve them. For I, 𐤉𐤄𐤅𐤄 your Elohim am a jealous El, visiting the crookedness of the fathers on the children to the third and fourth generations of those who hate Me, [6]but showing kindness to thousands, to those who love Me and guard My commands. [7]"You do not bring the Name of 𐤉𐤄𐤅𐤄 your Elohim to naught, for 𐤉𐤄𐤅𐤄 does not leave the one unpunished who brings His Name to naught.
[8]"Remember the Sabbath day, to set it apart. [9]"Six days you labor and shall do all your work, [10]but the seventh day is a Sabbath of 𐤉𐤄𐤅𐤄 your Elohim. You do not do any work – you, nor your son, nor your daughter, nor your male servant, nor your female servant, nor your cattle, nor your stranger who is within your gates. [11]"For in six days 𐤉𐤄𐤅𐤄 made the heavens and the earth, the sea, and all that is in them, and rested the seventh day. Therefore 𐤉𐤄𐤅𐤄 blessed the Sabbath day and set it apart. [12]"Respect your father and your mother, so that your days are prolonged upon the soil which 𐤉𐤄𐤅𐤄 your Elohim is giving you. [13]"You do not murder. [14]"You do not commit adultery. [15]"You do not steal. [16]"You do not bear false witness against your neighbor. [17]"You do not covet your neighbor's house, you do not covet your neighbor's wife, nor his male servant, nor his female servant, nor his ox, nor his donkey, or whatever belongs to your neighbor." [18]And all the people saw the thunders, the lightning flashes, the sound of the ram's horn, and the mountain smoking. And the people saw it, and they trembled and stood at a distance, [19]and said to Mosheh, "You speak with us and we hear, but let not Elohim speak with us, lest we die." [20]And Mosheh said to the people, "Do not fear, for Elohim has come to prove you, and in order that His fear be before you, so that you do not sin."

Where are Daniel's 490 years in the book of Revelation? Remember just one word translated out of context can be a huge stumbling block to our understanding. One mistranslated word can prevent Israel from understanding the true intent of the Scripture. In the Scripture below the phrase "about half an hour" is very important.

Revelation 8
[1]And when He opened the seventh seal, there came to be silence in the heaven for **about half an hour**. [2]And I saw the seven messengers who stand before Elohim, and to them were given seven trumpets.

The Greek word "hemiorion" means half of a particular time period, but it was **mistranslated as half an hour**. "Hemiorion" comes from another word "horah", which has four meanings.

1. a certain definite time or season fixed by natural law and returning with the revolving year of the seasons of the year, spring, summer, autumn, winter
2. the daytime (bounded by the rising and setting of the sun), **a day**
3. a twelfth part of the day-time, an hour, (the twelve hours of the day are reckoned from the rising to the setting of the sun)
4. any definite time, point of time, moment

We have already learned that a Day to ᎯYᎯZ is like 1,000 years. Half a day on Yahuah's clock is **about** 500 years. The thought that John was trying to communicate to the future generations of Israel, was that the First Fruits would experience **about** 500 years (486½ years to be exact) of living in Yahrushalayim, after OWYᎯZ gathers them from the nations back to northwestern Saudi Arabia at the opening of the 6th Seal. At the appointed time Nimrod's armies will sack the rebuilt city of Yahrushalayim. Most of the city will be captured and Yahuah's two witnesses slaughtered! But the remnant of Israel will be held up in the set apart precincts of the city. From year 483 to about year 486½ Yahuah's two witnesses will prophesy **once again** to the nations! Yahuah's two witnesses will play the same roles that Moses and Aaron played during the 1st Exodus from Mitsrayim. Moses and Aaron were Yahuah's two witnesses to Pharaoh in Mitsrayim during the 1st Exodus. On the Day of ᎯYᎯZ Yahuah's two witnesses will deliver Yahuah's messages to Nimrod just like Moses did with the Pharaoh of Mitsrayim. The two witnesses will deliver Yahuah's messages to the beast until their testimony is complete. ᎯYᎯZ commands the resurrected beast to "Let My People Go"! This sounds remarkably similar to the 1st Exodus scenario, doesn't it? However, this Exodus scenario will be much, much greater in scope and magnitude. The signs and wonders that OWYᎯZ will perform this time around will be **unparalleled** in the history of the earth! That's why the 1st Exodus as awesome as it was, will seem like a small thing in comparison to Israel's final worldwide Exodus on the Day of ᎯYᎯZ.

Ezekiel 38
^{8}"After many days you shall be called up **(the beast raised from he Abyss)**. In the latter years you shall come into the land of those brought back from the sword and gathered from many people on the mountains of Yisra'el, **which had been a continual waste**. But they were brought out of the gentiles, and all of them shall dwell safely.
^{9}"And you shall go up, coming like a storm, covering the land like a cloud, you and all your bands and many peoples with you."

Ezekiel 38, cont.

¹⁰'Thus said the Master ayaz, "And it shall be in that day that words arise in your heart, and you shall devise an evil plan: ¹¹"And you shall say, 'Let me go up against a land of unwalled villages, let me go to those at rest who dwell safely, all of them dwelling without walls, and having neither bars nor gates,' ¹²to take plunder and to take booty, to stretch out your hand against the waste places that are again inhabited, and against a people gathered from the gentiles, acquiring livestock and goods, who dwell in the middle of the land. ¹³"Sheba, and Dedan, and the merchants of Tarshish, and all their young lions shall say to you, 'Have you come to take plunder? Have you gathered your army to take booty, to bear away silver and gold, to take away livestock and goods, to take great plunder?' ¹⁴"Therefore, son of man, prophesy, and you shall say to Gog, 'Thus said the Master ayaz, "In that day when My people Yisra'el dwell safely, would you not know? ¹⁵"And you shall come from your place out of the far north, you and many peoples with you, all of them riding on horses, a great assembly and a mighty army. ¹⁶"And you shall come up against My people Yisra'el like a cloud **(cloud of locust)**, to cover the land – in the latter days it shall be. And I shall bring you against My land, in order that the gentiles know Me, when I am set apart in you, O Gog, before their eyes."

The nations will struggle to rebuild the infrastructure of the earth, which was devastated by the shaking of the heavens and the earth, when ayaz returned at the opening of the 6th Seal. Awesome and foreboding signs will occur in the heavens and on the earth at their appointed times during Daniel's 490 years. During the first 483 years the first six Trumpet Judgments of Revelation will occur. The First Fruits will rebuild and reinhabit the real Yahrushalayim during times of affliction! They will dwell in Yahrushalayim **safely** for 434 years. After 434 years have expired, the First Fruits will fight valiantly to defend themselves against the armies of Nimrod until the 7th Trumpet sounds! One mistranslated word can change everything. In Revelation 17 guess what word the English translators mistranslated as "one hour"? You guessed it. They mistranslated "hora" again. Hora is the same Greek word that appeared in Revelation 8 and the time period under discussion is the same, Daniel's 490 year prophecy.

Revelation 17
¹²"And the ten horns which you saw are ten sovereigns who have not yet received a reign, but receive authority as sovereigns with the beast for one hour. **Revelation 17**

Revelation 8
And when He opened the seventh seal, there came to be silence in the heaven for about half <u>an hour</u>.

What John trys to tell us is that, while the First Fruits are living in Yahudah and the restored Yahrushalayim, the rest of the world will be rebuilding its devastated infrastructure. There will be **a temporary halt in the shaking of the heavens.** However, at the appointed time the Trumpet Judgments of 𝐚𝐘𝐚𝐙 will begin for the inhabitants of the earth. These Trumpet Judgments of Revelation are designed by 𝐚𝐘𝐚𝐙 to pressure Nimrod to free His people and to pressure the unrepentant in the nations to repent of their apostasy, before it's too late. These seven plagues are very similar to the plagues experienced by Mitsrayim during the 1st Exodus, but much greater in scope and magnitude!

Seven Trumpets Plagues

Yahuah's Trumpet judgments are progressive. They will get worse and worse in both severity and magnitude. These plagues are designed to pressure Nimrod to free Yahuah's people and to humble the people still trapped in apostasy to repent. These plagues will torture the outright wicked as well as the unrepentant. Unless those sheep repent, they will be destroyed in the wrath of 𝐚𝐘𝐚𝐙. The last 3½ years of Daniel's 490 year prophecy will contain many significant events for the wicked and for the Righteous! War will take place in the heavens and on the earth simultaneously. Michael and the heavenly messengers of 𝐚𝐘𝐚𝐙 will battle Satan and his host of rebellious heavenly messengers. The time period between the 6th Trumpet and the 7th Trumpet is 3½ years, which is the same period of time in which Yahuah's two witnesses will be delivering their messages to the nations. When the 7th Trumpet is sounded, Satan and his hosts will battle Michael, the Prince and commander of Yahuah's heavenly army in the heavens! Satan's heavenly messengers rebelled against 𝐚𝐘𝐚𝐙 in the ancient past. They have been adversaries to 𝐚𝐘𝐚𝐙, since that time. When Adam lived on the earth, they were his adversaries. They are also **your** adversaries, if you belong to 𝐚𝐘𝐚𝐙. These heavenly adversaries of 𝐚𝐘𝐚𝐙 have been permitted to roam the heavens freely until the day of their judgment. For thousands of years they have brought great confusion, suffering, and violence on the earth! OW𝐘𝐚𝐙 will ultimately judge all of Yahuah's adversaries and throw them all into His Lake of Fire! Yahuah's heavenly messengers, who are led by Michael, will battle Satan and his messengers in the heavens above the earth, while at the same time Nimrod is warring against Israel on the earth! War is occurring in the heavens and on the earth at the same time.

YeshaYahu 24
²¹*And in that day it shall be that* 𐤀𐤄𐤉𐤄 *punishes on high the host of exalted ones, and on the earth the sovereigns of the earth.* ²²*And they shall be gathered together, as prisoners are gathered in the pit, and shall be shut up in the prison, and be punished after many days.* ²³*And the moon shall blush, and the sun shall be ashamed, for* 𐤀𐤄𐤉𐤄 *of hosts shall reign on Mount Tsiyon, and in Yahrushalayim, and before His elders, in esteem!*

Satan is permitted to open the Abyss at the 5th Trumpet blast and he sets free a huge army of **wicked warriors called Kittim** from the ancient past! These warriors will have already lived and died in the distant past! They were imprisoned by 𐤀𐤄𐤉𐤄 and reserved for the future appointed Day, when they will be used for judgment against the wicked and unrepentant of the earth. At the 5th Trumpet they are resurrected from the Abyss! These warriors have hideous bodies as described in Revelation 9. In their past lives these warriors were violent men, who lived and died by the sword in service to Nimrod. This wicked army of Kittim will be raised out of the Abyss to be used by 𐤀𐤄𐤉𐤄 as His tool to torture the wicked and rebellious in the nations! When these warriors are raised from the Abyss, they are given **monstrous** or **abominable** bodies that match their beastly natures! The leader of this army has been known by many, many names in the past. Some of these names are **Asshur**, Baal, Bel, Osiris, Bacchus, Mithra, **Apolluon**, Abaddon, Ninus, and **Nimrod**!

The Beast Asshur
Revelation 17
⁸*"The beast that you saw was, and is not, and **is about to come up out of the pit of the deep** **and goes to destruction**. And those dwelling on the earth, whose names are not written in the Book of Life from the foundation of the world, shall marvel when they see the beast that was, and is not, and yet is.*

Who is this beast? Many people over the years have speculated, who this beast will be. If you believe the testimony of the Scriptures, then you should know that this beast will be someone, who has **already died** in the distant past, but will be **resurrected** on the Day of 𐤀𐤄𐤉𐤄. He will be an instrument in Yahuah's hand just like the Pharaoh of Mitsrayim was in the 1st Exodus. Daniel warned us in the last days that many **Righteous people and many wicked people will be resurrected** to play out the roles that have been assigned to them by 𐤀𐤄𐤉𐤄 on His Day.

Daniel 9

*"Now at that time Mika'el shall stand up, the great head who is standing over the sons of your people. And there shall be a time of distress, such as never was since there was a nation, until that time. And at that time your people shall be delivered, every one who is found written in the book, ²and many of those who sleep in the dust of the earth wake up, **some to everlasting life**, and **some to reproaches, everlasting abhorrence**. ³"And those who have insight shall shine like the brightness of the expanse, and those who lead many to righteousness like the stars forever and ever.*

Based on evidence in the Scriptures, I believe that this beast resurrected from the Abyss is none other than **Nimrod**! He was the originator of the original apostasy and rebellion, after the Flood. Nimrod is the 4th horseman, who will be released at the opening of the 4th Seal of Revelation. In the Scriptures this beast is often referred to as **Asshur**! In Revelation he is called **Apolluon**. At the 5th Seal Satan is given the key to the Abyss to release his monstrous hordes called Kittim, who are imprisoned in the underworld. Remember the 4th horseman (Nimrod-the Destroyer), who will be followed by these wicked warriors from the underworld (Sheol). The spiritual apostasy that has overwhelmed this world for thousands of years originated with Ham, Cush, Nimrod, and Semiramis. The Scriptures teach that Ham, Cush, Nimrod, Semiramis, Constantine, and millions of other wicked men and women will be resurrected and gathered for their destruction in the valley of Yahushofet **(Yahuah's Judgment)**. These wicked souls will receive resurrected bodies to compliment their **beastly natures**. First the Kittim will be used to torture and later to destroy the wicked and the unrepentant sheep in the nations! This is recorded in the 5th and 6th Trumpet plagues. This army is resurrected for a short time to be used by ayaz for judgment. Then this wicked army will be completely destroyed in the valley of Yahushofet with the rest of Yahuah's adversaries! They will all ultimately face eternal annihilation in the Lake of Fire, which is the second death! On the Day of ayaz at the 7th Trumpet, OWYaZ will return as the Lion of Yahudah! He will gather all Israel from every generation to Mount Sinai and Mount Zion to receive their rewards! Conversely satan will be permitted to gather all his beloved children of wickedness from every generation to share in his defeat at the valley of Yahushofet and later His complete annihilation in the Lake of Fire!

It's an Army that You Won't Believe!
Revelation 9

And the fifth messenger sounded, and I saw a star **(Satan)** from the heaven which had fallen to the earth. **And the key to the pit of the deep was given to it.** ²And he opened the pit of the deep, and smoke went up out of the pit like the smoke of a great furnace. And the sun was darkened, also the air, because of the smoke of the pit. ³And out of the smoke **locusts (flying warriors that cover the sky)** came upon the earth, and authority was given to them as the scorpions of the earth possess authority. ⁴And it was said to them that they shall not harm the grass of the earth, or any green matter, **(Yahuah's Barley and Wheat)** or any tree, but only **those men who do not have the seal of Elohim upon their foreheads.** ⁵And it was given to them that **they should not kill them, but to torture (the wicked and unrepentant)** them **for five months.** And their torture was like the torture of a scorpion when it stings a man. ⁶And in those days men shall seek death and shall not find it. And they shall long to die, but death shall flee from them. ⁷And the locusts **looked like horses prepared for battle**, and **on their heads were crowns like gold, and their faces were like the faces of men**. ⁸And they **had hair like women's hair, and their teeth were like lions' teeth**. ⁹And **they had breastplates like breast plates of iron**, and the sound of their **wings** was like the sound of chariots of many horses running into battle. ¹⁰And **they have tails like scorpions, and stings**. And in their tails is **their authority to harm men five months.** ¹¹And they have over them a sovereign, the messenger of the pit of the deep, whose name in Hebrew is Abaddon**(destroyer)**, but in Greek he has the name Apolluon **(Nimrod)**. ¹²The first woe is past. See, two woes are still coming after this. ¹³And the **sixth messenger sounded**, and I heard a voice from the four horns of the golden altar which is before Elohim, ¹⁴saying to the sixth messenger who had the trumpet, "Release the four messengers, those having been bound at the great river Euphrates." ¹⁵And the four messengers, those having been prepared for the hour and day and month and year, were **released to kill a third of mankind.** ¹⁶And the number of the armies of the **horsemen was two hundred million, and I heard the number of them.** ¹⁷And this is how I saw the horses in the vision and those who sat on them, having **breast plates of fiery red, and hyacinth blue, and sulphur yellow**. And the heads of the horses were like the heads of lions, and out of their mouths came fire, and smoke, and sulphur. ¹⁸**A third of mankind was killed by these three plagues, by the fire and the smoke and the sulphur which came out of their mouths.** ¹⁹For the authority of the horses is in their mouth and in their tails, for their tails are like serpents, having heads. And with them they do harm.

Fig. 14.

Bull from Nimrod. From VAUX, p. 236.

The picture above and the exert below is from Alexander Hislop's, *The Two Babylons*. Alexander Hislop's book will help Israel gain an understanding of pagan worship of the sun, the moon, and the stars.

*"There was another way in which Nimrod's power was symbolized besides by the "**horn**." A synonym for **Gheber**, "The mighty one," was "Abir," while "Aber" also signified a "**wing**." **Nimrod**, as **Head and Captain** of those **men of war**, by whom he surrounded himself, and who were the **instruments of establishing** his power, was "**Baal-aberin**," "Lord of the mighty ones." But "Baal-abirin" (pronounced nearly in the same way) signified "The winged one," and therefore in symbol he was represented, not only as a horned bull, but as at once a horned and **winged bull**--as showing not merely that he was mighty himself, but that he had mighty ones under his command, who were **ever ready to carry his will into effect**, and to put down all opposition to his power; and to shadow forth the vast extent of his might, he was represented with great and wide-expanding wings."*

Abominations that cause Desolations on the Earth on the Day of 𐤉𐤄𐤅𐤄!

WINGED BULL (from British Museum)

Joel 2

Blow a ram's horn in Tsiyon, and sound an alarm in My set-apart mountain! Let all the inhabitants of the earth tremble, for the day of 𐤉𐤄𐤅𐤄 is coming, for it is near: ²a day of darkness and gloom, a day of clouds and thick darkness, like the morning clouds spread over the mountains – a people many and strong, the like of whom has never been, nor shall there ever be again after them, to the years of many generations. ³Ahead of them a fire (from their mouths) has consumed, and behind them a flame burns. Before them the land is like the Garden of Eden, and behind them (abominations that cause desolations) a desert waste. And from them there is no escape. ⁴Their appearance is like the <u>appearance of horses</u>, and they run like steeds. ⁵As the noise of chariots they leap <u>over mountain tops</u>, as the noise of a flaming fire consuming stubble, as a mighty people set in battle array. ⁶Before them <u>peoples are in anguish, all faces become flushed.</u> ⁷They run like mighty men, they climb the wall like men of battle, every one goes on his way, and they do not break ranks. ⁸And they do not press one another, every one goes in his path. <u>They fall among the weapons, but they do not stop.</u> ⁹They rush on the city, they run on the wall. They climb into the houses, they enter at the windows like a thief. ¹⁰The earth shall tremble before them, the heavens shall shake. Sun and moon shall be darkened, and the stars withdraw their brightness.

The image of the winged beast bears a striking resemblance to the winged horsemen called Kittim, who will be freed from the Abyss at the sound of the 5th Trumpet blast! The role of the Kittim will be to torture and then to kill the rebellious inhabitants of the earth. **These winged horsemen will be the abominations that will cause desolations across the whole earth!**

Habukkuk 1
^{5}"Look among the nations and see, and be amazed, be amazed! For a work is being wrought in your days which **you would not believe if it were told**. ^{6}"See, I am raising up the Chaldeans, a bitter and hasty nation, who is going through the breadth of the earth, to possess dwelling places that are not theirs. ^{7}"They are frightening and fearsome, their right-ruling and their exaltation proceed from themselves. ^{8}"Their horses shall be swifter than leopards, and more fierce than evening wolves. And their horsemen shall charge ahead, and their horsemen come from afar. They **fly as the eagle, rushing to eat**. ^{9}"All of them come for violence, the direction of their faces is like the east wind, and they gather captives like sand. ^{10}"And they scoff at sovereigns, and princes are a laughing matter to them. They laugh at every stronghold, for they pile up earth and seize it.

How does Nimrod rise to power? Daniel tells us.

Daniel 11
"And a sovereign of the South shall become strong, along with one of his princes who gains power over him and shall rule–his rule being a great rule. ^{6}"And at the end of years they shall join themselves together, and a daughter of the sovereign of the South shall come to the sovereign of the North to make an alliance. But she shall not retain the strength of her power, nor would he or his power stand. And she shall be given up, with those who brought her, and he who brought her forth, and he who supported her in those times. ^{7}"But from a branch of her roots one shall arise in his place, and he shall come into the defense and come into a stronghold of the sovereign of the North, and shall act against them, and shall prevail, ^{8}and also their mighty ones, with their princes and their precious utensils of silver and gold he shall seize and bring to Mitsrayim. And he shall stand more years than the sovereign of the North. ^{9}"Then he shall enter the reign of the sovereign of the South, but shall return to his own land. ^{10}"But his sons shall stir themselves up, and assemble a great army. And he shall certainly come and overflow and pass through, then return to his stronghold, and be stirred up. ^{11}"Then the sovereign of the South shall be enraged and go out to fight with him, with the sovereign of the North, who shall raise a large army.

Daniel 11, cont.
But the army shall be given into the hand of his enemy, [12]and he shall capture the army, his heart being exalted. And he shall cause tens of thousands to fall, but not prevail. [13]"And the sovereign of the North shall return and raise an army greater than the former, and certainly come at the end of some years with a great army and much supplies. [14]"And in those times many shall rise up against the sovereign of the South, while some violent ones among your people exalt themselves to establish the vision, but they shall stumble. [15]"Then the sovereign of the North shall come in and build a siege mound, and capture a city of strongholds. And the arms of the South shall not stand, nor his choice people, for there is no strength to stand. [16]"So his opponent shall do as he pleases–with no one standing against him – and stand in the Splendid Land with destruction in his hand. [17]"And he shall set his face to enter with the strength of his entire rule, and make an alliance with him. And he shall do so, and give him the daughter of women to corrupt her. But she shall not stand, neither be for him. [18]"Then he shall turn his face to the coastlands and capture many. But a ruler shall bring the reproach against them to an end. And with the reproach removed, he shall turn back on him. [19]"Then he shall turn his face toward the strongholds of his own land, but shall stumble and fall, and not be found. [20]"And in his place one shall stand up who imposes taxes on the adorned city of the rule, but within a few days he is destroyed, but not in wrath or in battle. [21]"**And in his place shall arise a despised one**, to whom they shall not give the excellency of the rule. But he shall come in peaceably, and seize the rule by flatteries. [22]"And the arms of the flood shall be swept away from before him and be broken, and also the prince of the covenant. [23]"And after they joined him, he shall work deceit, and shall come up and become strong with a small nation. [24]"He shall enter peaceably, even into the richest places of the province, and do what his fathers have not done, nor his forefathers: distribute among them plunder and spoil and supplies, and devise his plots against the strongholds, but only for a time. [25]"And he shall stir up his power and his heart against the sovereign of the South **with a great army (Kittim)**, and the sovereign of the South shall be stirred up to battle with a very great and mighty army, but not stand, for they shall devise plots against him. [26]"And those who have been eating his food shall destroy him, and his army be swept away, and many fall down slain. [27]"And both these sovereigns' hearts are to do evil, and speak lies at the same table, but not prosper, for the end is still for an appointed time. [28]"Then he shall return to his land with much supplies, and his heart be against the set-apart covenant. And he shall act, and shall return to his land. [29]"At the appointed time he shall return and go toward the south, but it shall not be like the former or the latter.

Daniel 11, cont.

³⁰"For ships from Kittim shall come against him, and he shall lose heart, and shall return in rage against the set-apart covenant, and shall act, and shall return and consider those who forsake the set-apart covenant. ³¹"And <u>strong ones shall arise</u> from him and <u>profane the set-apart place</u>, the stronghold, and <u>shall take away that which is continual, and set up the abomination that lays waste</u>. **(Nimrod sets up an image of himself to be worshipped in Yahrushalayim!)** ³²"And by flatteries he shall profane those who do wrong against the covenant, but the people who know their Elohim shall be strong, and shall act. ³³"And those of the people who have insight shall give understanding to many. And they shall stumble by sword and flame, by captivity and plundering, for days. ³⁴"And when they stumble, they shall be helped, a little help, but many shall join them, by flatteries. ³⁵"And some of those who have insight shall stumble, to refine them, and to cleanse them, and to make them white, until the time of the end, for it is still for an appointed time. ³⁶"And the sovereign shall do as he pleases, and exalt himself and show himself to be great above every mighty one, and speak incredible matters against the El of mighty ones, and shall prosper until the wrath has been accomplished – for what has been decreed shall be done –³⁷and have no regard for the mighty ones of his fathers nor for the desire of women, nor have regard for any mighty one, but exalt himself above them all. ³⁸"But in his place he shall give esteem to a mighty one of strongholds. And to a mighty one which his fathers did not know he shall give esteem with gold and silver, with precious stones and costly gifts. ³⁹"And he shall act against the strongest strongholds with a foreign mighty one, which he shall acknowledge. He shall increase in esteem and cause them to rule over many, and divide the land for gain. ⁴⁰"At the time of the end the sovereign of the South shall push at him, and the <u>sovereign of the North rush against him like a whirlwind, with chariots, and with horsemen, and with many ships</u>. And he shall enter the lands, and shall overflow and pass over, ⁴¹and shall enter the Splendid Land, and many shall stumble, but these escape from his hand: Edom, and Mo'ab, and the chief of the sons of Ammon. ⁴²"And he shall stretch out his hand against the lands, and the land of Mitsrayim shall not escape. ⁴³"And he shall rule over the treasures of gold and silver, and over all the riches of Mitsrayim, and Libyans and Kushites shall be at his steps. ⁴⁴"Then reports from the east and the north shall disturb him, and he shall go out with great wrath to destroy and put many under the ban, ⁴⁵and he shall pitch the tents of his palace between the seas and the splendid set-apart mountain, but shall come to his end with none to help him.

Yahuah's Two Olive Trees

After the 6th Trumpet judgment, OWYƎZ sends His two witnesses to prophesy to the nations for 3½ years! These two witnesses are instructed to measure how many of Yahuah's people are worshipping in Yahrushalayim on the Mount of Olives and on the Temple Mount! They deliver Yahuah's messages to Nimrod just like Moses and Aaron did to the Pharaoh of Mitsrayim did in the 1st Exodus! But like the 1st Exodus, Nimrod refuses to let Yahushua's people go! Yahuah's First Fruits are trapped in Yahrushalayim and His Wheat are trapped in the nations! This all sounds so very familiar, doesn't it? Do you remember the phrase "Let My People Go" from the 1st Exodus? Just as Moses and Aaron delivered Yahuah's message to the Pharaoh in the 1st Exodus, Yahuah's two witnesses will give Yahuah's demands to Nimrod on the Day of ƎYƎZ! Just like the Pharaoh of Mitsrayim, Nimrod refuses to obey ƎYƎZ! And just like the 1st Exodus, OWYƎZ brings plague after plague against Nimrod and the kings of the nations! Just like the 1st Exodus these events ramp up in magnitude and begin to climax with the last seven bowl plagues! Finally, just like the 1st Exodus, the climax occurs, when ƎYƎZ executes His final plague, the 7th Bowl judgment! Just as Moses and Aaron were the mouth pieces that ƎYƎZ used with the Pharaoh of Mitsrayim, the two end time witnesses will be the mouth pieces of ƎYƎZ for Israel's final Exodus! These two witnesses will deliver the messages of ƎYƎZ for the 3½ years of their testimony! Nimrod is powerless to stop them for 3½ years because it's Yahuah's will that they complete their witness! After the allotted time for the two witnesses' prophecy has been completed, Yahuah's two witnesses will be slaughtered in the streets of Yahrushalayim! After the bodies of Yahuah's two witnesses have laid in the streets of Yahrushalayim without a decent burial for 3½ days, the two witnesses will be resurrected and caught up into the heavens in front of their enemies! Then the two witnesses will be gathered with all the rest of Israel to Yahushua's great wedding banquet, when the 7th Trumpet sounds!

Who Are the Two Witnesses?

The two witnesses are two of Yahushua's servants from the **past**! They were hand picked by ƎYƎZ to prophesy **again** long ago. A lot of people have speculated about the identity of these two witnesses over the years. These two witnesses will be truly **qualified** to be Yahushua's witnesses during the Day of ƎYƎZ. One of the two witnesses knows by **first hand experience** the events that occurred before OWYƎZ came. The other witness knows exactly what happened during Yahushua's ministry. And of course, these two witnesses will be very, very familiar with the old set apart places in the Promised Land.

Many scholars teach that these two witnesses will be Moses and Elijah. Some believe that they will be Elijah and Enoch. I would be thrilled to follow either of those great men, wouldn't you? However, I believe based on the clues given in the Scriptures that these two witnesses will be none other than Yohanan, who was Yahushua's most beloved disciple known as John, and YeshaYahu, known as Isaiah! Who could be better witnesses for ayaz than Yohanan and YeshaYahu? Those two men have already supplied us with a tremendous amount of knowledge about the Day of ayaz in the books of Revelation and Isaiah. It's no accident that these two books give the most detailed information about Yahuah's end time Exodus. These two witnesses are like two book ends with Yahushua's Passover sacrifice in the middle. YeshaYahu was a leader among the prophets, before OWYAZ came. Yohanan was a leader and the most faithful of all Yahushua's twelve disciples. I love these two men, don't you?

Clues to the Identity of the Two Witnesses
Isaiah 6
³*And one cried to another and said, "Set-apart, set-apart, set-apart is* ayaz *of hosts; all the earth is filled with His esteem!"* ⁴*And the posts of the door were shaken by the voice of him who cried out, and the house was filled with smoke.* ⁵*And I said, Woe to me, for I am undone! Because I am a man of unclean lips, and I dwell in the midst of a people of unclean lips – for my eyes have seen the Sovereign,* ayaz *of hosts."* ⁶*And one of the seraphim flew to me, having in his hand a live coal which he had taken with the tongs from the altar.* ⁷*And he touched my mouth with it, and said, "See, this has touched your lips; your crookedness is taken away, and your sin is covered."* ⁸*And I heard the voice of* ayaz, *saying,* **"Whom do I send, and who would go for Us?"** *And I said,* **"Here am I** *(YeshaYahu volunteers)***! Send me**.*"* ⁹*And He said, "Go, and you shall say to this people, 'Hearing, you hear, but do not understand; and seeing, you see, but do not know.'* ¹⁰*"Make the heart of this people fat, and their ears heavy, and shut their eyes; lest they see with their eyes, and hear with their ears, and understand with their heart, and shall turn and be healed."* ¹¹*Then I said,* ayaz, *until when?" And He answered,* **"Until the cities are laid waste and without inhabitant, and the houses are without a man, and the land is laid waste, a ruin,** ¹²**and** ayaz **has removed men far away, and the forsaken places be many in the midst of the land.** ¹³*"But still, there is a tenth part in it, and it shall again be for a burning, like a terebinth tree and like an oak, whose stump remains when it is cut down. The set-apart seed is its stump!"*

John 21

¹⁹Now this He said, signifying by what death he would esteem Elohim. And having said this, He said to him, "Follow Me." ²⁰And Kepha, turning around, saw the taught one whom OWYƎZ loved following, who also had leaned on His breast at the supper, and said, "Master, who is the one who is delivering You up?" ²¹Seeing him, Kepha said to OWYƎZ, "But Master, what about this one?" ²² OWYƎZ said to him, "If I wish him to remain till I come, what is that to you? You follow Me." **²³Therefore this word went out among the brothers that this taught one would not die. However, OWYƎZ did not say to him that he would not die, but, "If I desire him to remain until I come, what is it to you?**

OWYƎZ did not say that Yohanan would not die, but that Yohanan would not die, until He returned. Yohanan will die, when he is slaughtered by Nimrod in the streets of Yahrushalayim! Yohanan was actually translated into Paradise **just like Enoch**. He remains in Paradise to this very day awaiting his call back to service as one of Yahuah's two witnesses on the Day of ƎYƎZ.

Revelation 4

After this I looked and saw a door having been opened in the heaven. And the first voice which I heard was like a trumpet speaking with me, saying, **"Come up here and I shall show you what has to take place after this."** ²And immediately I came to be in the Spirit and saw a throne set in the heaven, and One sat on the throne.

When Enoch was translated, he wrote what he saw and thus we have the *Book of Enoch*. When Yohanan was translated, he was shown the events of the Day of ƎYƎZ and as a result, we have the book of Revelation.

Revelation 11

⁸And the voice which I heard out of the heaven spoke to me again and said, "Go, take the little book which is opened in the hand of the messenger standing on the sea and on the earth." **(John instructed to prophesy again to the nations!)** ⁹And I went to the messenger and said to him, "Give me the little book." And he said to me, "Take and eat it, and it shall make your stomach bitter, but it shall be as sweet as honey in your mouth." ¹⁰And I took the little book out of the messenger's hand and ate it, and it was as sweet as honey in my mouth, but when I had eaten it, my stomach was made bitter. ¹¹And he said to me, "**You have to prophesy again** concerning many peoples and nations and tongues and sovereigns."

Revelation 11, cont.
And a reed like a measuring rod was given to me, and the messenger stood, saying, **"Rise and measure the Dwelling Place of Elohim, and the altar, and those worshipping in it.** *²"But cast out the court which is outside the Dwelling Place, and do not measure it, for it has been given to the gentiles, and they shall trample the set-apart city under foot for forty-two months. ³"And I shall give unto my two witnesses, and they shall prophesy one thousand two hundred and sixty days, clad in sack-cloth."*

These two witnesses are compared to two olive trees, which stand before ayaz. YeshaYahu was the olive tree, before OWYAZ came in the flesh. Yohanan was the olive tree, after OWYAZ came in the flesh. Both YeshaYahu and Yohanan are standing before OWYAZ right now waiting for the word to return to the earth to finish their assignment.

Revelation 11
⁴These are the two olive trees and the two lamp stands that are standing before the Elohim of the earth. *⁵And if anyone wishes to harm them, fire comes out from their mouth and consumes their enemies. And if anyone wishes to harm them, he has to be killed in that way. ⁶These possess* **authority to shut the heaven, so that no rain falls in the days of their prophecy. And they possess authority over waters to turn them to blood, and to smite the earth with all plagues, as often as they wish.**

ZekarYah 2
And I lifted up my eyes and looked, **and saw a man with a measuring line in his hand. (the two witnesses)** *²And I said, "Where are you going?" And he said to me,* **"To measure Yahrushalayim, to see what is its width and what is its length."** *³And see, the messenger who was speaking to me was going out. And another messenger was coming out to meet him, ⁴and he said to him, "Run, speak to this young man, saying, 'Yahrushalayim is to remain unwalled, because of the many men and livestock in it. ⁵'For I Myself am to her,' declares* ayaz, *'a wall of fire all around, and for esteem I am in her midst.' ⁶"Oh, Oh! And flee from the land of the north,"* **(Today's Palestine, which is North of the real Promised Land!)** *declares* ayaz, *"for I have scattered you like the four winds of the heavens," declares* ayaz. *⁷"Oh, Tsiyon! Escape, you who dwell with the daughter of Babel." ⁸For thus said* ayaz *of hosts (for the sake of esteem He sent me to the gentiles which plunder you): "For he who touches you touches the apple* **(pupil)** *of My eye. ⁹"For look, I am waving My hand against them, and they shall become spoil for their servants. And you shall know that* ayaz *of hosts has sent Me.*

ZekarYah 2, cont.

¹⁰"Sing and rejoice, O daughter of Tsiyon! For look, I am coming, and shall dwell in your midst," declares 𐤀𐤅𐤄𐤉. ¹¹"And many gentiles shall be joined to 𐤀𐤅𐤄𐤉 in that day, and they shall become My people. And I shall dwell in your midst. And you shall know that 𐤀𐤅𐤄𐤉 of hosts has sent Me to you. ¹²"And 𐤀𐤅𐤄𐤉 shall inherit Yehudah, His portion in the Set-apart Land.

ZekarYah 4

³"**And two olive trees are by it, one at the right of the bowl and the other at its left.**" ⁴Then I responded and spoke to the messenger who was speaking to me, saying, "What are these, my master?" ⁵And the messenger who was speaking to me answered and said to me, "Do you not know what these are?" And I said, "No, my master." ⁶And he answered and said to me, "This is the word of 𐤀𐤅𐤄𐤉 to Zerubbabel, 'Not by might nor by power, but by My Spirit,' said 𐤀𐤅𐤄𐤉 of hosts. ⁷'Who are you, great mountain, before Zerubbabel? A plain! And he shall bring forth the capstone with shouts of "Favor, favor to it!" ⁸And the word of 𐤀𐤅𐤄𐤉 came to me, saying, ⁹"The hands of Zerubbabel have laid the foundation of this House, and his hands shall complete it. And you shall know that 𐤀𐤅𐤄𐤉 of hosts has sent Me to you. ¹⁰"For who has despised the day of small beginnings? They shall rejoice when they see the plumb-line in the hand of Zerubbabel. These seven are the eyes of 𐤀𐤅𐤄𐤉, which diligently search throughout all the earth." ¹¹Then I responded and said to him, "**What are these two olive trees, one at the right of the lamp stand and the other at its left?**" ¹²**And I responded a second time and said to him, "What are these two olive branches which empty golden oil from themselves by means of the two gold pipes?**" ¹³And he answered me and said, "Do you not know what these are?" And I said, "No, my master." ¹⁴**And he said, "These are the two anointed ones, who stand beside the Master of all the earth."**

1260 days of the Two Witnesses Testimony

During years 483 through 486½, the two witness will prophesy to the nations! They will do their best to warn the people of the nations to repent, to come out of the Babylonian system, and to return to the Promised Land. Nimrod and His army of winged warriors from the Abyss refuse to let Yahushua's people go! Between the 6th and 7th Trumpet blasts, the two witnesses will deliver the messages for 𐤀𐤅𐤄𐤉.

The Beast Will Sack Yahrushalayim!

Matthew, Mark, and Luke describe how ayaz comes at the 7th Trumpet to rescue His people, who are trapped In Yahrushalayim.

Matthew 24

*Immediately after the tribulation **(Tribulation of the Righteous)** of those days shall the **sun be darkened, and the moon shall not give her light, and the stars shall fall from heaven, and the powers of the heavens shall be shaken:** And then shall appear the sign of the Son of man in heaven: and then shall all the **tribes of the earth mourn, and they shall see the Son of man coming in the clouds of heaven with power and great glory.** And he shall send his angels **(emissaries or disciples; see Isaiah 66)** with a great sound of a trumpet **(7th Trumpet)**, and **they shall gather together his elect from the four winds, from one end of heaven to the other. (Yahushua's Wheat harvest)***

Mark 13

*But take ye heed: behold, I have foretold you all things. But in those days, **after that tribulation (of the Righteous), the sun shall be darkened, and the moon shall not give her light,** And the **stars of heaven shall fall,** and **the powers that are in heaven shall be shaken.** And then shall they see the Son of man coming in the clouds with great power and glory. **And then shall he send his angels, and shall gather together his elect from the four winds, from the uttermost part of the earth to the uttermost part of heaven.***

Luke 21

*And there shall be signs in the **sun**, and in the **moon**, and in the **stars**; and upon the earth distress of nations, with perplexity; the **sea and the waves roaring**; Men's hearts failing them for fear, and for looking after those things which are coming on the earth: for the **powers of heaven shall be shaken.** And then shall they see the Son of man coming in a cloud with power and great glory.*

Zechariah 12

*The burden of the word of ayaz for Israel, saith ayaz, which stretcheth forth the heavens, and layeth the foundation of the earth, and formeth the spirit of man within him. Behold, **I will make Yahrushalayim a cup of trembling unto all the people round about, when they shall be in the siege both against Judah and against Yahrushalayim.** And in that day will **I make Yahrushalayim a burdensome stone for all people: all that burden themselves with it shall be cut in pieces, though all the people of the earth be gathered together against it.***

Zechariah 12, cont.

In that day, saith **𝐚𝐘𝐚𝐙**, I will smite every horse with astonishment, and his rider **(Nimrod's resurrected army of flying calvary)** with madness: and I will open mine eyes upon the house of Judah, and will smite every horse of the people with blindness. And **the governors of Judah shall say in their heart, The inhabitants of Yahrushalayim shall be my strength in 𝐚𝐘𝐚𝐙 of hosts their Elohim**. In that day will I make the governors of Judah like an hearth of fire among the wood, and like a torch of fire in a sheaf; and they shall devour all the people round about, on the right hand and on the left: and <u>Yahrushalayim shall be inhabited again in her own place, even in Yahrushalayim</u>. **𝐚𝐘𝐚𝐙** also shall save the tents of Judah first, that the glory of the house of David and the glory of the inhabitants of Yahrushalayim do not magnify themselves against Judah. In that day shall **𝐚𝐘𝐚𝐙** defend the inhabitants of Yahrushalayim; and he that is feeble among them at that day shall be as David; and the house of David shall be as Elohim, as the angel of **𝐚𝐘𝐚𝐙** before them. And it shall come to **pass in that day, that I will seek to destroy all the nations that come against Yahrushalayim**. And I will pour upon the house of David, and upon the inhabitants of Yahrushalayim, the **spirit of favor and of supplications: and they shall look upon me whom they have pierced, and they shall mourn for him, as one mourneth for his only son, and she will be in bitterness for him, as one that is in bitterness for his firstborn**. In that day shall there be a **great mourning in Yahrushalayim**, as the mourning of Hadadrimmon in the valley of Megiddon. And the land shall mourn, every family apart; the family of the house of David apart, and their wives apart; the family of the house of Nathan apart, and their wives apart; The family of the house of Levi apart, and their wives apart; the family of Shimei apart, and their wives apart; All the families that remain, every family apart, and their wives apart.

ZakarYah 14

See, a day shall come for **𝐚𝐘𝐚𝐙**, and your spoil shall be divided in your midst. ²And I shall gather all the gentiles to battle against Yahrushalayim. And <u>the city shall be taken</u>, the houses plundered, and the women ravished. Half of the city shall go into exile, but the remnant of the people shall not be cut off from the city. ³And **𝐚𝐘𝐚𝐙** shall go forth, and He shall fight against those gentiles, as He fights in the day of battle. ⁴And in that day <u>His feet shall stand upon the Mount of Olives</u>, which faces Yahrushalayim on the east. And <u>the Mount of Olives shall be split in two</u>, from east to west, a very great valley, and half of the mountain shall move toward the north and half of it toward the south.

ZakarYah 14, cont.

⁵And <u>you shall flee to the valley of My mountain – for the valley of the mountains reaches to Atsal</u> (Mount Sinai). And you shall flee as you fled from the earthquake in the days of Uzziyah sovereign of Yehudah. And ayaz my Elohim shall come (to Sinai)– all the set-apart ones with You. ⁶And in that day it shall be: there is no light, it is dark. ⁷And it shall be one day which is known to ayaz, neither day nor night, but at evening time there shall be light. ⁸And in that day it shall be that living waters flow from Yahrushalayim, half of them toward the eastern sea and half of them toward the western sea, in summer as well as in winter. ⁹And ayaz shall be Sovereign over all the earth. In that day there shall be one ayaz and His Name one.

When the city is sacked, Yahuah's two witnesses are killed on the streets of Yahrushalayim. Their bodies will lie in the streets of the city without a proper burial! After 3½ days, Yahuah's breath of life returns to their bodies! They stand up on their own two feet! The wicked are terrified! These two witnesses are caught up into the Heavens, before the very eyes of their enemies! **Then at the exact appointed time, the 7ᵗʰ Trumpet is blown!** At the sound of the 7ᵗʰ Trumpet, there are great sounds of thunder, a large earthquake, and great hail! **OWYaZ returns in tremendous glory and esteem as the Lion of Yahudah** to judge the wicked and rescue His people from Yahrushalayim! There is no more time! Nothing will ever be the same, after the 7ᵗʰ Trumpet sounds! When that Trumpet is sounded, ayaz will get the attention of the whole world! **The 7ᵗʰ Trumpet blast is the sound that will turn this world upside down!** No longer will ayaz hide His face from the inhabitants of the earth! OWYaZ is about to take **complete control** of the entire earth and establish His long awaited Kingdom! Yahushua's feet will land on the Mount of Olives, which is the very same Mountain on which OWYaZ was hung on a tree as Israel's Passover Lamb. It's also the very same mountain from which He ascended back into the heavens, after OWYaZ spent 40 days with His disciples in Galil district, after His resurrection! When Yahushua's feet touch the Mount of Olives, it will split apart and form a highway. That **HIGHWAY** will be for **Yahushua's set apart ones**! This set apart highway will be for Israel and it leads to Atsal, which is Mount Sinai! Remember the 1ˢᵗ Exodus, when Moses saw OWYaZ in the burning bush on Mount Sinai. Mount Sinai is the same Mountain where ayaz married Israel and it's the very same mountain where ayaz gave Israel His Torah.

Revelation 11
[15] And the seventh messenger sounded, and there came to be loud voices in the heaven, saying, "**The reign of this world has become the reign of our Master, and of His Messiah, and He shall reign forever and ever!**" [16] And the twenty-four elders sitting before Elohim on their thrones fell on their faces and worshipped Elohim, [17] saying, "We give You thanks, O ᴀʏᴀz El Shaddai, the One who is and who was and who is coming, because You have taken Your great power and reigned. [18] "And **the nations were enraged, and Your wrath has come, and the time of the dead to be judged, and to give the reward to Your servants the prophets and to the set-apart ones, and to those who fear Your Name, small and great, and to destroy those who destroy the earth.**" [19] And the Dwelling Place of Elohim was opened in the heaven, and the ark of His covenant was seen in His Dwelling Place. And there came to be lightnings, and voices, and thunders, and an earthquake, and great hail.

The First Fruits of Israel will escape to Mount Sinai **(Atsal)** on a fabulous highway formed over the mountain heights of Israel! At Mount Sinai the land will **become lush and well watered** again similar to the garden of ᴀʏᴀz! Israel will stand before ᴀʏᴀz at His set apart Mountain, while the rest of the world is experiencing great tribulation!

Isaiah 35 (YeshaYahu)
Let the wilderness and the dry place be glad for them, and let the desert rejoice, and blossom as the rose. [2] **It blossoms much and rejoices, even with joy and singing.** The esteem of Lebanon shall be given to it, the excellence of Karmel and Sharon. They shall see the esteem of ᴀʏᴀz, the excellency of our Elohim. [3] Strengthen the weak hands, and make firm the weak knees. [4] Say to those with anxious hearts, "Be strong, do not fear! See, your Elohim comes with vengeance, with the recompense of Elohim. "**He is coming to save you.**"(at the 7th **Trumpet**) [5] Then the eyes of the blind shall be opened, and the ears of the deaf be opened. [6] Then **the lame shall leap like a deer**, and **the tongue of the dumb sing**, because **waters shall burst forth in the wilderness, and streams in the desert (at Mount Sinai).** [7] And the **parched ground shall become a pool, and the thirsty land springs of water** – in the home for jackals, where each lay, grass with reeds and rushes. [8] **And there shall be a highway, and a way, and it shall be called "The Way of Set-apartness."** The unclean does not pass over it, but it is for those who walk the way, and no fools wander on it. [9] No lion is there, nor any ravenous beast go up on it, it is not found there. But the redeemed shall walk there.

Isaiah 35 (YeshaYahu), cont.

¹⁰And the ransomed of 𐤀𐤉𐤄𐤅 shall return and enter Tsiyon with singing, with everlasting joy on their heads. They shall obtain joy and gladness, and sorrow and sighing shall flee away.

Isaiah 41 (YeshaYahu)

¹⁷"When the poor and needy seek water, and there is none, and their tongues have failed for thirst, I, 𐤀𐤉𐤄𐤅, do answer them; I, the Elohim of Yisra'el, do not forsake them. ¹⁸"**I open rivers on bare hills, and fountains in the midst of valleys; I make a wilderness become a pool of water, and a dry land springs of water.** ¹⁹"**I set in the wilderness cedar, acacia and myrtle and oil tree; I place in the desert cypress, pine and box tree together.** ²⁰"So that they see and know, and consider and understand together, that the **hand of** 𐤀𐤉𐤄𐤅 **has done this, and the Set-apart One of Yisra'el has created it.**

Isaiah 19

²³**In that day there shall be a highway (highway for the Righteous)** from Mitsrayim to Ashshur, and Ashshur shall come into Mitsrayim and Mitsrayim into Ashshur, and Mitsrayim shall serve with Ashshur. ²⁴**In that day Yisra'el shall be one of three with Mitsrayim and Ashshur, even a blessing in the midst of the earth,** ²⁵whom 𐤀𐤉𐤄𐤅 **of hosts shall bless, saying, "Blessed is Mitsrayim My people, and Ashshur the work of My hands, and Yisra'el My inheritance."**

After the 7th Trumpet sounds, several events will take place. Mount Zion will become visible again in the heavens as she descends towards the earth! Zion will give birth to her Son, OWY𐤄𐤅! OWY𐤄𐤅 will come out of Zion with the Righteous, who were resurrected at the time of Yahushua's death! OWY𐤄𐤅 comes to rescue His First Fruits from Yahrushalayim. He leads his First Fruits to Mount Sinai for a gigantic wedding banquet on a set apart highway that will be exponentially better than the beloved yellow brick road seen in *The Wizard of Oz*! The Righteous dead, since Yahushua's death, will be resurrected and they will travel to Sinai with all the rest of Israel. The called out ones of Israel, who are alive at His coming will be reborn into incorruptible bodies! Israel will be called sons and daughters of 𐤀𐤉𐤄𐤅. But for the wicked and unrepentant the next 1260 days will be horrible! They will experience the full weight of Yahuah's wrath for their rebellion and their rejection of OWY𐤄𐤅! 𐤀𐤉𐤄𐤅 will reward them with His seven Bowl plagues! First they will be given Leprosy (1st Bowl), which is Yahuah's penalty for their rebellion! Then the sea, rivers, and springs will be turned to Blood (Bowls #2 and #3)! There will only be blood to drink! In the 4th Bowl plague 𐤀𐤉𐤄𐤅 turns up the heat of the sun so that it will scorche men horribly!

In the 5th Bowl plague 𐤀𐤉𐤄𐤆 will bring extreme darkness! The wicked and unrepentant will gnawe their tongues from the sores of their leprosy and the scorching heat of the sun, which they worshiped! For the 6th Bowl 𐤀𐤉𐤄𐤆 will dry up the River Pratt to prepare the way for the kings of the east to assemble at the Valley of Yahushofet for their personal banquet! At that banquet the wicked will be on the menu as OWY𐤄𐤆 will call the birds of prey to gorge themselves on their bloody corpses! Nimrod and all the wicked armies of all the nations will be gathered to the valley of Yahushofet for the battle of all battles against OWY𐤄𐤆 and all the valiant warriors of Israel! This battle will make the battle scenes in *The Lord of the Rings* look like a light skirmishes!

Dead Sea Scrolls-The War Rule
Then the]re shall be a time of salvation for the People of 𐤀𐤉𐤄𐤆, and a time of dominion for all the men of His forces, and **eternal annihilation** for all the forces of **Belial (satan)**. There shall be g[reat] panic [among] the sons of Japheth, Asshur **(Nimrod)** shall fall with no one to come to his aid, and the supremacy of the Kittim shall cease that wickedness be overcome without a remnant. There shall be no survivors of [all the **Sons of] Darkness**. Then [the Sons of Rig]hteousness shall <u>shine</u> to all ends of the world continuing to shine forth until end of the appointed seasons of darkness. Then at the time appointed by 𐤀𐤉𐤄𐤆, His great excellence shall shine for all the times of e[ternity;] for peace and blessing, glory and joy, and long life for all Sons of Light. On the day when the Kittim fall there shall be a battle and horrible carnage before the Elohim of Israel, for it is a day appointed by Him from ancient times as a **battle of annihilation for the Sons of Darkness**.

Revelation 19
[17] And I saw one messenger standing in the sun, and he cried with a loud voice, saying to all the birds that fly in mid-heaven, "Come and gather together for the supper of the great Elohim, [18] to eat the flesh of sovereigns, and the flesh of commanders, and the flesh of strong ones, and the flesh of horses and of those who sit on them, and the flesh of all people, free and slave, both small and great." [19] And I saw the beast, and the sovereigns of the earth, and their armies, gathered together to fight Him who sat on the horse and His army. [20] And the beast was seized, and with him the false prophet who worked signs in his presence, by which he led astray those who received the mark of the beast and those who worshipped his image.

In the 7th Bowl 𐤀𐤉𐤄𐤆 will cause massive (**100 pound**) hail stones to fall on wicked men, on Babel and the nations, as well as everything else that exalts itself against 𐤀𐤉𐤄𐤆! 𐤀𐤉𐤄𐤆 **will stone the wicked and unrepentant for their rebellion!**

At the sounding of the 7th Trumpet, the heavenly Mount Zion descends down from the heavens! OWYAZ comes out of Zion! Zion descends to her place in the wilderness of Sinai! Mount Zion and the New Yahrushalayim are clearly visible above Mount Sinai once again! (YeshaYahu 2, Mikah 1: 2-4, Mikah 4, Revelation 12, Tehillim-Psalms 68, Book of Enoch 1, Ibrim-Hebrews 11: 8-10; Hebrews 12: 18-26)

Revelation 12

And a great sign was seen in the heaven: a woman **(heavenly Mount Zion)** clad with the sun, with the moon under her feet **(Mount Zion descends)**, and on her head a crown of twelve stars. ²And being pregnant, she cried out in labor and in pain to give birth **(Zion ready to birth OWYAZ)**. ³And another sign was seen in the heaven: and see, a great, fiery red dragon having seven heads and ten horns, and seven crowns on his heads. ⁴And his tail draws a third of the stars of the heaven and throws them to the earth. And the dragon stood before the woman who was about to give birth, to devour her child as soon as it was born. ⁵And she bore a male child **(OWYAZ)** who was to shepherd all nations with a rod of iron. And her child was caught away to Elohim and to His throne. ⁶And the woman **(heavenly Mount Zion)** fled into the wilderness, where she has a place prepared by Elohim, to be nourished there one thousand two hundred and sixty days. ⁷And there came to be fighting in the heaven: Mika'el and his messengers fought against the dragon. And the dragon and his messengers fought, ⁸but they were not strong enough, nor was a place found for them in the heaven any longer. ⁹And the great dragon was thrown out, that serpent of old, called the Devil and Satan, who leads all the world astray. He was thrown to the earth, and his messengers were thrown out with him. ¹⁰And I heard a loud voice saying in the heaven, "Now have come the deliverance and the power and the reign of our Elohim, and the authority of His Messiah, for the accuser of our brothers, who accused them before our Elohim day and night, has been thrown down. ¹¹"And they overcame him because of the Blood of the Lamb, and because of the Word of their witness, and they did not love their lives to the death. ¹²"Because of this rejoice, O heavens, and you who dwell in them! Woe to the earth and the sea, because the devil has come down to you, having great wrath, knowing that he has little time." ¹³And when the dragon saw that he had been thrown to the earth, he persecuted the woman who gave birth to the male child. ¹⁴And the woman was given two wings of a great eagle, to fly into the wilderness to her place, where she is nourished for a time and times and half a time, from the presence of the serpent. ¹⁵And out of his mouth the serpent spewed water like a river after the woman, to cause her to be swept away by the river. ¹⁶And the earth helped the woman, and the earth opened its mouth and swallowed up the river which the dragon had spewed out of his mouth. ¹⁷And the dragon was enraged with the woman, and he went to fight with the remnant of her seed, those guarding the commands of Elohim and possessing the witness of OWYAZ Messiah.

Isaiah 61

¹⁰ *I greatly rejoice in* 𐤉𐤄𐤅𐤄, *my being exults in my Elohim. For He has put garments of deliverance on me, He has covered me with the robe of righteousness, as a bridegroom decks himself with ornaments, and as a bride adorns herself with her jewels.* **¹¹** *For as the earth brings forth its bud, as the garden causes the seed to shoot up, so the Master* 𐤉𐤄𐤅𐤄 *causes righteousness and praise to shoot up before all the nations!*

Isaiah 62

For Tsiyon's sake I am not silent, and for Yahrushalayim's sake I do not rest, until her righteousness goes forth as brightness, and her deliverance as a lamp that burns. **²** *And the nations shall see your righteousness, and all sovereigns your esteem. And you shall be called by a new name, which the mouth of* 𐤉𐤄𐤅𐤄 *designates.* **³** *And you shall be a crown of comeliness in the hand of* 𐤉𐤄𐤅𐤄, *and a royal head-dress in the hand of your Elohim.* **⁴** *No longer are you called "Forsaken," and no longer is your land called "Deserted." But you shall be called "Hephtsibah," and your land "Married," for* 𐤉𐤄𐤅𐤄 *shall delight in you, and your land be married.* **⁵** *For as a young man marries a maiden, so shall your sons marry you. And as the bridegroom rejoices over the bride, so shall your Elohim rejoice over you.* **⁶** *I have set watchmen on your walls, O Yahrushalayim, all the day and all the night, continually, who are not silent. You who remember* 𐤉𐤄𐤅𐤄, *give yourselves no rest,* **⁷** *and give Him no rest till He establishes and till He makes Yahrushalayim a praise in the earth.* **⁸** 𐤉𐤄𐤅𐤄 *has sworn by His right hand and by the arm of His strength, "No more do I give your grain to be food for your enemies, nor do sons of the foreigner drink your new wine, for which you have labored;* **⁹** *but those gathering it shall eat it, and praise* 𐤉𐤄𐤅𐤄. *And those collecting it shall drink it in My set-apart courts."* **¹⁰** *Pass through, pass through the gates! Prepare the way for the people. Build up, build up the highway! Remove the stones. Lift up a banner for the peoples!* **¹¹** *See,* 𐤉𐤄𐤅𐤄 *has proclaimed to the end of the earth: "Say to the daughter of Tsiyon, 'See, your deliverance has come; see, His reward is with Him, and His work before Him.'"* **¹²** *And they shall be called, "The Set-apart People, the Redeemed of* 𐤉𐤄𐤅𐤄." *And you shall be called, "Sought Out, a City Not Forsaken."*

After the 7th Trumpet sounds, 𐤀𐤋𐤉𐤄𐤅𐤄 will judge the kingdoms of this present world one by one! He will destroy every last one of the wicked! The last 3½ years of Daniel's 490 year prophecy will be filled with judgments against the wicked! 𐤀𐤋𐤉𐤄𐤅𐤄 will reward the Righteous and the wicked! Both the Righteous and the wicked will get what they rightly deserve!

Isaiah 11

And a Rod shall come forth from the stump of Yishai, and a Sprout from his roots shall bear fruit. ²The Spirit of 𐤀𐤉𐤄𐤅 shall rest upon Him– the Spirit of wisdom and understanding, the Spirit of counsel and might, the Spirit of knowledge and of the fear of 𐤀𐤉𐤄𐤅, ³and shall make Him breathe in the fear of 𐤀𐤉𐤄𐤅. **And He shall not judge by the sight of His eyes, nor decide by the hearing of His ears. ⁴But with righteousness He shall judge the poor, and shall decide with straightness for the meek ones of the earth, and shall smite the earth with the rod of His mouth, and slay the wrong with the breath of His lips.** ⁵And righteousness shall be the girdle of His loins, and trustworthiness the girdle of His waist. ⁶And a wolf shall dwell with the lamb, and a leopard lie down with the young goat, and the calf and the young lion and the fatling together, and a little child leads them. ⁷And cow and bear shall feed, their young ones lie down together, and a lion eat straw like an ox. ⁸And the nursing child shall play by the cobra's hole, and the weaned child shall put his hand in the adder's den. ⁹They do no evil nor destroy in all My set-apart mountain, for the earth shall be filled with the knowledge of 𐤀𐤉𐤄𐤅 as the waters cover the sea. **¹⁰And in that day there shall be a Root of Yishai, standing as a banner to the people. unto Him the gentiles shall seek, and His rest shall be esteem. ¹¹And it shall be in that day that 𐤀𐤉𐤄𐤅 sets His hand again a <u>second time</u> (the Wheat Harvest) to recover the remnant of His people who are left, from Ashshur and from Mitsrayim, from Pathros and from Kush, from Eylam and from Shin'ar, from Hamath and from the islands of the sea. ¹²And He shall raise a banner for the nations, and gather the outcasts of Yisra'el, and assemble the dispersed of Yehudah from the four corners of the earth.** ¹³And the envy of Ephrayim shall turn aside, and the adversaries of Yehudah be cut off. Ephrayim shall not envy Yehudah, and Yehudah not trouble Ephrayim. ¹⁴But they shall fly down upon the shoulder of the Philistines toward the west; together they plunder the people of the east, their hand stretching forth on Edom and Mo'ab, and the children of Ammon shall be subject to them. ¹⁵And 𐤀𐤉𐤄𐤅 shall put under the ban the tongue of the Sea of Mitsrayim, and He shall wave His hand over the River with the might of His Spirit, and shall smite it in the seven streams, and shall cause men to tread it in sandals. **¹⁶And there shall be a highway for the remnant of His people, those left from Ashshur, as it was for Yisra'el in the day when he came up from the and of Mitsrayim.**

At that time Yahuah's **Wheat** will be harvested and returned to the Promised Land. 𐤏𐤅𐤄𐤔𐤏 will hand pick fishermen from those rescued from Yahrushalayim. They will become fishers of men and will fish Yahushua's Wheat from the nations.

YeshaYahu (Isaiah) 66

[19] "And I shall set a sign among them, and shall send some of those who escape (from Yahrushalayim at 7th Trumpet) to the nations–Tarshish and Pul and Lud, who draw the bow, and Tubal and Yawan, the coastlands afar off who have not heard My report nor seen My esteem. And they shall declare My esteem among the gentiles. [20] "And they shall bring all your brothers as an offering to ayaz out of all the gentiles, on horses and in chariots and in litters, on mules and on camels, to My set-apart mountain Yahrushalayim," declares ayaz, as the children of Yisra'el bring an offering in a clean vessel into the House of ayaz. [21] "And from them too I shall take for priests–for Lewites," declares ayaz.

Enoch 57

[1] And it came to pass after this that I saw another host of wagons, and men riding thereon, and [2] coming on the winds from the east, and from the west to the south. And the noise of their wagons was heard, and when this turmoil took place the holy ones from heaven remarked it, and the pillars of the earth were moved from their place, and the sound thereof was heard from the one end of heaven [3] to the other, in one day. And they shall all fall down and worship the Lord of Spirits.

Yahushua's Wheat will be brought back from the north, the south, the east, and the west! At the sounding of the 7th Trumpet, they will be brought to Mount Sinai, which will be below the heavenly Mount Zion! All of Israel, who are Yahuah's overcomers from **every** generation, since Adam, will be gathered to the same set apart place at the same time for the greatest wedding celebration ever! HalleluYah! HalleluYah! HalleluYah!

Hebrews 12

[22] But you have drawn near to **Mount Tsiyon and to the city of the living Elohim, to the heavenly Yahrushalayim, to myriads of messengers,** [23] **to the entire gathering and assembly of the first-born having been enrolled in heaven, and to Elohim the Judge of all, and to the spirits of righteous men made perfect,** [24] **and to OWYaz the Mediator of a new covenant,** and to the blood of sprinkling which speaks better than the blood of Hebel. [25] Take heed not to refuse the One speaking. For if those did not escape who refused the warning on earth, much less we who turn away from Him from heaven, [26] whose voice shook the earth then, but now He has promised, saying, "**Yet once more I shake not only the earth, but also the heaven."**

The Harvest of the Wicked and Unrepentant

But what about the third Harvest? Yahushua's harvest of thorns and thistles will be His 3rd harvest. These over-ripened grapes will be thrown into the winepress of Yahuah's fury! **The wicked of every generation will <u>also</u> be resurrected and gathered to the Mountains of Israel for their judgment as Daniel and Enoch stated! The wicked of every generation** will be gathered to receive their rightful reward, which ayaz has <u>reserved</u> just for them! The seven bowls of Yahuah's wrath are reserved for the wicked, who have been resurrected and gathered to receive their just reward. The wicked will be gathered for **torture and physical destruction**! ayaz invites the wicked to a <u>feast</u> prepared just for them at the valley of Yahushofet! However for Yahuah's feast, **the wicked are on the main menu! OWYAZ calls for the birds of prey to feast on the flesh of these rich and mighty men**. And last, but not least, the wicked and unrepentant will face total annihilation in the Lake of Fire!

OWYAZ Takes Over the Reigns of this Earth!

Revelation 11
¹⁵And the seventh messenger sounded, and there came to be loud voices in the heaven, saying, "The reign of this world has become the reign of our Master, and of His Messiah, and He shall reign forever and ever!" ¹⁶And the twenty-four elders sitting before Elohim on their thrones fell on their faces and worshipped Elohim, ¹⁷saying, "We give You thanks, O ayaz El Shaddai, the One who is and who was and who is coming, because You have taken Your great power and reigned. ¹⁸"And the nations were enraged, and **Your wrath has come, and the time of the dead to be judged,** and **to give the <u>reward</u> to Your servants** the prophets and to the set-apart ones, and to those who fear Your Name, small and great, **and to destroy those who destroy the earth."**

Isaiah 10
²⁰And in that day it shall be that **the remnant of Yisra'el,** and those who **have escaped** of the house of Ya'aqob, never again lean upon him who defeated them **(at Yahrushalayim),** but shall lean upon ayaz, the Set-apart One of Yisra'el, in Truth. ²¹**A remnant shall return, the remnant of Ya'aqob, to the Mighty El.** ²²For though your people, **O Yisra'el, be as the sand of the sea, yet a remnant of them shall return–a decisive end, overflowing with righteousness.** ²³For the Master ayaz of hosts is making a **complete end, as decided, in the midst of all the earth.**

Isaiah 10, cont.

²⁴Therefore thus said the Master יהוה of hosts, "**My people, who dwell in Tsiyon, be not afraid of Ashshur (Nimrod), who beats you with a rod and lifts up his staff against you, in the way of Mitsrayim.** ²⁵"**For yet a little while and the displeasure shall be completed, and My displeasure be to their destruction.**" ²⁶And יהוה of hosts stirs up a lash for him as the smiting of Midyan at the rock of Oreb. And as His rod was on the sea, so shall He lift it up in the way of Mitsrayim. ²⁷**And in that day it shall be that his burden is removed from your shoulder, and his yoke from your neck, and the yoke shall be destroyed because of the anointing oil.**

Micah 4

"**And in the latter days it shall be that the mountain of the House of** יהוה **is established on the top of the mountains**, and shall be exalted above the hills. **And peoples shall flow to it.** ²And many nations shall come and say, "**Come, and let us go up to the mountain of** יהוה**, to the House of the Elohim of Ya'aqob, and let Him teach us His ways, and let us walk in His paths. For out of Tsiyon comes forth the Torah, and the word of** יהוה **from Yahrushalayim.** ³And He shall judge among many peoples, and reprove strong nations afar off. They shall beat their swords into plough- shares, and their spears into pruning hooks – nation shall not lift up sword against nation, neither teach battle any more. ⁴But each one shall sit under his vine and under his fig tree, with no one to make them afraid, for the mouth of יהוה of hosts has spoken. ⁵For all the peoples walk, each one in the name of his mighty one, but we walk in the Name of יהוה our Elohim forever and ever. ⁶"In that day," declares יהוה, "I gather the lame, and I bring together the outcast and those whom I have afflicted.

Isaiah 4

²In that day the Branch of יהוה shall be splendid and esteemed. **And the fruit of the earth shall be excellent and comely for the escaped ones of Yisra'el.** ³And it shall be that he who is left in Tsiyon and he who remains in Yahrushalayim is called set-apart, everyone who is written among the living in Yahrushalayim. ⁴When יהוה has washed away the filth of the daughters of Tsiyon, and rinsed away the blood of Yahrushalayim from her midst, by the spirit of judgment and by the spirit of burning, ⁵then יהוה shall create **above every dwelling place of Mount Tsiyon, and above her assemblies, a cloud and smoke by day and the shining of a flaming fire by night, (just like the first Exodus) for over all the esteem shall be a covering,** ⁶**and a booth for shade in the daytime from the heat, for a place of refuge, and for a shelter from storm and rain.**

Isaiah 25
⁴For You shall be a refuge to the poor, a refuge to the needy in his distress, a shelter from the storm, a shade from the heat. For the spirit of the ruthless is like a storm against a wall. ⁵You subdue the noise of foreigners, as heat in a dry place; as heat in the shadow of a cloud, the singing of the ruthless is subdued. ⁶And in this mountain 𐤉𐤄𐤅𐤄 of hosts shall make for all people a feast of choice pieces, a feast of old wines, of choice pieces with marrow, of old wines, well refined.
⁷**And He shall swallow up on this mountain the surface of the covering which covers all people, and the veil which is spread over all nations.** ⁸**He shall swallow up death forever, and the Master** 𐤉𐤄𐤅𐤄 **shall wipe away tears from all faces, and take away the reproach of His people from all the earth.** For 𐤉𐤄𐤅𐤄 has spoken. ⁹**And it shall be said in that day, See, this is our Elohim. We have waited for Him, and He saves us. This is** 𐤉𐤄𐤅𐤄**, we have waited for Him, let us be glad and rejoice in His deliverance.**"

Isaiah 13
²**"Lift up a banner on the high mountain, raise your voice to them; wave your hand, destroy in all My set-apart mountain, for the earth shall be filled with the knowledge of** 𐤉𐤄𐤅𐤄 **as the waters cover the sea.** ¹⁰And in that day there shall be a Root of Yishai, standing as a banner to the people. Unto Him the gentiles shall seek, and His rest shall be esteem. ¹¹And it shall be in that day that 𐤉𐤄𐤅𐤄 sets His hand again <u>a second time</u> to recover the remnant of His people who are left, from Ashshur and from Mitsrayim, from Pathros and from Kush, from Eylam and from Shin'ar, from Hamath and from the islands of the sea. ¹²**And He shall raise a banner for the nations, and gather the outcasts of Yisra'el, and assemble the dispersed of Yehudah from the four corners of the earth.** ¹³And the envy of Ephrayim shall turn aside, and the adversaries of Yehudah be cut off. Ephrayim shall not envy Yehudah, and Yehudah not trouble Ephrayim. ¹⁴But they shall fly down upon the shoulder of the Philistines toward the west; together they plunder the people of the east, their hand stretching forth on Edom and Mo'ab, and the children of Ammon shall be subject to them. ¹⁵And 𐤉𐤄𐤅𐤄 shall put under the ban the tongue of the Sea of Mitsrayim, and He shall wave His hand over the River with the might of His Spirit, and shall smite it in the seven streams, and shall cause men to tread it in sandals. ¹⁶And there shall be a highway for the remnant of His people, those left from Ashshur, as it was for Yisra'el in the day when he came up from the land of Mitsrayim.

The Resurrection of the Righteous
The 7th Trumpet blast signals the beginning of Yahushua's kingdom! But it also signals resurrection for Yahuah's Righteous!

These are the Righteous, who have died, since Yahushua's death on the tree. The physical bodies of these Righteous are in the dust of the earth right now, but their spirits are **alive** in **Sheol**. They are waiting for the 7th Trumpet to sound. When they hear the sound of the 7th Trumpet, the Righteous will arise! They will be reborn into brand new incorruptible bodies like Yahushua's body! The Righteous, who died before the death of OWYAZ, are already resurrected and are waiting in Paradise on the heavenly Mount Zion for the sounding of the 7th Trumpet! Then they will return riding on the clouds with OWYAZ!

Matthew 27
⁵⁰*And* OWYAZ *cried out again with a loud voice, and gave up His spirit.* ⁵¹*And see, the veil* **(the veil hiding the New Yahrushalayim)** *of the Dwelling Place was torn in two from top to bottom, and the earth was shaken, and the rocks were split,* ⁵²*and the tombs were opened, and* **many bodies of the set-apart ones who had fallen asleep (from Adam to Yahushua's death) were raised,** ⁵³*and* **coming out of the tombs after His resurrection**, *they went into the set-apart city* **(New Yahrushalayim)** *and appeared to many.* ⁵⁴*And when the captain and those with him, who were guarding* OWYAZ, *saw the earthquake and all that took place, they feared exceedingly, saying, "Truly this was the Son of Elohim!"*

All Israel will be gathered back to Mount Sinai for Yahushua's wedding banquet during the last 3½ years of Daniel's 490 year prophecy! All Israel includes **all the overcomers, who have ever lived** from Adam to the last soul of Israel at sounding of the 7th Trumpet! These overcomers **will be resurrected and receive incorruptible bodies like Yahushua's! The overcomers of Israel, who are alive, when the 7th Trumpet sounds, will be born again in the twinkling of an eye into their incorruptible bodies!** All of Yahushua's overcomers will be assembled at Mount Sinai! OWYAZ will shelter and protect Israel under His wings for the remaining 3½ years of Daniel's 490 year prophecy and forever more!

Enoch 1
The words of the blessing of Enoch, **wherewith he blessed the elect and righteous, who will be** ₂**living in the day of tribulation, when all the wicked and godless are to be removed.** *And he took up his parable and said --Enoch a righteous man, whose eyes were opened by* AYAZ, *saw the vision of the Holy One in the heavens, which the angels showed me, and from them I heard everything, and from them I understood as I saw,* **but not for this generation, but for a remote one which is** ₃**for to come.**

Enoch 1, cont.

Concerning the elect I said, and took up my parable concerning them: **The Holy Great One will come forth from His dwelling,** ₄ **And the eternal Elohim will tread upon the earth, (even) on Mount Sinai, [And appear from His camp]** And appear in the strength of His might from the heaven of heavens. ₅And all shall be smitten with fear And the Watchers **(Imprisoned in The Abyss)** shall quake, And great fear and trembling shall seize them unto the ends of the earth. ₆And the high mountains **shall be shaken,** And the high **hills shall be made low,** And shall melt like wax before the flame. ₇And the earth shall be wholly rent in sunder, And all that is upon the earth shall perish, And there shall be a judgment upon all (men). ₈But with the righteous He will make peace, And will protect the elect, And mercy shall be upon them. And they shall all belong to ᴀYᴀZ, and they shall be prospered, and they shall all be blessed. and He will help them all, and light shall appear unto them, and He will make peace with them. And behold! He cometh with ten thousands of His holy ones, to execute judgment upon all, and to destroy all the ungodly.

During the final 3½ years the nations of the world will experience Yahuah's seven bowl judgments! These contain Yahuah's <u>undiluted</u> wrath. It is a terrifying prospect to think of experiencing Yahuah's undiluted wrath. During the same time period, OWYᴀZ will send some of His Barley to the nations as fishermen and hunters.

Harvest of the Wheat

Jeremiah 16
¹⁴**"Therefore see, the days are coming," declares** ᴀYᴀZ, **"when it is no longer said, 'ᴀYᴀZ lives who brought up the children of Yisra'el from the land of Mitsrayim,' ¹⁵but, 'ᴀYᴀZ lives who brought up the children of Yisra'el from the land of the north and from all the lands where He had driven them.' For I shall bring them back into their land I gave to their fathers.** ¹⁶"See, I am sending for many **<u>fishermen</u>**," declares ᴀYᴀZ, "and **they shall fish them**. And after that I shall send for many hunters, and they shall hunt them from every mountain and every hill, and out of the holes of the rocks. ¹⁷"For My eyes are on all their ways; they have not been hidden from My face, nor has their crookedness been hidden from My eyes. ¹⁸"**<u>And first I shall repay double for their crookedness and their sin,</u>** **(Tribulation of the Righteous)** because they have defiled My land with the dead bodies of their disgusting matters, and have filled My inheritance with their abominations." ¹⁹O ᴀYᴀZ, my strength and my stronghold and my refuge, in the day of distress the gentiles shall come to You from the ends of the earth and say, "Our fathers have inherited only falsehood, futility, and there is no value in them."

Jeremiah 16, cont.
²⁰Would a man make mighty ones for himself, which are <u>not</u> mighty ones? ²¹"Therefore see, I am causing them to know, this time I cause them to know My hand and My might. **And they shall know that <u>My Name is</u> ᕁYᕁZ!"**

After the 7ᵗʰ Trumpet sounds, Yahushua's emissaries **will fish** His **Wheat** out of the nations during the last 3½ year period. Remember that OWYᕁZ told his <u>original</u> twelve disciples that they would be fishers of men. In the same way these end time fishermen will bring **Yahushua's Wheat** back to Mount Sinai in the Promised Land. These emissaries will serve OWYᕁZ in a role similar to the role played by Yahushua's original twelve disciples. OWYᕁZ will empower His fishermen to perform miracles, signs, and wonders just like His original twelve disciples did and better! **Yahushua's disciples will be empowered to <u>forgive</u> <u>sins</u> (bind and loose) in the name of OWYᕁZ and thereby to heal every type of disease, which they will encounter in the nations**! They will heal the sick, open blind eyes, and will do all kinds of wonderful miracles! And of course, they will bring back Yahuah's Wheat to Mount Sinai for Yahushua's great wedding feast! There's nothing better than a reunion of relatives and old friends! Reunions have lots of love, lots of great food, lots of wonderful stories, lots of joy, lots of laughter, and lots of thanksgiving! **For all Israel this reunion will be the greatest reunion of all time!** HalleluYah! HalleluYah! HalleluYah!

Hebrews 12
²²But you have drawn near to Mount Tsiyon and to the city of the living Elohim, to the heavenly Yahrushalayim, to myriads of messengers, ²³**to the entire gathering and assembly of the first-born having been enrolled in heaven**, and to Elohim the Judge of all, and to the spirits of righteous men made perfect, ²⁴and to OWYᕁZ the Mediator of a new covenant, and to the blood of sprinkling which speaks better than the blood of Hebel.

Yahuah's reunion of Israel is the gathering of all Yahuah's overcomers, who have ever lived from the days of Adam until the 7ᵗʰ Trumpet sounds. OWYᕁZ will reward His Righteous with rewards that are mind boggling and beyond my ability to fully understand or communicate! **The climax of this last 3½ years for the Righteous will be the marriage of OWYᕁZ to His people, to His city, (the New Yahrushalayim), and to His Land!** And last, but not least, **OWYᕁZ will lead His overcomers into His set apart city, the New Yahrushalayim!**

The Last Hurrah for the Wicked

The last 3½ years of Daniel's 490 year prophecy for the unrepentant **will be the most terrifying time period ever experienced by humanity**! Nimrod and his army of flying Kittim will cause terrible desolation in all the nations! They will be responsible for the torture and death of billions of people! **They will show no mercy!**

Isaiah 10
³"What shall you do in the day of visitation **(Yahushua's return)**, and in the ruin **(Nimrod and his army of winged warriors)** which comes from afar? To whom would you run for help? And where would you leave your wealth? ⁵"Woe to Ashshur **(Nimrod)**, the rod of My displeasure and the staff in whose hand is My displeasure. ⁶"Against a defiled nation I send him, and against the people of My wrath I command him to seize the spoil, to take the prey, and to tread them down like the mud of the streets. ⁷"But he does not intend so, nor does his heart think so, for it is in his heart to destroy, and cut off not a few nations. ⁸"For he says, Are not my princes sovereigns? ⁹'Is not Kalno like Karkemish? Is not Hamath like Arpad? Is not Shomeron like Damascus? **(Places Nimrod conquered in His first life!)** ¹⁰'As my hand has found the reigns of the idols, whose carved images excelled those of Yahrushalayim and Shomeron, ¹¹as I have done to Shomeron and her idols, do I not do also to Yahrushalayim and her idols?' ¹²"And it shall be, when ayaz has performed all His work on Mount Tsiyon and on Yahrushalayim, that I shall punish the fruit of the greatness of the heart of the sovereign of Ashshur **(Nimrod)**, and the boasting of his haughty looks. ¹³"For he has said, 'By the power of my hand I have done it, and by my wisdom, for I have been clever. **And I remove the boundaries of the people, and have robbed their treasuries. And I put down the inhabitants like a strong one.** ¹⁴'And my hand finds the riches of the people like a nest. And I have gathered all the earth like forsaken eggs are gathered. And there was no one who moved his wing, nor opened his mouth with even a peep.' "

Nimrod sets himself up as "God" the last 3½ years Daniel's prophecy!

Folly of the Wicked during the Day of ayaz
Enoch 99
₄In those days the nations shall be stirred up, And the families of the nations shall arise **(the resurrection of the wicked families)** on the day of destruction. ₅And in those days the destitute shall go forth and carry off their children, And they shall abandon them, so that their children shall perish through them: Yea, they shall abandon their children (that are still) sucklings, and not return to them, And shall have no pity on their beloved ones.

Enoch 99, cont.

₆,₇And again I swear to you, ye sinners, that sin is prepared for a day of unceasing bloodshed. And they who worship stones, and grave images of gold and silver and wood and clay, and those who worship impure spirits and demons, and all kinds of idols not according to knowledge, shall get no manner of help from them. ₈And they shall become godless by reason of the folly of their hearts, And their eyes shall be blinded through the fear of their hearts And through visions in their dreams. ₉Through these they shall become godless and fearful; For they shall have wrought all their work in a lie, And shall have worshiped a stone: **Therefore in an instant shall they perish.**

2 Thessalonians

As to the coming of our Master OWYAZ Messiah and **our gathering together (End Time Exodus, not rapture)** to Him, we ask you, brothers, ²not to become easily unsettled in mind or troubled, either by spirit or by word or by letter, as if from us, as if the day of AYAZ has come. ³Let no one deceive you in any way, because the falling away is to come first, and the man of lawlessness **(Nimrod)** is to be revealed, the son of destruction, ⁴who opposes and exalts himself above all that is called Elohim or that is worshipped, so that he sits as Elohim in the Dwelling Place of Elohim **(Yahrushalayim, after the 7ᵗʰ Trumpet)**, showing himself that he is Elohim. ⁵Do you not remember that I told you this while I was still with you? ⁶And now you know what restrains, for him to be revealed in his time. ⁷For the secret of lawlessness is already at work – only until he who now restrains comes out of the midst. **(the gates of Death in the Abyss now restrain Nimrod)** ⁸And then the lawless one shall be revealed, whom the Master shall consume with the Spirit of His mouth and bring to naught with the manifestation of His coming. ⁹The coming of the lawless one is according to the working of Satan, with all power and signs and wonders of falsehood, ¹⁰and with all deceit of unrighteousness in those perishing, because **they did not receive the love of the Truth, in order for them to be saved.**

AYAZ Pours Out the Bowls of His Wrath!

Yahuah's last seven Bowl judgments are progressive! They increase in magnitude and reach a climax at the 7ᵗʰ Bowl Judgment! These plagues are all horrible, but all carefully planned to satisfy Yahuah's wrath against the wicked from all the generations! AYAZ has stored up His wrath, since the time of the Flood! Can you imagine?

Revelation 15

And I heard a loud voice from the Dwelling Place saying to the seven messengers, "Go and pour out the bowls of the wrath of Elohim on the earth."

Revelation 15, cont.

²And the first went and poured out his bowl upon the earth, and an evil and wicked sore (𐤀𐤉𐤄𐤆 **rewards them with** <u>Leprosy</u>**, which they will have for 1290 days, just like** OWY𐤀𐤆) came upon the men, those having the mark of the beast and those worshipping his image. ³And the second messenger poured out his bowl on the sea, and it **<u>became blood</u>**, as of a dead one, and every living creature in the sea died. ⁴And the third messenger poured out his bowl on the rivers and fountains of water, and they **<u>became blood</u>**. ⁵And I heard the messenger of the waters saying, "You are righteous, O 𐤀𐤉𐤄𐤆, the One who is and who was and who shall be, because You have judged these." ⁶"Because they have shed the blood of set-apart ones and prophets, and You have given them blood to drink. For they deserve it." ⁷And I heard another out of the altar saying, "Yea, 𐤀𐤉𐤄𐤆 **El Shaddai**, true and righteous are Your judgments." ⁸And **the fourth messenger <u>poured out his bowl on the sun, and it was given to him to burn men with fire</u>**. ⁹And men were burned with great heat, and they blasphemed the Name of Elohim who possesses authority over these plagues. And they did not repent, to give Him esteem. ¹⁰And the **<u>fifth messenger poured out his bowl on the throne of the beast, and his reign became darkened</u>**. And they gnawed their tongues from pain. ¹¹And they blasphemed the Elohim of the heaven for their pains and their sores, and did not repent of their works. ¹²**And the sixth messenger poured out his bowl on the great river Euphrates, and its water was dried up, in order <u>to prepare the way of the sovereigns from the east</u>.** ¹³And I saw coming out of the mouth of the dragon, and out of the mouth of the beast, and out of the mouth of the false prophet, three unclean spirits, as frogs, ¹⁴for they are spirits of demons, doing signs, which go out to the sovereigns of the entire world, to **gather them to the battle of that great day of 𐤀𐤉𐤄𐤆 the Almighty.** ¹⁵"See, I am coming as a thief. Blessed is he who is staying awake and guarding his garments, lest he walk naked and they see his shame." ¹⁶And they gathered them together to the place called in Hebrew, Har Megiddo. ¹⁷And the **<u>seventh messenger</u> poured out his bowl into the air, and a loud voice came out of the Dwelling Place of the heaven, from the throne, saying, "It is done!"** ¹⁸And there came to be noises and thunders and lightnings. And there came to be a great earthquake, such a mighty and great earthquake as had not came to be since men were on the earth. ¹⁹And the great city became divided into three parts, and **the cities of the nations fell. And great Babel was remembered before Elohim, to give her the cup of the wine of the fierceness of His wrath.** ²⁰And every island fled away, and the mountains were not found.

Revelation 15, cont.
²¹And great hail from the heaven fell upon men, every hailstone about the weight of a talent. And men blasphemed Elohim for the plague of the hail, because that plague was exceedingly great.

Isaiah 13
³"I have commanded My set-apart ones; I have also called My mighty men for My displeasure, My proudly exulting ones." ⁴The noise of an uproar in the mountains, like that of many people! A noise of uproar of the reigns of gentiles gathered together! **𐤀𐤉𐤄𐤅 of hosts is gathering an army for battle.** ⁵They are coming from a distant land, from the end of the heavens, even 𐤀𐤉𐤄𐤅 and His weapons of displeasure, to destroy all the earth. ⁶Howl, for the day of 𐤀𐤉𐤄𐤅 is near! It comes as a destruction from the Almighty. ⁷Therefore **all hands go limp, every man's heart melts,** ⁸**and they shall be afraid. Pangs and sorrows take hold of them, they are in pain as a woman in labor; they are amazed at one another, their faces aflame!** ⁹See, the day of 𐤀𐤉𐤄𐤅 is coming, fierce, with wrath and heat of displeasure, to lay the earth waste, and destroy its sinners from it. ¹⁰For the stars of the heavens and their constellations do not give off their light. The sun shall be dark at its rising, and the moon not send out its light. ¹¹"And **I shall punish the world for its evil**, and the wrong for their crookedness, and shall **put an end to the arrogance of the proud, and lay low the pride of the ruthless.** ¹²"**I shall make mortal man scarcer than fine gold, and mankind scarcer than the gold of Ophir.** ¹³"So I shall make the heavens tremble, and the earth shall shake from her place, in the wrath of 𐤀𐤉𐤄𐤅 of hosts and in the day of the heat of His displeasure. ¹⁴"And it shall be as the hunted gazelle, and as a sheep that no man takes up – every man turns to his own people, and everyone flees to his own land. ¹⁵"Whoever is found is thrust through, and everyone taken falls by the sword. ¹⁶"**And their children are dashed to pieces before their eyes, their houses plundered and their wives ravished.**

Isaiah 5
²⁴Therefore, as a tongue of fire devours the stubble, and the flame consumes the chaff, their root is as rottenness, and their blossom goes up like dust –**because they have rejected the Torah of 𐤀𐤉𐤄𐤅 of hosts, and despised the Word of the Set-apart One of Yisra'el.** ²⁵Therefore the displeasure of 𐤀𐤉𐤄𐤅 has burned against His people, and He stretches out His hand against them and smites them, and the mountains tremble. And their carcass is as filth in the middle of the streets. With all this His displeasure has not turned back, and His hand is still stretched out! ²⁶And He shall lift up a banner to the nations from afar, and shall whistle to them from the end of the earth. And see, they come with speed, swiftly!

Isaiah 5, cont.
²⁷Not one of them is weary or stumbling, not one slumbers or sleeps. Not a belt shall be loosened on their loins, nor the thong of their sandals be broken.

The Valley of Yahushophet
Ezekiel 38
⁴"And I shall turn you around, and I shall put hooks into your jaws, and shall lead you out, with all your army, **horses and horsemen (5ᵗʰ Trumpet)**, clad perfectly, a great assembly with armour and shields, all of them handling swords. ⁵"Persia, Kush, and Put **(all parts of ancient Arabia)** are with them, all of them with shield and helmet, ⁶"Gomer and all its bands, the house of Togarmah from the far north and all its bands, many peoples with you. ⁷"Be ready, prepare yourself, you and all your assemblies that are assembled unto you. And you shall be a guard for them. ⁸"**After many days you shall be called up (Nimrod and his army resurrected). In the latter years you shall come into the land of those brought back from the sword and gathered from many people on the mountains of Yisra'el, (Final Exodus) which had been a** <u>continual</u> **waste (more proof that Israel today is a counterfeit). But they were brought out of the gentiles, and all of them hall dwell safely.** ⁹"And you shall go up, coming like a storm, covering the land like a cloud **(like locusts)**, you and all your bands and many peoples with you."¹⁰'Thus said the Master ayaz, "And it shall be in that day that words arise in your heart, and you shall devise an evil plan: ¹¹"And you shall say, 'Let me go up against a land of unwalled villages **(Yahrushalayim and the reinhabited cities of Yahudah)**, let me go to those at rest who dwell safely, all of them dwelling without walls, and having neither bars nor gates,' ¹²to take plunder and to take booty, to stretch out your hand against the waste places that are again inhabited, and against a people gathered from the gentiles, acquiring livestock and goods, who dwell in the middle of the land. ¹³"Sheba, and Dedan **(regions in Saudi Arabia)**, and the merchants of Tarshish, and all their young lions shall say to you, 'Have you come to take plunder? Have you gathered your army to take booty, to bear away silver and gold, to take away livestock and goods, to take great plunder?' ¹⁴"Therefore, son of man, prophesy, and you shall say to Gog, 'Thus said the Master ayaz, "In that day when My people Yisra'el dwell safely, would you not know? ¹⁵"And you shall come from your place out of the far north, you and many peoples with you, all of them riding on horses, a great assembly and a mighty army.

Ezekiel 38, cont.
[16]"And you shall come up against My people Yisra'el like a cloud **(Nimrod's flying warriors)**, to cover the land – in the latter days it shall be. And I shall bring you against My land, in order that the gentiles know Me, when I am set apart in you, O Gog, before their eyes."**(Just like Yahuah did with the Pharaoh of Mitsrayim at the crossing of the Sea)** [17]'Thus said the Master אYaZ, "Are you the one I spoke of in former days by My servants the prophets of Yisra'el, who prophesied for years in those days, to bring you against them? [18]"And it shall be on that day, on the day when Gog comes against the land of Yisra'el," declares the Master אYaZ, "that My wrath shall come up in My face. [19]"For in My jealousy and in the fire of My wrath I have spoken, 'On that day there shall be a great shaking in the land of Yisra'el, [20]so that the fish of the sea, and the birds of the heavens, and the beasts of the field, and all creeping creatures that creep on the earth, and all men who are on the face of the earth shall shake at My presence. And the mountains shall be thrown down, and the steep places shall fall, and every wall fall to the ground.' [21]"And I shall call for a sword against Gog on all My mountains," declares the Master אYaZ, "**the sword of each one being against his brother**. **(The wicked kill the wicked!)** [22]"And I shall judge him with pestilence and blood, and rain down flooding rain and hailstones, fire and sulphur, on him and on his bands and on the many peoples who are with him. [23]"And I shall exalt Myself and set Myself apart, and I shall be known in the eyes of many nations. And they shall know that I am אYaZ."

Ezekiel 39
And you, son of man, prophesy against Gog, and you shall say, 'Thus said the Master אYaZ, "See, I am against you, O Gog, the prince of Rosh, Meshek, and Tubal, [2]and shall turn you around and lead you on, and bring you up from the uttermost parts of the north, and bring you against the mountains of Yisra'el, [3]and shall smite the bow out of your left hand, and make the arrows fall from your right hand. [4]"On the mountains of Yisra'el you shall fall, you and all your bands and the peoples who are with you. To the birds of prey of every sort and to the beasts of the field I shall give you for food. [5]"On the face of the field you shall fall, for I have spoken," declares the Master אYaZ. [6]"And I shall send fire upon Magog and on those who live undisturbed in the coastlands. And they shall know that I am אYaZ. [7]"<u>And I shall make My set-apart Name known in the midst of My people Yisra'el, and not let My set-apart Name be profaned any more</u>. And the gentiles shall know that I am אYaZ, the Set-apart One in Yisra'el. [8]"See, it shall come, and it shall be done," declares the Master אYaZ. "This is the day of which I have spoken.

Ezekiel 39, cont.

⁹"And those who inhabit the cities of Yisra'el shall go out and set on fire and burn the weapons, both the shields and armour, the bows and arrows, the clubs and spears. And they shall make fires with them for seven years, ¹⁰and take no wood from the field nor cut down any from the forests, for with the weapons they make fire. And they shall plunder those who plundered them, and loot those who looted them," declares the Master 𐤀𐤅𐤄𐤅. ¹¹"And it shall be on that day that I give Gog a burial site there in Yisra'el, the valley of those passing by east of the sea, and stopping those passing by, because there they shall bury Gog and all his crowd, and shall call it the Valley of Hamon Gog. ¹²"And the house of Yisra'el shall bury them for seven months, in order to cleanse the land. ¹³"And all the people of the land shall bury them, and it shall be for a name to them on the day that I am esteemed," declares the Master 𐤀𐤅𐤄𐤅. ¹⁴"And they shall separate men who continually pass through the land, burying those who were passing through, those left on the surface of the ground, in order to cleanse it. At the end of seven months they shall search, ¹⁵and those passing through shall pass through the land, and when anyone sees a man's bone, he shall set up a sign beside it, till the buriers have buried it in the Valley of Hamon Gog. ¹⁶"And also a city named Hamonah shall be there. So they shall cleanse the land." ¹⁷"And you, son of man, thus said the Master 𐤀𐤅𐤄𐤅, 'Speak to <u>every sort of bird and to every beast of the field</u>, "Assemble yourselves and come, gather from all around to My offering which I am slaughtering for you, a great offering on the mountains of Yisra'el, and <u>you shall eat flesh and drink blood.</u> ¹⁸"Eat the flesh of the mighty, drink the blood of the princes of the earth, of rams and lambs, of goats and bulls, all of them fatlings of Bashan. ¹⁹"And you shall eat fat till you are filled, and drink blood till you are drunk, at My offering which I am slaughtering for you. ²⁰"And you shall be satisfied at My table with horses and riders, with mighty men and with all the men of battle," declares the Master 𐤀𐤅𐤄𐤅. ²¹"And I shall set My esteem among the gentiles. And all gentiles shall see My judgment which I have executed, and My hand which I have laid on them. ²²"And the house of Yisra'el shall know that I am 𐤀𐤅𐤄𐤅 their Elohim from that day onward. ²³"And the gentiles shall know that the house of Yisra'el went into exile for their crookedness, because they have trespassed against Me, so that I hid My face from them, and I gave them into the hand of their adversaries, and they all fell by the sword. ²⁴"According to their uncleanness and according to their transgressions I have dealt with them, and <u>hidden My face</u> from them." ' ²⁵"Therefore thus said the Master 𐤀𐤅𐤄𐤅, **'Now I am going to bring back the captives of Ya'aqob. And I shall have compassion on all the house of Yisra'el, and shall be jealous for My set-apart Name.**

Ezekiel 39, cont.
²⁶'And they shall have borne their shame, and all their trespass they committed against Me, when they dwell safely in their own land, with none to make them afraid, ²⁷when I have brought them back from the peoples and gathered them out of the lands of their enemies. And I shall be set apart in them before the eyes of many gentiles. ²⁸'And they shall know that I am 𐤉𐤄𐤅𐤄 their Elohim, who sent them into exile among the gentiles, **and then gathered them back to their own land, and left none of them behind.** ²⁹'And no longer do I hide My face from them, for I shall have poured out My Spirit on the house of Yisra'el,' declares the Master 𐤉𐤄𐤅𐤄."

Book of Enoch 100
₁And in those days in one place the fathers together with their sons **(families of the wicked)** shall be smitten and brothers one with another shall fall in death till the streams flow with their blood. ₂For a man shall not withhold his hand from slaying his sons and his sons' sons and the sinner shall not withhold his hand from his honored brother: From dawn till sunset they shall slay one another. ₃And the horse shall walk up to the breast in the blood of sinners, And the chariot shall be submerged to its height. ₄In those days the angels shall descend into the secret places and gather together into one place all those who brought down sin and the Most High will arise on that day of judgment to execute great judgment amongst sinners. ₅And over all the righteous and holy He will appoint guardians from amongst the holy angels to guard them as the apple of an eye, until He makes an end of all wickedness and all sin, and though the righteous sleep a long sleep, they have naught to fear. ₆And (then) the children of the earth shall see the wise in security, and shall understand all the words of this book, and recognize that their riches shall not be able to save them in the overthrow of their sins. The armies of the Beast and the false prophet are completely destroyed in the valley of Yahuah's judgment!

Revelation 19
And after these things I heard a great voice of much people in heaven, saying, HalleluYah; Salvation, and glory, and honour, and power, unto the 𐤉𐤄𐤅𐤄 our Elohim: For true and righteous are his judgments: for he hath judged the great whore, which did corrupt the earth with her fornication, and hath avenged the blood of his servants at her hand. And again they said, HalleluYah. And her smoke rose up for ever and ever. And the four and twenty elders and the four beasts fell down and worshipped 𐤉𐤄𐤅𐤄 that sat on the throne, saying, amein; HalleluYah!

Revelation 19, cont.
And a voice came out of the throne, saying, Praise our Elohim, all ye his servants, and ye that fear him, both small and great. And I heard as it were the voice of a great multitude, and as the voice of many waters, and as the voice of mighty thunderings, saying, Alleluia: for ᵃYᵃZ Elohim omnipotent reigneth. Let us be glad and rejoice, and give honour to him: for the marriage of the Lamb is come, and his wife hath made herself ready. And to her was granted that she should be arrayed in fine linen, clean and white: for the fine linen is the righteousness of saints. And he saith unto me, Write, Blessed are they which are called unto the marriage supper of the Lamb. And he saith unto me, These are the true sayings of ᵃYᵃZ. And I fell at his feet to worship him. And he said unto me, See thou do it not: I am thy fellow servant, and of thy brethren that have the testimony of OWYᵃZ: worship ᵃYᵃZ: for the testimony of OWYᵃZ is the spirit of prophesy. And I saw heaven opened, and behold a white horse; and he that sat upon him was called Faithful and True, and in righteousness he doth judge and make war. His eyes were as a flame of fire, and on his head were many crowns; and he had a name written, that no man knew, but he himself. And he was clothed with a vesture dipped in blood: and his name is called The Word of ᵃYᵃZ. And the armies which were in heaven followed him upon white horses, clothed in fine linen, white and clean. And out of his mouth goeth a sharp sword, that with it he should smite the nations: and he shall rule them with a rod of iron: and he treadeth the winepress of the fierceness and wrath of El-Shaddai. And he OWYᵃZ hath on his vesture and on his thigh a name written, KING OF KINGS, AND MASTER OF MASTERS. And I saw an angel standing in the sun; and he cried with a loud voice, saying to <u>all the fowls that fly in the midst of heaven</u>, <u>Come and gather yourselves together unto the supper of the great Elohim</u>; That ye may eat the flesh of kings, and the flesh of captains, and the flesh of mighty men, and the flesh of horses, and of them that sit on them, and the flesh of all men, both free and bond, both small and great. And I saw the beast, and the kings of the earth, and their armies, gathered together to make war against him that sat on the horse, and against his army. And the beast was taken, and with him the false prophet that wrought miracles before him, with which he deceived them that had received the mark of the beast, and them that worshipped his image. These both were cast alive into a lake of fire burning with brimstone. And the remnant were slain with the sword of him that sat upon the horse, which sword proceeded out of his mouth: and all the fowls were filled with their flesh.

After the great battle at the valley of Yahuah's judgment, the beast and the false prophet are thrown **alive** into the Lake of Fire, which is the second death!

Isaiah 14

How the oppressor **(Nimrod)** has ceased, the gold-gatherer ceased! ⁵"𝓐𝐘𝓐𝐙 has broken the staff of the wrong, the scepter of the rulers, ⁶he who smote the people in wrath with ceaseless blows, who ruled the gentiles in displeasure, is persecuted and no one restrains. ⁷"All the earth is at rest and at peace, they shall break forth into singing. ⁸**"Even the cypress trees rejoice over you, and the cedars of Lebanon (forest), saying, 'Since you were cut down, no woodcutter has come up against us (no more Christmas trees).'** ⁹"The grave from beneath is excited about you, to meet you at your coming; it stirs up the dead for you, all the chief ones of the earth; it has raised up from their thrones all the sovereigns of the gentiles. ¹⁰"All of them respond and say to you, 'Have you also become as weak as we? Have you become like us? ¹¹'Your arrogance has been brought down to the grave, and the sound of your stringed instruments; the maggot is spread under you, and worms cover you.' ¹²"How you have fallen from the heavens, O Helel, son of the morning! You have been cut down to the ground, you who laid low the gentiles! ¹³"For you have said in your heart, 'Let me go up to the heavens, let me raise my throne above the stars of El, and let me sit in the mount of meeting on the sides of the north; ¹⁴let me go up above the heights of the clouds, **(Remember the tower of Babel!)** let me be like the Most High.' ¹⁵"But you are brought down to the grave, to the sides of the Pit. ¹⁶"Those who see you stare at you, and ponder over you, saying, '**Is this the man who made the earth tremble, who shook reigns, ¹⁷who made the world as a wilderness and destroyed its cities, who would not open the house of his prisoners?**' ¹⁸"All the sovereigns of the gentiles, all of them, were laid in esteem, everyone in his own house; ¹⁹but you have been thrown from your grave like an abominable branch, like the garment of those who are slain, thrust through with a sword, who go down to the stones of the pit, like a trampled corpse. ²⁰"You are not joined with them in burial, for you have destroyed your land and slain your people. Let the seed of evil-doers never be mentioned. ²¹"Prepare his children for slaughter, because of the crookedness of their fathers, lest they rise up and possess the land, and fill the face of the world with cities." ²²"And I shall rise up against them," declares 𝓐𝐘𝓐𝐙 of hosts, "and shall cut off from Babel the name and remnant, and off-spring and descendant," declares 𝓐𝐘𝓐𝐙. ²³"And I shall make it a possession for the porcupine, and marshes of muddy water; and shall sweep it with the broom of destruction," declares 𝓐𝐘𝓐𝐙 of hosts.

Isaiah 14, cont.

24 יהוה of hosts has sworn, saying, "**Truly, as I have planned, so shall it be; and as I have purposed, so it stands:** 25 **"To break Ashshur in My land, and tread him down on My mountains. And his yoke shall be removed from them, and his burden removed from their shoulders.** 26 "This is the counsel that is counseled for all the earth, and this is the hand that is stretched out over all the nations. 27 "For יהוה of hosts has counseled, and who annuls it? And His hand that is stretched out, who turns it back?"

Isaiah 24

See, יהוה is making the earth empty and making it waste, and shall overturn its surface, and shall scatter abroad its inhabitants. 2 And it shall be–as with the people so with the priest, as with the servant so with his master, as with the female servant so with her mistress, as with the buyer so with the seller, as with the lender so with the borrower, as with the creditor so with the debtor; 3 the earth is completely emptied and utterly plundered, for יהוה has spoken this word. 4 The earth shall mourn and wither, the world shall languish and wither, the haughty people of the earth shall languish. 5 <u>**For the earth has been defiled under its inhabitants, because they have transgressed the Torot,**</u> changed the law, broken the everlasting covenant. 6 Therefore a curse shall consume the earth, and those who dwell in it be punished. **Therefore the inhabitants of the earth shall be burned, and few men shall be left.** 7 The new wine shall fail, the vine shall languish, all those glad at heart shall sigh. 8 The joy of the tambourine shall cease, the noise of those who rejoice shall end, the joy of the lyre shall cease. 9 No more do they drink wine with a song, strong drink is bitter to those who drink it. 10 The deserted city shall be broken down, every house shall be shut, no one enters. 11 There is a crying for wine in the streets; all joy shall be darkened, the gladness of the earth shall be gone. 12 The city is left in ruins, and the gate is stricken with destruction. 13 **For thus it is to be in the midst of the earth among the peoples, like the shaking of an olive tree, like the gleaning of grapes when the grape harvest is done.** 14 They lift up their voice, they sing of the excellency of יהוה, they shall cry aloud from the sea. 15 Therefore praise יהוה in the east, the Name of יהוה Elohim of Yisra'el in the coastlands of the sea. 16 From the ends of the earth we shall hear songs, "Splendor to the Righteous One!" But I say, "I waste away, I waste away! Woe to me! The treacherous betray, with treachery the treacherous betray." 17 Fear and the pit and the snare are upon you, O inhabitant of the earth. 18 And it shall be that he who flees from the noise of the fear falls into the pit, and he who comes up from the midst of the pit is caught in the snare.

Isaiah 24, cont.
For the windows from on high shall be opened, and the foundations of the earth be shaken. [19]The earth shall be utterly broken, the earth shall be completely shattered, the earth shall be fiercely shaken. [20]The earth shall stagger like a drunkard. And it shall totter like a hut, and its transgression shall be heavy upon it, and it shall fall, and not rise again. [21]And in that day it shall be that 𐤀𐤉𐤄𐤅 punishes on high the host of exalted ones, and on the earth the sovereigns of the earth. [22]And they shall be gathered together, as prisoners are gathered in the pit, and shall be shut up in the prison, and be punished after many days. [23]**And the moon shall blush, and the sun shall be ashamed, for 𐤀𐤉𐤄𐤅 of hosts shall reign on Mount Tsiyon, and in Yahrushalayim, and before His elders in esteem!**

After this OWY𐤄𐤅 chains the adversary in the Abyss for a thousand years! John saw thrones and authority being given to those, who had suffered and given their lives for 𐤀𐤉𐤄𐤅. The Righteous will be rewarded by OWY𐤄𐤅 and He will rule the earth with an iron rod! Many people will be spared from total annihilation because they helped one of Yahushua's called out ones. Because of this kindness, OWY𐤄𐤅 will remember and spare their lives. However, for those spared there will **not** be any rewards or crowns. During this 1,000 years the knowledge of 𐤀𐤉𐤄𐤅 will cover the earth! What the people in nations weren't told by their false Shepherds, will now be taught to them during this 1,000 years by Yahuah's Priests and Judges! These Priests and Judges will judge righteously using the Torah of 𐤀𐤉𐤄𐤅 **as the standard**! There will be no more bribes, no more favoritism, and the Torah will be observed by everyone **(one way or the other)**! I am so thankful that Yahuah's Ruach HaQodesh has already given me a love for His Truth!

II Thessalonians 2
[9]The coming of the lawless ones according to the working of Satan, with all power and signs and wonders of falsehood, [10]and with all deceit of unrighteousness in those perishing, because they **did not receive a love of the truth in order for them to be saved.**

OWY𐤄𐤅 will make sure that all the survivors in the nations will be thoroughly schooled for many years! Everyone will observe the Torah, like it or not! Many of Yahuah's overcomers will be appointed judges, priests, and Levites with OWY𐤄𐤅 in His kingdom. After 1,000 years, OWY𐤄𐤅 will allow satan to be freed from the Abyss to test the people in the nations one final time. As usual satan will stir up the nations to rebel against 𐤀𐤉𐤄𐤅. They will surround the New Yahrushalayim.

That will be a huge mistake! OWYAZ will quickly destroy satan's army with fire, which falls from the heavens! After that battle, it will be time for the final judgment of all of Yahuah's adversaries! They will all be judged and thrown into the Lake of Fire, where they will experience the second death! And at the appointed time OWYAZ will create a new earth! No idols will be found anywhere. The names of foreign elohim will <u>not</u> be on the lips of anyone! All traces of the foreign elohim will be burned up! There will be no more obelisks, no more steeples, no more edifices, no more Easter eggs, and no more Christmas trees!

Revelation 20
And I saw an angel come down from heaven, having the key of the bottomless pit and a great chain in his hand. And he laid hold on the dragon, that old serpent, which is the Devil, and Satan, and bound him a thousand years, And cast him into the bottomless pit, and shut him up, and set a seal upon him, that he should deceive the nations no more, till the thousand years should be fulfilled: and after that he must be loosed a little season. And I saw thrones, and they sat upon them, and judgment was given unto them: and I saw the souls of them that were beheaded for the witness of OWYAZ, and for the word of AYAZ, and which had not worshipped the beast, neither his image, neither had received his mark upon their foreheads, or in their hands; and they lived and reigned with Messiah a thousand years. But the rest of the dead lived not again until the thousand years were finished. This is the first resurrection. Blessed and holy is he that hath part in the first resurrection: on such the second death hath no power, but they shall be priests of AYAZ and of Messiah, and shall reign with him a thousand years. And when the thousand years are expired, Satan shall be loosed out of his prison, And shall go out to deceive the nations which are in the four quarters of the earth, Gog and Magog, to gather them together to battle: the number of whom is as the sand of the sea. And they went up on the breadth of the earth, and compassed the camp of the saints about, and the beloved city: and fire came down from AYAZ out of heaven, and devoured them. And the devil that deceived them was cast into the lake of fire and brimstone, where the beast and the false prophet are, and shall be tormented day and night for ever and ever. And I saw a great white throne, and him that sat on it, from whose face the earth and the heaven fled away; and there was found no place for them. And I saw the dead, small and great, stand before AYAZ; and the books were opened: and another book was opened, which is the book of life: and the dead were judged out of those things which were written in the books, according to their works. And the sea gave up the dead which were in it; and death and hell delivered up the dead which were in them: and they were judged every man according to their works.

Revelation 20, cont.
And death and sheol were cast into the lake of fire. This is the second death. And whosoever was not found written in the book of life was cast into the lake of fire.

𐤉𐤄𐤅𐤄 will create a fabulous new heaven and a fabulous new earth!

Revelation 21
And I saw a renewed heaven and a renewed earth, for the former heaven and the former earth had passed away, and the sea is no more. ^{2}And I, Yohanan, saw the set-apart city, renewed Yahrushalayim, <u>coming down</u> out of the heaven from Elohim, prepared as a bride adorned for her husband. ^{3}And I heard a loud voice from the heaven saying, "See, the Booth of Elohim is with men, and He shall dwell with them, and they shall be His people, and Elohim Himself shall be with them and be their Elohim. ^{4}"And Elohim shall wipe away every tear from their eyes, and there shall be no more death, nor mourning, nor crying. And there shall be no more pain, for the former matters have passed away." ^{5}And He who was sitting on the throne said, "See, I make all matters new." And He said to me, "Write, for these words are true and trustworthy." ^{6}And He said to me, "It is done! I am the 'Aleph' and the 'Taw', the Beginning and the End. To the one who thirsts I shall give of the fountain of the water of life without payment. ^{7}"The one who overcomes shall inherit all this, and I shall be his Elohim and he shall be My son. ^{8}"But as for the cowardly, and untrustworthy, and abominable, and murderers, and those who whore, and drug sorcerers, and idolaters, and all the false, their part is in the lake which burns with fire and sulphur, which is the second death."
^{9}And one of the seven messengers who held the seven bowls filled with the seven last plagues came to me and spoke with me, saying, "Come, I shall show you the bride, the Lamb's wife." ^{10}And he carried me away in the Spirit to a great and high mountain, and showed me the great city, the set-apart Yahrushalayim, descending out of the heaven from Elohim, ^{11}having the esteem of Elohim, and her light was like a most precious stone, like a jasper stone, clear as crystal, ^{12}and having a great and high wall, having twelve gates, and at the gates twelve messengers, and names written on them, which are those of the twelve tribes of the children of Yisra'el ^{13}three gates on the east, three gates on the north, three gates on the south, and three gates on the west. ^{14}And the wall of the city had twelve foundations, and on them were the names of the twelve emissaries of the Lamb. ^{15}And he who spoke with me had a golden measuring rod, to measure the city, and its gates, and its wall. ^{16}And the city lies four-cornered, and its length is as great as its breadth.

Revelation 21, cont.
And he measured the city with the rod: two thousand two hundred kilometers – the length, and the breadth, and height of it are equal. [17] And he measured its wall: sixty-five meters, according to the measure of a man, that is, of a messenger. [18] And the structure of its wall was jasper. And the city was clean gold, like clear glass. [19] And the foundations of the wall of the city were adorned with all kinds of precious stones: the first foundation jasper, the second sapphire, the third agate, the fourth emerald, [20] the fifth sardonyx, the sixth ruby, the seventh chrysolite, the eighth beryl, the ninth topaz, the tenth chrysoprase, the eleventh jacinth, and the twelfth amethyst. [21] And the twelve gates were twelve pearls – each one of the gates was a single pearl. And the street of the city was clean gold, like transparent glass. [22] And I saw no Dwelling Place in it, for 𐤀𐤉𐤀𐤆 El Shaddai is its Dwelling Place, and the Lamb. [23] And the city had no need of the sun, nor of the moon, to shine in it, for the esteem of Elohim lightened it, and the Lamb is its lamp. [24] And the gentiles, of those who are saved, shall walk in its light, and the sovereigns of the earth bring their esteem into it. [25] And its gates shall not be shut at all by day, for night shall not be there. [26] And they shall bring the esteem and the appreciation of the gentiles into it. [27] **And there shall by <u>no</u> means enter into it whatever is <u>unclean</u>, neither anyone doing abomination and falsehood, but only those who are written in the Lamb's Book of Life.**

Revelation 22
And he showed me a river of water of life, clear as crystal, coming from the throne of Elohim and of the Lamb. [2] In the middle of its street, and on either side of the river, was the tree of life, which bore twelve fruits, each tree yielding its fruit every month. And the leaves of the tree were for the healing of the nations. [3] And no longer shall there be any curse, and the throne of Elohim and of the Lamb shall be in it, and His servants shall serve Him. [4] And they shall see His face, and His Name shall be upon their foreheads. [5] And night shall be no more, and they shall have no need of a lamp or the light of the sun, because 𐤀𐤉𐤀𐤆 Elohim shall give them light. And they shall reign forever and ever. [6] And he said to me, "These words are trustworthy and true. And 𐤀𐤉𐤀𐤆 Elohim of the set-apart prophets has sent His messenger to show His servants what has to take place with speed. [7] "See, I am coming speedily! Blessed is he who guards the words of the prophecy of this book." [8] And I, Yohanan, saw and heard these matters. And when I heard and saw, I fell down to worship before the feet of the messenger who showed me these matters. [9] And he said to me, "See, do not!

Revelation 22, cont.
For I am your fellow servant, and of your brothers the prophets, and of those who are guarding the words of this book. Worship Elohim." **¹⁰*And he said to me, "Do not seal the words of the prophecy of this book, because the time is near.*** *¹¹"He who does wrong, let him do more wrong; he who is filthy, let him be more filthy; he who is righteous, let him be more righteous; he who is set-apart, let him be more set-apart. ¹²"And see, I am coming speedily, and My reward is with Me, to give to each according to his work. ¹³"I am the 'Aleph' and the Taw', the Beginning and the End, the First and the Last. ¹⁴"Blessed are those doing His commands, so that the authority shall be theirs unto the tree of life, and to enter through the gates into the city.*

What Time Is It?

In Daniel 9 a period of seventy weeks of years was discussed. Each of these seventy weeks represents a **seven year period.** So the **total** duration of this prophetic 70 weeks is **490** years **(70 × 7 years).** Daniel's prophecy of 490 years is consistent with the 10,000 year timeline discussed in *The Book of Enoch.* Enoch prophesied that OWYƷL will return for judgment in the **8th week** from Adam's fall! Each week is equivalent to 1,000 years. Earlier in this book, I discussed Yahuah's 10,000 plan. I believe that OWYƷL **did** in fact come as our Passover Lamb at the 5,500 year mark, after Adam's fall from Paradise! If the calendars are reasonably accurate, since Yahushua's Passover sacrifice, then Yahuah's clock is pointed at approximately the 7,500 year point right now! **The 7,500 year point is in the middle of the 8th week**! What does all this mean for you and me? **We are increditably close to the beginning of the Day of ƷYƷL** and Israel's final worldwide Exodus! OWYƷL is coming to get His First Fruits in the 8th week! **We are in the 8th week right now!** HalleluYah! HalleluYah! HalleluYah! **Now** is the time to break away from this world's religious apostasy and serve ƷYƷL!

Summary

The Day of ƷYƷL is a 1,000 year period, not a single 24 hour day. Daniel records that 490 years (or 70 weeks of years) will be required to accomplish the righteous milestones listed below.

(1) OWYƷL will put a **complete** end to iniquity, transgression, and sin against ƷYƷL!
(2) Crookedness will be righteously recompensed!
(3) Visions and prophecy of the Day of ƷYƷL will end!
(4) Everlasting righteousness will be established on the earth just as it is in the Heavens (Shamayim)!
(5) The New Yahrushalayim on the heavenly Mount Zion will be anointed!

When the first four Seals of Revelation are opened, four wicked kings from the regions of ancient Arabia will be loosed one by one. A classic confrontation will pit the king of the North against the king of the South. There will be wars, rumors of wars, oppression, and increasing affliction in all the nations! When the 4th Seal is opened a wicked and vile horseman will be resurrected from the Abyss (Sheol or the underworld)! Yahuah's prophets called him Abaddon, Apolluon, Bel, Baal, and Asshur, but he was known in Genesis as Nimrod! When the 6th Seal is opened, OWYAZ will return to gather the first of His three harvests on the Day of AYAZ. OWYAZ gathers His First Fruits back to the real Promised Land where they will rebuild and reinhabit the real Yahrushalayim and the other set apart cities of Yahudah on their own mounds. After 434 years have transpired in safety, the First Fruits will fight valiantly for many years to defend themselves against Nimrod and his confederacy of nations! At year 486½, after many years of war, Nimrod and His armies will sack Yahrushalayim! But, a remnant of the Righteous will remain held up on the Temple Mount and on the Mount of Olives (the altar)! At that time Yahuah's two witnesses will be slaughtered on the streets of Yahrushalayim by Nimrod and their bodies will lie in the streets of the city without a burial! After 3½ days, Yahuah's two witnesses will be resurrected in front of their enemies and will ascend into the heavens! When these events occur at the exact appointed time, OWYAZ will return with great power and esteem at the sounding of the 7th Trumpet! OWYAZ will return from the heavenly Mount Zion with the Righteous, who were resurrected at the time of His sacrifice on the Passover tree! OWYAZ will come to rescue His First Fruits from the fowler's (Nimrod's) snare! Then OWYAZ will send out fishermen and hunters to gather all the rest of Israel to His fabulous wedding banquet. At the 7th Trumpet blast the Righteous of Israel will be resurrected! Those alive will be reborn into spiritual bodies. Israel will travel on Yahuah's set apart highway across the mountain heights of Israel to the heavenly Mount Zion, which will have descended from the heavens and become a wedding canopy or Chuppah over Mount Sinai. Meanwhile Nimrod will erect an abominable image of himself on the Temple Mount. Sheep trapped in the nations will be intensely pressured to worship his image. Because He is merciful, AYAZ will dispatch three heavenly messengers to fly in the mid-heavens one after the other to warn the nations for the last time to repent of their apostasies, to worship AYAZ, to **refuse** the mark of the beast, and to **refuse** to fall down to his image! Nimrod and all the wicked from **every** generation will be gathered, progressively tortured, and then annihilated in the valley of Yahushofet! Seven bowls of Yahuah's undiluted wrath will be poured out on the wicked and **unrepentant** one by one! Woe, Woe, Woe be it to them!

Where Are the Good Shepherds?
Chapter 14

[11] "I am the good shepherd. The good shepherd lays down His life for the sheep. [12] "But the hireling, and not being a shepherd, one who does not own the sheep, sees the wolf coming and leaves the sheep and flees. And the wolf snatches the sheep and scatters them. Yohanan 10

I was in the church system for 43 years! I sincerely believed that I was saved based on the teaching of the church! Even though I am no longer a part of the church system, I still love the sincere sheep in the church system very much! Churches are full of many, many kind and compassionate people! There are thousands of church ministries that are carried out with very noble intentions by good, honorable, and giving people! In the churches that I attended the very best people were always the ones doing the most work! I believe that there are a great many very unselfish people, who have been serving in church ministries for no financial reward to themselves for many years! However, no matter how good the people are and how well intentioned their ministries, the sad Truth is the system itself is **in great apostasy**! The church system of Christianity was **defiled** and made **unclean**, when it was contaminated by the adoption of pagan practices and traditions long ago! In spite of wholesome outward appearances, Christianity does **not** teach the right **Way** to go! The **church system itself is a part of the religious system**, which the Scriptures try to warn us about! It's very, very deceptive! Most people in churches today don't even know the real set apart name of 𐤀𐤉𐤄𐤆, just as I didn't! Why don't they know? **Because their shepherds, who supposedly guide them, don't tell them**! The Scriptures testify over and over that we are to walk according to the Commandments of 𐤀𐤉𐤄𐤆, if we love our Messiah! That fact is down-played by today's preachers! Sadly the simple truth is that the church system has become contaminated with practices, icons, and philosophies that have their origins with the pagan worship of the sun! It's painful for me to say this, but **facts are facts** and the **truth is the truth**! This contamination started in the distant past, after the Flood with Nimrod! Nimrod was a son of Cush, who was a son of Ham, who was a son of Noah! Errors that originated with Nimrod have been passed down from generation to generation and are now taught in all Christian churches as doctrine! Now, **this may not bother you, but 𐤀𐤉𐤄𐤆 hates all forms of idolatry today just as much as He hated it in the time of Nimrod**! I know by first hand experience, how traumatic it is to find out that a system that you have believed in and trusted in, since your childhood, is actually based on lies and errors!

The church teaches the same deceptive doctrines that OWYAZ warned us to stay far away from! There is something terribly wrong with the doctrines of Christianity as well as all the other man made religions of the world, which don't acknowledge AYAZ and OWYAZ! **All these false religions have certain things in common no matter what they are called! They are all contaminated with traditions and doctrines rooted in the worship of the sun, the moon, and the stars!** They have all become defiled with idolatrous practices, icons, and false doctrines that are snares to the innocent sheep of this world! All forms of idolatry are **unclean** in Yahuah's eyes according to His Ten Commandments! We don't have to wonder what Yahuah's opinions are because the opinions of AYAZ were given to us at Mount Sinai! Yahuah's opinions are called His Torah! Yahuah's Torah is our guide for living the right Way! As strangers in this present world system, we need the Torah to be a lamp unto our feet and a light unto our path! On the Day of AYAZ everyone will finally realize that **Yahuah's opinions are the only opinions that really matter!** For thousands of years good people have incorrectly rationalized that AYAZ knows their hearts and therefore will excuse their disobedience to His Torah! But AYAZ **does know** their hearts and knows, when their hearts are in rebellion against His will! When a person chooses to continue to stay mired in religious apostasy, after he understands Yahuah's standards, then he proves that he actually loves the religious traditions of men **more than he loves** AYAZ and OWYAZ! AYAZ is unchanging! He still hates all forms of idolatry, paganism, and the mixing of the clean with the unclean! There are many counterfeit religious systems today that have entrapped the majority of Yahuah's people! These systems use covert deception and stealth! OWYAZ warned His twelve disciples that they would be persecuted by religious leaders just as He was! OWYAZ told them that a time was coming, when the people mired in apostasy would be so deceived that they would sincerely believe they were doing a holy service by killing Yahuah's people! That's pretty sick, isn't it?

John 16
These things have I spoken unto you, that ye should not be offended. They shall put you out of the synagogues: yea, the time cometh, that whosoever killeth you will think that he doeth AYAZ *service. And these things will they do unto you, because they have not known the Father, nor me.*

Isaiah 5
*Woe unto them that call evil good, and good evil; that put **darkness for light**, and **light for darkness**; that put bitter for sweet, and sweet for bitter!*

Isaiah 5, cont.
Woe unto them that are <u>wise in their own eyes, and prudent in their own sight!</u> Woe unto them that are mighty to drink wine, and men of strength to mingle strong drink: Which justify the wicked for reward, and take away the righteousness of the righteous from him! Therefore as the fire devoureth the stubble, and the flame consumeth the chaff, so their root shall be as rottenness, and their blossom shall go up as dust: because **they have cast away the law of ayaz of hosts, and despised the word of the Holy One of Israel**

As you know by now this **is not** a typical prophecy book! It's not like any of the popular prophecy books that are in the book stores today! In most cases this book <u>will be in direct conflict</u> with most of the teachings of the Christian prophecy writers! **But this book is true to the Word of ayaz!** Let My People Go attempts to <u>restore</u> the knowledge of the old ways, the location of the original Promised Land, and the original intent of prophecy in the Scriptures!

Jeremiah 6
Thus saith ayaz, Stand ye in the ways, and see, and ask for the old paths, where is **the good way, and walk therein, and ye shall find rest for your souls**.

I love the truth! I'm very hungry and thirsty for the knowledge and wisdom of ayaz! I'm frustrated and saddened at how much confusion and apostasy have entered into the religious traditions of mankind! I plan to do everything that I can to help good people **wake up** from their spiritual sleep, which the apostate religious systems have perpetuated! I feel so helpless, when I see the masses of good people, who are trapped in the snares of religious apostasy, <u>exactly where I was just a few years ago!</u> They don't even know that they are spiritually naked! Good people **sincerely want to know the Truth**, but they have trusted the false shepherds to teach them! They have unknowingly been led astray by false teaching and empty doctrines of men! The good people of the earth believe that these shepherds are correct in their doctrines! After all, they are highly educated and trained professionals aren't they? Don't these shepherds graduate from institutions of higher religious learning? Aren't these shepherds enlightened and qualified to correctly interpret the Scriptures for us? Doesn't higher learning qualify these shepherds as experts, who don't make mistakes as they interpret the Scriptures <u>for their sheep</u>? Sadly, most good sheep never study the Scriptures for themselves! The good sheep swallow the doctrines of the false shepherds without analyzing them against the Scriptures for themselves! These sheep don't challenge or even recognize the errors! They trust their false shepherds!

These shepherds are really wolves in sheep's clothing! These sheep do the same thing that **unclean** animals do! They swallow everything indiscriminately! These good sheep don't chew and evaluate their food, before they swallow! These sheep don't check the wolf shepherd's messages against the Scriptures, before they swallow! These sheep swallow everything whether it is true, false, or somewhere in between! But the saddest part is that the wolf shepherds have convinced the sheep that they **are already saved and that all is well**! The Truth is that most sheep are **completely naked and trapped** in a deadly snare! Tragically, they don't even realize it! Confusion abounds and their own wolf shepherds **show no mercy to their own sheep**! These shepherds are wolves and they have ravenous appetites! They make **merchandise** of the good sheep trapped in apostasy! The wolf shepherds speak lies against Yahuah's real overcomers, Israel! The people called Israel try their best to follow the Scriptures! They love OWYƎZ! They love the name of ƎYƎZ and they love to obey Yahuah's Commandments! However, Yahuah's real overcomers, Israel, are called legalists and extremists by the false shepherds!

The Sheep Are Blinded To The Truth!
Matthew 22
For many are called, but few are chosen.

Why are few chosen? Because even though many morally good sheep are called to be part of Israel by OWYƎZ, very few sheep take Yahuah's call seriously enough to make the necessary changes in their lives! Most sheep pull back! They will not repent of their harlotries with the religions of men! Very few sheep are willing to make the changes needed to fully embrace OWYƎZ and His messages!

Why Don't the Sheep Repent and Follow the Scriptures?
Most sheep, when confronted with the Truth of Scripture seem to understand, but are unwilling to give up the traditions of man's religious systems! Some sheep feel a great need to belong! Many point to the ministries of the churches as justification for their participation, even when they are exposed to the truth about the apostasy of the system! Some sheep believe that the charitable works done by churches more than offset for the errors of the system! Some like the apparent security offered by large numbers of people, who attend the churches with them! Many sheep rationalize that; if millions of sheep choose to go to church, then that must be the right way to go! Other sheep have established great friendships in the church and they love the social opportunities that the church offers!

Many sheep stay so busy in church that they don't have any time or energy to think about anything else! Some sheep are afraid of what the other sheep would say, if they came out of man's apostate religions! Lots of sheep try to super-impose their standards over Yahuah's Torah! They believe that 𐤀𐤉𐤀𐤆 will somehow overlook the errors that have crept into the church system because their "heart's right"! Finally many, many sheep just don't really have enough love for the Truth! These sheep love the lies of man's religious systems more than they love the OWY𐤀𐤆 himself! Many sheep give everything they have to their religious denominations! These sheep somehow **rationalize** that 𐤀𐤉𐤀𐤆 won't mind that their church's doctrine doesn't match the Truth in the Scriptures! Many sheep believe that giving goodwill boxes and *Toys for Tots* during Christmas will somehow please 𐤀𐤉𐤀𐤆! Somehow they believe that 𐤀𐤉𐤀𐤆 will overlook the pagan origins and icons of Christmas! Some sheep, when they are confronted with what the Scriptures actually teach just want to cover their ears! They simply don't want to hear it! It's very painful! Instead, they prefer to surround themselves with sheep, who **will affirm** their beliefs and rationalize away the Truth with them! I love these sheep and that's why it just breaks my heart to see so many sheep trapped in the snares of such deceitful systems!

Apostasy

The twelve tribes of Israel were exiled by 𐤀𐤉𐤀𐤆 to all the nations of the earth! They were warned by prophet after prophet, including OWY𐤀𐤆 Himself, to repent of their spiritual harlotry with the religious systems of the nations! Can you believe that today, after all these years, good people are still doing the exact same things and don't even realize it! Preachers follow the doctrines of their denominations at all cost, even when they must lie, twist, or tell half truths! These wolf shepherds have laid stumbling blocks in front of the sheep, but the sheep trust them to lead them in the right way! How ironic is that?

The Wolves Have Hidden the Set Apart Names!

The names of our heavenly Father and His Son are the two most important names in all the Heaven and the Earth! It hurts, when someone refuses to acknowledge you by your real name, doesn't it? It's rejection and it's disrespectful! It hurts, when someone doesn't respect you enough to learn your name and acknowledge you by calling you by that name! I cannot imagine how much it has grieved Yahuah's heart for thousands of years, when His name has been constantly disrespected and suppressed, even though He is the sustainer of all life! I am so thankful that Righteous sheep all over the world are coming into the knowledge of Yahuah's name! Israel will not be ashamed to use Yahuah's name!

The Wolves Have Done Violence to the Torah!
What a huge stumbling block pastors have created concerning the Ordinances and Commandments of 𝓐𝐘𝐀𝐙! These wolf shepherds have declared that anyone, who would follow the Torah doesn't understand the New Covenant and is still mired in legalism! **How far they are from the Truth!** The Truth is that the very behavior, which they readily condemn, is the evidence of our love for OWY𝐀𝐙 and 𝓐𝐘𝐀𝐙! I love OWY𝐀𝐙 and 𝓐𝐘𝐀𝐙 so much that I want to please them in every way! When you truly desire to please OWY𝐀𝐙 and 𝓐𝐘𝐀𝐙, then the Ruach HaQodesh will write Yahuah's Commandments on your heart! All Israel will love the Torah of 𝓐𝐘𝐀𝐙!

The Wolves Have Switched the Sabbath!
The Sabbath was created for man! The Truth is that 𝐀𝐘𝐀𝐙 knew that His people, Israel, would need the Sabbath to rest just as He rested from His work! The Sabbath reminds us that our lives will <u>not</u> always be filled with the hardships, pain, suffering, rejections, and struggles that we now face in this world! 𝐀𝐘𝐀𝐙 knew that His people needed a reminder every seven days that they **will experience** their eternal Sabbath Day rest <u>one day</u>! Instead of the truth, billions of people have been lead astray by the wolf shepherds to observe the day of the unconquerable sun instead of the real Sabbath! As a result, morally good people are participants in sun worship! When they hear the truth, they say, "Does it really matter as long as we observe a day of rest every week?" Well, it really, really matters to 𝐀𝐘𝐀𝐙!

The Wolves Teach Smooth Things Like the Rapture!
The rapture doctrine has done a lot of damage to the understanding of the good sheep, who are trapped in apostasy! The good sheep in the churches **have been set up** to believe a horrible rapture lie, which <u>will</u> cost them their eternal life in the end, if they don't change! This doctrine is a **terrible snare!** It has the sheep believing that there are two separate end time plans, one for the church and one for the Jews! These sheep have been led to believe that because they **believe** in the sacrifice of <u>Jesus</u> that they will be raptured up to meet Jesus in the air and be taken off into Heaven! These good sheep have been taught that only the poor Jews will have to be on the earth during the coming Tribulation! This doctrine is 180 degrees away from the real Truth! The Truth is exactly the opposite! There will be **no peace and safety** for those trapped in apostasy, <u>who do not</u> repent from their apostasy before the coming Tribulation! This Tribulation is designed to get the sheep to come out of <u>apostasy</u> because 𝓐𝐘𝐀𝐙 is **merciful!** The Righteous sheep in this world have experienced great tribulation and affliction, since OWY𝐀𝐙 hung on the tree!

And they will continue to experience even greater tribulation, until the 7th Trumpet sounds! At the sounding of the 7th Trumpet everything will turn upside down (flip flop) in this world! The <u>Righteous</u> will be at the <u>top</u> of Yahushua's Kingdom and the <u>wicked will be at the</u> <u>bottom</u>! At that time the Righteous will come into Yahuah's rest! It will be the wicked and unrepentant, who will experience terrible, terrible Tribulation! Yes, Christians **will be on the earth!** Many will lose their lives <u>because they will not repent of their apostasy</u>! Many Christians **will repent**, but some will lose their lives as martyrs for ayaz during the Tribulation because of the persecution of Nimrod! Don't wait until it's too late to repent! Teshubah, turn around now!

Men Have Underestimated ayaz!

The plans that ayaz has for the Righteous of the earth are far more wonderful and resplendent than anything that today's preachers are teaching! The Scriptures call the preachers blind guides and wells with no water! Men have greatly **underestimated** the glory and esteem that lies ahead for Yahuah's people, Israel! On the other side of the coin, the sheep in apostasy have grossly **underestimated** the horrors that lie ahead for the outright wicked and those, who refuse to come out of the counterfeit religious systems of man! The Torah contains Yahuah's instructions for fruitful living! It's applicable to **all** the generations and **all** the people of the earth! OWYAZ obeyed these instructions perfectly! OWYAZ is our example for living life Yahuah's Way! Sometimes the Truth is hard to swallow and it usually conflicts with the traditions of mankind, which were handed down to us by our forefathers! The Righteous sheep love ayaz and OWYAZ so much that they <u>are</u> willing to reject all the pagan traditions, which they once loved! Instead the people of Israel will want to do those things that really <u>please</u> ayaz!

Jeremiah 23
Woe be unto the pastors <u>that destroy and scatter the sheep of my</u> <u>pasture</u>! saith ayaz. Therefore thus saith ayaz Elohim of Israel against the pastors that feed my people; Ye have scattered my flock, and driven them away, and have not visited them: behold, I will visit upon you the evil of your doings, saith ayaz. ***And I will gather the remnant of my flock out of all countries whither I have driven them, and will bring them again to their folds; and they shall be fruitful and increase.*** *And I will set up shepherds over them which shall feed them: and they shall fear no more, nor be dismayed, neither shall they be lacking, saith ayaz. Behold, the days come, saith ayaz, that <u>I will raise unto David a righteous Branch</u> (OWYAZ), and a King shall reign and prosper, and shall execute judgment and justice in the earth.*

Jeremiah 23, cont.
In his days Judah shall be saved, and Israel shall dwell safely: and this is his name whereby he shall be called, 𐤀𐤉𐤄𐤆 *OUR RIGHTEOUSNESS. Therefore, behold, the days come, saith* 𐤀𐤉𐤄𐤆*, that they shall no more say,* 𐤀𐤉𐤄𐤆 *liveth, which brought up the children of Israel out of the land of Mitsrayim; But,* 𐤀𐤉𐤄𐤆 *liveth, which brought up and which led the seed of the house of Israel out of the north country, and from all countries whither I had driven them; and they shall dwell in their own land.*

Mine heart within me is broken because of the prophets; all my bones shake; I am like a drunken man, and like a man whom wine hath overcome, because of 𐤀𐤉𐤄𐤆*, and because of the words of his holiness. For the land is full of adulterers; for because of swearing the land mourneth; the* <u>pleasant places of the wilderness are dried up</u>*, and their course is evil, and their force is not right. For* <u>both prophet and priest are profane</u>*; yea, in my house have I found their wickedness, saith* 𐤀𐤉𐤄𐤆*. Wherefore their way shall be unto them as slippery ways in the darkness: they shall be driven on, and fall therein: for I will bring evil upon them, even the year of their visitation, saith* 𐤀𐤉𐤄𐤆*. And I have seen folly in the prophets of Samaria; they* <u>prophesied in Baal, and caused my people Israel to err</u>*. I have seen also in the prophets of Yahrushalayim an horrible thing: they commit adultery, and walk in lies: they strengthen also the hands of evildoers, that none doth return from his wickedness: they are all of them unto me as Sodom, and the inhabitants thereof as Gomorrah. Therefore thus saith* 𐤀𐤉𐤄𐤆 *of hosts concerning the prophets; Behold, I will feed them with wormwood, and make them drink the water of gall: for from the prophets of Yahrushalayim is profaneness gone forth into all the land. Thus saith* 𐤀𐤉𐤄𐤆 *of hosts, Hearken not unto the words of the prophets that prophesy unto you: they make you vain:* <u>they speak a vision of their own heart, and not out of the mouth of</u> 𐤀𐤉𐤄𐤆*.*

The Shepherds Deceive the Own Sheep for Personal Gain!
They say still unto them that despise me, 𐤀𐤉𐤄𐤆 *hath said,* <u>Ye shall have peace</u>*; and they* <u>say unto every one that walketh after the imagination of his own heart, No evil shall come upon you</u>*.* **(Think about the Rapture and the Prosperity doctrines!)** *For who hath stood in the counsel of* 𐤀𐤉𐤄𐤆*, and hath perceived and heard his word? Who hath marked his word, and heard it? Behold, a whirlwind of* 𐤀𐤉𐤄𐤆 *is gone forth in fury, even a grievous whirlwind: it shall fall grievously upon the head of the wicked. The anger of* 𐤀𐤉𐤄𐤆 *shall not return, until he have executed, and till he have performed the thoughts of his heart: in the latter days ye shall consider it perfectly.* <u>I have not sent these prophets</u>*, yet they ran: I have not spoken to them, yet they prophesied.*

Jeremiah 23, cont.
But if they had stood in my counsel, and had caused my people to hear my words, then they should have turned them from their evil way, and from the evil of their doings. **(Preachers have taught against the Torah!)** *Am I an Elohim at hand, saith* **𐤀𐤉𐤄𐤅**, *and not an Elohim afar off? Can any hide himself in secret places that I shall not see him? saith* **𐤀𐤉𐤄𐤅**. *Do not I fill heaven and earth? saith* **𐤀𐤉𐤄𐤅**. *I have heard what the prophets said,* <u>that prophesy lies in my name, saying, I have dreamed, I have dreamed</u>. *How long shall this be in the heart of the prophets that prophesy lies? yea, they are prophets of the* <u>deceit of their own heart</u>; *Which think to* **cause my people to** <u>**forget my name**</u> **by their dreams which they tell every man to his neighbor, as their fathers have forgotten my name for Baal.**

The Shepherds Have Hidden My Name!
Jeremiah 23, cont.
The prophet that hath a dream, let him tell a dream; and he that hath my word, let him speak my word faithfully. What is the chaff to the wheat? saith **𐤀𐤉𐤄𐤅**. *Is not my word like as a fire? saith* **𐤀𐤉𐤄𐤅**; *and like a hammer that breaketh the rock in pieces? Therefore, behold, I am against the prophets, saith* **𐤀𐤉𐤄𐤅**, *that steal my words every one from his neighbor. Behold*<u>, I am against the prophets</u>, *saith* **𐤀𐤉𐤄𐤅**, *that use their tongues, and say, He saith.*

The Shepherds Prophesy Falsely for Profit!
Behold, I am against them that prophesy false dreams, saith **𐤀𐤉𐤄𐤅**, *and do tell them, and cause my people to err by their lies, and by their lightness; yet I sent them not, nor commanded them: therefore they shall not profit this people at all, saith* **𐤀𐤉𐤄𐤅**. **(Most preachers need to take this message to heart!)** *And when this people, or the prophet, or a priest, shall ask thee, saying, What is the burden of* **𐤀𐤉𐤄𐤅**? *Thou shalt then say unto them, What burden? I will even forsake you, saith* **𐤀𐤉𐤄𐤅**. *And as for the prophet, and the priest, and the people, that shall say, The burden of* **𐤀𐤉𐤄𐤅**, *I will even punish that man and his house. Thus shall ye say every one to his neighbor, and every one to his brother, What hath* **𐤀𐤉𐤄𐤅** *answered? and, What hath* **𐤀𐤉𐤄𐤅** *spoken? And the burden of* **𐤀𐤉𐤄𐤅** *shall ye mention no more: for every man's word shall be his burden; for ye have perverted the words of the living Elohim, of* **𐤀𐤉𐤄𐤅** *of hosts our Elohim. Thus shalt thou say to the prophet, What hath* **𐤀𐤉𐤄𐤅** *answered thee? and, What hath* **𐤀𐤉𐤄𐤅** *spoken? But since ye say, The burden of* **𐤀𐤉𐤄𐤅**; *therefore thus saith* **𐤀𐤉𐤄𐤅**; *Because ye say this word, The burden of* **𐤀𐤉𐤄𐤅**, *and I have sent unto you, saying, Ye shall not say, The burden of* **𐤀𐤉𐤄𐤅**;

Jeremiah 23, cont.
Therefore, behold, I, even I, will utterly forget you, and I will forsake you, and the city that I gave you and your fathers, and cast you out of my presence: And I will bring an everlasting reproach upon you, and a perpetual shame, which shall not be forgotten.

Isaiah 56
His watchmen are blind: they are all ignorant, they are all dumb dogs, they cannot bark; sleeping, lying down, loving to slumber. Yea, they are greedy dogs which can never have enough, and they are shepherds that cannot understand: they all look to their own way, every one for his gain, from his quarter.

Jeremiah 25
And the slain of 𐤀𐤅𐤄𐤆 shall be at that day from one end of the earth even unto the other end of the earth: they shall not be lamented, neither gathered, nor buried; they shall be dung upon the ground. Howl, ye shepherds, and cry; and wallow yourselves in the ashes, ye principal of the flock: for the days of your slaughter and of your dispersions are accomplished; and ye shall fall like a pleasant vessel. And the shepherds shall have no way to flee, nor the principal of the flock to escape. A voice of the cry of the shepherds, and an howling of the principal of the flock, shall be heard: for 𐤀𐤅𐤄𐤆 hath spoiled their pasture. And the peaceable habitations are cut down because of the fierce anger of 𐤀𐤅𐤄𐤆.

Jeremiah 50
<u>My people hath been lost sheep: their shepherds have caused them to go astray</u>, they have turned them away on the mountains: they have gone from mountain to hill, they have forgotten their resting place. All that found them have devoured them: and their adversaries said, We offend not, because they have sinned against 𐤀𐤅𐤄𐤆, the habitation of justice, even 𐤀𐤅𐤄𐤆, the hope of their fathers.

Luke 20
Beware of the scribes, which desire to walk in long robes, and love greetings in the markets, and the highest seats in the synagogues, and the chief rooms at feasts; Which devour widows' houses, and for a shew make long prayers: the same shall receive greater damnation.

Matthew 15
Ye hypocrites, well did Isaiah prophesy of you, saying, This people draweth nigh unto me with their mouth, and honoreth me with their lips; but their heart is far from me. But <u>in vain they do worship me, teaching for doctrines the commandments of men.</u>

Ezekiel 34
And the word of אYהZ came unto me, saying, Son of man, prophesy against the shepherds of Israel, prophesy, and say unto them, <u>Thus saith the Master אYהZ unto the shepherds; Woe be to the shepherds of Israel that do feed themselves! Should not the shepherds feed the flocks? Ye eat the fat, and ye clothe you with the wool, ye kill them that are fed: but ye feed not the flock.</u> The diseased have ye not strengthened, neither **have ye healed that which was sick, neither have ye bound up that which was broken, neither have ye brought again that which was driven away, neither have ye sought that which was lost; but with force and with cruelty have ye ruled them.** And they were scattered, because there is no shepherd: and they became meat to all the beasts of the field, when they were scattered. My sheep wandered through all the mountains, and upon every high hill: yea, my flock was scattered upon all the face of the earth, and none did search or seek after them. Therefore, ye shepherds, hear the word of אYהZ; As I live, saith the Master אYהZ, surely because my flock became a prey, and my flock became meat to every beast of the field, because there was no shepherd, neither did my shepherds search for my flock, but the shepherds fed themselves, and fed not my flock; Therefore, O ye shepherds, hear the word of אYהZ; Thus saith the Master אYהZ; Behold, <u>I am against the shepherds</u>; and I will require my flock at their hand, and cause them to cease from feeding the flock; neither shall the shepherds feed themselves any more; for I will deliver my flock from their mouth, that they may not be meat for them. For thus saith the Master אYהZ; Behold, I, even I, will both search my sheep, and seek them out. As a shepherd seeketh out his flock in the day that he is among his sheep that are scattered; so will I seek out my sheep, and will deliver them out of all places where they have been scattered in the cloudy and dark day. **And I will bring them out from the people, and gather them from the countries, and will bring them to their own land, and feed them upon the mountains of Israel by the rivers, and in all the inhabited places of the country**. I will feed them in a good pasture, and <u>upon the high mountains of Israel</u> shall their fold be: there shall they lie in a good fold, and in a fat pasture shall they feed upon the mountains of Israel. I will feed my flock, and I will cause them to lie down, saith the Master אYהZ. I will seek that which was lost, and bring again that which was driven away, and will bind up that which was broken, and will strengthen that which was sick: but I will destroy the fat and the strong; I will feed them with judgment. And as for you, O my flock, thus saith the Master אYהZ; Behold, I judge between cattle and cattle, between the rams and the he goats.

Ezekiel 34
Seemeth it a small thing unto you to have eaten up the good pasture, but ye must tread down with your feet the residue of your pastures? and to have drunk of the deep waters, but ye must foul the residue with your feet? And as for my flock, they eat that which ye have trodden with your feet; and they drink that which ye have fouled with your feet. Therefore thus saith the Master aYaZ unto them; Behold, I, even I, will judge between the fat cattle and between the lean cattle. Because ye have thrust with side and with shoulder, and pushed all the diseased with your horns, till ye have scattered them abroad; Therefore will I save my flock, and they shall no more be a prey; and I will judge between cattle and cattle. And I will set up one shepherd over them, and he shall feed them, even my servant David; he shall feed them, and he shall be their shepherd. And I aYaZ will be their Elohim, and my servant David a prince among them; I aYaZ have spoken it. And I will make with them a covenant of peace, and will cause the evil beasts to cease out of the land: and they shall dwell safely in the wilderness, and sleep in the woods. And I will make them and the places round about my hill a blessing; and I will cause the shower to come down in his season; there shall be showers of blessing. And the tree of the field shall yield her fruit, and the earth shall yield her increase, and they shall be safe in their land, and shall know that I am aYaZ, when I have broken the bands of their yoke, and delivered them out of the hand of those that served themselves of them. And <u>they shall no more be a prey to the heathen</u>, neither shall the beast of the land devour them; but they shall dwell safely, and none shall make them afraid. And I will raise up for them a plant of renown, and they shall be no more consumed with hunger in the land, neither bear the shame of the heathen any more. Thus shall they know that I aYaZ their Elohim am with them, and that they, even the house of Israel, are my people, saith the Master aYaZ. And ye my flock, the flock of my pasture, are men, and I am your Elohim, saith the Master aYaZ.

Where are the good shepherds today?
I am convinced that aYaZ already has good shepherds selected! These good shepherds are being prepared as I write this book to serve aYaZ in the near future!

Yahushua the Ultimate Good Shepherd
John 10
Verily, verily, I say unto you, He that entereth not by the door into the sheepfold, but climbeth up some other way, the same is a thief and a robber. But he that entereth in by the door is the shepherd of the sheep.

John 10, cont.
To him the porter openeth; and the sheep hear his voice: and he calleth his own sheep by name, and leadeth them out. And when he putteth forth his own sheep, he goeth before them, and the sheep follow him: for they know his voice. And a stranger will they not follow, but will flee from him: for they know not the voice of strangers. This parable spake **OWYAZ** *unto them: but they understood not what things they were which he spake unto them. Then said* **OWYAZ** *unto them again, Verily, verily, I say unto you, I am the door of the sheep. All that ever came before me are thieves and robbers: but the sheep did not hear them. I am the door: by me if any man enter in, he shall be saved, and shall go in and out, and find pasture. The thief cometh not, but for to steal, and to kill, and to destroy: I am come that they might have life, and that they might have it more abundantly. I am the good shepherd: the good shepherd giveth his life for the sheep. But he that is an hireling, and not the shepherd, whose own the sheep are not, seeth the wolf coming, and leaveth the sheep, and fleeth: and the wolf catcheth them, and scattereth the sheep. The hireling fleeth, because he is an hireling, and careth not for the sheep. I am the good shepherd, and know my sheep, and am known of mine. As the Father knoweth me, even so know I the Father: and I lay down my life for the sheep. And other sheep I have, which are not of this fold: them also I must bring, and they shall hear my voice; and there shall be one fold, and one shepherd. Therefore doth my Father love me, because I lay down my life, that I might take it again. No man taketh it from me, but I lay it down of myself. I have power to lay it down, and I have power to take it again. This commandment have I received of my Father. There was a division therefore again among the Jews for these sayings. And many of them said, He hath a devil, and is mad; why hear ye him? Others said, These are not the words of him that hath a devil. Can a devil open the eyes of the blind? And it was at Yahrushalayim the feast of the dedication, and it was winter. And* **OWYAZ** *walked in the temple in Solomon's porch. Then came the Jews round about him, and said unto him, How long dost thou make us to doubt? If thou be the Messiah, tell us plainly.* **OWYAZ** *answered them, I told you, and ye believed not: the works that I do in my Father's name, they bear witness of me. But ye believe not, because ye are not of my sheep, as I said unto you. My sheep hear my voice, and I know them, and they follow me: And I give unto them eternal life; and they shall never perish, neither shall any man pluck them out of my hand.*

Hebrews 13

Now the Elohim of peace, that brought again from the dead our Master OWYAZ, that **great shepherd of the sheep**, through the blood of the everlasting covenant, Make you perfect in every good work to do his will, working in you that which is well pleasing in his sight, through OWYAZ the Messiah; to whom be glory for ever and ever. amein.

1 Peter 5

The elders which are among you I exhort, who am also an elder, and a witness of the sufferings of Messiah, and also a partaker of the glory that shall be revealed: Feed the flock of AYAZ which is among you, taking the oversight thereof, not by constraint, but willingly; not for filthy money, but of a ready mind; Neither as being masters over those entrusted to you, but being ensamples to the flock. And <u>**when the chief Shepherd shall appear, ye shall receive a crown of glory that fadeth not away.**</u>

Rewards for the Righteous
Chapter 15

¹²*"He who overcomes, I shall make him a supporting post in the Dwelling Place of My Elohim, and he shall by no means go out. And I shall write on him the Name of My Elohim and the name of the city of My Elohim, the renewed Yahrushalayim, which comes down out of the heaven from My Elohim, and My renewed Name.*
Revelation 3

Let My People Go would not be complete without a review of the rewards set aside for Yahuah's overcomers, Israel! However, I don't have the ability to describe the full extent of what AYAZ has planned for us! Scripture teaches that Yahushua's rewards are beyond the limits of anyone's wildest dreams!

Isaiah 64
For since the beginning of the world men have not heard, nor perceived by the ear, neither hath the eye seen, O Elohim, beside thee, what he hath prepared for him that waiteth for him.

1 Corinthians 2
⁹*But as it has been written, "Eye has not seen, and ear has not heard, nor have entered into the heart of man what Elohim has prepared for those who love Him."*

Until AYAZ determines that it's time to reveal the real OWYAZ to us, we will not be able to fully grasp truths hidden in the Scriptures. We truly do see through the glass dimly, but soon we will understand perfectly!

1Corinthians 13
For now we see through a glass, darkly; but then face to face: now I know in part; but then shall I know even as also I am known.

However, AYAZ reveals Himself step by step to those, who are sincerely hungry and thirsty for His water and His bread! Wisdom and understanding comes a little here and a little there!

Isaiah 28
⁹*Whom would He teach knowledge? And whom would He make to understand the message? Those weaned from milk, those taken from the breasts!* ¹⁰*For it is: command upon command, command upon command, line upon line, line upon line, here a little, there a little.*

Better than Sons and Daughters

𐤀𐤉𐤄𐤅 said that anyone, who keeps His Sabbaths, chooses to do the things that please Him, and takes hold of His Covenant, will have a position in His house <u>better than sons and daughters</u>! I can't even imagine the full magnitude of that statement! 𐤀𐤉𐤄𐤅 is no respecter of persons. 𐤀𐤉𐤄𐤅 doesn't discriminate at all! 𐤀𐤉𐤄𐤅 doesn't reject someone for being sick with a disease, for being crippled, or someone with a very, very bad physical appearance! 𐤀𐤉𐤄𐤅 does not <u>reject</u> a person because he is too short, too fat, too tall, too skinny, bald, black, red, white, weak, freckled, or red headed! Nor does 𐤀𐤉𐤄𐤅 <u>reject</u> a person, who is lonely, who has no family, who has no husband or wife, who has no children, who has no money, who has no house, who has no career, who has no degree, or who is simple minded! 𐤀𐤉𐤄𐤅 doesn't reject a person for being unattractive or not fitting into this world's system! This world rejects people for <u>all</u> those things and more, but <u>not</u> 𐤀𐤉𐤄𐤅! Why doesn't 𐤀𐤉𐤄𐤅 reject those kinds of people? Because 𐤏𐤅𐤄𐤔𐤏 experienced those kinds of rejections Himself, when He humbled himself as our Passover Lamb!

1 Corinthians 1

²⁵For the foolishness of Elohim is wiser than men, and the weakness of Elohim is stronger than men. ²⁶For look at your calling, brothers, that there were not many wise according to the flesh, not many mighty, not many noble. ²⁷But Elohim has chosen the foolish matters of the world to put to shame the wise, and Elohim has chosen the weak of the world to put to shame the strong. ²⁸And Elohim has chosen the low-born of the world and the despised, and the ones that are not, that He might bring to naught the ones that are, ²⁹so that no flesh should boast in His presence. ³⁰And of Him you are in Messiah 𐤏𐤅𐤄𐤔𐤏, who became for us wisdom from Elohim, righteousness also, and set-apartness and redemption, ³¹that, as it has been written, "He who boasts, let him boast in 𐤀𐤉𐤄𐤅."

Anyone who truly loves 𐤀𐤉𐤄𐤅 and 𐤏𐤅𐤄𐤔𐤏 with their whole heart <u>will choose</u> to do the things that please 𐤀𐤉𐤄𐤅! They will receive the rewards of 𐤏𐤅𐤄𐤔𐤏! Yahuah's people undergo Yahuah's process of being set apart in this world! That process will circumcise the heart and will qualify Israel to receive Yahushua's rewards!

Deuteronomy 30

And 𐤀𐤉𐤄𐤅 thy Elohim will circumcise thine heart, and the heart of thy seed, to love 𐤀𐤉𐤄𐤅 thy Elohim with all thine heart, and with all thy soul, that thou mayest live.

When we reach perfection, we will be echad, completely united with Yahuah's dreams and desires and we will be united with each other!

We will be called sons and daughters of **ayaz!** We will all have **One Heart!**

Jeremiah 32
Behold, I will gather them out of all countries, whither I have driven them in mine anger, and in my fury, and in great wrath; and I will bring them again unto this place, and I will cause them to dwell safely: And they shall be my people, and I will be their Elohim: And I will give them **one heart, and one way**, that they may fear me for ever, for the good of them, and of their children after them:

Isaiah 56
Thus saith **ayaz, Keep ye judgment,** and **do justice**: for my salvation is near to come, and my righteousness to be revealed. Blessed is the man that doeth this, and the son of man that layeth hold on it; that **keepeth the sabbath** from polluting it, and **keepeth his hand from doing any evil**. Neither let the son of the stranger, that hath joined himself to **ayaz**, speak, saying, **ayaz** hath utterly separated me from his people: neither let the eunuch say, Behold, I am a dry tree. For thus saith **ayaz** unto the eunuchs that keep my sabbaths, and choose the things that please me, and take hold of my covenant; Even unto them will I give in mine house and within my walls a place and a name **better than of sons and of daughters**.

In this present world system the people of Israel **will not typically be the rich and famous people, or the powerful people!** **ayaz** chooses the weak and rejected people of this world to confound the strong and powerful! Satan's world system gives people the opportunity to achieve some of their fleshly desires! You can choose to love this world instead of Yahuah's promises! However, in order to be found acceptable to **ayaz**, we must reject the lustful desires of this world just as **OWYaz** did! In this present world, Israel will be afflicted and tried in Yahuah's crucible in order to prove us and try us in the same way **ayaz** has tried all the members of Israel, since Adam! **ayaz did not even spare His only begotten son**, but He tried **OWYaz** in **every way possible,** even to the ultimate breaking point! **OWYaz** did not even flinch! **OWYaz** overcame every obstacle, every pressure, every struggle, every sickness, every disease, every pain, every rejection, and every form of humiliation! What an example we have in **OWYaz**! I am not worthy of such a **OWYaz**! How about you? **OWYaz** is truly qualified to be our High Priest! **OWYaz** is the only one, who can truly speak with authority as the ultimate overcomer of all human struggles! **OWYaz** even overcame death itself!

Protection For the First Fruits
Revelation 3
*And to the angel of the assembly in Philadelphia write; These things saith he that is holy, he that is true, he that hath the key of David, he that openeth, and no man shutteth; and shutteth, and no man openeth; I know thy works: behold, I have set before thee an open door, and no man can shut it: for thou hast a little strength, and hast kept my word, and hast not denied my name. Behold, I will make them of the synagogue of Satan, which say they are Jews, and are not, but do lie; behold, I will make them to come and worship before thy feet, and to know that I have loved thee. Because thou hast kept the word of my patience, **I also will keep thee from the hour of temptation, which shall come upon all the world, to try them that dwell upon the earth.***

After Yahushua's final judgment, there will be no more death, no more sicknesses, no more diseases, no more pain, no more poverty, no more insecurity, no more loneliness, no more hunger, no more thirst, no more crying, no more sorrow, and no more curses! HalleluYah! HalleluYah! HalleluYah!

No more Sickness, Disease, or Death
Revelation 21
*And ayaz shall wipe away all tears from their eyes; and there shall be no **more death**, **neither sorrow, nor crying**, neither shall there be any more **pain**: for the former things are passed away.*

No more Crying and Sorrow
Revelation 7
*And I said unto him, Sir, thou knowest. And he said to me, These are they which came out of great tribulation, and have washed their robes, and made them white in the blood of the Lamb. Therefore are they before the throne of ayaz, and serve him day and night in his temple: and he that sitteth on the throne shall dwell among them. They shall **hunger no more**, **neither thirst any more**; neither shall the **sun light on them, nor any heat**.*

No more Loneliness
Psalms 68
Let Elohim arise, let his enemies be scattered: let them also that hate him flee before him. As smoke is driven away, so drive them away: as wax melteth before the fire, so let the wicked perish at the presence of Elohim. But let the righteous be glad; let them rejoice before Elohim: yea, let them exceedingly rejoice. Sing unto Elohim, sing praises to his name: extol him that rideth upon the heavens by his name ayaz, and rejoice before him.

Psalms 68, cont.
A father of the fatherless, and a judge of the widows, is Elohim in his holy habitation. <u>Elohim setteth the solitary in families</u>: he bringeth out those which are bound with chains: but the rebellious dwell in a dry land.

Israel Will Shine with a Bright Appearance like Yahushua!
Revelation 3
He that overcometh, the same shall be clothed in **white raiment**; and I will not blot out his name out of the book of life, but I will confess his name before my Father, and before his angels.

Enoch 104
I swear unto you, that in heaven the angels remember you for good before the glory of the Great $_2$One: and your names are written before the glory of the Great One. Be hopeful; for aforetime ye were put to shame through ill and affliction; but now <u>ye shall shine as the lights of heaven,</u> $_3$ ye shall shine and ye shall be seen, and the portals of heaven shall be opened to you. And in your cry, cry for judgment, and it shall appear to you; for all your tribulation shall be visited on the $_4$ rulers, and on all who helped those who plundered you. Be hopeful, and cast not away your hope; $_5$ for ye shall have great joy as the angels of heaven. What shall ye be obliged to do? Ye shall not have to hide on the day of the great judgment and ye shall not be found as sinners, and the eternal $_6$ judgment shall be far from you for all the generations of the world. And now fear not, ye righteous, when ye see the sinners growing strong and prospering in their ways: be not companions with them, $_7$ but keep afar from their violence; for ye shall become companions of the hosts of heaven. And, although ye sinners say: "All our sins shall not be searched out and be written down," nevertheless $_8$ they shall write down all your sins every day. And now I show unto you that light and darkness, $_9$ day and night, see all your sins. Be not godless in your hearts, and lie not and alter not the words of uprightness, nor charge with lying the words of the Holy Great One, nor take account of your $_{10}$ idols; for all your lying and all your godlessness issue not in righteousness but in great sin. And now I know this mystery, that sinners will alter and pervert the words of righteousness in many ways, and will speak wicked words, and lie, and practice great deceits, and write books concerning $_{11}$their words. But when they write down Truthfully all my words in their languages, and do not change or minish ought from my words but write them all down Truthfully -all that I first testified $_{12}$ concerning them. <u>Then, I know another mystery, that books will be given to the righteous and the $_{13}$wise to become a cause of joy and uprightness and much wisdom.</u>

Enoch 104, cont.
And to them shall the books be given, and they shall believe in them and rejoice over them, and then shall all the righteous, who have learnt therefrom all the paths of uprightness be recompensed.'

No More Curses Only Blessings

Deuteronomy 28
And it shall come to pass, if thou shalt hearken diligently unto the voice of 𐤀𐤉𐤄𐤅 thy Elohim, to observe and to do all his commandments which I command thee this day, that 𐤀𐤉𐤄𐤅 thy Elohim will set thee on high above all nations of the earth: And all these blessings shall come on thee, and overtake thee, if thou shalt hearken unto the voice of 𐤀𐤉𐤄𐤅 thy Elohim. Blessed shalt thou be in the city, and blessed shalt thou be in the field. Blessed shall be the fruit of thy body, and the fruit of thy ground, and the fruit of thy cattle, the increase of thy kine, and the flocks of thy sheep. Blessed shall be thy basket and thy store. Blessed shalt thou be when thou comest in, and blessed shalt thou be when thou goest out. 𐤀𐤉𐤄𐤅 shall cause thine enemies that rise up against thee to be smitten before thy face: they shall come out against thee one way, and flee before thee seven ways. 𐤀𐤉𐤄𐤅 shall command the blessing upon thee in thy storehouses, and in all that thou settest thine hand unto; and he shall bless thee in the land which 𐤀𐤉𐤄𐤅 thy Elohim giveth thee. 𐤀𐤉𐤄𐤅 shall establish thee an holy people unto himself, as he hath sworn unto thee, if thou shalt keep the commandments of 𐤀𐤉𐤄𐤅 thy Elohim, and walk in his ways. And all people of the earth shall see that thou art called by the name of 𐤀𐤉𐤄𐤅; and they shall be afraid of thee. And 𐤀𐤉𐤄𐤅 shall make thee plenteous in goods, in the fruit of thy body, and in the fruit of thy cattle, and in the fruit of thy ground, in the land which 𐤀𐤉𐤄𐤅 sware unto thy fathers to give thee. 𐤀𐤉𐤄𐤅 shall open unto thee his good treasure, the heaven to give the rain unto thy land in his season, and to bless all the work of thine hand: and thou shalt lend unto many nations, and thou shalt not borrow. And 𐤀𐤉𐤄𐤅 shall make thee the head, and not the tail; and thou shalt be above only, and thou shalt not be beneath; if that thou hearken unto the commandments of 𐤀𐤉𐤄𐤅 thy Elohim, which I command thee this day, to observe and to do them: And thou shalt not go aside from any of the words which I command thee this day, to the right hand, or to the left, to go after other elohim to serve them.

OWYAZ promises the Righteous a wonderful life for all <u>eternity</u> in His Kingdom! OWYAZ will lead Israel to eat from His Tree of Life and to drink from His Fountain of Life! Israel will be given responsibility in Yahushua's Kingdom in proportion to how they lived in this present world! Those, who OWYAZ judges as perfect, will serve Him as Judges and Priests!

OWYAZ will give every overcomer of Israel a new name! Our appearance will have a bright nature like Yahushua's glorious appearance! The Righteous will shine like stars and will be clothed with Yahuah's light! Ultimately there <u>will</u> <u>be</u> <u>no</u> more sickness, no more disease, no more sin, and no more death! HalleluYah! Every sacrifice made in this present world will be <u>recompensed</u> to the Righteous a <u>hundred fold</u>! When Israel receives their rewards, **they will <u>not</u> <u>be</u> <u>sorry</u> for their decision to follow OWYAZ!** Israel will forget all the troubles, afflictions, rejections, and hardships that they suffered in this present world for their decision to follow OWYAZ!

Israel Shall Reign on Earth!
Revelation 5
And they sung a new song, saying, Thou art worthy to take the book, and to open the seals thereof: for thou wast slain, and hast redeemed us to AYAZ by thy blood <u>out of every kindred, and tongue, and people, and nation</u>; nd hast made us unto our Elohim **kings and priests: and we shall reign on the earth.**

Israel Eat from the Tree of Life
Revelation 2
He that hath an ear, let him hear what the Spirit saith unto the assemblies; To him that overcometh will I give to **eat of the tree of life, which is in the midst of the paradise of Elohim.**

Israel Will Drink from the Fountain of Life!
Revelation 21
And he said unto me, It is done. I am Alpha and Omega, the beginning and the end. **I will give unto him that is athirst of the fountain of the water of life freely.** He that overcometh shall inherit all things; and I will be his Elohim, and **he shall be my son.**

Israel Is Given Hidden Manna and a New Name!
Revelation 2
He that hath an ear, let him hear what the Spirit saith unto the assemblies; To him that overcometh will I give to eat of the **hidden manna**, and will give him **a white stone**, and in the stone **a new name** written, which no man knoweth saving he that receiveth it. And he that overcometh, and keepeth my works unto the end, <u>to him will I give power over the nations</u>: And he shall rule them with a rod of iron; as the vessels of a potter shall they be broken to shivers: even as I received of my Father. And I will give him the morning star.

Matthew 19
And every one that hath forsaken houses, or brethren, or sisters, or father, or mother, or wife, or children, or lands, for my name's sake, shall **receive an hundredfold**, and **shall inherit everlasting life**. But many that are first shall be last; and **the last shall be first.**

OWYAZ has rewards for Israel, which include everlasting life with Him in the New Yahrushalayim! This is the city, which Abraham and all the prophets of old looked for! This is Yahuah's city of perfection, which has been prepared especially for His children! Not only is OWYAZ giving us access into the New Yahrushalayim, but He will completely rework the Heavens and the Earth! Who can imagine what kind of new Heaven and new Earth OWYAZ will create! It will be the absolute best work of OWYAZ! You can count on that! How wonderful it is to dream of Israel's future!

Israel Will Again Be Satisfied in Yahuah's Promised Land!

Deuteronomy (Debarim) 8
[7] "For AYAZ your Elohim is bringing you into a good land, a land of streams of water, of fountains and springs, that flow out of valleys and hills, [8] a land of wheat and barley, of vines and fig trees and pomegranates, a land of olive oil and honey, [9] a land in which you eat bread without scarcity, in which you do not lack at all, a land whose stones are iron and out of whose hills you dig copper. [10] "And you shall eat and be satisfied, and shall bless AYAZ your Elohim for the good land which He has given you.

Eternal Life within The New Yahrushalayim
Revelation 3
Him that overcometh will I make a pillar in the temple of my Elohim, and he shall go no more out: and I will write upon him the name of my Elohim, and the name of the **city of my Elohim, which is New Yahrushalayim, which cometh down out of heaven from my Elohim: and I will write upon him my new name.** To him that overcometh will I grant to sit with me in my throne, even as I also overcame, and am set down with my Father in his throne.

Revelation 21
And he carried me away in the spirit to a great and high mountain, and shewed me that great city, the holy Yahrushalayim, descending out of heaven from AYAZ, Having the glory of AYAZ: and her light was like unto a stone most precious, even like a jasper stone, clear as crystal; And had a wall great and high, and had **twelve gates, and at the gates twelve angels, and names written thereon, which are the names of the twelve tribes of the children of Israel:**

Revelation 21,cont.
On the east three gates; on the north three gates; on the south three gates; and on the west three gates. And the wall of the city had twelve foundations, and in them the names of the twelve apostles of the Lamb. And he that talked with me had a golden reed to measure the city, and the gates thereof, and the wall thereof. And the city lieth foursquare, and the length is as large as the breadth: and he measured the city with the reed, twelve thousand furlongs. The length and the breadth and the height of it are equal. And he measured the wall thereof, an hundred and forty and four cubits, according to the measure of a man, that is, of the angel.

Eternal Life With in The New Yahrushalayim, cont.

And the building of the wall of it was of jasper: and the city was pure gold, like unto clear glass. And the foundations of the wall of the city were garnished with all manner of precious stones. The first foundation was jasper; the second, sapphire; the third, a chalcedony; the fourth, an emerald; The fifth, sardonyx; the sixth, sardius; the seventh, chrysolite; the eighth, beryl; the ninth, a topaz; the tenth, a chrysoprasus; the eleventh, a jacinth; the twelfth, an amethyst. And the twelve gates were twelve pearls; every several gate was of one pearl: and the street of the city was pure gold, as it were transparent glass. And I saw no temple therein: for ayaz El-Shaddai and the Lamb are the temple of it. And the city had no need of the sun, neither of the moon, to shine in it: for the glory of ayaz did lighten it, and the Lamb is the light thereof. And the nations of them which are saved shall walk in the light of it: and the kings of the earth do bring their glory and honour into it. And the gates of it shall not be shut at all by day: for there shall be no night there. And they shall bring the glory and honour of the nations into it.

Revelation 22

And he shewed me a **pure river of water of life, clear as crystal, proceeding out of the throne of ayaz and of the Lamb.** In the midst of the street of it, and on either side of the river, was there the **tree of life**, which bare twelve manner of fruits, and yielded her fruit every month: and **the leaves of the tree were for the healing of the nations.** And there shall be **no more curse**: but the throne of ayaz and of the Lamb shall be in the city! And they shall see his face; and his name shall be in their foreheads. And there shall be no night there; and they need no candle, neither light of the sun; for ayaz Elohim giveth them light: and they shall reign for ever and ever.

And he said unto me, These sayings are faithful and true: and 𐤀𐤉𐤄𐤆 Elohim of the holy prophets sent his angel to shew unto his servants the things which must shortly be done. Behold, I come quickly: blessed is he that keepeth the sayings of the prophecy of this book. And I John saw these things, and heard them. And when I had heard and seen, I fell down to worship before the feet of the angel which shewed me these things. Then saith he unto me, See thou do it not: for I am thy fellow servant, and of thy brethren the prophets, and of them which keep the sayings of this book: worship 𐤀𐤉𐤄𐤆. And he saith unto me, Seal not the sayings of the prophecy of this book: for the time is at hand. He that is unjust, let him be unjust still: and he which is filthy, let him be filthy still: and he that is righteous, let him be righteous still: and he that is holy, let him be holy still. And, behold, I come quickly; and my reward is with me, to give every man according as his work shall be.

What Shall We Do?
Chapter 16

15Do your utmost to present yourself approved to Elohim, a worker who does not need to be ashamed, rightly handling the Word of Truth. **2 Timothy 2**

I hope that by now you are convinced that ayaz really has planned an end time Exodus for His people, Israel! Israel will all be gathered back to the real Promised Land in today's northwestern Saudi Arabia! All of Yahuah's people, since Adam, have looked forward to the Day of ayaz! The final worldwide Exodus of Israel from the nations is a central theme of the Good News, which OWYaz and His prophets taught repeatedly! We all should look forward with great expectation to Yahuah's Day! Even the Sabbath Day is a reminder of that wonderful Day, when all Israel will come together to enjoy her Sabbath Day's rest with OWYaz! Please understand that the Scriptures clearly teach that **anyone**, who loves ayaz and OWYaz with their whole **heart**, **is accepted** as a member of the **Commonwealth of Israel**! The people of Israel will choose to guard Yahuah's Commandments because of their love for ayaz and OWYaz not because of any legalism! No matter how many preachers teach otherwise, the Scriptures clearly teach that Yahuah's people are called Israel, **not the Church**! The word "church" was substituted for the word "Israel" by men! Yahuah does not have two separate peoples and two separate agendas! There's not a Church agenda and a separate Israel agenda! **There is only one agenda and that's Yahuah's agenda for Israel**! If you are truly thirsty for Yahuah's Truth, then Yahuah's Spirit of Truth will be your teacher and your guide! Yahuah's Ruach HaQodesh will remove the useless teachings of men from your heart and mind! Instead Yahuah's Ruach HaQodesh will write Yahuah's eternal Commandments on your heart! Then you will realize that you really do love Yahuah's Commandments and His name! Please study the Scriptures in their Hebraic context for yourself! Learn the difference between the traditions of men and Yahuah's Commandments and Ordinances! Guard Yahuah's Commandments to the best of your ability! Do it with joy and gladness! Consider the traditions of men as just traditions to be considered only, when they do not conflict with Yahuah's Commandments in any way! When you do sin, be quick to ask forgiveness for that sin in the name of OWYaz and teshubah (repent)! Try your best not to sin that way again! Determine in your heart to live in a way that hits Yahuah's mark for the rest of your life! Determine to finish the rest of your life well! Make the necessary changes in your life as the Ruach HaQodesh reveals issues to you!

Change where change is needed! Below are a few of the central themes of *Let My People Go!* Check out these topics for yourself! Study to show yourself approved! Seek wisdom and understanding!

- The Heavenly Father's real set apart name is 𐤀𐤅𐤄𐤉 and His Son's set apart name is 𐤏𐤅𐤄𐤔𐤉. These names have been removed from nearly all the recent translations of the Scriptures! When transliterated into English, their names are pronounced Yahuah and Yahushua!

- The prophets saw the final <u>supernatural</u> Exodus of Israel! Yahuah's overcomers will return from all the nations where they are now scattered! Israel will return to the original Promised Land that 𐤀𐤅𐤄𐤉 promised Abraham, Isaac, and Jacob! The Scriptures teach that the coming worldwide Exodus will completely overshadow the 1st Exodus! In fact, men won't even discuss the 1st Exodus because the final Exodus will be so spectacular!

- The real location of the Promised Land is in today's northwestern Saudi Arabia, **not in Palestine**!

- The point of origin of the first Exodus was **not** Egypt! It was **Mitsrayim** in northwestern Arabia just **as the original Hebrew Scriptures record**! World renowned researchers like Hugo Winckler, Fritz Hommel, and T. K. Cheyne discovered the real truth about Mitsrayim by translating ancient inscriptions in the Middle East!

- The prophets taught that 𐤏𐤅𐤄𐤔𐤉 will return to the earth and set up His Kingdom! He will rule the earth from the New Yahrushalayim! The rapture doctrine is a fabrication of religious men designed to tickle the sheep's ears! It's a deadly snare to you, if you choose to believe that lie!

- 𐤏𐤅𐤄𐤔𐤉 has prepared a city called the New Yahrushalayim for Israel! The New Yahrushalayim was named in honor of 𐤀𐤅𐤄𐤉! It is a city, which was **not** built with human hands! The New Yahrushalayim will come down into the full view of mankind above the Mountains of Israel on the Day of 𐤀𐤅𐤄𐤉, **when the 7th Trumpet sounds**!

- There is <u>nothing supernatural</u> about the origin of today's State of Israel! The State of Israel is entirely a endeavor of powerful men! It was accomplished by powerful political and military entities! Today's State of Israel was established by the strength of men, not by Yahuah's **supernatural** power!

- When OWYAZ returns and establishes His Kingdom, Yahuah's Sabbath Days, His Seven Festivals, and His New Moons will be set apart by everyone, who survives! They will obey Yahuah's Commandments, not men's useless traditions! Everyone will know and respect the set apart names of ayaz and OWYAZ! The names of the world's counterfeit elohim will no longer be spoken! There will be no more Sunday Sabbaths, no more Christmas trees, no more Easter eggs, no more Valentine's Day, no more unclean unclean shrimp, lobster, oysters, ham, no more Greek counterfeit Jesus, no more nameless lords and gods, no more fairy tale raptures, no more competing denominations, no more tithes of money to wolf shepherds, no more unrecompensed lawlessness, no more tolerance for deceit, no more incurable diseases, and no more war! HalleluYah! HalleluYah! HalleluYah!

- Mixing of pagan practices, icons, and observances with Scriptural themes has contaminated the religious traditions of men for thousands of years! However, religious confusion greatly escalated, when Constantine the Roman Emperor in 321 AD, rejected Yahuah's real set apart times and instituted hybrid pagan festivals mixed with "Christian" themes instead! Most Christians and many Jews, both Messianic and Orthodox do not clearly recognize the difference between the clean and the unclean **anymore**! As I write *Let My People Go* many Christians, Messianic Jews, Orthodox Jews, and other sheep all over the earth are being set apart by ayaz! We are all works in progress!

- Isaiah, YeshaYahu, said in Isaiah 53, "Who has believed our report?" It's painful to explain, but Yahushua's extremely **repulsive physical appearance was the reason** that OWYAZ was not recognized and accepted as Israel's Messiah by the masses of Israel at His 1st coming! Just as it is in today's society, people make quick judgments based on the outward physical appearance of a person, rather than the inner substance of a person! Because of Yahushua's dreadful outward appearance, the masses of Israel did **not** receive Him! They considered OWYAZ wretched, cursed, and a person to be despised! YeshaYahu taught that Yahushua's appearance was marred more than any man's appearance! As Yahushua's healing ministry progressed, OWYAZ experienced more and more sicknesses and diseases by **first hand experience**!

At that time OWYAZ **literally** carried Israel's sicknesses and diseases in His own body! Yahushua's appearance progressively degraded as He healed those sheep! OWYAZ literally carried the sins, the sicknesses, and the diseases of those people! Many of those people **mocked, jeered, and waged their heads in disgust** at OWYAZ! They looked down on OWYAZ! They believed He was cursed! Others hid their faces and the faces of their children from OWYAZ! OWYAZ was rejected and despised by men because of the awful appearance of His **body** and His **face**! He was terribly **disfigured and emaciated**! OWYAZ suffered **much more** than we can really comprehend! Since I've learned more about the true nature of Yahushua's sufferings, **I have fallen even more in love with** OWYAZ! OWYAZ has truly led by example! If you love OWYAZ, then follow His narrow Way!

I hope that *Let My People Go* has stirred up your spirit about AYAZ and OWYAZ! Please seek out the Truth for yourself! Don't hold on to your family's religious traditions, **if they are in error**! Remember "close" only counts in the game of "Horse Shoes"! Participation in apostasy will cost you everything in the long run, **if you cling to it**! Don't depend on the religious institutions of men to lead you to the Truth! If you do, you will get nowhere! False shepherds have become rich by fleecing their sheep for many years! False shepherds have a conflict of interest with the real OWYAZ! The false shepherd's conflict of interest with OWYAZ is all about their wealth, their security, and their careers! False shepherds love their money, their careers, and their temporary security **more than** they love OWYAZ! Be relentless in your pursuit of the Truth of AYAZ! Study the Scriptures diligently in their original Hebraic context. Look up the original Hebrew meanings of English words in the Bible using a Strong's Concordance or a good Bible Search engine on the internet! The Blue Letter Bible is a good one! Investigate for yourself how the Sabbath day was changed to Sunday by men and how contaminated pagan days like Sunday, Christmas, Easter, and Valentine's Day, came to be accepted, instead of Yahuah's real set apart days! Yahuah's appointed times of worship and meditation are His weekly Sabbath and His seven festivals! These include the Passover, Unleavened Bread, First Fruits, Shabuoth, the Feast of Trumpets, Yom Kippur, and the Feast of Tabernacles! We should worship AYAZ every morning and evening with our praises and our prayers! We should also recognize that the sighting of the New Moons are special times to AYAZ, which will be observed by **everyone**, when OWYAZ sets up His Kingdom! If you are hungry, many wonderful books are available on all these subjects!

Many good servants of 𐤀𐤉𐤄𐤅 are trying to warn the sheep, before it's too late! Learn as much as you can about the Roman emperor, Constantine, and the changes that Constantine brought about! Ask 𐤀𐤉𐤄𐤅 to be your teacher, your comforter, and your guide! Ask 𐤀𐤉𐤄𐤅 to show you and your family the <u>Right Way</u> <u>to GO</u>! If you seek OWY𐤄𐤅 with our <u>whole</u> <u>heart</u>, then OWY𐤄𐤅 will reveal Himself to you! He will show you the <u>Right Way to GO</u>! Sadly most people refuse to enter Yahushua's narrow gate because Yahushua's **Way** <u>is afflicted</u> with much trouble! <u>Very</u> few people go that way! When we follow OWY𐤄𐤅 in this life, we will get a <u>taste</u> of the afflictions, rejections, and persecutions faced by OWY𐤄𐤅! Sadly most people still choose to enter the wide gate, which leads to destruction, even after being exposed to Yahuah's Truth! The wide gate is <u>easy</u>! <u>Many</u> people choose to go through that gate! However, beware that gate leads to <u>certain</u> and <u>absolute</u> destruction!

How Shall We Live?

OWY𐤄𐤅 said that many are called, but few are chosen! **If many are called by 𐤀𐤉𐤄𐤅, then why aren't many chosen?** 𐤀𐤉𐤄𐤅 reaches out to multitudes of morally good people all over the world in <u>every</u> <u>nation</u> at different times in their lives! 𐤀𐤉𐤄𐤅 uses afflictions, troubles, and hardships in the lives of good people so that they will be humbled enough to seek **Him** with their whole hearts! The process of overcoming afflictions, troubles, and hardships should motivate good people to diligently search the Scriptures for answers! Yahuah's called out ones <u>will</u> truly seek the real creator of the Heavens and the Earth, when they are in Yahuah's furnace of affliction! When a person is truly humbled and gets to the point where they can truthfully say, "I Give Up and I Want To Live Life Your Way!", then 𐤀𐤉𐤄𐤅 will reveal Himself to them! Nothing will ever be the same for them again! Over time they will be completely set apart to 𐤀𐤉𐤄𐤅 step by step!

Matthew 7
<u>Ask, and it shall be given you</u>; <u>seek, and ye shall find</u>; <u>knock, and it shall be opened</u> unto you: For <u>every</u> <u>one</u> that <u>asketh</u> <u>receiveth</u>; and <u>he that seeketh findeth</u>; and to him that knocketh it shall be opened.

Unfortunately, when confronted with the true message of the Scriptures, most people, who are called, do <u>not</u> <u>answer</u> Yahuah's call!

Isaiah 65 Therefore will I number you to the sword, and ye shall all bow down to the slaughter: <u>because when I called, ye did not answer;</u> <u>when I spake, ye did not hear; but did evil before mine eyes, and did</u> <u>choose that wherein I delighted not</u>.

Isaiah 66
I also will choose their delusions, and will bring their fears upon them; because <u>when I called, none did answer</u>; when I spake, they did not hear: but they did evil before mine eyes, and chose that in which I delighted not.

Sadly, most people, even when exposed to the apostasy in man's religious systems, are still <u>unwilling</u> to give them up! It's hard to believe, but most people <u>choose to</u> <u>love</u> the <u>lies</u> of religious tradition <u>more than the Truth of</u> ayaz! That's very sad! Most people including the preachers, pastors, and popes shrink back and refuse to follow the "Way of OWYAZ"! How does ayaz want us to live? The <u>best</u> possible <u>pattern</u> to follow is that of OWYAZ!

1 John 2
My little children, I write this to you, so that you do not sin. And if anyone sins, we have an Intercessor with the Father, OWYAZ Messiah, a righteous One. ²And He Himself is an atoning offering for our sins, and not for ours only but also for all the world. ³And by this we know that we know Him, <u>if we guard His commands</u>. ⁴The one who says, "I know Him," and does not guard His commands, is a liar, and the Truth is not in him. ⁵But <u>whoever guards His Word, truly the love of Elohim has been perfected in</u> him. By this we know that we are in Him. ⁶The one who says he stays in Him <u>ought himself also to walk, even as He walked</u>.

Yahushua's Personal Invitation
Revelation 22
*And, behold, I come quickly; and <u>my reward is with me, to give every man according as his work</u> shall be. I am Alpha and Omega, the beginning and the end, the first and the last. <u>Blessed are they that do his commandments</u>, that <u>they may have right</u> to <u>the tree of life</u>, and <u>may enter in through the gates into the city</u>.(**the New Yahrushalayim**) For without are dogs, and sorcerers, and whoremongers, and murderers, and idolaters, and whosoever loveth and maketh a lie. I ayaz have sent mine angel to testify unto you these things in the assemblies. I am the root and the offspring of David, and the bright and morning star.* **And the Spirit and the bride say, Come. And let him that heareth say, Come. And let him that is <u>athirst</u> come. And whosoever will, let him take the water of life freely.**

Our Story

²⁸And we know that all matters work together for good to those who love Elohim, to those who are called according to His purpose. **Romans 8:28**

I grew up in a middle class southern household in Augusta, Georgia. My parents were both Christians, who faithfully attended the same Baptist church for almost 50 years! My parents were very good to my brother and me! They gave us both what we needed to be successful in this life! My mother is retired now, but she was an outstanding school teacher, who was old school all the way! She still helps many people, especially older people, who are home bound or just experiencing hard times! My father was a real "Field and Stream" man! Hunting and fishing were his great passions! He helped me over the years numerous times, when I really needed it! When my brother and I were both young, my parents ensured that we both attended Sunday school and church every Sunday, unless we were out of town! At nine years old I attended our church's annual two week revival! It was at that time that I first felt the Ruach HaQodesh convicting my heart! Of course at that time I didn't know anything about Hebrew or the Ruach HaQodesh, but I did know that I was feeling extreme pressure, while sitting on my pew! The visiting evangelist, who was preaching that revival, was Adrian Rogers! Adrian Rodgers became a very well known Baptist preacher! He was broadcast nationally on television for many years! Ironically, the sermon that night was titled "Armageddon"! That sermon was the first teaching on the end times that I had ever heard! Whenever a visiting preacher came to the church for a revival, it was a tradition for the children to get the autograph of the visiting preacher in their Bibles, after the service! The children would line up for the visiting preacher to sign his autograph and write a Bible verse inside their Bibles! When Adrian Rodgers signed my Bible, he wrote Romans 8:28!

Romans 8: 28
²⁸And we know that all matters work together for good to those who love Elohim, to those who are called according to His purpose.

Little did I know back then, but that verse was to become my life's verse! It has been a constant source of hope and comfort to me from that day forward! As a young adult, I was very naive about people and the ways of this world! As many people do, I married the first girl, who came along! As a young person I was good by the standards of society!

I taught Sunday school in the Youth Department for several years, but never could figure out why those kids weren't more excited about the Scriptures and their promises! After three years of marriage, my wife decided that I wasn't what she wanted! She left along with our six month old daughter, Leslie! That was heart breaking for me! When my wife left, I was crushed! I did the only thing that I knew to do! I searched the Scriptures for answers! It was then that I read the Scriptures from cover to cover for the very first time! During that first crisis and every crisis, since then, I have survived by consuming the Scriptures! Now the Scriptures are my food and my water everyday! I study and meditate on the Scriptures everyday for my very own personal survival! <u>All</u> my dreams and desires hang on Yahuah's promises! Yahuah's Word has <u>sustained</u> me <u>all my life</u>! The immediate aftermath of that marriage was an extremely difficult time for me and my family! I give 𐤀𐤉𐤄𐤅 <u>all</u> the credit for carrying me through the grieving process, even though I didn't even know Yahuah's name back then! After a while, I married an unusually strong and virtuous young woman named Vicki Lynn Barnes! Vicki and I have been married for 23 years! We are alike in a lot of ways! We are both extremely family oriented! We love each other and we love our children! We even love the same movies! Vicki is a very rare commodity in today's world because in the end she follows her husband no matter what! That characteristic has proven to be very important, when we finally decided to follow Yahuah's ways and <u>not</u> the ways of this world, no matter what! Vicki nurtures the whole family each and everyday! I know that 𐤀𐤉𐤄𐤅 hand picked Vicki for us because of her strength, toughness, and determination! 𐤀𐤉𐤄𐤅 knew that our family would need a woman like that in order to fulfill our destiny! Vicki and I have three children! Kasey is twenty years old and she's our oldest daughter! Kasey epitomizes the daughter that I always saw in my dreams! She is beautiful inside and out! She's very creative, very insightful, and very kind to everyone no matter what their abilities or disabilities! Kasey is a stellar student, an obedient daughter, and she has always been extremely virtuous! Christian is fifteen and he's my first born son! Christian was named in honor of the promise that I made to 𐤀𐤉𐤄𐤅, when I asked 𐤀𐤉𐤄𐤅 for a son! Of course, when I prayed Hannah's prayer, I didn't even know, who Hannah was, or the name of the mighty one that I was created to serve! Christian is a wonderful son in everyway! He was created, after my own image, but only better! Christian has a very quiet nature and he's very practical! He has the wisdom of a wise old man, but he has a warrior's spirit, which manifests itself on the baseball field! Christian never quits on the baseball field and will never quit on 𐤀𐤉𐤄𐤅, no matter what! Our youngest son Chad is fourteen!

Chad is the most amicable of all our children! He has a very kind and compassionate heart! Chad has great compassion for people, who are suffering with diseases, especially children! Chad loves his family very much and is often brought to tears, when saying his goodbyes! Chad is very tough and gets the most out of every minute of every day! He absolutely loves the outdoors! Chad never goes anywhere without making new friends and he's always willing to help with a project! Tools, clothes, and shoes, especially tennis shoes and boots, are Chad's favorite material things! The makeup of our family would not be complete without a discussion about Leslie! Leslie is twenty-five and my daughter from my first marriage! Leslie and I were both born on November 15th in the same hospital twenty five years apart! Leslie is a very kind and very gentle person on the one hand, but she has no trouble taking charge in critical situations! I guess that's why Leslie is such a good nurse in the Heart Intensive Care unit at the local hospital! Leslie is a great story teller, she has boundless enthusiasm, and she is always ready for an adventure!

Our lives made a quantum change, when Chad contracted Juvenile Diabetes, when he was two years old! Chad almost died, when the doctors misdiagnosed his disease twice before finally recognizing the problem weeks later! Since that time Chad and the whole family have been profoundly affected by Chad's continuous struggle with that disease! A few years later Christian was diagnosed with Perthes Disease, which causes the femur bones to disintegrate in the hip sockets! Last year Kasey was diagnosed with a thyroid and a heart condition, which has caused Kasey to experience dizziness, numbness, and weight loss! We are fighting that battle right now! In January of 2006 I was working in New Mexico and living alone in an apartment, far away from my family and my familiar Georgia surroundings! A few months earlier I was laid off from a job that I had held for 24 years because of company downsizing! While I was working in New Mexico, my father was very, very sick at home in Augusta, Georgia! My life seemed to be overflowing with problems and I was sixteen hundred miles from home! But I remembered Romans 8:28 and I meditated on it often, while there! Just in time 𐤀𐤉𐤀𐤆 brought me back home to work at the same place where I had worked for the previous 24 years! The day, after I got home, my father went back into the hospital for the last time! He died a few days later with my family and my mother present in the room! I closed his eyes for the last time! I started this book, while I was alone in New Mexico! Looking back 𐤀𐤉𐤀𐤆 must have known that I needed solitude and undivided time to start *Let My People Go!*

In a very strange way the pressures of Chad's Diabetes, Christian's Perthes Disease, Kasey's condition, and all the other struggles have been the catalysts that have provoked me to zealously search the Scriptures for answers and hope! I understand a little bit about how Jacob must have felt, when He was questioned by the Pharaoh of Mitsrayim, after Jacob was reunited with Joseph!

Genesis 47
[7] *And Yoseph brought in his father Ya'aqob and set him before Pharaoh. And Ya'aqob blessed Pharaoh.* [8] *And Pharaoh said to Ya'aqob, "How old are you?"* [9] *And Ya'aqob said to Pharaoh, The days of the years of my sojournings are one hundred and thirty years.* <u>*Few and evil have been the days of the years of my life*</u>*, and they have not reached the days of the years of the life of my fathers in the days of their sojournings."*

I started searching for answers about my sons' diseases first, but I found out so much more! I did <u>not</u> understand it back then, but my real destiny hangs on the knowledge that I have learned about 𐤀𐤉𐤄𐤅! The wisdom and understanding that Yahuah's Ruach HaQodesh has given me already has far surpassed my wildest imaginations! Yahuah's Scriptures are becoming more and more clear to me everyday! Yahuah's Ruach HaQodesh teaches me the right Way to go and has given me a love for the people of Israel! About eight years ago this love surfaced and led me to investigate the Hebrew roots of the Scriptures! For several years I financially supported *The Wings of Eagles*, which is an organization that airlifts Jews out of Russia to the State of Israel! I also supported several settlements in the State of Israel as well as other ministries there as well! At that time we were going to a full gospel church, which stressed, "Healing is for today!" There were many very sincere Christians at that church, who we still love, but there were many red flags that we saw there as time went by! The pastor held a strange mesmerizing hold over her sheep! She was very charismatic and a great communicator! She had the power to lead a large group of people in a certain direction, which <u>she determined</u>, of course! Her church was a "feel good kind of place" with a lot of dancing and celebration, but as I was to discover over time, deception and control reigned supreme there!

Revelation 2
[20] *"But I hold against you that you allow that woman Izebel, who calls herself a prophetess, to teach and lead My servants astray to commit whoring and to eat food offered to idols.* [21] *"And I gave her time to repent of her whoring, and she did not repent.* [22] *"See, I am throwing her into a sickbed, and those who commit adultery with her into great affliction, unless they repent of their works.*

After a while I no longer felt comfortable in that church! I left and started attending a very small Messianic congregation! I was at a crossroad and Vicki had to determine, if she would follow my lead! I did not pressure Vicki at all, but Kasey and Vicki studied on their own and convinced themselves that I was indeed telling the truth! When they determined to follow me, they didn't realize it then, but they were about to go further and further against the grain of popular opinion as we traveled on our spiritual journey! It was at that time that Vicki and the rest of the family stopped celebrating Christmas, Easter, and all the rest of the contaminated Christian holidays! Vicki, who had been a huge Christmas person all her life, took both of our artificial trees, her wooden reindeer, all her lights, and all the other trappings and put them at the road for the garbage collector! Wow, I was so proud of Vicki and Kasey that day! That had to be 𐤀𐤉𐤄𐤆, who caused such a huge change in Vicki! Like I said, Vicki's one in a million! Initially, I felt like that Messianic congregation must be where we belonged, but as I kept studying and learning, I knew that something was still missing! I knew that somehow there was so much more! While that Messianic congregation did celebrate the Shabbat and the Festivals, they didn't use the real names of 𐤀𐤉𐤄𐤆 and OWY𐤄𐤆 at all! That puzzled me greatly! I noticed that Messianic Judaism had its own gaggle of man-made traditions, which many times over-shadowed the real Commandments of 𐤀𐤉𐤄𐤆! All the people in our congregation observed Yahuah's Festivals, but had no problem with celebrating the pagan Festivals of Christmas, Easter, etc. too! That inconsistency vexed me! At that time I read *The Two Babylons, Fossilized Customs*, and *Come Out of Her My People* for the very first time! I was reading everything that I could get my hands on about the origins of paganism and the history of the Christian church! At that time I came to the shocking realization of what apostasy was all about and how sinister its deception is! The pieces were coming together for me and my eyes were wide open! I was upset, terrified, and broken hearted because of the depth of the deception that has snared so many millions of well meaning people over so many generations! I'm sorry, but I have stop right here just a minute and be painfully honest! If you are a preacher serving as a shepherd over any congregation of sheep and you've been exposed to the truth about Christmas, Easter, and the set apart names of 𐤀𐤉𐤄𐤆 and OWY𐤄𐤆, then you should be very ashamed and sorry for your participation in apostasy against 𐤀𐤉𐤄𐤆! Not only have you and your family lived the lies yourself, but you have led innocent sheep under your care deeper and deeper into apostasy against 𐤀𐤉𐤄𐤆 and OWY𐤄𐤆! If you can't teach the undiluted truth where you are, then leave that profession and get another job to make a living! But it's not over until it's over!

Repent while there's still time to repent and walk in Yahuah's ways! If you continue to refuse to repent, then you and your family are really no different that the prophets of Baal! Like them you will face total destruction in the Lake of Fire, if you do not change! **It's still not too late!** After a couple of years with that Messianic group, I could no longer tolerate the observance of the unless traditions of men, while many weightier Commandments of AYAZ were being ignored! No one, but me saw any harm in observing the pagan holidays along with Yahuah's festivals or the harm in suppressing Yahuah's name! I had to leave those sheep, but we had no place to go! So what should we do? Our family had decided once and for all to follow AYAZ and OWYAZ, even if no one else did! Of course we know that right now there are tens of thousands of overcomers all over the earth, who have similar stories! We are very thankful that AYAZ has been so merciful to us! AYAZ called us to follow Him and **we have answered His call!** However, we have found the Way of OWYAZ to be very, very narrow and very hard pressed! Yahushua's Way is hard pressed and full of tribulations, rejections, sorrows, and afflictions! Very few people choose to travel that Way!

Matthew 7
^{13}"Enter in through the narrow gate! Because the gate is wide – and the way is broad – that leads to destruction, and there are many who enter in through it. ^{14}"Because the gate is narrow and the way is hard pressed which leads to life, and there are few who find it.

At this time we have our own family Shabbat times and our own Festival times! Vicki and I teach Yahuah's ways to our children everyday as we encounter the problems that arise that day! We have recently learned of a few other families in our area, who also serve AYAZ with their whole heart! HalleluYah! HalleluYah! HalleluYah! I have been asking AYAZ for some like minded friends!

During our spiritual journey, we made stops in the Baptist and the Full Gospel denominations of Christianity! Then we made a stop in Messianic Judaism, but we knew in our hearts that something was still missing! At each one of those stops, we met many kind individuals, who were doing what they truly believed was right at the time! At each stop we noticed that more and more people got off the narrow Way of OWYAZ! We have felt more and more alone as we have continued along on our journey! The good news is that as we have traveled the way of AYAZ, we have fallen more and more in love with AYAZ and OWYAZ! Now we want Yahuah's plans and desires to be completely fulfilled in our lives as well as in the lives of all Yahuah's overcomers, Israel! Doesn't AYAZ, who fashioned our hearts and minds have the capability of experiencing feelings and desires? Doesn't AYAZ feel joy, happiness, and gratification?

Well, of course 𐤀𐤉𐤀𐤆 can, and to degrees that we cannot even imagine! My heart's desire is that my family would **exceed** Yahuah's own expectations and desires for us, if that's possible! We would like to totally fulfill Yahuah's desires for our family and gratify His heart beyond measure!

By the way, 𐤀𐤉𐤀𐤆 miraculously healed Christian of Perthes Disease, while we were in Dr. Bailey's office at the University Hospital in Augusta! Christian had been in traction for three months and was missing the 1st grade! I had prayed in my prayer room that even though I didn't understand why Christian had to have the disease, I understood that Christian belonged to 𐤀𐤉𐤀𐤆! Christian's father submitted to Yahuah's will that night! Whatever was to be Yahuah's will, I knew that I could accept it because I knew in my heart that 𐤀𐤉𐤀𐤆 truly loved Christian **even more than I did**! A few days later, I literally carried Christian as usual up to the ninth floor of the hospital for his scheduled appointment! The nurses took Christian back for X-rays as usual, but this time it took about 45 minutes for them to come back, when normally an X-ray took about 20 minutes! When they did come back, Dr. Bailey asked Christian, "Are you going to play baseball this summer?" Christian looked perplexed and said, "No sir, I can't!" Dr. Bailey asked Christian, "Why can't you play?" Christian looked confused and said, "Because of my hip!" Then Dr. Bailey said to Christian, **"What if I said that you can play baseball, if you promise me that you will hit a .400 batting average!"** Dr. Bailey told us that miraculously there was absolutely no sign of Perthes disease in Christian's hips and femur bones, which they verified by taking two sets of x-rays! Christian walked out of the hospital on his own two legs that day and has been playing baseball and hitting .400 ever since! Chad still has Juvenile Diabetes **for the moment** because 𐤀𐤉𐤀𐤆 is still **using the pressure of that struggle to accomplish His purposes** in all of our lives! But I have asked 𐤀𐤉𐤀𐤆 to let me see with my own two eyes, when He heals Chad from that disease! HalleluYah! HalleluYah! HalleluYah!

Well, that's the quick version of the Bragg's spiritual journey to this point! Even though I am not a polished writer, as you can certainly see, I was convicted that I must write Let My People Go for Yahuah's overcomers, **Israel**! I believe in the end the right people will read Let My People Go and Yahuah's purposes will be accomplished in their lives as well! HalleluYah! HalleluYah! HalleluYah! The Bragg family's message to all of Israel, is to **finish this race of patient endurance well! WE love you very, very much!**

Around the Arc

My 15 year old son Christian pitches for his High School baseball team! His team, the Westside Patriots, has a play that I believe reinforces the "Verse to Remember"! The play is called "Around the Arc"! This year the play worked several times! With a runner on second in a close game, the coach will yell out "Arc"! The pitcher spins around on the pitcher's mound and throws the ball to second base to try to pick off the runner, who has a big lead! The runner scurries back to second sliding head first! Meanwhile the shortstop and second baseman both leave their feet and dive behind second base to cut off the errant pickoff throw! The next thing you see is the center fielder running frantically to the outfield wall! The pitcher has a dejected look on his face and shakes his head in disgust! The first baseman exhorts the outfielders to get the ball back in quickly! The runner on second gets up, after his slide back into second! He hears the fans, his teammates, and the third base coach exhorting him to "Run-n-n" to third! The runner takes off to third! He's very confident that he will make it safely to third and possibly even score! However, after the runner has fully committed and is half way between second and third, the pitcher very nonchalantly pulls the ball out of his glove where it has been <u>hidden</u> from the very beginning and throws it to third! Of course the runner is <u>dead</u> <u>meat</u>! He is tagged out in a very embarrassing moment for the runner, which he will <u>never</u> forget! It was all a trick and an illusion, which was designed to take advantage of the confusion and erroneous communications built into the play! Of course, the pitcher never really threw the ball to second, but all the actions of the players, the fans, and the coaches gave the <u>appearance</u> that the ball had really been thrown! It <u>appeared</u> that the ball had gotten past the infielders and was rolling to the outfield wall!

[24] *"Do not judge according to appearance, but judge with righteous judgment."* Yohanan (John) 7

This trick play is another practical analogy that I hope will help you remember Yahushua's "Verse to Remember"! Please do <u>not</u> judge spiritual things or anything else for that matter by their appearances! If you don't judge using righteous judgment, then you will be dead meat too just like the runner, who was cut down at third base! The runner truly believed that he had done the right thing, but he was dead wrong as well as all the other people, who encouraged him to run! Study the Torah of ayaz diligently for yourself! Follow <u>all</u> the Scriptures to the very best of your ability, period! Let The Scriptures be a lamp unto your feet and a light unto your path! May ayaz bless you!

The Little Red Hen

"Follow Me, and I shall make you fishers of men." **MattiYahu 4**

Remember the time, when Kepha (Peter), Ya'aqob (James), and Yohanan (John) had been fishing all night, but hadn't caught any fish! These men were professional fisherman! They certainly had to know their business! They surely had all the right equipment and knew the best spots, but the fish just weren't going into their nets! However, **when Yahushua came** at the **appointed** time, then everything changed! They caught **so many fish** that the weight of their catch almost sank their two boats!

Luke 5
³*And entering into one of the boats, which belonged to Shim'on, He asked him to pull away a little from the land. And He sat down and was teaching the crowds from the boat.* ⁴*And when He ceased speaking, He said to Shim'on, "Pull out into the deep and let down your nets for a catch."* ⁵*And Shim'on answering, said to Him, "Master, <u>we have toiled all night and caught none, but at Your word I shall let down the net.</u>"* ⁶*And when they did so, <u>they caught a great number of fish, and their net was breaking</u>,* ⁷*and they motioned to their partners in the other boat to come and help them. And they came and filled both the boats, so that they were sinking.* ⁸*And when Shim'on Kepha saw it, he fell down at the knees of* OWYAZ, *saying, "Depart from me, for I am a man, a sinner, O Master!"* ⁹*For astonishment had seized him and all those with him, at the catch of fish which they took,* ¹⁰*so too were Ya'aqob and Yohanan, the sons of Zabdai, who were partners with Shim'on. Then* OWYAZ *said to Shim'on, "Do not fear, <u>from now on you shall catch men.</u>"*

Day by day, I try my best to tell the Good News of OWYAZ to as many spiritually minded people as possible! However, most of the time, I don't catch <u>any</u> fish! When I explain to morally good people about the apostasy that exists all around us, they seem interested and very attentive! However, once these people realize that changes and sacrifices are needed in their own lives, then those fish just swim away back to their familiar and comfortable waters! There are a very few fish, a remnant, who do swim into Yahushua's net! I have found in my experience that the ones, who seem to be the most willing to put Yahuah's words into action are those, who are in the midst of being sorely tested and afflicted! Immersion by fire into Yahuah's furnace of affliction brings out the <u>best</u> in us, doesn't it? Isn't that interesting? Remember Romans 8:28!

Kepha and his friends were <u>toiling</u> all night in the <u>darkness</u>! But in the <u>morning</u>, when OWY𐤔Z came, everything changed dramatically! Kepha, Ya'aqob, and Yohanan caught so many fish that it was almost overwhelming! We are toiling for OWY𐤔Z in great <u>darkness</u> in this present world! Sometimes it may <u>look</u> like we aren't catching any fish or doing any good at all! **However take heart!** In the <u>morning</u>, when OWY𐤔Z **comes to take us back to the Promised Land, then everything will change**! Then we will catch so many fish that it will almost overwhelm us too! What fun that will be!

SHIR haSHIRIM (Song of Soloman) 2

⁸The voice of my beloved! See, <u>he is coming</u>, Leaping on the mountains, skipping on the hills. ⁹My beloved is like a gazelle or like a young stag. See, he is standing behind our wall, Looking through the windows, Peering through the lattice. ¹⁰My beloved responded and said to me, "<u>Rise up, my love, my fair one, and come away</u>." ¹¹"<u>For look, the winter is past, the rain is over</u>, gone. ¹²"The <u>flowers have appeared in the earth</u>; The <u>time of singing has come</u>, And the voice of the turtledove has been heard in our land. ¹³"The fig tree has ripened her figs, And the vines with the tender grapes have given a good fragrance. Rise up, my love, my fair one, and <u>come away</u>! ¹⁴"O my dove, <u>in the clefts of the rock</u>, In the covering of the cliff, Let me see your appearance, Let me hear your voice; For your voice is sweet, And your appearance is lovely." ¹⁵Catch the foxes for us, The little foxes that spoil the vines, And our vines are all blossom. ¹⁶My beloved is mine, and I am his.

YirmeYahu 16

¹⁴"Therefore see, the days are coming," declares 𐤀Y𐤔Z, "<u>when it is no longer said,</u> '𐤀Y𐤔Z <u>lives who brought up the children of Yisra'el from the land of Mitsrayim</u>,' ¹⁵but, 𐤀Y𐤔Z lives who brought up the children of Yisra'el from the land of the north and from all the lands where He had driven them.' For <u>I shall bring them back into their land I gave to their fathers</u>. ¹⁶"See, <u>I am sending for many fishermen</u>," declares 𐤀Y𐤔Z, "and they shall fish them.

Sometimes Yahushua's narrow Way seems very lonely, very frustrating, and very afflicted! I offer this simple story to you in the hope that it will give you encouragement! I'm sure this story will be very familiar to many of you! However, I believe that *The Little Red Hen* is a story worth remembering and meditating on! May your light shine brightly in this world until you see the face of 𐤀Y𐤔Z, OWY𐤔Z!

The Little Red Hen

One day as the Little Red Hen was scratching in a field, she found a grain of wheat.
"This wheat should be planted," she said. "Who will plant this grain of wheat?"
"Not I," said the Duck.
"Not I," said the Cat.
"Not I," said the Dog.
"Then I will," said the Little Red Hen. And she did.
Soon the wheat grew to be tall and yellow.
"The wheat is ripe," said the Little Red Hen. "Who will cut the wheat?"
"Not I," said the Duck.
"Not I," said the Cat.
"Not I," said the Dog.
"Then I will," said the Little Red Hen. And she did.
When the wheat was cut, the Little Red Hen said, "Who will thresh the wheat?"
"Not I," said the Duck.
"Not I," said the Cat.
"Not I," said the Dog.
"Then I will," said the Little Red Hen. And she did.
When the wheat was threshed, the Little Red Hen said, "Who will take this wheat to the mill?"
"Not I," said the Duck.
"Not I," said the Cat.
"Not I," said the Dog.
"Then I will," said the Little Red Hen. And she did.
She took the wheat to the mill and had it ground into flour. Then she said, "Who will make this flour into bread?"
"Not I," said the Duck.
"Not I," said the Cat.
"Not I," said the Dog.
"Then I will," said the Little Red Hen. And she did.
She made and baked the bread. Then she said, "Who will eat this bread?"
"Oh! I will," said the Duck.
"And I will," said the Cat.
"And I will," said the Dog.
"No, No!" said the Little Red Hen. "I will do that." And she did.

In this present world system with all its distractions, most people make their decisions based totally on what they see and not what the Scriptures actually say! Following the Way of OWYAZ requires trust and action!

We must trust that 𐤉𐤄𐤅𐤄 does exist and that His word is true! Then we must put the words of 𐤉𐤄𐤅𐤄 into action in our lives! We must do our best to obey His Torah each day! By our obedience, **we prove that we really do love** 𐤉𐤄𐤅𐤄 and OWY𐤄𐤋 even though we cannot see the reality of Mount Zion, until the Day of 𐤉𐤄𐤅𐤄! But, when we truly trust and obey, then we will be prepared for Yahushua's return! Oh, how blessed we really are to have eyes to really see and ears to really hear! Todah, todah, todah OWY𐤄𐤋! Today most of the morally good people reason that somehow everything will be alright in the long run because they mean well in their hearts! Very few people are actually willing to make the changes needed in their lives today so that they can become laborers in Yahushua's harvest! Unfortunately, most people are totally consumed with the cares of this life!

Because they can't see the reality of Yahushua's kingdom with their own eyes, there seems to be no urgency to change! These sheep are on **dangerously thin ice** and don't even realize it! Some things haven't changed at all, since OWY𐤄𐤋 first came! Most sheep today still make their decisions based entirely on what they **see** with their eyes and what they hear with their ears! Remember that character trait was the stumbling block, which prevented so many sheep from recognizing OWY𐤄𐤋! Those sheep were blinded to the truth, when OWY𐤄𐤋 came as our Passover Lamb because they judged OWY𐤄𐤋 **by His physical appearance, which was very, very, very BAD!** When Yahushua returns and people see Mount Zion, then masses of sheep will become very, very interested! The Scriptures report that even Yahushua's enemies will bow their knees to OWY𐤄𐤋! However, when OWY𐤄𐤋 returns many, many sheep will be rejected because they did not act, when 𐤉𐤄𐤅𐤄 called them to repent! So, after having said all that, the moral of the story of *The Little Red Hen* is this! **Do not judge things by how they look now!** Sometimes you may feel that you are laboring alone for 𐤉𐤄𐤅𐤄, but one day soon you will reap the rewards for your labor! Yes, Israel will face great struggles, many afflictions, and countless rejections, but there will come a Day, when all that will be forgotten! Always remember **"Yahushua's Verse to Remember"**! When it appears that nobody cares about the feelings of OWY𐤄𐤋 and 𐤉𐤄𐤅𐤄 including your own family members and close friends, then take heart! Remember that like OWY𐤄𐤋, you too will be exalted on the Day of 𐤉𐤄𐤅𐤄!

Then you will <u>not</u> be sorry for your decision to follow the Way of OWYAZ!

Matthew 19
²⁸And OWYAZ said to them, "Truly I say to you, when the Son of Adam sits on the throne of His esteem, you who have followed Me in the rebirth, shall also sit on twelve thrones, judging the twelve tribes of Yisra'el. ²⁹"And everyone who has left houses or brothers or sisters or father or mother or wife or children or lands, for My Name's sake, <u>shall receive a hundredfold, and shall inherit everlasting life</u>. ³⁰"But many who are first shall be last, and the last first.

The END

Todah! Todah! Todah!

Thank You AYAZ and OWYAZ for giving me the privilege of writing *Let My People Go!*

Acknowledgements

Thank you for reading this humble book! I hope that *Let My People Go* has stirred up your love for 𐤉𐤄𐤅𐤄 and 𐤉𐤄𐤅𐤔𐤏! Thank you mother and dad for your loving-kindness all my life! Thank you Vicki for helping me to fulfill my destiny, which includes writing *Let My People Go* for Israel! Thank you Kasey for your art work and computer help! Thank you Christian for proof reading! Thank you Chad for helping me with *The Little Red Hen!* Thank you Jim and Penny Caldwell for the use of your picture of the summit of Jebel al Lawz! Thank you Mrs. Mildred Goolsby for your kindness and for educating me on the printing business!

Source References:

Restored Name King James Version

The Scriptures, Institute of Scripture Research

The Two Babylons, Alexander Hislop

Fossilized Customs, Lew White

The Book of Enoch, Restored Name Version

CHIZAYON (PNV), Todd Effren

Book of Adam and Eve, Restored Name Version from R. H. Charles

Book of Yashar, Restored Name Version

The Cave of Treasures, Restored Name Version

Northern Arabia, Alois Musil

Altorientalische Forschungen, Hugo Winckler

North Arabia Mitsrayim and the Old Testament, Catholic Encyclopedia

Dead Sea Scrolls, Michael Wise, Martin Abegg, Jr., & Edward Cook

American Leprosy Missions http://www.leprosy.org/LEPdisease.html

Illustrations:

The Fall of the Children of Seth, *Forgotten Books of Eden*

Map of Arabia, *Northern Arabia*

Map of Northwestern Arabia, *Atlas of the Kingdom of Saudi Arabia*

Bull of Nimrod, *The Two Babylons*